BELIEFS ABOUT TEXT
AND INSTRUCTION
WITH TEXT

BELIEFS ABOUT TEXT AND INSTRUCTION WITH TEXT

Edited by

RUTH GARNER
Washington State University

PATRICIA A. ALEXANDER
Texas A & M University

LEA LAWRENCE ERLBAUM ASSOCIATES, PUBLISHERS
1994 Hillsdale, New Jersey   Hove, UK

Copyright © 1994 by Lawrence Erlbaum Associates, Inc.
   All rights reserved. No part of the book may be reproduced in
   any form, by photostat, microform, retrieval system, or any other
   means, without the prior written permission of the publisher.

Lawrence Erlbaum Associates, Inc., Publishers
365 Broadway
Hillsdale, New Jersey, 07642

Library of Congress Cataloging-in-Publication Data

Beliefs about text and instruction with text / edited by Ruth Garner,
   Patricia A. Alexander.
       p.   cm.
   Includes bibliographical references and indexes.
   ISBN 0-8058-1426-4. — ISBN 0-8058-1427-2 (pbk.)
   1. Reading, Psychology of. 2. Reading—Public opinion.
   3. Literacy—Psychological aspects. I. Garner, Ruth.
   II. Alexander, Patricia A.
   BF456.R2B35 1994
   418′.4′019—dc20   94-239
                                                                         CIP

Books published by Lawrence Erlbaum Associates are printed on acid-free
paper, and their bindings are chosen for strength and durability.

Printed in the United States of America
10 9 8 7 6 5 4 3 2 1

Contributors

Patricia A. Alexander, *Texas A & M University, College Station, TX 77843*

Donna E. Alvermann, *University of Georgia, Athens, GA 30602*

Patricia L. Anders, *University of Arizona, Tucson, AZ 85721*

Hilda Borko, *University of Colorado, Boulder, CO 80309*

Vay Bott, *Washington State University, Vancouver, WA 98663*

Marilyn J. Chambliss, *Stanford University, Stanford, CA 94305*

Michelle Commeyras, *University of Georgia, Athens, GA 30602*

Kathryn H. Davinroy, *University of Colorado, Boulder, CO 80309*

Filip J. R. C. Dochy, *Open University, Heerlen, Netherlands*

Janice A. Dole, *University of Utah, Salt Lake City, UT 84112*

Karen S. Evans, *University of Arizona, Tucson, AZ 85721*

Maurene D. Flory, *University of Colorado, Boulder, CO 80309*

Ruth Garner, *Washington State University, Vancouver, WA 98663*

Mark G. Gillingham, *Washington State University, Vancouver, WA 98663*

Richard Hansis, *Washington State University, Vancouver, WA 98663*

Elfrieda H. Hiebert, *University of Colorado, Boulder, CO 80309*

Rosalind Horowitz, *University of Texas, San Antonio, TX 78249*

Emily Hutton, *Washington State University, Vancouver, WA 98663*

Nia Johnson-Crowley, *University of Washington, Seattle, WA 98195*

Jonna M. Kulikowich, *University of Connecticut, Storrs, CT 06269*

Susan Bobbitt Nolen, *University of Washington, Seattle, WA 98195*

Penelope L. Peterson, *Michigan State University, East Lansing, MI 48823*

Marlene Schommer, *Wichita State University, Wichita, KS 67260*

Gale M. Sinatra, *University of Utah, Salt Lake City, UT 84112*

Jan Spiesman, *Washington State University, Vancouver, WA 98663*

Audrey Thompson, *University of Utah, Salt Lake City, UT 84112*

Suzanne Wade, *University of Utah, Salt Lake City, UT 84112*

William Watkins, *University of Utah, Salt Lake City, UT 84112*

Claire Ellen Weinstein, *University of Texas, Austin, TX 78712*

Joanna P. Williams, *Teachers College, Columbia University, New York, NY 10027*

Samuel S. Wineburg, *University of Washington, Seattle, WA 98195*

Michael F. Young, *University of Connecticut, Storrs, CT 06269*

Contents

Foreword

The Importance of Examining
Beliefs About Text

Joanna P. Williams
Teachers College, Columbia University

What do you believe about reading and about learning to read? Chances are, if you are reading this book, that you think that reading is one of the most important things that a child learns in school, that it is a skill that opens up worlds of knowledge and understanding and pleasure, that the inventions of the alphabet and the printing press rank very high in cultural history, and that, indeed, the ability to read and write is a veritable hallmark of a civilized person. You probably remember that as a child you were eager to learn to read and that your parents were pleased and proud of your accomplishment.

Until recently our work on reading comprehension and instruction via text assumed without question that everybody felt this way. But we have learned better. We realize, for example, that sometimes children in the inner city reject the idea that literacy is important, because to want to become literate is to buy into the white establishment's value system, and that is verboten. If these children buckle down in school and make any effort to learn, they are mocked by their friends. Literacy in this case is a burden, not a joy; it means alienation and isolation. We understand, too, that in some traditional cultures in which only males are expected to read and write, both men and women may reject a woman who takes on roles involving literacy. And there are other instances where so much importance is placed on being able to read and write that it is inhibiting; some adults will go to great lengths to hide their illiteracy from employers, neighbors, and their own children because they are ashamed.

Psychological and educational research has demonstrated the profound influence of belief. Most of today's theories of motivation put heavy weight on cognitions and beliefs. Dweck (1986) has shown that children who attribute their school achievement to an external source such as luck perform less well than do children who attribute it to their own intelligence or effort. Similarly, Seligman (1975) has shown that the amount of overall control that people feel they have over their destiny makes a huge difference: If you believe that you are helpless, you stop trying. We also know that teachers' opinions of their students matter greatly: Rosenthal and Jacobson (1968) demonstrated that a teacher who expects children to do well behaves in a way conducive to their doing well. Unfortunately, the converse also holds: A teacher's expectation that a child will fail may in fact move that child toward failure.

We act on these insights; we exhort teachers to work at raising students' self-esteem, on the grounds that it will improve their school performance. We attempt to make the teachers themselves feel competent as well as confident that they can work constructively with children, so that their expectations will be positive and their impact strong and effective.

Researchers in the field of reading have discovered that a consideration of beliefs also illuminates other issues beyond those of motivation. One of the biggest insights we have gained from cognitive theory is that comprehension is based on the integration of multiple knowledge sources, and that people rely very heavily on prior knowledge in any and all comprehension. We also recognize that prior knowledge is not simply "cold cognition"; it includes beliefs, attitudes, and values as well (Alexander, in press).

Moreover, the influence of our beliefs on our understanding is not necessarily always advantageous. Perceptions and values can make it difficult to comprehend material that does not conform to those values (Pace, Marshall, Horowitz, Lipson, & Lucido, 1989). Williams (1991), for example, found that adolescents predicted that story characters would do what they themselves would do in a similar situation even in the face of textual information that clearly pointed in another direction.

These considerations hold for any kind of comprehension, but the fact that we are talking specifically about the comprehension of text makes a difference. People have particular beliefs about text itself. Some books—the Bible, the Koran—are sacred, and they are approached and understood and used in special, sacred ways. But books in general seem special to some extent: How many of us have overcrowded shelves and closets simply because we cannot bear to throw away books?

This specialness of text is promoted actively. For example, a deep respect for the written word is reflected in the Jewish tradition of dropping honey on a book for children to taste so they will grow up with a love of learning. (In fact, similar approaches have sometimes backfired. Years ago, school children were taught how to open a new book properly, a few pages at a time, so that the binding wouldn't break; but this often taught them to revere books as valuable physical objects and thereby rendered them less approachable as texts to enjoy. Today we rejoice in the availability of inexpensive paperbacks.)

Without a doubt, text is special. Children often think that everything they read is true. If it says so in print, it must be believed. Some adults think the same thing. Even when we know better, it is difficult not to be seduced by the printed page. We may be able to read *The National Enquirer* (only in supermarket check-out lines!) for momentary amusement and not for "facts," but we may be tempted to swallow *The New York Times* whole.

How do these beliefs develop? As children grow up, and as they begin to learn to read, they gradually become aware of many things about reading—that certain things are easier to read than others, that there are many different purposes for reading and many different strategies used in reading. These observations, sometimes helped along by parents, teachers, and peers, form the basis of what we call metacognition, or, in other words, knowledge about reading (Garner, 1987). But children do not all make the same observations nor do they have the same experiences, and so their knowledge will be somewhat different, that is, they will develop what we call beliefs and attitudes. It is important that children grow up with healthy, constructive attitudes about books and about reading, in part because as development proceeds, beliefs and metacognitive knowledge correlate increasingly with reading achievement, suggesting that achievement depends to some degree on these factors.

Wagner, Spratt, Gal, and Paris (1989) found much the same pattern of development in Morocco, a culture quite different from our own, involving two distinct school systems (Islamic and French), an instructional emphasis on learning religious text and rote memorization, and until recently, a much lower proportion of literacy in the population. There were, however, interesting differences: There were no gender differences in reading achievement, as there are in other countries, even though vocational and social advantages clearly accrue to males in Morocco. More of this cross-cultural comparison might yield new insights: For example, much is currently made of the high proficiency of Japanese children in reading; it is notable that Asian school children believe that effort is the most important factor in determining reading proficiency—and that they consider effort to be more important than do American children (Stevenson, Lee, & Stigler, 1982).

We certainly know how important belief systems are and that they are a strong determinant of academic success. But there are many things we still don't know. What are the processes by which beliefs and attitudes develop and become interrelated with reading? How does motivation mediate the relationship? And we have not identified all of the beliefs about the self and about the larger society that may affect one's attitude toward reading and one's achievement.

A major reason for doing such research, of course, is to determine what kinds of instructional programs should be undertaken. Over the last few years we have made substantial progress in delivering instruction to adults who lack basic reading and writing skills, for example. But given the ordinary requirements of daily living—demands of employment, family, etc.—plus the need for privacy and confidentiality, it has been a challenge. There is a high dropout rate in adult training programs. The field is crying out for new insights and approaches.

One such approach is to focus on family literacy. We acknowledge that parents' attitudes toward reading and literacy, their own interests and needs, and their evaluation of schools and teachers can impact considerably on the achievement of their children, and so we try to change these attitudes, if need be. And intergenerational literacy programs are also aimed at helping the parents themselves improve in reading, via capturing and capitalizing on their aspirations for their children.

But we must do much more work to determine the ways in which cultural and social factors influence perceptions and beliefs about literacy. If we do not develop our instructional efforts with these considerations in mind, they will not be successful.

Read this book and you will realize how important beliefs are and how powerfully they can influence our judgments and actions. Read it as a scholar; it is an area that is just opening up, and there is fascinating research to be done. Read it as a concerned educator for its ideas about how to promote constructive beliefs in our students and in our teachers. And read it as one of those teachers (which many of us are) and indeed as a human being looking for insights into your own life. It is much easier to think that other people are biased or closed-minded than to understand that if everyone else sees the world through his own construction of it, then you yourself must be doing the same. What beliefs and assumptions do you bring to your consideration of the issues?

And one more point: For which of these beliefs and assumptions do you actually have evidence? It may be difficult to differentiate *belief* and *knowledge* (Abelson, 1979), but there is a clear difference between *belief* and *evidence*. We have evidence that beliefs matter. But this is a general statement, and we know that research is most meaningful in context. Ask always what we have evidence *for*. Will changing teachers' beliefs change their instructional practices? Obviously, we believe so; but we must find out for sure, that is, gather evidence relevant to the particular situation and context involved. And when we find such evidence, we must go one step further and ask whether changing those instructional practices does in fact improve student performance. That, too, must sooner or later be demonstrated in the appropriate context.

Ruth Garner and Pat Alexander have assembled a collection of provocative and timely research reports that are worthy of careful consideration. As a group, they define the field as it is currently emerging as an important focus for study, and they have much to tell us about a very important area indeed.

REFERENCES

Abelson, R. P. (1979). Differences between belief and knowledge systems. *Cognitive Science, 3*, 355–366.

Alexander, P. A. (in press). The interplay between domain and general strategy knowledge: Exploring the influence of motivation and situation. In A. J. Pace (Ed.), *Beyond prior knowledge.* Norwood, NJ: Ablex.

Dweck, C. (1986). Motivational processes affecting learning. *American Psychologist, 41*, 1040–1048.

Garner, R. (1987). *Metacognition and reading comprehension.* Norwood, NJ: Ablex.

Pace, A. J., Marshall, H., Horowitz, R., Lipson, M., & Lucido, P. (1989). When prior knowledge doesn't facilitate text comprehension: An examination of some of the issues. *National Reading Conference Yearbook, 33,* 213–224.

Rosenthal, R., & Jacobson, L. (1968). *Pygmalion in the classroom: Teacher expectation and pupils' intellectual development.* New York: Holt, Rinehart and Winston.

Seligman, M. E. P. (1975). *Helplessness.* San Francisco: Freeman.

Stevenson, H. W., Lee, S. Y., & Stigler, J. W. (1982). Reading disabilities: The case of Chinese, Japanese, and English. *Child Development, 33,* 1164–1181.

Wagner, D. A., Spratt, J. E., Gal, I., & Paris, S. G. (1989). Reading and believing: Beliefs, attributions, and reading achievement in Moroccan school children. *Journal of Educational Psychology, 881,* 283–293.

Williams, J. P. (1991). Learning-disabled adolescents' difficulties in solving personal/social problems. In J. Baron & R. V. Brown (Eds.), *Teaching decision-making to adolescents.* Hillsdale, NJ: Lawrence Erlbaum Associates.

Preface

Every day in classrooms, teachers and students think about, and with, text. Their beliefs about what text is, who created it, and how to evaluate it are an influence, often a profoundly important one, on how they use text.

Consider the rituals of textbook distribution and collection that Luke, de Castell, and Luke (1983) describe: Someone (occasionally a teacher or a group of teachers, never students) selects a single textbook; students are told which parts of the book are to be read at which times; marking in the book is penalized; what is tested in the classroom is tied explicitly to what is in the book; and the textbook is withdrawn when content has supposedly been mastered. Whether they reflect on beliefs underlying these practices or not, teachers who participate in this ritual year after year reinforce the authority of textbooks. Students in these classrooms are highly likely to view the textbook as icon.

Beliefs about where text comes from (i.e., about authorship) are also important. Although some textbooks compiled by committees of authors are so drab and fact-laden that one is hard put to see an author's presence, text is always a human creation. It is written in a particular time and place, and always with particular intentions. The consequence of failing to remember that text is authored is that both teachers and students can forget that they are reading only one particular construction of reality. Wineburg's clever study (1991) involving eyewitness accounts, newspaper articles, a piece of historical fiction, and an excerpt from an American history textbook on the topic of the Battle of Lexington underscores this point. Even bright, college-bound students rated the textbook excerpt as most trustworthy among the sources, despite the fact that it contradicted primary accounts from both British and American sides and was rather obviously written to aggrandize the heroism and resolve of the colonists.

Tied to beliefs about textbooks as authorless truth is an apparently widespread belief that school text is not be to be evaluated critically. Text, by virtue of its permanence, is available for reinspection and critical scrutiny in a way that speech is not; however, there are few instances in classroom discourse of teachers modeling, and students risking, analysis and criticism of school text (Baker & Freebody, 1989; Haas & Flower, 1988). As Olson and Astington (1993) put it, there are few instances of intent to interpret text, rather than merely learn it.

Beliefs about text is an active area of inquiry—particularly in cognitive, developmental, and social psychology; curriculum; linguistics; literacy education; and rhetoric. We have called this volume on the subject *Beliefs about Text and Instruction with Text* in order to emphasize its two themes: that children and adults have beliefs about text, and that these beliefs influence what is taught and what is learned in classrooms. It is our intent to illustrate what a cross-disciplinary body of work looks like, what varied insights are possible, when the central concerns are beliefs and text.

The book is organized into three main sections. The first section, Children's, Adolescents', and Adults' Beliefs About Text (Chapters 1–5), addresses the first theme of the book (i.e., that children and adults have beliefs about text).

In Chapter 1, Horowitz examines adolescents' understanding of oral and written language. She reports that she presented a set of very diverse forms of discourse (e.g., an oral autobiography transcribed to text, an excerpt from the Texas drivers' manual, lyrics to a rap song, a narrative from a teen magazine) to 10 adolescents enrolled in a summer-long, federally funded program in San Antonio. Two of the interesting findings reported in the chapter are that adolescents were willing to express strong personal constructs and convictions (beliefs) in response to the discourse presented, and that they reported encountering a very limited range of discourse types in school.

Schommer's Chapter 2 presents findings from a series of carefully crafted studies of high school and college students' beliefs about the nature of knowledge and learning. She concludes that individuals' beliefs are multidimensional and that they affect comprehension, metacomprehension, and critical evaluation of text.

In Chapter 3, Nolen, Johnson-Crowley, and Wineburg turn readers' attention from general epistemological beliefs to beliefs about a particular subset of texts: expositions on the topic of correlation. Nolen et al. compare female college students' responses to an excerpt from a standard statistics textbook (they describe it as "considerate, but from a distance") and to an aside on the same topic that appears in a *New York Times* best-seller. To the surprise of Nolen and her colleagues, the main finding is that increased visibility of author yields "a bigger target" (i.e., more for readers to like or dislike).

Both Chapters 4 and 5 address thinking about, and with, persuasive text. In Chapter 4, Garner and Hansis recount how they collected a set of the ubiquitous, mostly unremarkable texts that one is handed on the street (what they call "street texts"). After examining the structure and content of a representative subset of the street texts, Garner and Hansis presented them to 50 adults and examined the adults' understanding, evaluation of source, and reports of likely action (i.e., tossing immediately, keeping for reexamination, or acting on the written request). The authors discuss how beliefs about what the world is like and what actions have value influence comprehension of street texts.

Chambliss devotes the first half of Chapter 5 to descriptions of how we might analyze persuasive text. She relies on philosopher Stephen Toulmin as a foundation for structural analysis and on Aristotle as a basis for content analysis. In the second half of the chapter, Chambliss turns her attention to why it is that persuasive text typically fails to change reader beliefs; she proposes a model of Ideal Reader, Typical Reader, and Good Reader—who engage text in quite different ways.

The second theme of the book (i.e., that beliefs about text influence what is taught and what is learned in classrooms) emerges in the second section, Teachers' Beliefs About Text and Instruction With Text (Chapters 6–11). The authors of the chapters in this section share a concern about classrooms, whether the emphasis is primarily on beliefs about *what* should be taught or on beliefs about *how* particular content should be taught and assessed.

In Chapter 6, Peterson argues convincingly that educational researchers have beliefs that are often "invisible," but that influence their research in classrooms. These beliefs are situated within the context of individual researchers' personal and professional lives and within the professional discourse of the time. Peterson traces the evolution of her own beliefs from a time when work was usually done by academics and handed to teachers "all figured out" to the present when most researchers and teachers work together to construct knowledge about classrooms.

All of the remaining chapters in the second section provide us with pictures of classroom events—and of the teacher beliefs that support these events. Hutton, Spiesman, and Bott, in Chapter 7, describe writing events in four elementary classrooms, where "writing" ranges from practicing handwriting and transcribing someone else's text in two rooms to expressing one's own ideas and editing them in the other two. It is only in the latter two rooms where children display genuine understanding of authorship.

In Chapter 8, Anders and Evans discuss interviews and classroom-video-tape viewings over a period of 4 years with teachers in grades 4, 5, and 6.

Findings about reading instruction are both general (beliefs predict practice) and specific (perceptions of what constitutes adequate assessment change—often dramatically). Anders and Evans make the important point that changes in fundamental beliefs and practices for instruction and assessment come slowly; textbooks, basal readers, and teachers' concern with accountability to external sources all serve to impede change.

In Chapter 9, Borko, Davinroy, Flory, and Hiebert also discuss classroom goals and practices. They describe the first semester of a year-long staff development project. As part of the project, a group of third-grade teachers worked together to plan assessment compatible with their instructional goals in the area of text summarization. Borko and her colleagues remind us, as Anders and Evans did earlier, that teachers' concern about subjectivity in their assessments and their long-held beliefs about a relatively restricted set of assessment tools impede change in assessment practices—at least in the short run.

Chapters 10 and 11 continue to provide us with pictures of classroom events, but they also encourage us to restructure our notions of two key components of classrooms: discussion and text. In Chapter 10, Alvermann and Commeyras describe traditional discursive practices—and alternative ones. They note that language conventions for holding the floor, interrupting, and introducing new topics are traditionally bound up with power relationships among discussion participants. An extended example of an alternative situation, where students feel it is safe to share multiple readings of a controversial text, is provided.

In Chapter 11, the focus is text—what it is. Gillingham, Young, and Kulikowich note that nonlinear text (i.e., text that differs from linear text in its structure or lack of it, text that is usually presented electronically) can be an immensely powerful classroom tool. Students can retrieve ideas from a multimedia encyclopedia on CD-ROM and can, in turn, store their reports, essays, and journals for classmates to retrieve and read. Unfortunately, Gillingham and his colleagues report that they found that in-service teachers enrolled in an instructional computing course did not, by and large, consider nonlinear text to be text.

The final section of the volume, Issues in Research on Beliefs About Text (Chapters 12–14), addresses some of the issues that arose in previous chapters. In Chapter 12, Alexander and Dochy attempt to establish conceptual boundaries for knowing and believing. They provide personal perspectives on the matter and then ask various groups of adults (undergraduates, graduate students and faculty in educational psychology, and educational researchers engaged in the study of knowledge or beliefs) to talk about knowing and believing. One of the interesting findings that emerges is that undergraduates, in general, maintain that it represents strength of character to resist doubt and to ignore information that runs counter to one's beliefs. No wonder Schommer found so much certainty (see Chapter 2) and Chambliss found so little changing of beliefs (see Chapter 5)!

The last two chapters, Chapters 13 and 14, introduce readers to the social psychology literature on beliefs and to recent work on ideology. We learn from Dole and Sinatra, in Chapter 13, that social psychologists have paid considerable attention to beliefs—how we acquire them and how likely we are to change them. One reliable finding emerging from this body of work is that our beliefs survive virtually intact despite evidence, often overwhelming evidence, that runs counter to those beliefs. The species appears to rely very little on evidence, preferring, as Howard Gardner (1991) put it, "dominant images, prevalent stereotypes, or favored ways of framing a problem" (p. 170).

Then, we learn from Wade, Thompson, and Watkins, in Chapter 14, that dissonance between a reader's ideology (belief system) and an author's can cause the reader to distance herself from a text and to read in a resistant, critical manner. Ideology is foregrounded. Another reader might set aside ideology and read the author appreciatively. This notion that readers can approach a text in a variety of ways is reminiscent of Nolen and her colleagues' point (see Chapter 3) that readers with similar "entering characteristics" (e.g., topic knowledge) can, nonetheless, have wholly different interactions with the same text.

The three main sections of the book are preceded by a Foreword and followed by an Afterword. In the Foreword, Williams discusses the importance of studying beliefs about text, including beliefs about the "specialness" of text (i.e., deep respect for the written word). In the Afterword, Weinstein comments on what insights are possible with sustained scrutiny of beliefs about text. She also offers sage advice to researchers (e.g., judge respondents' statements about beliefs against their actions, and work toward theories and models of belief systems that combine the "pieces of a very complex puzzle" presented discretely here).

We invite readers to explore the varied perspectives offered in this volume. The chapters are not decontextualized pieces, delivered unto readers from nowhere by nobody, *unsponsored* texts, to use Bruner's (1990) term; rather, they are pieces framed in a time and place, with particular intentions. One of those intentions is that they, separately and as a whole, stimulate discussion about beliefs and text.

REFERENCES

Baker, C. D., & Freebody, P. (1989). Talk around text: Constructions of textual and teacher authority in classroom discourse. In S. de Castell, A. Luke, & C. Luke (Eds.), *Language, authority, and criticism: Readings on the school textbook* (pp. 263–283). London: Falmer.

Bruner, J. (1990). *Acts of meaning*. Cambridge, MA: Harvard University Press.

Gardner, H. (1991). *The unschooled mind: How children think and how schools should teach.* New York: Basic Books.

Haas, C., & Flower, L. (1988). Rhetorical reading strategies and the construction of meaning. *College Composition and Communication, 39,* 167–183.

Luke, C., de Castell, S., & Luke, A. (1983). Beyond criticism: The authority of the school text. *Curriculum Inquiry, 13,* 111–127.

Olson, D. R., & Astington, J. W. (1993). Thinking about thinking: Learning how to take statements and hold beliefs. *Educational Psychologist, 28,* 7–23.

Wineburg, S. S. (1991). On the reading of historical texts: Notes on the breach between school and academy. *American Educational Research Journal, 28,* 495–519.

R.G.
P.A.A.

PART ONE

CHILDREN'S, ADOLESCENTS', AND ADULTS' BELIEFS ABOUT TEXT

CHAPTER ONE

Adolescent Beliefs About Oral and Written Language

Rosalind Horowitz
The University of Texas—San Antonio

In the past decade, linguists, psychologists, and educators have worked diligently to describe the different discourse genres that exist inside and outside of schools. One goal has been to characterize the varieties of oral and written language. Another goal has been to describe different genres of oral language and explain, specifically, how natural conversation differs from, or combines with, forms of literate language—particularly academic, written language. Still another goal has been to understand the difficulties students experience in learning to process different text types.

A review that I conducted of the theories about oral and written language over the past century conveys the recency of the study of written language (Horowitz & Samuels, 1987). It was not until the 1930s when the differences between the functions of oral and written language were highlighted by the Prague School of Linguistics, and it was not until much later, in the 1970s and 1980s when discourse analysis systems were developed that allowed for serious study of written English texts (Biber, 1988; Chafe & Danielewicz, 1987; Halliday, 1987; Tottie & Backlund, 1986). Attention was focused by linguists on the oral—the sound system—given that most languages have been exclusively oral and most individuals users of oral language. The study of oral extended discourse has become a relatively recent activity enhanced to some extent by the use of tape recorders, video tapes, and computers.

A review of the literature in 1987 also revealed that most comparisons and contrasts of oral and written discourse have used adult samples of language. Further, the analyses of oral and written discourse were based on the observations of adult experts—not the general public—certainly not students. As students move up the grades they are likely to hold different beliefs about language and respond to different oral and written language based on these beliefs.

In this chapter, I describe adolescent beliefs about and interpretations of a range of oral and written discourse. Although I was invited to write a chapter about children's beliefs about oral and written language, I have chosen to focus on adolescents. This is an age group that has interested me for a number of years. Further, adolescents are a unique population to investigate for the study of beliefs about texts. First, there is little research to turn to which addresses adolescent beliefs about language, their expression of these beliefs (their use of a metalanguage to describe their beliefs) and their beliefs about the social identity of interlocutors—those producing or receiving communication. However, we do know from the research on adolescents that they have a strong interest in others (the peer group) and that they often have strong opinions (likes and dislikes) about others and beliefs about self and others. They routinely express beliefs about what they hear and read. Adolescents frequently analyze people, social relationships, social situations, and communication acts. Their beliefs have been studied, however, in a sparse literature (e.g., Csikszentmihalyi & Larson, 1984; Csikszentmihalyi, Rathunde, & Whalen, 1993; Livesley & Bromley, 1973; Worell & Danner, 1989).

Second, recommendations have been made and are being sought to determine the kinds of materials that might be suitable for building the literacy and cognitive development of adolescents. I recently reviewed a popular publication produced by the National Council of Teachers of English, *Books and the Teenage Reader. A Guide for Teachers, Librarians and Parents* (Carlsen, 1980), that identifies texts for adolescents and found that the books recommended were mostly narratives. Topics, such as health and sports, were listed and presented primarily through narratives. Another more recently published book by the International Reading Association, *Teens' Favorite Books*, 1992, suggested reading material across a broad range of categories. Their recommended books, including books dealing with issues such as obesity, were also largely narratives. Although narratives are highly valuable reading, there was little to be found that represented the range of authentic nonfiction or oral genres of the kinds that I consider in this chapter. There has been little attempt to provide adolescents with oral or written discourse that comes directly from other living teenagers in the world adolescents know today.

Third, an examination of oral and written language can benefit by taking into account the beliefs and attitudes of language users beyond those of professional linguists and psychologists. Adolescents are exposed to a variety of oral genres in the real world that may complement and contribute to their intuitions about and understanding of written language—even that used in schools. However, to date, little is known about these oral genres and the ways in which adolescents relate to them particularly when they are presented in writing.

Fourth, when they are invited to do so, adolescents may be quite able to insightfully talk about texts on a higher-order level than children and particularly when they realize that their ideas are valued and appreciated.

This chapter, thus, examines adolescent beliefs about oral and written language. The study of beliefs is a relatively new and an undeveloped area of research. There is a varied research literature that emerged in the 1970s and 1980s and is being carried on in the 1990s that is particularly powerful for its overlap with and potential contributions to the study of beliefs. This includes work in social psychology and social cognition (Abelson, 1986; Fiske & Taylor, 1991; Schank & Abelson, 1977; Perner, 1988, 1991; Ross, 1987; Wyer & Srull, 1984), attribution theory (Jones et al., 1987), person perception (Livesely & Bromley, 1973), speech-communications and persuasion (Kernan, Sbasay, & Shinn, 1988), and language and interpersonal relations (Berger & Bradac, 1982; Cushman & Cahn, 1985; Gregory & Carroll, 1978; Gudykunst & Ting-Toomey, 1988).

Beliefs have been examined as part of the study of the development of theories of mind in children (Astington, Harris, & Olson, 1988). David R. Olson (1988) points out that "... perhaps the central question, in cognitive science discourse is the role that 'intentional states,' that is, representational states including beliefs, desires, intentions, and sentiments, play in the explanation of behavior" (p. 414). Beliefs may be conceived as minitheories of the mind, ways of characterizing language and behavior and ascribing mental states to people. Beliefs are, I believe, profoundly personal and delicate constructs that represent convictions. They are a part of the social and cultural truths to which individuals try to adhere in daily living. They are often difficult, however, to pinpoint and describe because they are interwoven with individual philosophies, habits, experiences, and social histories that are emotional and personal. They may also be propositional or image-like in form or conceptualized as attitudes. In some respects, they may defy analysis and classification. Nevertheless, researchers who wish to study oral and written discourse can substantially benefit by trying to understand the beliefs adolescent learners hold about oral and written language and "demystify mentalities" maintained by this age group. The study of adolescent beliefs would help us to know more about adolescents and their perceptions about language. This study would also help us to select discourse and plan for text processing in the range of content fields offered in the upper grades.

THE RESEARCH PROJECT

Subjects

During the summer of 1993, adolescents participating in the San Antonio Jobs for Progress, Project SER (Spanish for "to be"), a summer youth employment training project, were selected for the present research. This summer, federally funded program pays low-income, urban adolescents to go to school and/or for work on given job sites in the city. Students lived in San Antonio, Texas. This research follows other studies that I have designed to understand this urban population (see Horowitz, 1991). There were 10 students, an even number of males and females. The students participating in this project were Hispanic, specifically Mexican-American, and one was Black. They were selected for the project based on the *McGraw Hill Test of Adult Basic Education.* Students were designated as low, middle, and high ability readers. Those in the lower ability group performed from a grade level of 6.1 to 8.0, the middle level group performed from 8.1 to 10.0, and the upper level group performed at a grade level of 10.1 to 12.9. Students were entering the 10th or 11th grade in the Fall of 1993 and were between 15 and 17 years of age. All but one was at the correct age for their grade.

Two graduate students who were interested in adolescents and had taught this age group conducted the study. Each adolescent in our study met with one graduate student privately and was asked to read and listen to passages that were carefully selected for the research. The graduate students spent some time introducing themselves and getting to know each subject prior to the actual study.

Passages

Nine passages were selected for this project in the following manner: The Director of Project SER, graduate students, and principal investigator selected real-world passages that adolescents might be exposed to through a variety of media. We were particularly interested in discourse which was composed by adolescents or by adults for adolescents. We sought a range of discourse from varieties of oral and written genres—with particular attention to the oral genres. Thus, we included spoken texts from the verbal arts, some designed to be performed, such as rap music and opera, others including letters to the editor, that had a speech-like quality, an interview transcribed to text, and a newspaper report for the general public. We were interested in moving beyond the great division of oral versus written discourse (Ong, 1982). We considered variations of speech-like language presented *within* writing (Horowitz, in press). The passages were from 1 to 6 paragraphs in length, usually about two paragraphs, were typed on a sheet of paper in large size font, centered on the page, with questions and Likert scales that followed on subsequent sheets of paper.[1]

Procedures

A graduate student read the following instructions to each adolescent subject:

> We are studying the different kind of language that is used in different places. We have selected some passages which were either written or spoken. We would like you to read or listen to these passages and answer some questions about them. We would like you to use your best judgment and tell us what you believe the passage might be communicating. You are free to reread or relisten to a passage until you feel comfortable enough to answer a question. This is not a test. There will be no grades. This is part of a project we are doing to learn more about teenagers and their beliefs about language. Your name will never be identified with your responses.

The graduate student presented each passage in counterbalanced order, alternating the presentation with the first passage as either for listening or reading. Students read the passages silently. The oral presentation of the passages was on a cassette taperecorder. The passages were taped by an individual who had been a theater major, however, the reading of each passage was done in a Dan Rather, announcement-style, which was not dramatic and was easy to follow. The style was announcement-like in order to avoid influencing the students' interpretations. A graduate student recorded the responses of each subject and, then, transcribed, from notes, onto computer, in more complete language the students' responses.

RESULTS

In this section, I provide information about each of the passages used in the research, a discussion of some of the questions posed about those passages, and the beliefs expressed by the adolescents about the oral and written language studied. The Likert Scales used and questions presented for each passage can be found in the Appendix (pp. 23–24).

A number of the passages used in this research represented a range of oral genres in the arts which had been converted, at some juncture, to written language. Intentionally, there was no context presented for the passages. I hoped that the adolescents would be able to imagine a context

---

[1]The taperecording of the passages used in this research may be obtained by contacting the author.

that would be appropriate for each discourse sample. Further, we were interested in the adolescents' perceptions and beliefs about the interlocutors—speakers/writers and audience listeners/readers—by whom the messages were produced and for whom the messages were intended and designed, the adolescents' perceptions and beliefs about the language used and the messages expressed. The nine passages and adolescent beliefs about these passages are presented next and followed by a discussion of the research findings.

Passage #1

> My parents were in a state about me. One day they invited our minister to
> our house, because I had been close to him before all this stuff started
> happening. They thought maybe I'd listen to him. But on that day, my friends
> and I were hanging out again. We were drinking beer and popping pills—some
> really strong downers. I could hardly walk and I had no idea what I was
> saying. Well, instead of letting me sleep it off or keeping me where I was,
> my friends dropped me off in front of my house. (Haring, 1991, p. 19)

The Text

Passage #1 was an oral autobiography by Keith Haring, a visual artist—painter, sculptor, print-maker. His oral presentation was an interview, that was later transcribed to text, *The Authorized Biography*, with probably some editing. This editing makes it sound more like written discourse. The passage is written in first-person which may actually make it sound speech-like. It contains vocabulary that might be construed as street language—"all this stuff started happening," "hanging out," "popping pills." One of my undergraduate students, however, felt the text had an aura of intelligence about it; to her, it appeared organized, moreso than the organization one would expect to find in informal, everyday conversation of the street. The clauses used were short, swift, and conversation-like.

Adolescent Beliefs

In this chapter, beliefs expressed by our 10 subjects are reported. The beliefs reported by two Mexican-American females, San Juana and Roseanne, are highlighted. These two students produced responses which showed particularly good insights about the language presented and creative theorizing about the interlocutors and the situational contexts represented. San Juana (a common name in Mexico, St. Jane) was in the low ability reading group as she read at 8.2 and was 15 going into the 11th grade. Roseanne was in the high ability category of reading. This 16-year-old, 11th grader, read at a 12.9 grade level. Responses by the other subjects are reported where appropriate and a complete report of the responses of all of the subjects can be obtained by contacting the author.

Passage #1 was repeatedly identified as spoken and rated as highly believable. When San Juana was asked about what the passage was trying to convey, she succinctly expressed her theoretical beliefs about friendships: "You can have friends. But you can't have some friends." Roseanne expressed her philosophy about writing and made intertextual comparisons: "It reminds me of the *Diary of Ann Frank.* Do you know that story? She wrote that for herself. It was later that someone else found it and read it," insinuating that Haring's discourse was really self-talk, a prelude to authorship.

When asked about how believable the passage was another subject noted, "It's all fake. I've never gotten drunk. I've never done drugs." Several of our Hispanic students turned the Minister referred to in Passage #1 into a Priest, consistent with their cultural schemata of the clergy. We had hoped that these adolescents would consider the language, grammar, and punctuation— but the adolescents' remarks were focused on the content of the message and the language only indirectly. When the researchers asked whether Passage #1 might be used in school, the majority said no because of vocabulary such as "popping pills." A Likert Scale item was designed to ask students about the audience for whom this passage was intended. Roseanne noted the change of text quality. "It started for an intimate friend. Self. Later (in time) it became public." This is an example of Roseanne's awareness and beliefs about the evolving nature of texts as discourse. They begin for the private self but become vehicles for public expression of ideas.

Passage #2
HOW TO PASS ON A TWO-LANE ROAD

1. Stay well back from car ahead so you can see ahead. Check rearview and side mirrors, also turn your head and look back—someone may be passing you. Signal left.
2. Check well ahead for "No Passing Zone" and oncoming cars. Be sure you have time and space enough to overtake the car ahead and return to the right lane before an approaching car comes within 200 feet of you.
3. Tap your horn when necessary to alert the driver ahead.
4. Pass on the left and do not return to the right lane until safely clear of overtaken vehicle. Wait until you can see the car you have just passed in your rearview mirror before returning to right lane.
5. Signal right turn to return to right lane. Be sure to turn signal off.

(*Texas Drivers Handbook,* 1992)

The Text

Passage #2 was an excerpt from the *Texas Drivers Manual.* It represents a sample of planned, formal, directions.

Adolescent Beliefs

There was little interest in this passage. The adolescents may not have had driver's education in school, or a license. Nevertheless, many of the adolescents regarded the passage as highly believable and true because it was written in the manual. Roseanne thought it was probably true. She focused on the multiple ways a text can communicate a message. "But like an opinion everyone may have a different way of explaining it. Maybe, you don't need to do it (drive) exactly like that (the way the manual says)." She knows the passage can be questioned. San Juana noted on a Likert Scale item that "Maybe. Everyone has their own way of doing things when driving." We asked specifically about whether the students thought that this passage was stated in a way that one could understand and perform what was being described. Henry felt it was necessary to do multiple readings.

Passage #3

Clear the way for the prophets of rage
Engagin' on the stage, on a track
Tell Jack stay in the back
I was born
Every level I'm on
You're warned
Just in case you forgot
I pump up the kilowatts
To let 'em know which direction
To go what's up I want to know
I test the front row
Forgivinen the givin' while the livin' is livin' it up
So many people is sleepin' while standin' up
'Cause the name of the game
Don't give 'em checks above the necks
Some don't realize the same side
Siddity in the city
Suburbs or projects
But we're livin' in a different time
Some speed, some lead
While some jus' pump rhymes
Then again all in the same gang
Info to flow
And heal all below
Let's go and find
The piece of mind that's taken
Or else the black
Or start breakin' . . .
Public Enemy no! (*Apocalypse 91*, 1991)

The Text

Passage #3 is a rap song entitled "Lost at Birth" from the album *Apocalypse 91, The Enemy Strikes Back*, sung by Public Enemy and produced in 1991. It refers to the power of space and time, the different kinds of people at different strata of society, and addresses the tensions of seeking upward mobility. We asked our adolescents: What discourse community is the individual from who is saying this? Texts evolve out of communities of speakers or writers. Some texts convey these communities more directly than others. Some also convey conflicts among communities or cultures and call for certain kinds of stances by the reading/listening communities. Our questionnaire also asked: How does the speaker/writer's community influence what is said? What does the speaker/writer believe and feel about the people receiving this message?

Adolescent Beliefs

One student who knew the lyrics to this rap song thought it sounded more like Shakespeare or classic poetry. San Juana appeared to become angry during her reading of the text. Roseanne was more contemplative. She did not want to stereotype or make judgments about the speaker/writer or the discourse. When asked about whether this passage would appear in school, she indicated: "First, it was confusing to me, and, then, I put myself in that situation and I communicated with it. . . . Prejudiced people are everywhere. No, not for school—people don't care." San Juana noted: "She (the author) doesn't like rich people."

The researchers asked: What discourse community is the individual from who is saying this? Likert Scales were used that asked the adolescents to consider whether the speaker was rich or poor, maintained very distant, very friendly or extremely close relationships and asked the student to determine where the author stood with regards to literacy, whether they might be illiterate or of high literacy. San Juana referred to the speaker as a "he" and thought he was above average in intelligence because he could explain himself. To her, the discourse "sounded friendly." She said: "Most people put down people who are below average . . . and rich people. . . . It's like they see a god. Below average—you don't belong here." Leticia, a Black, in the low-ability reading group, reading at 7.8 grade level, 16 years of age and going into the 11th grade said: "He started out down here. Now he's successful—so he's moved up." Leticia distinguishes two kinds of literacy. "You know with the slang and the spelling it may not be very good speaking or writing but he *was* smart. He knew what he was talking about and said it in a different way."

Passage #4

Jesabel, the other migrant farm worker I'm supposed to meet, lives in the last trailer in the park, right next to a strawberry field. Spare parts of bicycles, rusted tires and crumpled beer cans are scattered across the yard. She meets us out front along with her sister Aneni, 14, and two boys from the area. Jesabel has long jet-black hair and is wearing an off-the-shoulder white top. The first thing she does is joke about the living conditions her family has to deal with. "One time the pipe in our trailer, it broke, right? So nobody could use the bathroom," she says. "We had to use our neighbor's toilet for a month and a half. When the parts came in, the plumber didn't fix it right. Three weeks later, it broke again. That was during the hurricane. Water was, like, coming in the window and the carpet was getting wet——" Her voice rises dramatically. Everyone chortles.

"How can you laugh?" I ask.

"It's funny to us because whenever it rains, no matter what, something gets wet. Awful. And there's a whole bunch of cats under our trailer, right? They go up through the floor inside our trailer. They make holes. Yeah." She shakes her head. More hysterics. "Smells nasty." (Ann, 1993, p. 85)

The Text

Passage #4 is about Jesabel, a 16-year-old, and her living quarters. Jesabel is described in *Sassy*, a teen magazine, as a migrant farm worker, living under difficult conditions. She told Mary Ann, the author of "These Girls Live Like Slaves," which appeared in the 1993 edition of *Sassy*, all about "living in overcrowded trailers, working from dawn till dusk, missing school and treating pesticide burns with alcohol." Her family is among the first- and second-generation Mexican immigrants working in Texas. We were interested in seeing if our Texas-based adolescents could determine the community that Jesabel was from and whether or not it was the same community as that of the author's community. We thought that the author came from an upper class culture based on some of the details that she focuses on in her description of Jesabel. Finally, this text was written in third person and has linguistic features that make it seem more written-like—including longer clauses, more detailed vocabulary, no slang but still appears to be written by a young adult.

Adolescent Beliefs

The method of presentation may have influenced the beliefs about whether the Jesabel passage was written or spoken discourse. The adolescents were sure about their assessment of the passages. They rated the passages consistently as highly likely to be written or highly likely to be spoken. However, this passage resulted in considerable variation in beliefs about the believability of the discourse. Students just were not sure about the authenticity of this passage. Our subject San Juana related this passage to her family situation. "There's going to be one (a Jesabel) in every family that puts the family down." . . . "I can relate because we have had problems before. I could understand what the girl was feeling and in a way I could relate to the family too." San Juana's response is highly personal and empathic.

Half of our adolescents indicated that this was not a passage that was likely to appear in school. At this age level and given teenage views of privacy, the treatment of the migrants' dwellings of this poor caliber and toilet problems seemed inappropriate for school text and discourse.

Our adolescents characterized Jesabel's community as "ugly," "low-income," "poor," "not safe," a "ranch type," and "a bad slum, somewhere with a lot of storms." Our low ability reader, Leticia, a Black female, thought that "the author might actually be Jesabel" and that Jesabel spoke in the third person because she didn't want to use "I" and reveal her identity.

Passage #5

Do you know they just don't make clothes for people who wears glasses. There's no pockets anymore. So if you take your glasses off. They're easy to lose or break. Well New York a Phonic Center has the answer to your problem. Contactless lenses and the new soft lenses. The Center gives you thirty days and see if you like them. And if you don't. They could refunds your money. (Except for the examination fee). So if you're tired of glasses. Go to New York a Phonic Center on Eleven West Forty-Second Street near fifth Avenue for sight with no hassle. Please call BR9-5555......Would it get some wind for the sailboat. And it could get those for it is. It could get the railroad for these workers. It could be a balloon. It could be Franky, it could be very fresh and clean, it could be. It could get some gasoline shortest one it could be. Al these are the days my friends and these are the days my friends. Look....batch catch hatch latch match patch watch snatch
scratch..Look.
SWEARIN TO GOD   WHO LOVES YOU
FRANKIE VALLIE   THE FOUR SEASONS
(*Knowles*, 1976)

The Text

We expected a range of responses to Passage 5. It is an opera written by an autistic teenager at age 17, who worked with Christopher Knowles. This opera was adapted to written text. The autistic teenager was a talented performer, choreographer, poet, and visual artist, born with severe brain-damage. The language is autistic and is incomprehensible at times. Words such as "wears" and "refunds" are strange when presented within this context, and sentences are incomplete, ungrammatical, and lack cohesion and direction.

Adolescent Beliefs

As with the previous passage, students who listened to this passage regarded it as oral language, and those who read the passage regarded it as written language. The teens who identified it as written language were less certain in their judgments than those who listened and identified it as spoken. (For one student, the medium always dictated whether it was spoken or written.) Some thought it was a radio or TV commercial. As soon as the text became bizarre, they turned off and blocked out the text. Roseanne thought it was writing intended to be spoken. One reader, Leticia, reached, "go to the New York a Phonic Center on eleven west 42nd street, near fifth avenue for sight with no hassle" . . . "would it get some wind for the sailboat," and paused. She lifted her head up and said, "What happened?," then, went back to reading.

We asked: If you were a teacher how would you grade this and why? Responses varied, from grades of A to D. San Juana read the passage and said: "This text is worthy of a D. The text seemed phony as an advertisement." She regarded the person as stupid to write this. "Everybody is smart. Nobody is stupid in this world. They really need to express and take the time to write what they are feeling." Another student thought Frankie Valli wrote this with The Four Seasons.

Those who read this gave it a low score for believability. Those who listened to this varied in their perceptions of the passage. One of our graduate students who conducted the research noted: "What I think I see going on here, is that being able to look at the passage, they are able to identify mechanical inconsistencies." The teens who listened to this passage seemed to rate it higher because of perceptions of originality—but scored it lower for believability, a judgment that reappears in this research following listening. The passage sounded like a commercial; the teenagers have been taught not to believe what "sounds" like a commercial. Listeners based judgment of the passage on content; the readers on form. This is consistent with what we know about reading and listening to school discourse. In listening one can focus on the meaning—one doesn't need to worry about the code—but while reading one is engaged in decoding and comprehending, concurrently, and the visual presentation (even handwriting) may influence the process of understanding and the interpretation of the text.

Punctuation is important here; for one student, the rhyming words required commas. The sentences attracted the student's attention. Many of our subjects thought this was an advertisement. For these students, such advertising represents exaggeration in language and form.

Passage #6

I'm 16 years old and am heavily into lowered mini-trucks. I don't have a truck of my own yet, but I'm working on that problem. I'm considering a Chevy or Nissan. I was wondering what's the best truck to slam? I was wondering if you could tell me what's the least expensive way to lower my truck, and can I do it myself or should I have a shop do it? Is it hard to put a convertible on, and do they come in hard and soft tops? Could you tell me what the best stereo system to buy is? Thanks for the great tips and thanks for a great magazine. (DeBlasio, 1992)

The Text

This passage is from a 1992 edition of *Mini Truckin'* and is a letter to the editor of a magazine. Letters to editors by individuals seeking advice have recently caught the attention of discourse analysts in that they seem to represent a common and unique genre of discourse worthy of linguistic analysis (Horowitz, in press). They are comments about the individuals, our society, and the needs of different people. Without prompting, my graduate students found this passage to be an honest attempt at producing a letter to the editor.

Adolescent Beliefs

Of the students who read this passage, they all unequivocally identified it as written. These readers accurately identified the discourse as a letter to the editor of a magazine. Of those who listened to it, half identified it as spoken and were quite certain about its speech-like quality.

When judging this passage for school, their initial judgment was on the content and not on the form. They initially indicated the topic of minitrucks was not acceptable for school. When prompted to separate content from form, and asked whether the style would be found in school, then they all indicated letter writing was done frequently in schools and was acceptable.

We asked one question unique to this passage. Is this a Texan speaking/writing? One subject said it was a Texan because it was about a Chevy and "Texans buy Chevy's," Texans brag about trucks more. "There aren't a lot of people here with minitrucks." Roseanne said: "I can't tell. That would be a judgment." She is extremely careful about the judgments that she makes.

Passage #7

Edmund stared at the page, horrified. He recalled Mr. Dupin's questions and his own answers. These lines were much more than that. He reread them. When he reached the word, *death*, that word so often written, he shuddered,

closed the book, and pushed it away. There was something very wrong with
Mr. Dupin. (Avi, 1989, p. 83)

The Text

This passage is from *The Man who was Poe* (1989), a novel that one of our
graduate students could not take out of the hands of his son. It is not
conversational-like discourse. It is in third person. We expected that it would
sound like a novel to our adolescents.

Adolescent Beliefs

Leticia said: "Oh, this is Steven King." Steven King is very popular among
adolescents in Texas. He has created horror stories and supernatural novels
which have been adapted as films. Once again, those who read the text,
generally saw it as written and those who listened to the text, generally
perceived it as spoken. As anticipated, the passage was usually identified
as fiction. The believability of the passage was low; they recognized this
passage as a story. This passage was not particularly revealing. Students
talked about their views of death: "It was prepared by someone who was
afraid of the word death, because of the way he expresses himself and
because of the way he wrote the word death."

Passage #8

For example, in a study of fighting among teen-agers in a tough, inner-city
Boston neighborhood, Dr. Levitt described the attitudes of a 14-year old girl:
"She sees fighting as an inevitable law of nature, something people have to
do when they get angry. She doesn't connect it to anything about her life,
but sees it as an impersonal rule." Dr. Levitt said this type of thinking reflected
the lowest level of the development hierarchy.

At a slightly higher level, a 14-year old boy said he would fight to stick up
for his family. His credo about fighting came from his mother, who he said
had told him, "If someone starts it, you beat them up." This attitude, Dr. Levitt
said, reflects a rule that has some degree of personal meaning. (Goleman,
1993, p. 35)

The Text

This passage is from a section called a "Study on Fighting" an excerpt from
The New York Times Science section and which appeared in an article
entitled, "Teen-agers are Called Shrewd Judges of Risk." Unlike the other
samples of discourse, this one is written by an adult who is a psychologist
and who is reporting her knowledge about adolescents and the laws by
which they live and fight. We asked our adolescents to tell us whether they
believed the remarks expressed to be true.

Adolescent Beliefs

Again, the mode of presentation influenced students' judgments of whether this was oral or written language. Students found Passage #8 to be highly believable (Likert Scale scores were 4 or 5). One graduate student felt that this high believability was influenced by the fact that the speaker is identified as a doctor and that the passage was viewed as authentic because it was about fighting—a topic that they know about.

The majority, nine, of the adolescents said it was produced by a doctor and one subject indicated a "nosey reporter." The passage was regarded as formal writing for a general audience, the public, parents, teenagers, or there was no idea whom the audience might be. A number saw fighting as a topic teachers would bring up in the classroom. San Juana said: "Yes, I'd like to see this presented in my school. The word can get across to control your fight, control your temper." One male saw this text as cohesive, "Yes, it sticks to the facts, it sticks to the topic." Another student, Juan, said he would not like to see this used in school, "If a teacher gave it to me, I'd give it back to them."

Leticia said, "We just got done talking about this topic. It was on the Texas Assessment of Academic Skills Test (TAAS)." She would like to listen to the text (as a private experience) and not talk about it.

We asked: "Do you believe what this says is true?" San Juana indicated that she believed this text to be true, "If I had to defend my family. I would do it. And if my parents would tell me, if I fight, beat them up. My understanding of this statement is, if you are going to fight, don't lose it." One male said, "My mom says, if I throw the first punch I'd be in trouble, I'd better throw the last."

Passage #9

When considering the best liked cities on earth, Paris looms large among them. Paris is one of the world's greatest tourist attractions. And not without reason, for Paris has much to offer. Paris does not have a multiplicity of skyscrapers like New York, but it has much beauty and elegance. And Paris has an illustrious background of history.

In Paris there is a number of young men who are very beautiful, very charming, and very lovable. Paris is called "The city of lights." But these young men who are very beautiful, very charming, and very lovable, prefer the darkness for their social activities.

One of the most beautiful streets of Paris is called "Les Champs Elysee," which means: "The Elysian Fields." It is very broad, bordered with trees, and very pleasant to look at.

One of the most beautiful things of Paris is a lady. She is not too broad, bordered with smiles, and very, very, very pleasant to look at. When a gentleman contemplates a lady of Paris, the gentleman is apt to exclaim: "Oo la la," for the ladies of Paris are very charming. And the ladies of Paris are dedicated to the classic declaration, expressed in the words: "L'amour, toujours l'amour!" (Johnson, 1976)

The Text

This discourse was written to be heard. It is a contemporary opera libretto, from *Einstein on the Beach*. Nevertheless, it has features which would suggest it is written, literate language. The first paragraph may have seemed to our students like a tour-guide book, particularly if one read the passage silently. It has song-like phrases, dialogue which could almost be sung to some tune and one of my students called it a "Patriotic Ode to Paris."

Adolescent Beliefs

Half of our adolescents saw this passage as speech, the other half as writing. Unlike the previous passages, the mode of presentation did *not* determine the decision about the language. Those who identified it as written ranked themselves as highly certain of it being written. Those who identified it as spoken were less certain of the believability. Across most of the subjects, the believability of this passage was high. Some adolescents were quite literal in their processing. Students thought this was produced by someone who had been to Paris or someone who lived in Paris. The females liked the text, while the males did not.

When asked about whether they might read or listen to this in school, females said yes, males said no. Roseanne noted the topic would be used in school, but not language such as this. She indicated that she would like to see more of this kind of passage used in school and that it would make school fun.

San Juana indicated that she would like to see this used in schools: "It would give guys the hint that the way women are in Paris as charming, they are the same way here."

All subjects indicated that this passage might be both speech and writing. However, they did not know which elements might be speech-like or writing-like. Juan thought this sounded like a commercial. The language and the purpose were more like writing.

DISCUSSION OF THE FINDINGS

The Research Questions

Each subject received the same eight questions per passage. As noted, there were additional questions to most of the passages designed to consider content specific to particular passages and to contribute to our understanding of adolescent beliefs about oral genres and written language.

In this study, we were particularly interested in several questions.

1. *Was this a written or spoken passage?* Why or why not? We wanted to know whether the adolescents would judge the passages as speech or writing. Seeing the passages caused the passages to be rated as higher toward the writing end of the scale (except for text #1 and #3). This study showed that modality of presentation determined whether a passage was believed to be oral or written language. These adolescents did not appear able to talk about their beliefs about differences between speech and writing. However, they seemed to understand that oral and written language represent different creative acts. Teachers usually do not teach or distinguish what it is that makes language speech or writing, yet student essays may be criticized for use of speech in writing. Little time is typically spent with analysis of oral language in schools.

2. *We wanted to know how authentic and believable the students perceived each passage to be.* Texts were more believable when read. The research literature has begun to emphasize the importance of authenticity in classroom discussion and writing activities (Horowitz, 1994). Less attention has been directed to whether students believe certain oral or written language incorporated into classes is natural, authentic discourse. This concern for authenticity is important. It may be useful to know about what adolescents regard as authentic, believable oral and written genres, and why.

In this research, our question about believability resulted in a shift in responses. In some instances, students were responding to believability with regard to the text genre, and at other times with regard to the ideas expressed in the text. The believability of the specific features of the language seemed of less concern to them, or, at best, the text was treated holistically. The concept of believability may be particularly helpful for teachers—for choosing texts, for generating writing, and for holding discussions.

3. *A number of questions were designed to prompt the reader/listener to decide who may have been the author of a passage, and to consider the topic, audience, and purpose of the passages.* Also, a question was asked about their desire to pursue reading on this topic and their feelings about the passage. Noteworthy is that these adolescents had distinct mental representations about the speaker/author and audiences a composer had in mind.

4. *Another major concern had to do with the likelihood of teachers using such a passage in school—for reading or listening lessons.* We wanted to obtain some information about adolescents' beliefs concerning the kinds of texts that appear in school settings and the kinds that do not. Thus, we asked students whether they would like to see the passage or one like it used in school. Once again, there were distinct beliefs and mental representations about what would or could be used in schools.

The last section of our study asked students to rank order the 9 passages according to (a) student interest, (b) difficulty, and (c) the likelihood of the passage being used in school. While ranking the passages, students manipulated the written texts in order to determine their rank for each passage. These rankings were limited by the fact that the subjects had an opportunity during the ranking to read the texts of those passages that they had earlier listened to and also spent additional time exploring the written texts. Thus, it should be noted that their rankings of the passages may not have been strictly based upon the mode of presentation in which they initially received each passage. Results for each of these rankings is reported next.

RANKING OF PASSAGES

Interest

Those passages that were perceived as being "speech" (when subjects were asked, is this spoken or written), irrespective of the actual modality of presentation, were rated higher on the interest ranking and, conversely, in nearly every case, on the passages ranked as low interest, only 4 were perceived as being "speech." To elaborate, more than half ranked Passage #6 (the mini-truckin' passage) as first or second, and these were largely the male adolescents. (Females ranked this as lowest of interest.) We also found that passage to be consistently ranked as low in difficulty. Passage #1 (the Haring passage) was ranked among half of the subjects as of first or second in interest. This passage did not seem to be quite as sensitive to gender.

Those who read the rap discourse typically ranked this at the bottom of their lists in terms of interest and these same adolescents ranked it at the very top in terms of difficulty. When Passage #2 (from the *Drivers Manual*) was read, it was ranked among the lowest of interest. When it was listened to, it was ranked as higher in interest. Interest in a passage was clearly determined by modality. Consistently, in my research with these adolescents, I have found differences in attitudes toward text depending upon whether the material was read or heard. Texts heard were rated as more interesting than those read.

Text Difficulty

Regardless of modality, the rap song was typically ranked as high in difficulty. We found that 6 out of 10 subjects selected this passage as the most difficult. Our adolescent subjects were largely Mexican-American. The rap song is coming out of Black culture. Our one Black student ranked it as the easiest passage. She also recognized the text as rap. Because the oral reading of this passage was done without dramatization, many of the students had no idea what it was.

In contrast, the passage on Truckin' was repeatedly ranked at the lower half of the scale on difficulty. We believe that this may be because it is close to teen talk and is on a topic of interest to our Texas teens.

Texts Used in Schools

Almost all passages were ranked at least by one subject as likely to be used in schools. More than any other passage, Passage #8, on fighting, was ranked highly as likely to appear in school. It was one of the few passages in this research that was written by an adult. It is also the most formal and academic sounding of the passages, perceived to be produced by an authority. The rap song was ranked as the lowest in terms of likelihood to be used in schools by several adolescents. Earlier in our study when we asked the question about the use of the Truckin' passage in school, the adolescents thought this was not appropriate for school when they considered the content. But, when they considered the form, a letter to the editor, it seemed like a familiar style for schoolwork. Now, when they went to rank this, 6 out of 10 adolescents placed this passage at the bottom of their rankings, with low likelihood of it being used in school; so they reverted back to their notion of this passage topic as being the guiding force determining its use. This project revealed that among these adolescents, there is a constant tug and pull between content and form. When the form becomes so strange as the rap song or bizarre as the autistic piece, the adolescent seems to block out the form and solely focus on the content that makes sense.

CONCLUSION

This research has revealed that the study of adolescent beliefs about texts can be an intriguing contribution to our knowledge of discourse and the various genres that exist in our world and school settings. Discourse may be judged for believability and used differently across age and cultural groups. In this project, we studied primarily low-income, urban Mexican-American adolescent beliefs about discourse from the oral verbal arts. The study showed that the boundaries separating different discourse types are difficult to define and are subject to change. The boundaries that we hold in mind for separating discourse types and their functions are determined, it appears, to some extent by the mode of presentation, but also by the reader/listener and the speech community that an audience comes from, as well as by the community of the author/speaker and by message contents.

The ways of categorizing text may vary depending upon conventions readers/listeners come to expect in given social contexts and situations, for example, school versus nonschool settings.

Teachers have used a limited range of discourse types in schools. This research has confirmed a long held belief of mine. That is, teachers may need to expand the possible range of genres that they bring into their classrooms—particularly if they are to stretch the imaginations and thinking skills of students engaged in listening and reading (Scott, in press). Adolescents, in particular, are capable of responding to text variations, as our study revealed, and have beliefs about these texts. These beliefs influence what they read or hear, how they read or listen, and what interpretations they take away from a discourse. In this study, our questions prompting beliefs and interpretations were sometimes yes/no questions—but with the possibility of answering "why's or why not's" designed to allow the adolescent to express what they believed.

There are some kinds of passages or texts that urban and ethnic minority teens do not want to get involved with and with which they cannot cope. They will not listen to or read these passages. We need to find out what such discourse might be and why adolescents choose to ignore these passages. We also need to consider whether or not the avoidance is okay and whether believability of the discourse is at issue or adolescent beliefs about given subject areas are in conflict with the text. Research has repeatedly shown that expository texts are less appealing than narratives, but it remains unclear exactly what it is about expository text and adolescent beliefs about or representations of expository texts, that creates the difficulty or disinterest (Langer, 1985; Langer, Applebee, Mullis, & Foertsch, 1990). The seriousness of this matter cannot be underestimated, given that most upper grade schoolwork requires use of expository text.

In textbook publishing, there may be value in considering adolescent attitudes and feelings about different language styles—e.g., whether difficult vocabulary, or spoken as opposed to written discourse with particular intentionality and illocutionary force, is more likely to be processed, understood, and enjoyed. Would an adolescent's attitude change if the vocabulary difficulty were changed, and the syntax modified, or an oral genre presented as written or vice versa? Do adolescents value other adolescent discourse more than adult discourse? If so, under what conditions should adolescent discourse be more frequently utilized in schools?

I wish to conclude with a final note regarding beliefs. Adolescents should be given an opportunity to judge language and to consider the variables that influence messages and their interpretations. Classroom activities that ask students to express their beliefs, discuss speech and writing linguistic features and content, and convey the ways in which they, as adolescents, cognitively represent a message can be instrumental in teaching students about language and its purposes in various contexts.

ACKNOWLEDGMENTS

Special appreciation is extended to Hal Courtice and Kathy Martinez for their help with the project and for conducting the interviews. Dennis Poplin helped identify many of the passages used in the research. Tara Edwards helped with the reporting of the research and the manuscript editing.

REFERENCES

Abelson, R. P. (1986). Beliefs are like possessions. *Journal for the Theory of Social Behavior, 16*(3), 223-250.

Ann, M. (1993, August). These girls live like slaves. *Sassy,* p. 85.

Astington, J. W., Harris, P. L., & Olson, D. R. (Eds.). (1988). *Developing theories of mind.* Cambridge, England: Cambridge University Press.

Avi, (1989). *The man who was Poe.* New York: Avon Books.

Berger, C. R., & Bradac, J. J. (1982). *Language and social knowledge. Uncertainty in interpersonal relations.* London: Edward Arnold.

Biber, D. (1988). *Variation across speech and writing.* Cambridge, England: Cambridge University Press.

Carlsen, G. R. (1980). *Books and the teenage reader: A guide for teachers, librarians and parents* (rev. ed.). New York: Harper & Row.

Chafe, W. & Danielewicz, J. (1987). Properties of spoken and written language. In R. Horowitz & S. J. Samuels (Eds.), *Comprehending oral and written language* (pp. 83-113). London and San Diego: Academic Press.

Csikszentmihalyi, M., & Larson, R. (1984). *Being adolescent: Conflict and growth in the teenage years.* New York: Basic Books.

Csikszentmihalyi, M., Rathunde, K., & Whalen, S. (1993). *Talented teenagers: The roots of success and failure.* Cambridge, England: Cambridge University Press.

Cushman, D. P., & Cahn, D. D., Jr. (1985). *Communication in interpersonal relationships.* Albany, NY: State University of New York.

DeBlasio, T. (1992, May). Future mini trucker. *MiniTruckin', 6*(3) p. 12.

Fiske, S. T., & Taylor, S. E. (1991). *Social cognition.* New York: McGraw Hill.

Goleman, D. (1993, March 2). Teen-agers called shrewd judges of risk. *The New York Times. Science,* B5.

Gregory, M., & Carroll, S. (1978). *Language and situation: Language varieties and their social contexts.* London and Boston: Routledge & Kegan Paul.

Gudykunst, W. B., & Ting-Toomey, S. (1988). *Culture and interpersonal communication.* Newbury Park, CA: Sage.

Halliday, M. (1987). Spoken and written modes of meaning. In R. Horowitz & S. J. Samuels (Eds.), *Comprehending oral and written language* (pp. 55-82). London and San Diego: Academic Press.

Haring, K. (1991). *Keith Haring, the authorized biography.* Englewood Cliffs, NJ: Prentice-Hall.

Horowitz, R. (in press). Orality in literacy: The uses of speech in written language by bilingual and bicultural writers. In D. Rubin (Ed.), *Social identity in writing.* Hillsdale, NJ: Lawrence Erlbaum Associates.

Horowitz, R. (Guest editor). (1991). A reexamination of oral versus silent reading. *Text.* Special guest edited issue. *Studies of orality and literacy: Critical issues for the practice of schooling, 11*(1), 133-166.

Horowitz, R. (Guest editor). (1994, April). Classroom talk about text: What teenagers and teachers come to know about the world through talk about text. *Journal of Reading, 37*(7).

Horowitz, R., & Samuels, S. J. (1987). Comprehending oral and written language: Critical contrasts for literacy and schooling. In R. Horowitz & S. J. Samuels (Eds.), *Comprehending oral and written language* (pp. 1-55). London and San Diego: Academic Press.

Johnson, S. M. (1976). Paris (an opera). In R. Wilson-Phillip Glass. *Einstein on the beach, an opera in four acts.* Dunvagen Music.

Jones, E. E., Kanouse, D. E., Kelley, H. H., Nisbett, R. E., Valins, S., & Weiner, B. (1987). *Attribution: Perceiving the causes of behavior.* Hillsdale, NJ: Lawrence Erlbaum Associates.

Kernan, K.T., Sabsay, S., & Shinn, N. (1988). Discourse features as criteria in judging the intellectual ability of speakers. *Discourse Processes, 11*(2), 203-220.

Knowles, C. (1976). Do you know they just don't make clothes for people that wears glasses (an opera). In R. Wilson-Phillip Glass. *Einstein on the beach, an opera in four acts.* Dunvagen Music.

Langer, J. A. (1985). Children's sense of genre: A study of performance on parallel reading and writing tasks. *Written Communication, 9,* 157-187.

Langer, J. A., Applebee, A., Mullis, I.V., & Foertsch, M. (1990, June). *Learning to read in our nation's schools: Instruction and achievement in 1988 at grades 4, 8, and 12.* Princeton, NJ: National Assessment of Educational Progress and Educational Testing Service.

Livesley, W. J., & Bromley, D. B. (1973). *Person perception in childhood and adolescence.* London & New York: Wiley.

Olson, D. R. (1988). On the origins of beliefs and other intentional states in children. In J. W. Astington, P. L. Harris, & D. R. Olson (Eds.), *Developing theories of mind* (pp. 414-426). Cambridge, England: Cambridge University Press.

Ong, W. (1982). *Orality and literacy: The technologizing of the word.* New York: Methuen.

Perner, J. (1988). Higher-order beliefs and intentions in children's understanding of social interaction. In J. W. Astington, P. L Harris, & D. R. Olson (Eds.), *Developing theories of mind* (pp. 271-294). Cambridge, England: Cambridge University Press.

Perner, J. (1991). *Understanding the representational mind.* Cambridge, MA: MIT Press.

Ross, L. (1987). The problem of construal in social inference and social psychology. In N. E. Grunberg et al. (Eds.), *A distinctive approach to psychological research* (pp. 118-150). Hillsdale, NJ: Lawrence Erlbaum Associates.

Schank, R. C., & Abelson, R. P. (1977). *Scripts, plans, goals and understanding. An inquiry into human knowledge structures.* Hillsdale, NJ: Lawrence Erlbaum Associates.

Scott, C. M. (in press). A discourse continuum for school-age students: Impact of modality and genre. In G. Wallach & K. Butler (Eds.), *Language learning disabilities in school-age children and adolescents: Some underlying principles and applications* (2nd ed.). Columbus, OH: Merrill-MacMillan.

Teens' favorite books: Young adults' choices 1987-1992 (1992). Newark, DE: International Reading Association.

Texas drivers handbook (1987). How to pass on a two-lane road. p. 8-2.

Tottie, G., & Backlund (Eds.). (1986). *English in speech and writing: A symposium.* Stockholm: Almqvist & Wiksell International.

Worell, J., & Danner, F. (Eds.). (1989). *The adolescent decision maker: Applications to development and education.* San Diego, CA: Academic Press.

Wyer, R. S., Jr., & Srull, T. K. (Eds.). (1984). *Handbook of social cognition. Volume 2.* Hillsdale, NJ: Lawrence Erlbaum Associates.

APPENDIX

The following eight questions were presented to the adolescents following each passage presentation:

QUESTIONS FOR ALL PASSAGES

1. Is this a written or spoken passage?
   How sure are you?   Why?

1_____	1_____	1_____	1_____	1_____
1	2	3	4	5
SPOKEN	APPROACHING SPOKEN	UNCERTAIN	APPROACHING WRITTEN	WRITTEN

2. Who do you think wrote or said this?
   Why do you think it was prepared by _____?
                    (the response from 1st question)
   Do yuou think it was prepared by someone else other than the person "speaking" in the text?
   Is this authentic/real?
   How believable is this passage?   Why?

1_____	1_____	1_____	1_____	1_____
1	2	3	4	5
NOT TRUE NO ONE REALLY EXPRESSED THIS	UNLIKELY TO BE BELIEVABLE	SOMEWHAT BELIEVABLE	LIKELY TO BE BELIEVEABLE	EXTREMELY BELIEVABLE SOMEONE REALLY EXPRESSED THIS

3. What does the passage try to say?
4. For whon was the passage designed or prepared?
5. Is this something you would want to read more about?
6. How do you feel about the passage?
7. Is this something you would expect to read of "listen to" in school? Why or why not?
8. Would you like to see this passage or one like it used in school? Why or why not?

PASSAGE 1

A.   How believable is this passage?   Why?

1_____	1_____	1_____	1_____	1_____
1	2	3	4	5
NOT TRUE NO ONE REALLY EXPRESSED THIS	UNLIKELY TO BE BELIEVABLE	SOMEWHAT BELIEVABLE	LIKELY TO BE BELIEVEABLE	EXTREMELY BELIEVABLE SOMEONE REALLY EXPRESSED THIS

B.   Who is the audience?   What makes you think this?

1_____	1_____	1_____	1_____	1_____
1	2	3	4	5
STRANGER "PUBLIC AUDIENCE"	NEIGHBOR	CLASSMATE	FRIEND	INTIMATE FRIEND

PASSAGE 2

A.   Is this stated in a way that you can understand the information and perform what is described?   Explain.

1_____	1_____	1_____	1_____	1_____
1	2	3	4	5
IMPOSSIBLE TO DO	PROBABLY NOT	MAYBE	PRETTY SURE	CERTAINLY CAN BE DONE

PASSAGE 3

A.   What discourse community is the individual from who is saying this?   Why?

1_____	1_____	1_____	1_____	1_____
1	2	3	4	5
POOR	BELOW AVERAGE	MIDDLE INCOME	ABOVE AVERAGE	RICH

1_____	1_____	1_____	1_____	1_____
1	2	3	4	5
VERY DISTANT RELATIONSHIP	UNFRIENDLY	FRIENDLY COOPERATIVE	FRIENDLY	EXTREMELY CLOSE RELATIONSHIP

1_____	1_____	1_____	1_____	1_____
1	2	3	4	5
ILLITERATE	BELOW AVERAGE	APPROPRIATE FOR AGE	ABOVE AVERAGE	HIGH LITERACY

    B.   How does the speaker / writer's community influence what is said?
    C.   What does the speaker / writer believe and feel about the people receiving this message?

PASSAGE 4

    A.   What community is Jesabel from?
    B.   Is it the same as the author's community?   Why?

PASSAGE 5

    A.   If you were a teacher how would you grade this and why?
    B.   What do you think about the words used?
    C.   What do you think about the sentences used?
    D.   What do you think about the punctuation the sentences used?

PASSAGE 6

    A.   Is this a Texan speaking/writing?

PASSAGE 7   (No specific questions)

PASSAGE 8

    A.   Do you believe what this says is true?   Why or why not?

PASSAGE 9

    A.   Might this passage be both speech and writing?
    B.   What elements might be speech like?
    C.   What elements might be written like?

RANK SHEET

Instructions to Interviewer:

Students should be able to manipulate the pages of the passages.

    A.   Rank the passages on your interest for each one. How interesting was this passage?

RANKING: HIGH ___ ___ ___ ___ ___ ___ ___ ___ ___ LOW

    B.   Rank the passages in how easy to hard they seemed to you.
          How easy/hard was this passage to understand?

RANKING: HARD ___ ___ ___ ___ ___ ___ ___ ___ ___ EASY

    C.   Rank the passages on their likelihood to be used in school.
          Which texts are more likely to be used in school?

RANKING: HIGH ___ ___ ___ ___ ___ ___ ___ ___ ___ LOW

An Emerging Conceptualization of Epistemological Beliefs and Their Role in Learning

Marlene Schommer
Wichita State University

All around us there are clues to suggest that individuals' beliefs about the nature of knowledge and learning may be influencing how they approach learning. For example, a college undergraduate declares, "When I went to my first lecture, what the man said was just like God's word, you know. I believed everything he said, because he was a professor. . ." (Perry, 1968, p. 18).

Beliefs, such as this, may contribute to the numerous problems of poor learners. For example, some students fail to think critically. Some fail to integrate information. Some fail to see the complexity and uncertainty of information. Some fail to persist in their studying at the first sign of making an error. And lest you think that these problems will go away in time, I invite you to imagine these students as adults. These problems can be re-framed in day-to-day adult life. For example, some adults follow cultist leaders without question. Some fail to see the big picture in world events. Some give up on themselves at the first sign of difficulty. It would seem addressing these problems at the student level may decrease the problems at the adult level.

Recently, researchers started investigating students' beliefs about the nature of knowledge and learning, or epistemological beliefs (e.g., Feltovich, Spiro, & Coulson, 1989; Schoenfeld, 1983, 1985; Steinbach, Scardamalia, Burtis, & Bereiter, 1987) in an attempt to determine some of the contributing factors to problems like these. For example, if students believe that knowledge is characteristically isolated bits, then they may assume that being able to list and define terms in a chapter qualifies as understanding. In other words, this belief

25

in simple knowledge serves as a standard for understanding. In turn, if "to understand" means being able to define terms, then the student would select a study strategy consistent with achieving this standard, namely memorizing. The ultimate consequence of this chain of events would be an oversimplified knowledge representation of the chapter content.

One possible objection to this line of research is that beliefs are far too messy to study in an objective, scientific, and scholarly manner. Pajares (1992) has suggested that in order to cope with the fuzziness of beliefs, we need to clearly conceptualize them, articulate precise meanings, and test key assumptions. With this advice in mind I have written this chapter for several purposes: (a) to introduce an emerging theory of individuals' beliefs about the nature of knowledge and learning, or epistemological beliefs, (b) to review research that tests aspects of this theory, and (c) to highlight the critical role of epistemological beliefs in learning. My ultimate goal is to entice researchers, practitioners, and philosophers to question, test, and revise the theory that I present.

Underlying assumptions of this line of work are that individuals have an unconscious system of beliefs about what knowledge is and how it is acquired. These epistemological beliefs have subtle, yet important effects on how individuals comprehend, monitor their comprehension, problem solve, and persist in the face of difficult tasks. Epistemological beliefs are likely to have direct effects on individuals' intellectual performance, as well as indirect effects that are mediated through other aspects of cognition. In this chapter I do acknowledge limitations of this theory. Each limitation serves as an invitation to the reader, to revise the theory after thoughtful questioning and careful investigation. In the first section of this chapter I present a brief history of the study of epistemological beliefs. This is followed by the introduction of a theory of epistemological beliefs, research that tests aspects of the theory, limitations of the theory, and final comments.

A BRIEF HISTORY

Although there have been several attempts to describe personal epistemology as a component of human development (Broughton, 1978; Chandler, 1987; Gilligan & Murphy, 1979) and personality (Pepper, 1942; Royce & Powell, 1983; Toulmin, 1972), it has been William Perry, Jr.'s (1968) theory of college students' beliefs about the nature of knowledge that has received substantial attention among researchers interested in education (e.g., Knefelkamp & Slepitza, 1976; Touchton, Wertheimer, Cornfeld, & Harrison, 1977). Based on interviews and survey responses of college undergraduates, Perry theorized that students progress through a series of nine intellectual stages. In the early stages students see knowledge as either right or wrong with authority figures knowing the answers (dualism). As students progress through college they encounter conflicting opinion among experts. In time, they come to recognize different points of view, yet persist in searching for the right answer. Eventually students conclude that one point of view is as good as another (multiplicity). As students enter new stages of development they begin to perceive knowledge as correct relative to various contexts (relativism). The right/wrong belief is now subordinate to relativistic thinking. According to Perry, when students reach the final stage of development, they realize that there are multiple possibilities for knowledge and that there are times when one must make a strong, yet tentative commitment to some ideas (commitment).

Early attempts to link epistemological beliefs to metacomprehension based on Perry's work have produced mixed results. Ryan (1984), using several items from Perry's questionnaire, classified students as either highly dualistic (knowledge is right or wrong) or highly relativistic (validity of knowledge is context dependent). When students were asked what their criteria were for determining if they had comprehended a textbook chapter, dualists reported using fact-oriented standards, such as free recall, whereas relativists reported using context-oriented standards, such as paraphrasing and application. In contrast, Glenberg and Epstein (1987), using Ryan's scale to predict students' accuracy in monitoring their comprehension, found that the scale "accounted for little variance and, thus tended to waste degrees of freedom" (p. 87).

AN EMERGING THEORY OF EPISTEMOLOGICAL BELIEFS

In order to resolve these conflicting results, I have reconceptualized epistemological beliefs and initiated a series of experiments to test aspects of this reconceptualization. This reconceptualization is presented as an initial effort to generate a loose-knit theory of epistemological beliefs.

Like Perry, I approach epistemological beliefs with a psychologist's background rather than with a philosopher's background. Unlike Perry, I have chosen to label my theory with the umbrella term epistemology. I borrow this philosophical term because the focus of this theory is on individuals' beliefs about what knowledge is and how knowledge is acquired.

Personal Epistemology is a System of More or Less Independent Beliefs

Ryan's interpretation of Perry's work assumes that personal epistemology is unidimensional and develops in a fixed progression of stages. A more plausible conception is that personal epistemology is a system of more or less independent dimensions. That is, epistemological beliefs may be far too complex to be captured in a single dimension. Consequently, I propose that epistemological beliefs be conceived as a system of relatively independent beliefs.

By *system* of beliefs, I mean that there is more than one epistemological dimension to consider. I have proposed five epistemological dimensions, each dimension having a range of possible values: *CERTAINTY* of knowledge, ranging from knowledge is absolute to knowledge is tentative; the *STRUCTURE* of knowledge, ranging from knowledge is organized as isolated bits and pieces to knowledge is organized as highly interwoven concepts; the *SOURCE* of knowledge, ranging from knowledge is handed down by authority to knowledge is derived through reason, the *CONTROL* of knowledge acquisition, ranging from the ability to learn is fixed at birth to the ability to learn can be changed; and the *SPEED* of the knowledge acquisition, ranging from knowledge is acquired quickly or not-at-all to knowledge is acquired gradually. Although these five epistemological dimensions do not encompass all possible aspects of epistemological beliefs, they do serve as a starting point into this line of investigation.

Several studies support the notion of a system of epistemological beliefs. In order to test the multidimensionality of an epistemological belief system, a questionnaire (Schommer, 1990) was developed that tapped individuals' preferences to statements about knowledge and learning. For example, "Successful students learn quickly," "Scientists can ultimately get to the truth," and "Most words have one clear meaning." The questionnaire was administered to 260 college undergraduates. Factor analysis yielded four factors suggesting four epistemological dimensions. Factor titles stated from the naive perspective are as follows: (a) *fixed ability*, (b) *simple knowledge*, (c) *certain knowledge*, and (d) *quick learning*. This factor structure has been replicated with another college group of over 400 students (Schommer, Crouse, & Rhodes, 1992), with over 1,000 high school students (Schommer, 1993), and by different investigators (Dunkle, Schraw, & Bendixen, 1993).

Other researchers have found evidence for all five epistemological dimensions. Jehng, Johnson, and Anderson (1993) developed a questionnaire by revising the Schommer (1990) questionnaire and adding aspects of Spiro's (1989) questionnaire. Using confirmatory factor analysis, Jehng et al. indicate that there is evidence of five epistemological dimensions that reflect the five beliefs hypothesized.[1] Although additional means of measuring epistemological beliefs needs to be developed, these studies support the multidimensionality of personal epistemology.

---

[1]Jehng et al. (1993) chose to reconceptualize the epistemological dimension I refer to as the structure of knowledge. In their questionnaire this factor, stated from the naive perspective, reflects a belief in orderly process. This bears a strong resemblance to my conception that knowledge is simple. Jehng et al.'s emphasis is that the *process* of learning is simple, whereas my conceptualization emphasizes that *knowledge*, itself, is simple.

I have also hypothesized that these epistemological beliefs are relatively independent. By that I mean that individuals are not *necessarily* sophisticated (or naive) in all beliefs concurrently. For example, individuals may believe that the solution to poverty is highly complex, yet once the solution is found, it will be an absolute solution.

Some supporting evidence for the independence of epistemological dimensions within epistemological belief systems is found in Schommer and Dunnell's study (1994). The development of gifted and non-gifted high school students' epistemological beliefs was compared. In the early years of high school, no differences were found in epistemological beliefs between groups. By the end of high school, the gifted students were less likely to believe in simple knowledge and quick learning, yet they maintained less sophisticated beliefs in fixed ability and certain knowledge. At least in this sample of students, there was no evidence to suggest that gifted students' beliefs were developing in synchrony.

Epistemological Beliefs are Characterized as Frequency Distributions

I propose that individuals' epistemological beliefs are best characterized as frequency distributions, rather than a single point along each dimension. With this characterization of epistemological beliefs, the distinction between the naive learner and the sophisticated learner becomes a matter of the shape of the distribution. Figure 2.1 shows two hypothetical epistemological distributions. Individuals with a sophisticated epistemological belief in the certainty of knowledge would believe that there are a few things in this world that are certain, some things that are temporarily uncertain, and many things that are either unknown or constantly evolving. With this particular distribution a sophisticated learner by default would be a critical reader, that is, always questioning what is read since many facts may be tentative or unknown. Yet, with enough accumulated evidence, the sophisticated individual would hold a small set of facts as basic concepts that hold true through time.

I also show the hypothetical epistemological distribution of naive learners. They would have a restricted epistemological belief distribution. Naive individuals would believe much knowledge is absolute and the remainder of knowledge is temporarily unknown. In time, experts may find the answers. Their epistemological distribution either does not include any notion that some knowledge is constantly evolving or the likelihood of uncertainty is so slim, that it would take an extraordinary event for them to acknowledge uncertainty. With this epistemological distribution, naive individuals will, by default, fail to read critically. When information is explicitly or implicitly stated as tentative, they may distort information.

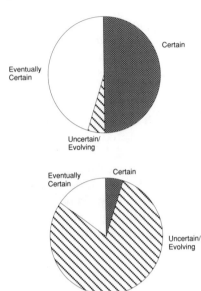

FIG. 2.1. The upper pie chart shows the hypothesized belief in certainty distribution of a naive learner. The lower pie chart shows the hypothesized belief in certainty distribution of a sophisticated learner.

For example, naive individuals may be more susceptible to advertisements for the cure of baldness or the best diet yet. They may also be more susceptible to phone market scams that promise great prizes or cheap luxurious property in a retirement village. Alternatively, sophisticated individuals will be more skeptical of these solicitations. Furthermore, when sophisticated individuals read newspapers and magazines articles, they may be more likely to question factual, as well as editorial articles. Yet, when enough evidence is accumulated, sophisticated readers can be influenced to believe what they read.

Support for the distribution hypothesis is found in Perry's descriptions of students' educational views, as well as research examining the effects of epistemological beliefs on learning. Although Perry (1968) has not characterized personal epistemology as a distribution, his description of incoming college freshmen is consistent with it. He reported that the freshmen did not entertain any possibility of uncertain knowledge. And he theorized that when students began to believe in relativistic knowledge, then dualistic beliefs took on a subordinate function. The right/wrong belief was an exception to the rule. In agreement with Perry, I am suggesting that sophisticated individuals do entertain the possibility of absolutes.[2] They believe there are few absolutes and many uncertainties.

---

[2]I suspect that an individual who has the opposite belief, that is, never entertains the notion of certainty, may have problems as well. This may lead to depression and despair. Chandler (1987) has theorized that adolescents are incredible skeptics and this can account for certain aspects of identity crises during development.

Although there is no empirical evidence to support the "distribution" hypothesis, per se, there is research evidence that supports the notion that a strong belief in certainty hinders text comprehension. In two separate studies (Schommer, 1988, 1990) college students were presented text information that was explicitly tentative. After reading the passages, students rated their confidence in their comprehension. The final paragraph at the end of each passage had been omitted. Students were asked to imagine that they were the authors of the passage. They were to write a concluding paragraph based on what they had just read. Students' concluding paragraphs were coded for the reflection of certainty or uncertainty. Analyses revealed that the more students believed in certain knowledge, the more likely they were to write inappropriately absolute conclusions. There is also research evidence that suggests strong beliefs in quick learning, simple knowledge, and fixed ability hinder learning, as well.

A strong belief in quick all-or-none learning has been found to predict the comprehension of mathematical, social, and physical science texts. Based on extensive analysis of mathematical problem solving protocols of experts and novices, Schoenfeld (1983, 1985) suggests that many high school students (novices) believe mathematics problems should be solved in less than 10 minutes. Students considered more mental investment as a waste of time. In the Schommer (1990) study, students read either a physical science passage or social science passage. In addition to writing a concluding paragraph, students rated their confidence in understanding the passage and completed a mastery test. To measure depth of students' understanding, conclusions were categorized according to the degree to which students elaborated on the passage information. To test their comprehension, tests were scored for accuracy. And to test for comprehension monitoring, the degree of agreement between students' confidence in their comprehension and their actual test performance was compared. After controlling for verbal ability, regression analyses indicated that the more students believed in quick learning, the more likely they were to write impoverished conclusions, perform poorly on the mastery test, and be over confident in their understanding of the text material.

In a more recent study (Schommer, 1993), the epistemological beliefs of over 1,000 high school students were assessed. After controlling for general intelligence, regression analyses revealed that the more students believed in quick learning, the more likely they were to have a low overall grade point average.

Strong belief in simple knowledge (i.e., knowledge is fragmented and isolated) has been found to predict medical science, physical science, and mathematical text comprehension. In a provocative study of medical students' understanding of biomedicine, Feltovich et al. (1989) indicate that epistemological beliefs influence students' understanding of complex medical concepts. The major roadblock to conceptual understanding was a "reductive bias" or tendency to oversimplify and reduce new information into a single framework. Students tended to oversimplify complex and irregular structures, rely on single mental representations, and compartmentalize knowledge components. Songer and Linn (1991) examined students' views of science and their effect on an integrated understanding of thermodynamics. Students were asked questions about the work of scientists; about the nature of scientific knowledge; and about the relevance of science outside the classroom. Students who held a rich, integrated view of science, for example, related science in the classroom with science outside the classroom and who recognized the interrelationship among scientific concepts, outperformed students with the opposite views in understanding thermodynamics. Schommer, Crouse, and Rhodes (1992) found that the more students believed in complex, interrelated knowledge, the more likely they were to successfully comprehend statistical text.

There is evidence to suggest a strong belief in fixed ability predicts children's persistence in learning. Work done by Dweck (see Dweck & Leggett, 1988) in the last 10 years provides evidence for the influence of children's beliefs about the nature of intelligence and persistence. She has found that some children have a predominant belief that intelligence is a fixed entity, whereas others believe it is incremental, that is, it can be improved. When engaging in an easy task, these two groups of children will perform similarly. When confronted with a difficult task, children with an entity theory will interpret the situation as reflecting a lack of intelligence. They will display "helpless" behavior. That is, they will engage in negative self-talk, such as "I'm failing," perseverate on the same study strategy, and finally cease to try. Incremental theorists, on the other hand, will perceive the difficulty of the task as a challenge. They will engage in positive self-talk, such as "I must try harder and longer." They will also try alternative study strategies. Ultimately, although both groups have similar ability, the incremental theorists will outperform the fixed theorists.

Epistemological Beliefs Have Both Direct and Indirect Effects

I propose that epistemological beliefs have indirect, as well as direct effects on other aspects of cognition. The indirect effects of epistemological beliefs make their manifestation subtle. Nonetheless, the effects are important. For example, if individuals believe knowledge is organized as isolated bits and pieces, this belief in turn may effect the standards by which they judge accurate comprehension (Baker, 1984, 1985) and the study strategies they select when studying. In this example, they might be convinced that reciting definitions constitutes comprehension, and rehearsing definitions would be a means to meet this standard of comprehension.

Research from text comprehension studies provides some support for the direct and indirect effects of epistemological beliefs. The finding that students with strong beliefs in certain knowledge tend to write absolute conclusions for tentative text information (Schommer, 1990) provides some evidence of the direct effect of epistemological beliefs. Evidence for indirect effects comes from the investigation of statistical text comprehension (Schommer et al., 1992). College students completed the epistemological questionnaire, a study strategy inventory (Weinstein, Palmer, & Schulte, 1987), read a statistical passage, rated their confidence in their comprehension, and completed a mastery test. Regression analyses revealed that the less students believed in simple knowledge, the better they performed on the mastery test and the more accurately they assessed their own understanding. Path analyses indicated both direct and indirect effects of belief in simple knowledge. The less students believed in simple knowledge, the more sophisticated study strategies they reported using. The more sophisticated study strategies they used, the better they performed on the mastery test.

This conclusion must be considered tentative however, since students were asked to rate how they *typically* studied (rather than how they studied for the task they had just completed) and the assessment was based on self report, rather than with on-line measures. Nevertheless, this study does provide enough evidence to suggest future research on the interaction of epistemological beliefs with other aspects of cognition is likely to reveal the subtle, yet important influence of these beliefs.

Epistemological Beliefs are Influenced by Experience

An important issue to address is the development and modification of epistemological beliefs. Whether children are born with an "epistemological scheme" is unclear. What does seem evident is the influence of environmental factors that instill and modify children's beliefs about knowledge. In 1984 at the presidential address for the annual meeting of the American Educational Research Association, Richard C. Anderson stated that:

> It stands to reason that beliefs about knowledge that a child develops will be influenced by those of his parents. Parents' beliefs about knowledge will be conditioned by educational and occupational status. . . . Later, teachers become mediators of experience. (1984, p. 8)

I propose that individuals' beliefs are influenced by experience. Although empirical evidence is limited as to the sources of epistemological beliefs, there is some research that points to the contribution of both teaching and upbringing to personal epistemology. Beers (1988) in interviewing teachers regarding their classroom goals, found their objectives to be less content oriented and more philosophically oriented.

Few were interested in transmitting their content per se. . . . It seemed that these teachers were primarily concerned with helping them [students] develop particular attitudes and thinking styles. A biologist, for example, said that she "hated facts," and spoke of "getting students excited about the way the world works." . . . When these teachers were discussing their educational goals, they were referring to a set of epistemological assumptions. . . . Teachers . . . may be unaware of the role that epistemological assumptions play in their interactions with students, but this role may be profound. (p. 87)

Indeed, Schoenfeld (1983) has suggested that students' beliefs about quick and easy mathematical solutions and failure to integrate mathematical concepts may be a product of how they are taught. For example, teachers may emphasize memorizing formulas and ignore conceptual understanding in their teaching and/or testing of mathematics.

I am presently conducting research to investigate the development of epistemological beliefs. In the first year of a 4-year longitudinal study (Schommer, 1993), the epistemological beliefs of students in a high school were assessed. Differences in epistemological beliefs between students across high school years and between genders were examined. Belief in simple knowledge, certain knowledge, and quick learning decreased from freshman to senior years. Girls were less likely to believe in quick learning and fixed ability. Results from the longitudinal study will be needed to determine if the difference in epistemological beliefs across the school years is due to sophisticated students remaining in school through their senior year and less sophisticated students dropping out, or students' beliefs actually changing. As intriguing as this longitudinal study is, we will not be able to tease apart the influence of education versus life's experiences on students' epistemological beliefs.

To control for the confound between personal experiences and formal education, I carried out a study examining the epistemological beliefs of adults (Schommer, 1992). To decrease the confound between age (a measure of experience) and education, adults from all walks of life were studied. One third of the sample of adults had no more than a high school degree. Another third of the sample had no more than a college undergraduate degree. The remaining portion of the adults had been exposed to postgraduate work. These adults completed the epistemological questionnaire and a demographic/upbringing survey. Epistemological factor scores were regressed, first, on age and demographic/upbringing variables, then, on educational level.

Demographic characteristics and upbringing factors predicted the adults' epistemological beliefs. The older adults were, the less likely they were to believe in fixed ability. The more they had been allowed to question their parents, the less likely they were to believe in fixed ability and quick learning. The less they had been pushed to get good grades, the less likely they were to believe in simple knowledge. The less strict they had perceived their parents to be, the less likely they were to believe in quick learning. The more they had been allowed to make their own decisions, the less likely they were to believe in certain knowledge. And the more education their father had, the less likely they were to believe in simple knowledge and certain knowledge. Women were less likely to believe in quick learning and certain knowledge.[3] In short, the more their parents encouraged them to think deeply and to think for themselves, the more likely they were to hold sophisticated epistemological beliefs as adults.

When background knowledge was controlled, education also predicted epistemological beliefs.[4] The higher educational level achieved, the less likely adults believed in simple and certain knowledge. It is interesting to note aspects of epistemological beliefs that deal with knowledge, per se, are predicted by education. Beliefs about self, the speed and control of learning, are predicted by personal experience. In other words, beliefs about knowledge, which the perceivers can *think* is distant from them, may be modified by education. On the other hand, beliefs about the learning which intimately involves the self, may be firmly established early in the individual's home life and resistant to change from factors outside the family.

Although these results reveal that education predicts personal epistemology above and beyond, age, parents' education, and upbringing, interpretation of the data must be made with caution. As in the high school study (Schommer, 1993), we cannot determine if adults' beliefs change because they experienced formal education or if adults who decided to pursue higher education have more sophisticated epistemological beliefs. Future longitudinal studies may help resolve this issue.

Domain Independence of Epistemological Beliefs Varies With Experience

Throughout all the research I have reported an underlying assumption is that epistemological beliefs are domain independent. There is one recent study that suggests college students in different majors have different epistemological beliefs (Jehng et al., 1993). But we cannot tell from this information if students in a particular domain believe consistently across domains. For example, business majors may believe *all knowledge* is cut and dried. Whereas, social science majors may believe *all knowledge* is tentative. Jehng et al. do not address the domain specificity issue, per se. I

---

[3] In an earlier study (Schommer & Dunnell, 1994), high school girls were less likely to believe in fixed ability and quick learning.

[4] The statistical confound between age and education was decreased substantially. The zero-order correlation between age and education was −.11.

am presently conducting a series of studies to address this issue. For now I would like to theorize just how complex this investigation is likely to be.

I propose that the issue of domain specificity is far more complex than simply saying epistemological beliefs either are, or are not, domain independent. Essentially, I suggest that the issue of domain specificity may be intimately related with individuals' experiences.

A hypothesis to be tested is that the degree of domain specificity will vary with either age or education. Setting aside for the moment the issue of whether age or education (or both) affects individuals' epistemological views, let us assume that experience is the influence. Now let me present to you a testable hypothesis. Young children will most likely have domain-independent beliefs. The level of sophistication of these beliefs is directly dependent on the home environment of the child. When the child enters school, the teacher and the child's peers now begin to influence his or her epistemological beliefs. It may be at this time in children's lives that they begin to acquire stereotypes of domains resulting in different epistemological beliefs for different domains. The domain specificity tendency may continue until sometime in adulthood. When an individual acquires a substantial amount of experience, they will develop a sophisticated epistemological point of view in the domain of their expertise. The real mystery is whether their epistemological bent for their area of expertise will generalize to other domains. It is such a tentative point, that I prefer to wait for empirical evidence before I draw any conclusions. The main point is that the question of domain specificity is not easily resolved. There may be times in an individuals' life when their beliefs are consistent across domains and other times, when their beliefs will vary across domains.

REFLECTIONS ON THE EPISTEMOLOGICAL THEORY

It is important to consider the LIMITATIONS of this loose-knit epistemological theory and the supporting research.

1. I write this theory with a psychologist's background, rather than a philosophers' background. This adds strength to the theory in that aspects of the theory are based on empirical findings and psychological explanations of human learning. On the other hand, the conceptualization of epistemological beliefs, that is, the description of individual dimensions and the completeness of the *system* of beliefs would be enhanced by a philosopher's contribution to the theory.

2. This theory is influenced by my own personal background and from the background of the psychologists who have influenced me with their

research and thinking. Hence, the theory is written from a limited cultural perspective. Contributions from individuals with different cultural perspectives and different areas of expertise are likely enrich the conceptualization of epistemological beliefs.

3. The assertion as to what constitutes naive and sophisticated epistemological beliefs is somewhat vague and perhaps presumptuous. Essentially, I entertain the notion that as long as individuals are willing to consider all possibilities, for example, both certain knowledge and uncertain knowledge, and their default is uncertain knowledge, then they are sophisticated. This is controversial. And although never explicitly asserted, I have come to believe that great scholars share similar epistemological beliefs across all domains. Perhaps this is not so. It may be that great engineers need to have a different epistemological beliefs compared to great sociologists.[5] These issues remain to be tested.

4. Varied measures of epistemological beliefs are needed to confirm the notion of a *system* of beliefs and to be sensitive to the *distribution* of beliefs. No single measure could possibly capture all aspects of individuals' epistemological belief systems. Belief systems in general, will almost always need to be inferred (Rokeach, 1960). By using multiple measures such as questionnaires (e.g., Jehng et al., 1993; Perry, 1968; Schommer, 1990; Spiro, 1989), dilemma resolutions (e.g., Kitchener, 1986), and interviews (e.g., Perry, 1968), a more complete picture of individuals' epistemological beliefs may be derived.

5. The suggestion that epistemological beliefs have both direct and indirect effects only begins to address the complexity of their effects. It is likely that within individuals' system of beliefs, certain patterns of beliefs may have unique effects on learning. For example, does an individual who has strong beliefs in certain and complex knowledge approach a learning task differently compared to an individual who has strong beliefs in uncertain and simple knowledge?

6. Finally, I have not addressed the issue of affect. The study of epistemological beliefs is clearly dealing with "hot cognition." Beliefs, by definition, are emotion-laden. That is why beliefs can drive behavior. That is why they are resistant to change. Presently, I am in the process of analyzing epistemological interviews in search of affective information.

---

[5]Although I report that Jehng et al. (1993) found students in different majors have different epistemological beliefs, I do not consider these students as "great experts." They were in the early stages of developing their expertise. For example, based on conversations with professors in physics, psychology, and education, I come to suspect that naive beliefs in certainty last into the early years of graduate school.

FINAL COMMENT

To summarize the epistemological theory to date, I have proposed an epistemological belief system that is multidimensional. These epistemological dimensions are more or less independent. At least five beliefs have been considered including the Source, Structure, and Certainty of Knowledge, and the Speed and Control of the Acquisition of Knowledge. Individuals' beliefs are better described in terms of distributions rather than a single point along each continuum. Epistemological beliefs affect learning both directly and indirectly. Their effects are often mediated by other aspects of cognition. The development of these beliefs may be due to cultural, familial, and educational influences. Whether epistemological beliefs are domain-specific or not depends on the developmental level of the individual.

To summarize the research to date, there is evidence that suggests epistemological beliefs affect comprehension, metacomprehension, interpretation, and persistence. These effects have been found among individuals of all ages and with varied educational backgrounds. These effects may be mediated by other aspects of cognition. There is evidence to suggest that both upbringing and education influence individual's epistemological beliefs.There appear to be age and gender differences, as well.

I hope I have achieved my goals for writing this chapter. If you have finished reading this chapter and are now convinced that epistemological beliefs, as difficult as they may be to conceive and measure, are too important to ignore, then I have achieved my most important goal. If you find yourself in doubt about the conception, the measure, and the findings of epistemological beliefs, to date, then I have achieved another goal, to entice you to reflect, research, and revise the conceptualization of epistemological beliefs. I do not believe that a single conceptualization of epistemological beliefs, a single measure of epistemological beliefs, or a single researcher of epistemological beliefs, will successfully capture this complex phenomenon. By explicitly writing this theory, I hope to encourage teachers to consider the epistemological beliefs of their students, as well as themselves during instruction and testing, and to entice researchers to embrace this conceptually challenging phenomenon in their thoughts and in their investigations.

REFERENCES

Anderson, R. C. (1984). Some reflections on the acquisition of knowledge. *Educational Researcher, 13*(9), 5-10.

Baker, L. (1984). Children's effective use of multiple standards for evaluating their comprehension. *Journal of Educational Psychology, 76*, 588-597.

Baker, L. (1985). Differences in the standards used by college students to evaluate their comprehension of expository prose. *Reading Research Quarterly, 20*, 297-313.

Beers, S. E. (1988). Epistemological assumptions and college teaching: Interactions in the college classroom. *Journal of Research and Development in Education, 21,* 87-93.

Broughton, J. (1978). Development of concepts of self, mind, reality, and knowledge. *New Directions for Child Development, 1,* 75-100.

Chandler, M. (1987). The Othello effect. *Human Development, 30,* 137-159.

Dweck, C. S., & Leggett, E. L. (1988). A social-cognitive approach to motivation and personality. *Psychological Review, 95,* 256-273.

Dunkle, M. F., Schraw, G. J., & Bendixen, L. (1993, April). *The relationship between epistemological beliefs, causal attributions, and reflective judgment.* Paper presented at the annual meeting of the American Educational Research Association, Atlanta, GA.

Feltovich, P. J., Spiro, R. J., & Coulson, R. L. (1989). The nature of conceptual understanding in Biomedicine: The deep structure of complex ideas and the development of misconceptions. In D. Evans & V. Patel (Eds.), *The cognitive science in medicine* (pp. 113-172). Cambridge, MA: MIT Press.

Gilligan, C., & Murphy, J. M. (1979). Development from adolescence to adulthood: The philosopher and the dilemma of the fact. *New Directions for Child Development, 5,* 85-99.

Glenberg, A. M., & Epstein, W. (1987). Inexpert calibration of comprehension. *Memory & Cognition, 10,* 597-602.

Jehng, J. J., Johnson, S. D., & Anderson, R. C. (1993). Schooling and students' epistemological beliefs. *Contemporary Educational Psychology, 18,* 23-35.

Kitchener, K. S. (1986). The reflective judgment model: Characteristics, evidence, and measurement. In R. A. Mines & K. S. Kitchener (Eds.), *Adult cognitive development* (pp. 76-91). New York: Praeger.

Knefelkamp, L. L., & Slepitza, R. (1976). A cognitive-developmental model of career development: An adaptation of the Perry Scheme. *The Counseling Psychologist, 6,* 53-58.

Pajares, M. F. (1992). Teacher's beliefs and educational research: Cleaning up a messy construct. *Review of Educational Research, 62,* 307-332.

Pepper, S. C. (1942). *World hypotheses.* Berkeley: University of California Press.

Perry, W. G., Jr. (1968). *Patterns of development in thought and values of students in a liberal arts college: A validation of a scheme.* Cambridge, MA: Bureau of Study Counsel, Harvard University. (ERIC Document Reproduction Service No. ED 024315)

Rokeach, M. (1960). *Open and closed mind.* New York: Basic Books.

Royce, J. R., & Powell, A. (1983). *Theory of personality and individual differences: Factors, systems, and processes.* Englewood Cliffs, NJ: Prentice-Hall.

Ryan, M. P. (1984). Monitoring text comprehension: Individual differences in epistemological standards. *Journal of Educational Psychology, 76,* 248-258.

Schoenfeld, A. H. (1983). Beyond the purely cognitive: Beliefs systems, social cognitions, and metacognitions as driving forces in intellectual performance. *Cognitive Science, 7,* 329-363.

Schoenfeld, A. H. (1985). *Mathematical problem solving.* New York: Academic Press.

Schommer, M. (1988, April). *Dimensions of tacit epistemology and comprehension.* Paper presented at the annual conference of the American Educational Research Association, New Orleans.

Schommer, M. (1990). Effects of beliefs about the nature of knowledge on comprehension. *Journal of Educational Psychology, 82,* 498-504.

Schommer, M. (1992, October). *Predictors of epistemological beliefs: Comparing adults with only a secondary education to adults with post-secondary education.* Paper presented at the Mid-western Educational Research Association, Chicago.

Schommer, M. (1993). Epistemological development and academic performance among secondary students. *Journal of Educational Psychology, 85,* 1-6.

Schommer, M., Crouse, A., & Rhodes, N. (1992). Epistemological beliefs and mathematical text comprehension: Believing it's simple doesn't make it so. *Journal of Educational Psychology, 84,* 435-443.

Schommer, M., & Dunnell, P. A. (1994). A comparison of epistemological beliefs between gifted and non-gifted high school students. *Roeper Review, 16,* 207–210.

Songer, N. B., & Linn, M. C. (1991). How do students' views of science influence knowledge integration? *Journal of Research in Science Teaching, 28,* 761-764.

Spiro, R. J. (1989). *Epistemological beliefs questionnaire.* University of Illinois, Center for the Study of Reading, Champaign, IL. [Unpublished raw data]

Steinbach, R., Scardamalia, M., Burtis, P. J., & Bereiter, C. (1987). Children's implicit theories of knowledge and learning. Presented at *The American Educational Research Association,* Washington, D.C.

Touchton, J. G., Wertheimer, L. G., Cornfeld, J. L., & Harrison, K. H. (1977). Career planning and decision-making: A developmental approach to the classroom. *The Counseling Psychologist, 6,* 42-47.

Toulmin, S. (1972). *Human understanding: Volume I: General introduction and part I.* Princeton, NJ: Princeton University Press.

Weinstein, C., Palmer, D. R., & Schulte, A. C. (1987). *Learning and study strategies inventory.* Clearwater, FL: H & H Publishing Co.

CHAPTER THREE

Who Is This "I" Person, Anyway? The Presence of a Visible Author in Statistical Text

Susan Bobbitt Nolen
Nia Johnson-Crowley
Samuel S. Wineburg
University of Washington, Seattle

Considerable research has explored ways to design expository texts that are cognitively "considerate"—that is, which facilitate understanding, learning, and remembering (Armbruster, 1984; Garner, Brown, Sanders, & Menke, 1992). In even the most considerate textbook, however, the author remains largely invisible, assuming a stance that Crismore (1984) has called the "anonymous authoritative 'author' " (p. 279). Although there is evidence that sophisticated readers do consider the author when reading some kinds of expository text when they read (see Shanahan, 1992; Wineburg, 1991), the "invisibility" of textbook authors likely lessens the probability that this will occur. What happens when a textbook author becomes clearly visible to readers? Is the author seen as friend, foe, or neutral dispenser of information? In this chapter, we explore readers' emerging beliefs about the author, and their relationship to that author, during an expository reading task. In the process we examine our own beliefs about readers and texts, and how those beliefs were challenged by our data.

The data we report here are drawn from a larger study of how features of expository text, individual differences in motivation and confidence, and comprehension of difficult concepts interact when students study text. We examined women's response to statistics texts for two reasons: First, we felt such text would be perceived as difficult. In addition, statistics text might engender anxiety through its association with mathematics or statistics' position as a potential "gatekeeper" for graduate study. A considerable body of evidence shows that mathematics affect and mathematics attitudes contribute to selection of coursework and careers, especially among women

41

(e.g., Hyde, Fennema, Ryan, Frost & Hopp, 1990; Linn & Hyde, 1989; Meyer & Koehler, 1990).

THE STUDY

The study grew, in part, from our belief that textbook authors perform a function not unlike that of teachers. As is true for teachers, a textbook author's style of presentation might serve to help or hinder learning through students' affective responses. Thus, although both texts we chose for our study introduce the statistical novice to basic concepts underlying Pearson's Product-Moment correlation coefficient, they represent two different styles of expository writing. The first passage we used was excerpted from a standard textbook (Glass & Hopkins, 1984, *Statistical methods in education and psychology*), and takes a dispassionate, clear, but somewhat remote and lecture-like approach to exposition. It is considerate, but from a distance. The second passage is an instructional aside taken from Gould's (1981) *The mismeasure of man*, a *New York Times* best-seller criticizing the reification of intelligence and the checkered history of intelligence testing. Understanding this history requires a general understanding of the concepts of correlation and factor analysis, so Gould takes the time to "teach" these concepts to his readers. Consistent with the rest of the book, Gould adopts a personal, collaborative tone in this passage.

The rhetorical choices made by the authors of the two texts set up different relationships with their readers, similar to those described by Gragson and Selzer (1990). Building on Ong's (1975) thesis that *all* authors "fictionalize" their audiences, Gragson and Selzer demonstrated how authors of expository text construct a role for their readers through their use or deliberate violation of expository conventions. Gould strives to establish an equality or empathy with the reader through his use of rhetorical devices, such as writing in the first person. He accords the reader a certain kinship by the frequent use of "we" and references to the things "we do," such as "our" natural tendency to infer causation from correlation. Perhaps in an effort to reduce the psychological distance between the expert author and novice reader, Gould makes occasional self-deprecatory remarks (e.g., referring to himself as "a bratty little kid," p. 243). Although Glass and Hopkins relate the statistical concept of correlation to familiar examples, they write in the third person, maintaining a distant relationship of lecturer-expert to listener-student. In Table 3.1, excerpts from the two texts illustrate these contrasts.

At the beginning of this investigation, we believed that texts with invisible, authoritative authors might exacerbate the anxieties of students who doubt their ability to understand a subject. If an author took a visible, more egalitarian stance, anxious students might relax, trusting in the author to help them understand difficult material. Such an author might be able to

TABLE 3.1
Opening Paragraphs of Texts Used in the Larger Study

From Glass and Hopkins (1984) *Statistical Methods in Education and Psychology:*

"Measures of correlation are used to describe the degree of relationship between two variables. Moreover, correlation is an integral part of many other statistical techniques. In this chapter the meaning, use, and computation of measures of relationship are studied.

Researchers are often concerned with the association between two variables for a group of persons, schools, cities, or the like. For example: Is absenteeism related to socioeconomic status? Is class size related to gains in achievement during the course of a school year? Do less competitive cultures have a smaller incidence of peptic ulcers? To answer questions such as these, measures of relationship or correlation are needed." (p. 79)

From Gould (1981) *The Mismeasure of Man:*

"The spirit of Plato dies hard. We have been unable to escape the philosophical tradition that what we can see and measure in the world is merely the superficial and imperfect representation of an underlying reality. Much of the fascination of statistics lies embedded in our gut feeling— and never trust a gut feeling—that abstract measures summarizing large tables of data must express something real and fundamental than the data themselves. (Much professional training in statistics involves a conscious effort to counteract this gut feeling). The technique of *correlation* has been particularly subject to such misuse because it seems to provide a path for inferences about causality (and indeed it does, sometimes—but only sometimes)." (p. 239)

---

convince readers of the importance of learning the material, and so increase their commitment to the task of comprehension. In the classroom, Midgley and Eccles (1990) found that students who perceive their math instructors to be supportive tend to value mathematics learning more than those who perceive the teachers to be unsupportive. We wanted to know if these same relationships hold for the independent study of text.

We recruited and paid 47 female volunteers from upper-division courses at a research university to participate in the study. Women were randomly assigned to one of the two texts, which were edited slightly to be roughly equivalent in difficulty, concepts covered, and length. The study was presented as an investigation of different styles of textbook writing, and both passages were introduced as "text on the topic of statistics."

The second author elicited modified think-aloud protocols from twenty of the women, ten in each text condition. Each text was divided into 6 parts, two parts to a page. At the end of each part, readers were asked to "tell the researcher what you are thinking and feeling." Responses were tape-recorded and transcribed. Before reading, and at the end of the second, fourth, and final segments, all readers responded to a questionnaire adapted from the work of Csikszentmihalyi and his colleagues (Csikszentmihalyi & Csikszentmihalyi, 1988). Readers rated their responses to reading the text, including feelings of confusion, challenge, perceptions of their own skill level, mood, and continuing motivation to read the text. These measurements provided a profile across the course of the reading task.

After finishing the text, we asked the twenty women who completed think-alouds to imagine the author in an interpersonal situation (sharing a taxicab). All participants then imagined the author as a statistics instructor, and rated the likelihood that he would exhibit each of a list of teaching behaviors. Finally, the women completed an open-ended transfer test which required them to interpret two brief reports of correlational studies.

THE VISIBLE AUTHOR: FRIEND OR FOE?

As we expected, women reading the Gould text were more likely to form a clear image of the author and to interact with the author during reading than were women reading the more formal Glass and Hopkins text. When discussing their own understanding during the think-aloud, women reading Gould mentioned the author six times more often than did women reading Glass and Hopkins. But our beliefs about the positive effects of having a *visible author* were rooted in a simplistic notion of what is essentially a human interaction. A visible author is not only a potential ally, but equally a potential target for blame when comprehension is difficult. For the remainder of this chapter, then, we take a closer look at the women who read the passage from Gould. (We encourage the reader to read the entire passage, which is printed in the Appendix, before continuing.)

The cases of two women, Mary and Karen, nicely illustrate the range of readers' responses to a visible author in this study. Although the two shared many entering characteristics (level of self-efficacy for statistics, career choice, difficulty with previous math classes, experience with statistics), their beliefs about the author, and their interactions with him, were quite different.

Mary

Mary was a 32-year-old English major planning to be a teacher. She had never taken statistics, but would expect to get "lower than a C." She rated her previous math courses as very hard and her performance in them as not very good. Her score on a 5-point Statistics Self-Efficacy scale was 2.8. She was moderately interested in statistics and thought it would be very useful to know some basic statistics, but expected an introductory statistics class to be "very difficult."

After reading the first paragraph (see Appendix, section 1) Mary stated that she had difficulty with the last sentence. But, she went on, she "caught the drift of what they were trying to say," and that they were trying to "get an abstractive or philosophical presentation of statistics." From the beginning, then, Mary spoke of the author(s) as trying to communicate with the reader.

The next paragraph (section 2) describes positive, negative, and zero correlations, which raised the specter of math anxiety for Mary. She stated that it automatically put her "in the mode of, 'Oh, I don't know what you're talking about because it's about numbers.' " But the presentation of this information in words rather than formulae mitigated this reaction somewhat. She understood the closing sentences, which stated that correlations are not always causal (the central theme). Without a graphic representation, though, she was not confident that she understood the different kinds of correlations.

The next section (section 3) begins with the introduction of the correlation coefficient, which Mary claimed she "kept up with," connecting it to the material on the first page. Scatterplots of high, medium, and low positive correlations were displayed at the bottom of the page in the participants' materials. She said she didn't understand how the coefficients related to the scatterplots, and so was further confused about positive, negative, and zero correlations. Her reaction to her comprehension difficulties was muted. She stated that she didn't "have the investment as I do when I'm in a class," and so didn't feel strong negative emotions, although she would "invite" more explanation from "somebody." In describing her thoughts and feelings while reading this page, Mary did not refer to the author, but instead seemed to treat the text itself as the source of information.

The author reemerged in the next paragraph (section 4) for Mary. She became increasingly lost in the explanation as she read about correlations simplifying data. She stated, "They don't do a very good job of explaining it to me—to help me understand what they're getting at." When asked about her feelings, she claimed to not have any, other than she supposed it would be useful to know some statistics, though she didn't "feel strongly enough about it at this point in my life right now to learn it."

On the last page, the author took on more definite form. After reading the fifth section, Mary began to refer to the author as "her." She suggested ways for the author to help her understand the examples by providing more information (in one case, the numbers to go along with the conceptual example). She was intrigued by the author's reference to Halley's Comet, which tapped into Mary's existing interest in astronomy, and wished for a more detailed explanation, but recognized that "it wasn't her [the author's] . . . intent to get me thinking about astronomy." She expressed curiosity and a little frustration that she had "more questions than . . . answers at this point."

In the last section (section 6), Mary was momentarily put off by the sentence, "Few people would be fooled by such a *reductio ad absurdum* as the age-gas correlation". She said, "It kind of struck me at first as 'Oh I fooled you trying to make a correlation between age and the price of gas' and I wasn't sure at first if I was just being stupid and didn't understand age and price correlation, or if that was just one of those opening sentences to . . . try to make a distinction between that and 20 children playing baseball. Which I think that's what it was." She continued to have difficulty understanding. "I have no idea where that high r comes from. Perhaps she . . . just put it in there." And "I saw at least how . . . the different things in the equation . . . what sex they are, practice, training, upbringing, can make the correlations more ambiguous. I had a vague sense of that." About the summary statement that correlations tell nothing about cause, she said, "I'm not sure I understand that. (Pause) Yeah, yeah that leaves me more, that leaves me more in question then, [because I don't understand the relationship between the examples and the scatterplots]." She believed she "understood that there's a difference between correlation and cause," but suspected she knew that prior to reading.

Mary was left feeling that she didn't understand the concept of correlation well enough to use it; that she knew no more after reading the text than she did before. But despite her struggle to understand, she ended the session motivated to learn more. "The one thing that I can say about the whole entire lesson is that, or this text or whatever it is, is that it's presented in to, in a way that I would like to know more."

Clues to this statement came when she was asked to imagine sharing a cab with the author. She pondered why she saw the author as a woman:

> . . . mainly because . . . [seeing the author as female] was an unexpected reaction. And I thought that maybe . . . it was because the author was, I think somewhat good at bringing up—how to say this . . . this author seemed to do a lot, whether they did it successfully or not for me, they did a lot of visualization. A lot of examples and a lot of real life experiences and trying to implement them in there, and I could at least access the material by having those examples. And, and I would say probably, probably this little tiny text was more successful in getting closer to, if nothing else, breaking down barriers of, that I can't do it, than the whole [algebra class I took] was.

Mary's response to the author of her text was consistent with our initial beliefs about readers of statistical texts. Gould's rhetorical techniques left her seeing the author as an ally, trying valiantly to help her understand and confident that she could. Further, Mary indicated a willingness to continue to work on understanding, even though it might be frustrating. But Karen showed us that our rosy notion of reader interaction with a visible author was oversimplified.

Karen

Karen was a 23-year-old Communications major in the teacher education program. She had never taken statistics, but would expect to get a 2.5 (C+/B–). Like Mary, Karen rated her previous math courses as very hard and her performance in them as not very good. Her score on the 5-point

Statistics Self-Efficacy scale was 1.8. She was not very interested in statistics, but indicated that it would be useful to know some basic statistics.

As she read the first paragraph (section 1), Karen became increasingly confused. It didn't match her idea of a statistics text either in content (Plato, gut feelings) or in comprehensibility. Since "because you're having me read it it should make sense," she wondered if this was an experimental "set-up" to confuse her. She states,

> I mean, I think of statistics as being more numbers, you know, just from what I'd known, you know like, hearing about, like Statistics 120, or thinking about taking the class. And I never really thought about it relating to Plato and gut feeling. I didn't see what that had to do with statistics . . . And it like it changed ideas way too many times in that small of a paragraph. . . . It doesn't seem like it flows together at all. Like kind of different pieces of random information.

Karen understood the second section better, and felt more relaxed and confident. She contrasted it with the first section, where she "didn't feel very intelligent." But her confusing experience with the first section continued to intrude on her thoughts as she read on. Why couldn't she understand the beginning if she understood the later sections? Should she have been able to relate the new material to that first paragraph? She was not interested in rereading the offending section, however, and declined the researcher's offer with a laugh, saying "I don't really *want* to read the first one again."

While reading section 3, Karen began to refer to an author or authors. This began with a shift from *it* (as in "it changed ideas") to *they* ("I didn't understand what they were talking about.") She had trouble understanding the scatterplot illustrations, and when Gould stated that his point "can be illustrated by example", she hoped for a reprieve. These hopes were dashed when the explanation didn't help. The author(s) "lied":

> And then they said . . . when I read the first sentence, I thought that they were going to clarify the questions that I kind of have been having when I read the top part, and it only confused me more . . . So it seemed to, seemed like their first sentence, they kind of lied, because they didn't do . . . They said they were going to use example to clarify the interpretation of the graphs and they—and I don't really understand that.

(This reaction was echoed later when she discussed her image of the author as an instructor: someone who wouldn't or couldn't help students understand the material.) She expressed her frustration that she didn't understand it well enough to explain it to anybody, ". . . and I don't know who this 'I' person is."

In section 5, Karen grasped Gould's example of noncausal correlation: his age and the price of gas [during the 1970s], but not the companion example of "anything that has been decreasing steadily in recent years and the distance between Earth and Halley's Comet." She began to suspect that the sense she made of earlier segments didn't match what the author was trying to say.

Finally, reading the last segment (section 6), Karen felt more confident in her understanding of the baseball example. She took issue with the author's apparent assumption that she would think all of the kids in the example were boys (later she referred to him as sexist.) She commented that she didn't feel as "stressed out" and stated "I liked the fact that I almost could question, question the author." She had "thoughts about it more than the other ones," where she "just was trying to understand them and not really thinking beyond what exactly was . . . in the paragraph."

As she struggled through the passage, an uneasy relationship developed between Karen and the author. He took on form and substance, and entered into the interaction between Karen and the text. As in Mary's think-aloud, it appeared that the text became a vehicle for communication between author and reader. Karen's stance at the end of the passage contrasts with the way she treated the text in the beginning, as an authorless entity from which she should be able to pry some meaning.

When asked to imagine the author sharing a cab with her, she describes him as "one of those people that are very knowledgeable about what they know about correlations and cause, so much so that, he's not very clear on how to explain it to somebody who doesn't understand it." Embodied in this criticism is a belief that the author is in large measure responsible for her difficulty in understanding the text. This is consistent with other comments she made during the think-aloud.

The responses of Mary and Karen illustrate the complexity that accompanies textual voice. These two women, similar in experience with statistics, belief in its usefulness, self-efficacy for understanding statistical content, and career aspirations, construct equally visible yet qualitatively different authors. For Mary, the author's presence is comforting; trusting that Gould believes in her and is willing to help her understand, she, in turn, is willing to commit to further effort. Karen shows us that when comprehension is difficult, the visible author becomes an inviting target for blame. In three short pages, Mary and Karen create two different authors, as shown in Table 3.2.

The differences in Mary's and Karen's authors are representative of the variety of images constructed by other readers in our study. Of the 10 women who had not taken a statistics course, half saw Gould more likely to be a distant lecturer, unconcerned with student learning; half saw him as involving students actively, being flexible, and being interested in their understanding. Among women who had taken a statistics course prior to this study, the majority constructed an author that resembled Mary's. But even in this group there was considerable disparity among readers' beliefs about the author.

TABLE 3.2
Mary and Karen Describe the Author

Mary	Karen
...I'm going into teaching. First of all, I see myself as being that kind of a teacher myself, and I'm really interested in teaching that way. And constantly thinking of ideas and concepts and ways to get them across. So maybe I saw myself in the author and I made the, you know distinction. ...[As a teacher the author is] energetic, enthused about the material that they're doing. Real dedicated to the idea that anyone can access to this information if I teach it in the right way. An egalitarian as it were...is that a good word? Somewhat [empathic], concern for the students. Willing to assist in the remediation, enrichment end of the deal if it's needed.	And he'd keep standing at the podium and, talk, and talk, and talk, and talk, and talk, and talk, and not really care who was there and who wasn't there and not real concerned about who was understanding and who wasn't understanding. I don't think he'd care to make anybody understand. I don't-think, I don't think that he's the type of person... He wouldn't try to adapt his teaching to make it clear, for anyone. He'd probably have his way of teaching it. If he knew his stuff wouldn't understand why others couldn't. And he would feel it was his job to give the lecture and give the test and that was about it. Not at all concerned about making me understand.

Joan, who plans to teach German, found Gould's rhetorical style "friendly": ". . . this is really easy to understand. And I particularly liked the fact that it was in the first person. That feels friendly to me. And I noticed that my mood kind of changed. That was like, 'Oh, we're working on this together.' (Laughs) And I liked that." On the other hand, Nancy, an anthropology major, grew increasingly angry at the author as she read. In particular, she found his style "condescending" and "manipulative." Her reaction to the use of "we," for example, is far removed from Joan and Mary's. ". . . I feel condescended to. Like, 'we all know this, and we all know that, and we all know this, and it leads to something that even a moron knows.' "

The very fact that the author *was* visible seemed to antagonize Nancy. Early in the passage, she stated, "I think the paragraph kind of . . . starts to disintegrate when the person puts it's own, his own or her own point of view." And by the end of the passage, she claims,

> . . . actually I can't tell you what the interesting points were, because I got too involved with the author's personal agenda and what it was. And, in fact, I guess I got turned off that there *was* a personal agenda of the author. And so the, whether or not correlations are causal or non-causal I just, it's still up in the air for me.

Nancy's beliefs about the author's "agenda" led her to dismiss the content of the passage along with the author himself.

VIOLATING READERS' ASSUMPTIONS

The appearance of an author in expository text is not unusual in trade books and magazine articles (Crismore, 1984), and so Gould's passage on correlation is not atypical of its genre. But it *is* unusual to "see" the author of a textbook. The participants in our study expected to read an excerpt from a statistics textbook. Beginning with the first sentence, "The spirit of Plato dies hard," Gould writes in a way that violates the conventions of textbook writing. By invoking Plato, moreover, he broadens the context, situating correlation in the wider realm of human efforts to explain their world.

For some readers, this toying with convention may violate a tacit social contract between textbook author and student to present necessary information as straightforwardly and predictibly as possible. Karen seemed to be thrown off by Gould's introduction, and spent much of the think-aloud wondering why it was there (even suspecting an experimental "trick") and why it didn't seem to fit into the rest of the material. Nancy interpreted this section as evidence that "the author is coming from a negative perspective, that, that they're trying to evoke a negative response." A breach of trust early in the relationship may lead the reader to suspect that the author is either inept (e.g., Karen's view) or malicious (Nancy's view.) Mary and Joan, on the other hand, seemed to accept Gould's introduction, taking it as a legitimate entry into the topic.

CHANGING OUR BELIEFS ABOUT TEXTS AND READERS

The presence of a visible author creates additional variance in readers' responses to textbooks. We suppress that variance when we present information as from an "anonymous authoritative author." By using this conventional technique, textbooks constrain the possible relationships between author and reader. By the time students reach upper division coursework, they have come to expect and, for the most part, accept these constraints. When we tamper with readers' expectations of text by making the author a living, breathing human, we open the door to a wider variety of author-reader relationships.

We initially believed that this was a positive thing, and that anxious students might be comforted by the human presence of the author. It is clear from the responses of the women in our study that our beliefs need modification. Authors who emerge from the text may be welcomed, if students believe them to be generally helpful and supportive. But because human relationships are inherently unpredictable, we cannot assume that this will be the case. Students may perceive a visible author to be obstructive, inept, or manipulative—in short, the author may be seen as the reason the reader doesn't understand.

The more the author presents him- or herself, the bigger the target; the more we know about the author, the more we have to like or dislike. Part of an author's stance is communicated through the assumptions projected about the reader, what Ong (1975) called fictionalizing the audience. Gould clearly fictionalizes his audience as intelligent and well-read, and as having at least a nodding acquaintance with the philosophy and history of science. His opening sentence, "The spirit of Plato dies hard," signaled to our readers that Gould expected to share a common framework with his audience. This is clearly illustrated by Nancy's assertion that

> . . . there's no reason to have the first sentence, "The spirit of Plato dies hard." It doesn't, *he* knows what he's talking about, but unless you're versed in philosophy, and as I said, . . . unless you're versed in European philosophy from a male perspective, *you* don't know what he's talking about. Not everybody in the world knows what the cause and effect of Plato's ideas were. So I think that really, that really makes an assumption that's harmful.

But Gould is not merely trying to communicate his expectations about his readers' prior knowledge. He is trying to frame statistics as part of the human endeavor to make sense of the world, and as such, part of a much broader context. As Mary states, Gould is ". . . trying to . . . get an abstractive or philosophical presentation of statistics." We believed that making these connections to general human concerns would make statistics seem less narrow, less alien, and thus, less intimidating. Once again, our initial beliefs proved inadequate to predict the complex interaction between author and reader. Our data suggest that the very narrowness of statistics, along with the predictability afforded by textbook conventions, make it seem to some extent controllable. Like visiting the dentist, studying statistics may involve pain, but it is manageable because it is circumscribed and short-term pain. Attempts to broaden the context of statistics may be seen primarily as distractions: Don't bring Plato into it when I know I'm going to be tested on formulas.

So what are the implications of our revised beliefs about the relationship of readers to visible authors? We could retreat into convention, designing bland, authorless texts. This would serve to suppress the variance produced by interactions with a human author, rendering readers' cognitive and affective responses more predictable. Perhaps such visible authors are best viewed as a "seductive detail" (Garner et al., 1992), distracting readers from the important information. If we undertake to write introductory statistics texts, we might go further and limit "real-world" connections only to concrete applications of statistics, rather than portraying it as a human construction subject to question and debate.

Unfortunately, all this would serve to perpetuate the myth that mathematics in general, and statistics in particular, are immaculately conceived tools for the divining of truth, handed down from nameless, faceless "authorities." Such tools produce questionable results only when used incorrectly. Students and others in possession of only elementary knowledge about such tools are thus not in a position to question their use by those presumed to have access to higher knowledge. But the alternative, embodied here in Gould's lesson on correlation, presents its own dilemmas. Students who feel confused, led astray, or left behind by a visible author may take aim at the author's retreating back, and then turn their ire on the discipline itself. Statistics cast as a human invention might invoke less awe and greater distrust, especially among those who feel let down by an author unable to help them grasp its intricacies. And yet those who feel supported, guided, and included by the author may respond, as Mary and Joan did, by feeling that understanding statistics may be interesting, valuable, and, above all, accessible. This tantalizing possibility is what will keep us, and, we hope, others, engaged in further research on the effects of visible authors in text for some time to come.

REFERENCES

Armbruster, B. B. (1984). The problem of "inconsiderate text." In G. G. Duffy, L. R. Roehler, & J. Mason (Eds.), *Comprehension instruction: Perspectives and suggestions* (pp. 202-217). New York: Longman.

Crismore, A. (1984). The rhetoric of textbooks: Metadiscourse. *Journal of Curriculum Studies, 16*, 279-296.

Csikszentmihalyi, M., & Csikszentmihalyi, I. S. (1988). *Optimal experience: Psychological studies of flow in consciousness.* Cambridge, England: Cambridge University Press.

Garner, R., Brown, R., Sanders, S., & Menke, D. J. (1992). "Seductive details" and learning from text. In K. A. Renninger, S. Hidi, & A. Krapp (Eds.), *The role of interest in learning and development.* Hillsdale, NJ: Lawrence Erlbaum Associates.

Glass, G. V., & Hopkins, K. D. (1984). *Statistical methods in education and psychology* (2nd Ed.). Englewood Cliffs, NJ: Prentice-Hall.

Gould, S. J. (1981). *The mismeasure of man.* New York: Norton.

Gragson, G., & Selzer, J. (1990). Fictionalizing the readers of scholarly articles in biology. *Written Communication, 7*, 25-58.

Hyde, J. S., Fennema, E., Ryan, M., Frost, L. A., & Hopp, C. (1990). Gender comparisons of mathematics attitudes and affect. *Psychology of Women Quarterly, 14*, 299-324.

Linn, M. C., & Hyde, J. S. (1989). Gender, mathematics, and science. *Educational Researcher, 18*, 17-19; 22-27.

Meyer, M. R., & Koehler, M. S. (1990). Internal influences on gender differences in mathematics. In E. Fennema & G. C. Leder (Eds.), *Mathematics and gender.* New York: Teachers College, Columbia University.

Midgley, C., & Eccles, J. S. (1990, April). *The classroom environment during math instruction and the transition to junior high school.* Paper presented at the annual meeting of the American Educational Research Association, Boston.

Ong, W. (1975). The writer's audience is always a fiction. *PMLA, 90*, 9-21.

Shanahan, T. (1992). Reading comprehension as a conversation with an author. In M. Pressley, K. Harris, & J. Guthrie (Eds.), *Promoting academic competence and literacy in schools.* San Diego, CA: Academic Press.

Wineburg, S. S. (1991). Historical problem solving: A study of the cognitive processes used in the evaluation of documentary and pictorial evidence. *Journal of Educational Psychology,* *83*, 73-87.

APPENDIX

Text from S. J. Gould's (1981) *The mismeasure of man,* as presented to participants. Section numbers not in participants' materials. (Directions to participants shown in brackets.)

Section 1
Correlation and cause

The spirit of Plato dies hard. We have been unable to escape the philosophical tradition that what we can see and measure in the world is merely the superficial and imperfect representation of an underlying reality. Much of the fascination of statistics lies embedded in our gut feeling—and never trust a gut feeling—that abstract measures summarizing large tables of data must express something more real and fundamental than the data themselves. (Much professional training in statistics involves a conscious effort to counteract this gut feeling.) The technique of *correlation* has been particularly subject to such misuse because it seems to provide a path for inferences about causality (and indeed it does, sometimes—but only sometimes).

[Tell the researcher what you are thinking and feeling]

Section 2

Correlation assesses the tendency of one measure to vary in concert with another. As a child grows, for example, both its arms and legs get longer; this joint tendency to change in the same direction is called a *positive correlation.* Not all parts of the body display such positive correlations during growth. Teeth, for example, do not grow after they erupt. The relationship between first incisor length and leg length from, say, age ten to adulthood would represent *zero correlation*—legs would get longer while teeth changed not at all. Other correlations can be negative—one measure increases while the other decreases. We begin to lose neurons at a distressingly early age, and they are not replaced. Thus, the relationship between leg length and number of neurons after midchildhood represents *negative correlation*—leg length increases while number of neurons decreases. Notice that I have said nothing about causality. We do not know why these correlations exist or do not exist, only that they are present or not present.

{Participants fill out questionnaire, then tell researcher what they are thinking and feeling.}

Section 3

The standard measure of correlation is called Pearson's product moment correlation coefficient or, for short, simply the correlation coefficient, symbolized as r. The correlation coefficient ranges from +1 for perfect positive correlation, to 0 for no correlation, to −1 for perfect negative correlation.[1] In rough terms, r measures the shape of an ellipse of plotted points (see Fig. 6.1). Very skinny ellipses represent high correlations—the skinniest of all, a straight line, reflects an r of 1.0. Fat ellipses represent lower correlations, and the fattest of all, a circle, reflects zero correlation (increase in one measure permits no prediction about whether the other will increase, decrease, or remain the same).

[Tell the researcher what you are thinking and feeling]

Section 4

The correlation coefficient, though easily calculated, has been plagued by errors of interpretation. These can be illustrated by example. Suppose that I plot arm length vs. leg length during the growth of a child. I will obtain a high correlation with two interesting implications. First, I have achieved *simplification*. I began with two dimensions (leg and arm length), which I have now, effectively, reduced to one. Since the correlation is so strong, we may say that the line itself (a single dimension) represents nearly all the information originally supplied as two dimensions. Secondly, I can, in this case, make a reasonable inference about the *cause* of this reduction to one dimension. Arm and leg length are tightly correlated because they are both partial measures of an underlying biological phenomenon, namely growth itself.

{Participants fill out questionnaire, tell researcher what they're thinking and feeling.}

Section 5

Yet, lest anyone become too hopeful that correlation represents a magic method for the unambiguous identification of cause, consider the relationship between my age and the price of gasoline during the past ten years. The correlation is nearly perfect, but no one would suggest any assignment of cause. The fact of correlation implies nothing about cause. It is not even true that intense correlations are more likely to represent cause than weak ones, for the correlation of my age with the price of gasoline is nearly 1.0. I spoke of cause for arm and leg lengths not because their correlation was high, but because I know something about the biology of the situation. The

---

[1] Pearson's r is not an appropriate measure for all kinds or correlation, for it assesses only what statisticians call the intensity of linear relationship between two measures—the tendency for all points to fall on a single straight line. Other relationships of strict dependence will not achieve a value of 1.0 for r.

inference of cause must come from somewhere else, not from the simple fact of correlation—though an unexpected correlation may lead us to search for causes so long as we remember that we may not find them. The vast majority of correlations in our world are, without doubt, noncausal. Anything that has been decreasing steadily during the past few years will be strongly correlated with the distance between the earth and Halley's comet (which has also been decreasing of late)—but even the most dedicated astrologer would not discern causality in most of these relationships. The invalid assumption that correlation implies cause is probably among the two or three most serious and common errors of human reasoning.

[Tell the researcher what you are thinking and feeling]

Section 6

Few people would be fooled by such a reductio ad absurdum as the age-gas correlation. But consider an intermediate case. I am given a table of data showing how far twenty children can hit and throw a baseball. I graph these data and calculate a high r. Most people, I think, would share my intuition that this is not a meaningless correlation; yet in the absence of further information, the correlation itself teaches me nothing about underlying causes. For I can suggest at least three different and reasonable causal interpretations for the correlation (and the true reason is probably some combination of them):

1. The children are simply of different ages, and older children can hit and throw farther.

2. The differences represent variation in practice and training. Some children are Little League stars and can tell you the year that Rogers Hornsby hit .424 (1924—I was a bratty little kid like that) others know Billy Martin only as a figure in Lite beer commercials.

3. The differences represent disparities in native ability that cannot be erased even by intense training. (The situation would be even more complex if the sample included both boys and girls of conventional upbringing. The correlation might then be attributed primarily to a fourth cause—sexual differences; and we would have to worry, in addition, about the cause of the sexual difference: training, inborn constitution, or some combination of nature and nurture).

In summary, most correlations are noncausal; when correlations are causal, the fact and strength of the correlation rarely specify the nature of the cause.

{Participants fill out questionnaire, then tell researcher what they are thinking and feeling.

CHAPTER FOUR

Literacy Practices Outside of School: Adults' Beliefs and Their Responses to "Street Texts"

Ruth Garner
Richard Hansis
Washington State University, Vancouver

Recently, we took a look at literacy in a rather novel way. We ignored how readers acquire skill in constructing meaning from school texts and looked, instead, at how they *do* reading outside of school. Specifically, we looked at how adults respond to fliers, those mostly unremarkable texts that one encounters frequently on the street. Actually, that is what we came to call this genre of text: "street texts."

We became interested in street texts last summer because we began to notice just how ubiquitous they really are. Having been handed fliers of one sort or another in Portland ("Vote to shut down Trojan nuclear power plant"), Seattle ("Learn Japanese in 3 short weeks"), Chicago ("Buy a leather skirt at the remarkable price of only $14.95") and Cannon Beach, Oregon ("Sign a petition opposing short-term rental restrictions for coastal properties"), we resolved to look more closely at the genre. We wanted to know more about street texts as text, and we wanted to know how readers respond to them. Do they understand most of them? Do they assess them for trustworthiness? Do they generally keep them or toss them?

COLLECTING STREET TEXTS

One of us decided to accept all fliers offered during a single summer month. It was July of a Presidential election year, and we expected to have little difficulty in collecting a set of street texts. Most flier collection was done in Portland, though four days were spent in Seattle and a number of hours were spent in the Oregon countryside. Downtown and campus areas of both cities had the highest yield. In all, 134 different fliers were collected, 117 of which were single-page texts of approximately comparable length.

It is noteworthy, because of later discoveries, that the flier distributors are not particularly memorable. Recently, we reread a *New York Times* article (Rimer, 1992) with great interest, for the author of the article made much the same point about the invisibility of flier distributors on city streets:

> Hundreds of people pass by—tourists wielding cameras, teenagers on class trips tagging after chaperones, men and women in office garb rushing to appointments. The tourists look up at the buildings, the New Yorkers look straight ahead, and almost no one seems to notice the 52-year-old man with the thick glasses wordlessly holding out fliers. (p. 22A)

The *Times* piece also contained a clue as to why street texts are so common. The author reported that they are a very cheap means of soliciting action. It costs about $20.00 to print 1000 single-page fliers, and most flier distributors are paid only about $4.25 an hour, without any benefits.

One of us and a colleague independently examined the 117 single-page fliers that had been collected, each attempting to generate categories of action requested in the texts; 100% agreement was reached on the following categories: (a) Write to express concern, (b) make a donation, (c) participate in illegal activity, (d) sign a petition, (e) buy a product, (f) engage in specific private activity, usually of a spiritual nature, and (g) change public behavior. Most frequently observed categories among the 117 fliers in our set were "buy a product" ($n = 37$) and "make a donation" ($n = 30$), with each other category observed with approximately equal frequency (i.e., n = about 10). We then worked together to select an exemplar that best represented each category. We intended to examine seven of the street texts, one from each category, more closely.

ANALYZING STREET TEXTS AS TEXT

In an earlier analysis (Garner & Chambliss, in press) of persuasive texts (i.e., editorials, fliers, and all other texts written primarily to transform knowledge and beliefs of readers so that they will then act in a particular way), it was noted that this sort of text has not been examined thoroughly by the same researchers who have addressed construction of meaning from texts written primarily to inform or to entertain. Garner and Chambliss relied on work in philosophy and rhetoric for their analysis, and we followed much the same approach here with the seven street texts.

For example, we accepted Toulmin's (1958) assumption that effective reasoning, whether in speech or in print, is not capricious but orderly, and with an identifiable structure. We adopted two components from Toulmin's model of argument structure: claim and evidence. According to Toulmin's model, the *claim* is an assertion exacting a listener's or reader's attention (e.g., Presidential leadership in a new national health-care policy is desperately needed). *Evidence* is the set of facts or examples offered in support of the claim (e.g., the U.S. infant mortality rate is substantially higher than that in all other developed countries; in many parts of the rural United States, medical diagnosis and treatment have not advanced beyond what was available a century ago; and, many Americans are uninsured and can no longer afford either routine or emergency medical care). Claims are invariably superordinate to evidence.

The seven fliers that we examined were structured quite similarly. All presented a single claim, each claim was explicit and was mentioned either in a heading or in the first sentence of text, and graphic signaling of the claim (usually large, bold print) was used. All were remarkably similar in amount of evidence presented explicitly in support of a claim: Five fliers presented four facts or examples, and the remaining two presented three. In one flier, evidence was pictorial (a "before and after" set of photographs).

We concluded that the texts were intended to be comprehensible to a broad audience of readers, for they were relatively short (none over 600 words) and used little jargon. Explanatory sketches and photographs often accompanied texts.

At a very general level, the content of the seven texts was the same: a set of facts to prove the truth of a claim about a significant social issue. However, the specific issues addressed were quite varied: clearcutting of old-growth forests, homeless adolescents, urban rioting, presidential leadership, economic uncertainty, abortion, and endangered species. For each issue, we agreed that there exists some controversy, ranging from mild disagreement (e.g., differences in opinion about appropriate shelters for homeless adolescents) to acrimonious dispute (e.g., opposing views about the legitimacy of legalized abortion).

In addition to examining each flier's structure and content, we also noted its source. With historical documents, historians routinely look first to the source of a document so that they can then develop hypotheses about what is likely to be in the body of the document, what stance it might take, and how truthful it might be (Wineburg, 1991). We wondered if this information was available to readers who engage the "sourcing heuristic" as part of assessing trustworthiness of the texts.

All but one of the seven street texts presented a source explicitly. Many provided addresses and phone numbers for further inquiries. Only a flier advocating participation in street rioting against the police failed to provide a source—for obvious reasons.

A CLOSER LOOK AT ONE STREET TEXT

During the summer and fall, a single-page flier was distributed widely in Portland. We received it in July outside a local food co-op. The action requested in this particular flier was clear: Readers were advised to "Write or call! Say you want the Forest Park Wildlife Corridor protected before it is too late!"

The structure of the Forest Park flier was similar to that of many others. It was short (190 words) and without scientific jargon. To capture readers' attention, the flier included a claim in large, bold print at the top of the text: Forest Park's Wildlife Corridor is being destroyed at an alarming rate. Development and clearcutting are taking their toll.

A set of facts supported this claim: (a) Historically, there has been little economic incentive to develop the wildlife corridor, but times have changed as real estate speculators are clearcutting forests and then subdividing for residential development; (b) approximately 50% of close-in corridor lands have been clearcut in the past two years, and follow-up subdivisions are planned; and (c) whereas from 1980 to 1990 the corridor averaged only 4 dwelling permits per year, last year, 23 permits were issued.

Additional evidence was pictorial. Just above the text (taking about 1/3 of the entire page), two aerial photographs appeared. One was captioned "Forest Park Wildlife Corridor in 1989," the other "Forest Park Wildlife Corridor in 1991." They showed the same hills, but the images were markedly different. Whereas the 1989 picture showed hills covered with trees, the 1991 picture showed hills marked by contiguous clearcuts.

For readers who might look to the source of the flier for information about likely stance, the source—Friends of Forest Park—was presented explicitly. In addition, a county commissioner and county planning director who might be contacted were noted, and their addresses and phone numbers were given.

If one were to use the text comprehension literature to inform an evaluation, the Forest Park street text would surely be judged effective for any number of reasons. For one, for a cheaply produced, easily distributed text, it contained much interesting textual and (especially) pictorial information, making it more likely that the impact of clearcuts would be understood and recalled (Renninger, Hidi, & Krapp, 1992). The text itself was not long and jargon-laden, and it did not require background knowledge unavailable to, say, food co-op customers (Anderson, 1984). The claim was presented explicitly at the start of the discourse, signaled as important so that unwarranted inferences about the point of the flier were less likely (van Dijk & Kintsch, 1983). Evidence given served as positive exemplars of the claim (Williams, 1984). The information was clearly arrayed in a pattern (photographs at the top, text in the middle, addresses and phone numbers to be used at the bottom) that would support readers' reinspecting the text for information that they had read, but not remembered (Garner, 1987). Finally, it presented a simple argument (i.e., a single claim supported by evidence) of the sort readily comprehended by competent readers (Chambliss, 1989).

Judging from where we received the Forest Park street text, it was apparently distributed to adults likely to agree with the authors about development, clearcutting, and wildlife corridors. Given this distribution, rather than creating a flier to convince, the authors needed only to create one to move like-minded individuals to action.[1] Structurally, this meant that the text could do without components that would have lengthened it and made it more complex—components that would have been needed to persuade opponents to the corridor position: backing (elaborative treatment or repetition of the claim), rebuttal (consideration of a potential counterargument), or qualification (slight modification of the main argument in light of the counterargument). Chambliss (1989) demonstrated that more complex argument structures cause many readers comprehension challenges. The Forest Park flier authors, with their distribution decision, avoided the need to persuade opponents, and thus avoided the need for a complex argument structure that might have led to widespread reader confusion.

EXAMINING READERS' RESPONSES TO STREET TEXTS

As we mentioned, we wanted to know about street texts as text, but we also wanted to know something about how readers respond to them. We were curious about whether adult readers generally understand them, whether they ever assess them for trustworthiness, and, perhaps most basically, whether they even bother to read them before discarding them.

We tried to envision a naturalistic study of the sort that Jean Lave and her colleagues had designed. Lave, Murtaugh, and de la Rocha (1984) had been interested in how adults do numeracy outside of school, in much the same way that we were interested in how they do reading outside of school. Lave and her colleagues observed 25 expert grocery shoppers in Southern California. They asked the shoppers to strap a tape recorder over their shoulders and to think aloud in conversation with anthropologists who accompanied them through a large supermarket.

When one shopper found an unusually high-priced package of cheese in a bin, he suspected a pricing error. Rather than mentally dividing weight into price and comparing the result with the price per pound printed on the label (a procedure that he probably learned in school), he searched through the bin for a package weighing the same amount and inferred from

---

[1]We are indebted to Deb McCutchen for pointing out the importance of distribution decisions.

the discrepancy in prices that one was in error. His comparison to other packages established which one was the erroneously priced package.

This discovery that, at least for cheese shopping in Southern California, problem-solving skills acquired in school may not be very useful outside of school is very important. The discovery is central to the growing literature on what has been labeled "authentic activity" (Brown, Collins, & Duguid, 1989), "everyday reasoning" (Perkins, Farady, & Bushey, 1991), or "everyday cognition" (Rogoff, 1984)—in short, the literature on what people do in ordinary cycles of activity (Lave, 1988).

The problem with adapting this paradigm to our literacy problem is that we could only seek out flier distributors as informed participants. Taping their thoughts as they offered fliers might yield fascinating information, but it would tell us nothing about readers' responses. Also, by videotaping exchanges, we might observe whether adults accepted fliers or refused them; however, videotapes would not record adults' cognitions about the fliers.

If we chose, instead, to interview passersby who accepted fliers, asking them about the meaning of a particular text and what action they might take in response to it, we felt certain that Bower's point would be relevant: "In normal conversation, even with a child, the answer you get to a question depends very much on what your listener assumes you want" (Bower, 1978, p. 350). We could envision adults reporting that, yes, they had just received an interesting flier; that, yes, it was easily understood; and that, yes, they surely would be sending off a contribution soon. We thought that anonymity of response, impossible with this interviewing method, would yield more valid data about reader response.

Thus, we arrived at what might be called a *quasi-naturalistic* method. We borrow that term from Revelle, Wellman, and Karabenick (1985), who designed a data-collection setting where task, stimuli, and situation were simple and familiar to the participants; however, certain aspects of the situation were structured by the investigators. In the case of the street texts, the reading of short texts, the texts themselves, and the task of deciding upon a response were familiar to the adults with whom we worked; however, we selected the particular texts (the seven that we had analyzed) and presented them in a packet, rather than requiring the adults to walk through Portland and Seattle to collect them.

Twenty-five graduate students received partial course credit for assisting us, and each student recruited another adult participant. The group of 50 was predominantly female ($n = 32$) and in their 30s or 40s (M age = 39). All of the participants were Caucasian. Most (85%) lived in the Portland suburbs. It is important to note that each participant was asked if he or she (a) was routinely offered street texts, and (b) at least occasionally accepted them; all 50 responded "yes" to both questions. It seems that we had at hand a relatively homogeneous group of flier takers.

The stimulus materials (street texts) were "natural texts"; they appeared exactly as they had when we collected them, except that they were photocopied. We assembled the texts into packets in three different randomly generated orders, which were then randomly assigned to the 50 adults. In the packets, a blue sheet was provided after each text for two sets of anonymous responses from the adults: retrospective verbalizations and responses to questions.

The verbalizations were prompted only very generally ("Make notes on each blue sheet about what you are thinking. Try to write down everything that you are thinking"), and there were no predetermined boundaries for response, such as every sentence or paragraph. We had found in pilot study that the least disruptive method was the one that yielded the richest retrospective data. We directed participants to determine when they wanted to interrupt their reading of a particular street text in order to respond to it on the blue sheet. The 50 adults had an opportunity to practice this activity for a topically unrelated text and then continued, unassisted, with the seven street texts under consideration. The amount of time between reading and reporting was short, thus enhancing validity of the retrospective data (Garner, 1987; Kail & Bisanz, 1982).

The adults were directed to respond to three questions after reading and reporting about each flier. The questions were: Who do you think would hand you this flier? Where do you think that you would receive it? What would you do with it—toss it, keep it for reexamination, or act immediately?

Readers' Responses: Comprehension

In categorizing readers' retrospective verbalizations for further analysis (comprehension vs. miscomprehension, attention to source vs. absence of attention to source), we asked a rater who was unfamiliar with the data to categorize the responses independent of us. Interrater agreement between that rater and one of us exceeding 95% was achieved in both cases, and any disagreements were resolved in conference before we proceeded with additional analyses.

We assessed comprehension only indirectly—by tallying instances of miscomprehension in the retrospective verbalizations. We used a Neisser (1981) criterion for comprehension: a response that is roughly faithful to the argument of the original text. Because of text features already mentioned (length, amount of specialized vocabulary, presence of adjunct sketches and photographs, argument structure), we expected the seven fliers to be readily comprehensible to the 50 adult readers.

Among 350 blue sheets (7 for each of the 50 participants), there were only 8 responses (2% of the total) that contained instances of miscomprehension. One response included the comment, "I might be interested in this newsletter, if I knew exactly how much the subscription costs," when the cost was printed in bold type on the flier. Two responses questioned the legitimacy of a local agency providing training and housing to homeless adolescents ("Does this group really exist?" and "Is this a legitimate operation?") despite considerable (and recent) local media attention devoted to the agency's needle-exchange program.

The other instances were similar to each other; all were questions about the Forest Park street text along the lines of "Where exactly is this place? Is it near here? What is a wildlife corridor and why is there one near here?" These comments were an unexpected index to low background knowledge of the surrounding area, in that the 4800-acre park is generally conceded to be one of the largest city parks in the world, known earlier in this century to the Olmstead brothers (of Central Park fame), but apparently not to some adults living 5-10 miles away.

Given the low overall incidence of miscomprehension in the retrospective verbalizations, we concluded that the 50 adults, in general, understood the seven street texts. Miscomprehension, it appeared, would not be a factor in decisions that they made about what to do with the texts.

Readers' Responses: Sourcing

In addition to wondering about whether the 50 adults who read the fliers understood them, we also wondered whether any of them used a sourcing heuristic as part of evaluating the texts. That is, we wondered if any of the adults looked first to the source of the document so that they could then develop hypotheses about content, stance, and accuracy. Wineburg (1991) pointed out that "when texts are viewed as human creations, what is said becomes inseparable from who says it" (p. 510).

Judging from comments (or the absence of them) in the retrospective verbalizations, we concluded that the sourcing heuristic was seldom used. In fact, we found only two instances of use. One woman read a flier advocating catching, but then releasing, wild steelhead (fish) and wrote:

> This flier comes from the state Department of Fish and Wildlife, so it must have some good ideas.

However, apparently after reading on, she noted:

> Well, this idea is ludicrous. Why catch fish in the first place if you intend to release them? It sounds like torture for the poor fish. Well, maybe you might catch a steelhead while fishing for something else, and then it would make sense. I'm going to ask my friend who works at Fish and Wildlife if he knows anything about this!

The woman was not particularly impressed by the claim that "You can learn to catch and release wild steelhead, thus ensuring more fish to catch in the future" and in fact proposed an alternative one: "Don't fish for wild steelhead." Her claim, like the Fish and Wildlife one, was supported by textual evidence about the value of the natural resource. What interested us at this point, however, was that the woman was attentive to source. She expected sage advice from Fish and Wildlife and then expressed surprise at the advice that was given. She even reported her intention to consult the source on her own!

The second adult who was attentive to source was a man who had a different reaction to the overall content of the same street text:

> Oh, this is from the state Department of Fish and Wildlife. It's probably a plan about conservation.

Later, he wrote:

> This is useful. I'm glad that the department is trying to be proactive.

As with all concurrent and retrospective verbalizations, we could not be certain that everything that was thought by the adults was actually verbalized. Nonetheless, based on the paucity of comments about sourcing among the 50 adults, we concluded that decisions about what to do with the fliers were more likely to have been based on content (what was said in the street texts), rather than on source (who said it).

Readers' Responses: Likely Action

Understanding and evaluating the street texts are important, but the whole point of the genre is, as we have said, to prompt action on the part of flier takers (writing, donating, signing, etc.). Were these 50 adults moved to action by these seven fliers? To answer this question, we studied both retrospective verbalizations and responses to the three questions asked about each flier.

Eight of the adults (16%) reported that they would toss all seven fliers, rather than acting on them or keeping them for reexamination. Remembering that all 50 adults had reported that they at least occasionally accept fliers, we wondered if the content of these seven street texts had particularly offended them. Retrospective verbalizations indicated that, on the contrary, these eight adults may take street texts from a flier distributor, but they seldom read them in entirety and they very seldom act on them. One adult wrote:

I always have mixed feelings about pamphlets I receive on the street. I always wonder if the organizations are on the level. I feel guilty if I don't donate a little bit of money, but I worry that if I do, I'll discover later that the whole thing was a scam. I like pamphlets that don't ask for money.

In a similar vein, another adult wrote:

Fliers bring out the cynic in me. Because I'm in school now, I live from month to month on a very limited income. I don't have money to give to organizations that aren't close to my heart. I don't trust a lot of them either. What I usually do with fliers is read a few lines, decide if they might have anything to offer, and then decide not to read on.

Still another adult from the group of eight wrote:

Most fliers are written and handed out by fanatics. I don't usually agree with them. Then, they ask for money that I can't spare. I just throw most of these things away.

These comments were representative of those from the adults who reported that they would toss away all seven fliers. Two factors were consistently mentioned: concern about being duped and inability to spare any money.

The other 42 adults reported that they would keep some of the fliers, but not all. No adult reported wanting to toss away fewer than three, so some selection was taking place. In fact, none of the 50 adults decided to keep two fliers that encouraged them to either participate in street rioting against the police or pray for forgiveness for having an abortion. We wondered why rejection was the universal outcome for these two street texts (as opposed to, for instance, the wild steelhead text, which 25 of the adults reported they would keep, 13 to reexamine it and 12 to act on it immediately).

We considered, and ultimately discarded, the idea that all 50 adults were right-leaning politically and objected to the shrill call for violent demonstrations against injustice expressed in the riot flier, just as we considered and discarded the idea that all were left-leaning and objected to the strident Right to Life position expressed in the abortion flier. Because all 50 adults decided that they would toss *both* fliers, and because the generally positive response to the steelhead text seemed mostly apolitical, we concluded that political stance was not the most salient factor in selection decisions.

Another factor emerged when we contrasted the adults' retrospective verbalizations for the riot and abortion fliers with their verbalizations for the wild steelhead flier. Whereas the former set of texts was discussed in very negative terms (e.g., "angry and scary"; "hateful"; "a really depressing thing"; "so sick that I can't even read it"; "gag, it's trying to make me feel guilty"; "the writers are angry, and they're making me angry"; "so negative"; "really extreme"; and "terribly gloomy, way too political for me"), the wild steelhead flier was discussed—by the half of the group that reported that they would keep it—in entirely different terms (e.g., "sensible"; "wise idea"; "interesting, something we should all try, should have thought of a long time ago"; "doesn't sound like it would take away any pleasure at all"; and "educational").

This factor is reminiscent of what Abelson (1986) labeled as "happy talk" in his discussion of Reagan's victory over Mondale in the 1984 presidential race with a combination of vague themes and cheerful chatter. Much as the voters rejected Mondale's occasionally gloomy discussions and generally serious tone, the 50 adult readers apparently rejected the undeniably gloomy content and serious tone of the riot and abortion fliers. The riot (1), abortion (2), and wild steelhead (3) segments below give a sense of content and tone differences:

1. There can be no illusion about the purpose of the police. They are just another instrument of the racist ruling class to keep the rest of society from threatening their power. They are not a neutral force and do not exist to protect us. The police are not for our benefit. They are tools of the state essential in keeping power in the hands of white male corporate Amerika.

2. Jesus picked up the pieces of my life and put it back together again. Sure, sometimes I still grieve for my aborted child. I wonder what he (or she) would have been like and I sorrow that I denied myself the joy of nurturing him. . . . Abortion is not just a misguided act, a carrying out of an unfortunate decision. It is sin.

3. Wild steelhead are too valuable a resource to be caught only once. When you release wild steelhead, they will be able to spawn and produce a new generation. A fish released today is a fish *you* have an opportunity to catch tomorrow.

One way of explaining the 50 adults' preference for happy talk in street texts is to acknowledge that the students among them are required to read informational text in large quantities for graduate work. Perhaps the adults expect that, outside of school and work, they should be able to indulge in what Resnick (1991) called "pleasurable literacy" (i.e., reading of self-selected material for enjoyment). Gloomy facts and requests for time or money may interfere with pleasurable literacy and may, in fact, induce discomfort among readers.

Readers' Responses: Biased Processing

One set of findings would not have emerged if we had been clever enough to manage to design a wholly naturalistic study in which we observed what flier takers did when approached on the street and subsequently observed their honest responses to any fliers that they accepted. In that elusive paradigm, the flier takers would, of course, see the flier distributors.

In the quasi-naturalistic method that we actually used, flier takers (the 50 adults) did *not* see the distributors, but they guessed at the "who" and "where" of the flier exchange in two of the three questions that they were asked about each flier. It was in response to these questions that some very interesting information emerged.

The 50 adults gave very embellished descriptions of flier distributors and sites, particularly for the texts that they decided to toss. The clearest example of this pattern emerged for the riot flier, which no adult kept.

Although we had received this flier one sunny afternoon from two young, Caucasian males on the University of Washington campus in Seattle, nearly every adult ($n = 44$, 88% of the group) responded that the likely distributor was an adolescent, African-American male ("possibly a gang member" 10 adults suggested) who handed us the flier at night in a dangerous downtown location.

The richness of description of the (unseen) riot flier distributor is seen in these representative comments: "a Black militant at a downtown shopping area, after hours"; "a minority male attending a loud rally against the police downtown, a rally that quickly gets out of hand"; "an 'in your face' young Black man at a Safeway parking lot, a dark corner, in a bad part of town"; "a Black gang member hanging out with a group of guys on MLK Boulevard"; "a young male gang member standing, with troublemakers, near an entrance to a seedy tavern downtown"; "a Black, who is frustrated, angry, and has been in trouble with the law, who is hanging around at the downtown bus station."

It is certainly possible that explicit references to racism in the riot text led the adults to infer that the flier distributor was African-American (untrue, but a reasonable inference). However, there was no textual reference to gangs, seedy locations, or night. What was the source of this information (misinformation)?

Lee Ross and his colleagues (see, for example, Griffin & Ross, 1991; Ross, 1987) have examined sources of human misunderstanding. Their work suggests that something like the following occurs: People are not governed by recognition of some invariant objective reality; rather, they construct the events that unfold around them, sometimes using stereotypes and other schemas without awareness. However, people view their own subjective constructions as objective reality. Epistemologically, this is naive realism— "The world is as I see it" (Hansis, 1976).

It is surely not unimportant, in this regard, that the 50 adults who read the riot flier were mostly female, mostly 30- or 40-something, mostly suburban, and exclusively Caucasian. The imagined flier distributors were different from them in all imaginable ways (i.e., gender, age, neighborhood, and race). Ross and his colleagues might suggest that once the adults determined (falsely) that the flier distributors were African-American, they brought to the flier distribution scenario a whole package of "stereotypes and other schemas" about African-Americans. This process might be considered to be reverse sourcing (where the messenger, rather than the message, is hypothesized about).

Part of the reverse sourcing may have been a phenomenon that Fiske and Taylor (1991) called "illusory correlation." Illusory correlation is an *expectation* that two variables are related (e.g., race and gang membership). Given this expectation, people often overestimate the degree of relationship that exists or impose a relationship when none actually exists. Illusory correlation is particularly likely to occur when the two groups (expecting and expected about) have little regular contact, for, as Kuhn (1992) wrote, "Social interaction offers a natural corrective to the egocentrism of individual minds" (p. 174); when interaction is missing, so too is the corrective.

The flier distribution context that was so richly hypothesized about by the adults is one context of interest in this work. Another context that must be acknowledged is the one where a known instructor (one of us) distributed research packets to 25 of the adults who were attending a graduate class (the other 25, it will be recalled, were recruited by the students and were not previously known to the instructor).

Recalling Orne's (1962) cautions about experimental setting, we must admit that a professor-student imbalance of authority and an investigator-subject imbalance of authority both existed here. Orne suggested that one of the most interesting things that may occur in such a situation is remarkable compliance among subjects, even in performing boring, unrewarding tasks.

Orne gave an incredible example: In pilot work, he asked subjects to perform serial additions of adjacent pairs of numbers on sheets filled with rows of random numbers. To complete a single sheet, 224 calculations were required, and a stack of some 2000 sheets was presented to each subject! Subjects were told simply, "Continue to work; I will return eventually."

In general, subjects tended to continue to work for several hours, usually with little decrement in performance. As if this were not shocking enough, an even more frustrating task that was devised produced similar results: Subjects were asked to perform the same task described above, but were also told that when finished with each sheet, they should pick up a card nearby for additional instructions. That card (and every other card) instructed them to tear up the sheet that they had just completed into a minimum of 32 pieces and then to go on to the next sheet and card. Orne and his colleagues expected that subjects would discontinue the task as soon as they realized that each card carried the same wording, and that the task was wholly meaningless. Instead, they found that subjects tended to persist in the task for several hours with relatively little sign of overt hostility. Removal of a one-way screen made little difference. Subjects invariably attributed meaning to their performance.

So, just as we have argued that the participants' stereotypes and other schemas seem to have made a difference in their responses to the street texts, so too should we argue, apparently, that we (at least the one of us present during completion of the task) might have made a difference in those responses. If we were African-American researchers, perhaps the more stereotypic responses to questions would not have emerged. If we were not authority figures, perhaps less embellished, effortful responses would have been the norm.

ON DOING READING OUTSIDE OF SCHOOL

At the beginning of this chapter, we said that we wanted to see how readers do reading outside of school. We collected street texts, analyzed them as text, and then examined adult readers' comprehension, evaluation, and likely action in response to them. Among other things, we observed an unexpectedly large number of responses that involved stereotyping. What conclusions can be drawn from all of this?

Our basic conclusion is that text comprehension researchers have been insufficiently attentive in the past to the importance of reader beliefs. We have acknowledged for some time that *knowledge* structures matter, that in the absence of a schema for topic X, reading about X can be very difficult (Anderson & Pearson, 1984); however, we have been slow to recognize that *belief* structures also matter.

Beliefs about what people are like, what the world is like, and what actions have value have been shown to influence readers' evaluations of plot and character in school narratives (Beach & Hynds, 1991). Now we know that these beliefs also influence readers' understanding of street texts. Many of the adults brought to the riot text a set of stereotypes and other schemas about African-Americans and then misinterpreted both context and text. When we assessed miscomprehension narrowly (counting factual errors, comments in retrospective verbalizations that were not faithful to a particular flier text), we found little evidence of miscomprehension. However, when we looked at misunderstanding a bit more broadly (noting, for example, the intrusion of stereotypic response in answers to questions), we found constructions that could in no way be traced to text. Bruner's (1990) call to specify the structure and larger contexts (including belief systems) in which specific meanings (for instance, of particular texts) are created and transmitted demands our attention.

Beliefs about text itself also matter. Marlene Schommer and her colleagues (Schommer,1990; Schommer, Crouse, & Rhodes, 1992) have demonstrated that belief in simple knowledge is negatively associated with both comprehension and metacomprehension in school expositions. Now we know that readers' beliefs about whether or not one can trust street texts affect whether the texts are read carefully—or even read at all. Many adults reported that they were worried about being duped by fanatics who write most street texts; they reported that they would skim these fliers quickly or simply throw them away unread.

One aspect of the street texts that particularly interests us is that they differ so much from textbook passages. Many of us have spent many years examining textbooks or textbook-like passages. These texts have a number of features in common: They introduce too many concepts in too few words (Beck, McKeown, & Gromoll, 1989); they rarely contain interesting or entertaining material "written in any rhetorically purposeful way" (Hidi & Baird, 1988, p. 468); and they often contain topically irrelevant information (Garner, Alexander, Gillingham, Kulikowich, & Brown, 1991). Perhaps worst of all, they are anonymously authoritative. As Apple (1992) and Luke, de Castell, and Luke (1983) have noted, textbooks are often written by committees—without any linguistic hedges to indicate that they present one perspective out of a set of many possible perspectives about black holes, the Revolutionary War, sonnets, or whatever. They give few clues to the social world in which they originated. They appear to be authorless truth.

Street texts are quite different. The ones that we examined presented a single claim and three or four facts to support the claim, and had almost no distracting detail. They had a clear purpose (to persuade a reader to act) and, toward that end, they were engaging (i.e., anecdotal, short, with vivid pictures, and without jargon). They were not authoritative in tone. If one were to characterize their rather uniform tone, it might be as hopeful ("Won't you at least think about these ideas?"). The source of each text was visible (except in the case of the riot flier), and the stance of each was straightforward.

In looking at literacy in a rather novel way, we have encountered texts that differ from textbooks, and we have seen reader responses that are driven less by procedures learned in school than they are by basic beliefs about people and events. The experience has broadened our sense of what *doing* reading is all about, and we commend it enthusiastically to others.

REFERENCES

Abelson, R. P. (1986). Beliefs are like possessions. *Journal for the Theory of Social Behaviour, 16*, 223-250.

Anderson, R. C. (1984). Some reflections on the acquisition of knowledge. *Educational Researcher, 13*, 5-10.

Anderson, R. C., & Pearson, P. D. (1984). A schema-theoretic view of basic processes in reading comprehension. In P. D. Pearson (Ed.), *Handbook of reading research* (pp. 255-291). New York: Longman.

Apple, M. W. (1992). The text and cultural politics. *Educational Researcher, 21*, 4-11, 19.

Beach, R., & Hynds, S. (1991). Research on response to literature. In R. Barr, M. L. Kamil, P.B. Mosenthal, & P. D. Pearson (Eds.), *Handbook of reading research* (Vol. 2, pp. 453-489). New York: Longman.

Beck, I., McKeown, M. G., & Gromoll, E. W. (1989). Learning from social studies texts. *Cognition and Instruction, 6*, 99-158.

Bower, G. H. (1978). Representing knowledge development. In R. S. Siegler (Ed.), *Children's thinking: What develops?* (pp. 349-362). Hillsdale, NJ: Lawrence Erlbaum Associates.

Brown, J. S., Collins, A., & Duguid, P. (1989). Situated cognition and the culture of learning. *Educational Researcher, 18*, 32-42.

Bruner, J. (1990). *Acts of meaning.* Cambridge, MA: Harvard University Press.

Chambliss, M. J. (1989). *Processes good readers use to construct the gist of texts with an argument structure.* Unpublished doctoral dissertation, Stanford University.

Fiske, S. T., & Taylor, S. E. (1991). *Social cognition* (2nd ed.). New York: McGraw-Hill.

Garner, R. (1987). *Metacognition and reading comprehension.* Norwood, NJ: Ablex.

Garner, R., Alexander, P. A., Gillingham, M. G., Kulikowich, J. M., & Brown, R. (1991). Interest and learning from text. *American Educational Research Journal, 28*, 643-659.

Garner, R., & Chambliss, M. J. (in press). Do adults change their minds after reading persuasive text? In A. J. Pace (Ed.), *Beyond prior knowledge: Issues in text processing and conceptual change.* Norwood, NJ: Ablex.

Griffin, D. W., & Ross, L. (1991). Subjective construal, social inference, and human misunderstanding. In M. P. Zanna (Ed.), *Advances in experimental social psychology* (Vol. 24, pp. 319-359). San Diego, CA: Academic Press.

Hansis, R. (1976). *Ethnogeography and science: Viticulture in Argentina.* Unpublished doctoral dissertation, The Pennsylvania State University.

Hidi, S., & Baird, W. (1988). Strategies for increasing text-based interest and students' recall of expository texts. *Reading Research Quarterly, 23*, 465-483.

Kail, R. V., Jr., & Bisanz, J. (1982). Cognitive strategies. In C. R. Puff (Ed.), *Handbook of research methods in human memory and cognition* (pp. 229-255). New York: Academic Press.

Kuhn, D. (1992). Thinking as argument. *Harvard Educational Review, 62*, 155-178.

Lave, J. (1988). *Cognition in practice: Mind, mathematics and culture in everyday life.* Cambridge, England: Cambridge University Press.

Lave, J., Murtaugh, M., & de la Rocha, O. (1984). The dialectic of arithmetic in grocery shopping. In B. Rogoff & J. Lave (Eds.), *Everyday cognition: Its development in social context* (pp. 67-94). Cambridge, MA: Harvard University Press.

Luke, C., de Castell, S., & Luke, A. (1983). Beyond criticism: The authority of the school text. *Curriculum Inquiry, 13*, 111-127.

Neisser, U. (1981). John Dean's memory: A case study. *Cognition, 9*, 1-22.

Orne, M. T. (1962). On the social psychology of the psychological experiment: With particular reference to demand characteristics and their implications. *American Psychologist, 17*, 776-783.

Perkins, D. N., Farady, M., & Bushey, B. (1991). Everyday reasoning and the roots of intelligence. In J. F. Voss, D. N. Perkins, & J. W. Segal (Eds.), *Informal reasoning and education* (pp. 83-105). Hillsdale, NJ: Lawrence Erlbaum Associates.

Renninger, K. A., Hidi, S., & Krapp, A. (Eds.). (1992). *The role of interest in learning and development.* Hillsdale, NJ: Lawrence Erlbaum Associates.

Resnick. L. B. (1991). Literacy in school and out. In S. R. Graubard (Ed.), *Literacy* (pp. 169-185). New York: Noonday.

Revelle, G. L., Wellman, H. M., & Karabenick. J. D. (1985). Comprehension monitoring in preschool children. *Child Development, 56,* 654-663.

Rimer, S. (1992, May 3). For flier distributors, peskiness can be a virtue. *New York Times,* p. 22A.

Rogoff, B. (1984). Introduction: Thinking and learning in social context. In B. Rogoff & J. Lave (Eds.), *Everyday cognition: Its development in social context* (pp. 1-8). Cambridge, MA: Harvard University Press.

Ross, L. (1987). The problem of construal in social inference and social psychology. In N. E. Grunberg, R. E. Nisbett, J. Rodin, & J. E. Singer (Eds.), *A distinctive approach to psychological research: The influence of Stanley Schachter* (pp. 118-150). Hillsdale, NJ: Lawrence Erlbaum Associates.

Schommer, M. (1990). Effects of beliefs about the nature of knowledge on comprehension. *Journal of Educational Psychology, 82,* 498-504.

Schommer, M., Crouse, A., & Rhodes, N. (1992). Epistemological beliefs and mathematical text comprehension: Believing it is simple does not make it so. *Journal of Educational Psychology, 84,* 435-443.

Toulmin, S. E. (1958). *The uses of argument.* Cambridge, England: Cambridge University Press.

van Dijk, T. A., & Kintsch, W. (1983). *Strategies of discourse comprehension.* New York: Academic Press.

Williams, J. P. (1984). Categorization, macrostructure, and finding the main idea. *Journal of Educational Psychology, 76,* 874-879.

Wineburg, S. S. (1991). On the reading of historical texts: Notes on the breach between school and academy. *American Educational Research Journal, 28,* 495-519.

CHAPTER FIVE

Why Do Readers Fail to Change Their Beliefs After Reading Persuasive Text?

Marilyn J. Chambliss
Stanford University

In an *Education Week* article, "When a Teacher's Red Pen Can Liberate" (Lew, 1993), English teacher Ann Lew shares the following belief. "For generating topics, exchanging stories, and helping one another develop them, the writing process, as I learned it, is still a valuable, humanizing activity. But for editing, proofreading, and correctness, I am convinced that the teacher must intervene" (p. 30). Ms. Lew presents examples of her current approach, describes the instructional needs of her multicultural classes, offers possible counter arguments that she dismisses with subarguments. Her carefully crafted article tries to convince readers to accept her claim.

How is her article likely to affect readers? It depends. Readers who have never given much thought to good writing pedagogy will likely adopt her belief. Gilbert (1991) argues forcefully that humans have a propensity to accept newly encountered beliefs as true. Other readers who come to the text believing strongly that a teacher's red pen crushes rather than liberates student literacy will likely reject the claim. Research in social psychology (e.g., Lord, Ross, & Lepper, 1979) and more recent cognitive and developmental work (e.g., Kuhn, 1992) suggest that people do not readily exchange strongly held initial beliefs with opposing positions.

Garner and I (Garner & Chambliss, in press) have suggested elsewhere that *written* persuasion might lead to more belief change than less permanent forms. Once spoken, utterances disappear. Written text is permanent. Writers may design their persuasion more carefully than speakers can. The permanence of written persuasion allows writers to recycle through their text as readers, recrafting the text accordingly (Spivey, 1990). Speakers certainly can backtrack and correct themselves occasionally, but excessive "editing on the spot" could make a speech difficult for the speaker to deliver and for the listener to comprehend and remember. Readers can reinspect written text sentence by sentence if necessary. Such careful processing could enhance reader comprehension of and memory for written text over the same content presented as utterance. Listeners may have difficulty remembering both the new belief and its evidence once the persuasive event is over.

Unfortunately, recent work suggests that written persuasion is no more potent a medium than any other persuasive type. Garner and I (Garner & Chambliss, in press) have reported that reading a persuasive text apparently neither enhances reader memory nor prompts readers to change strongly held prior beliefs. This chapter explores the issues by identifying the characteristics of persuasive text and analyzing three models to explain how readers process persuasion and why reader beliefs are so resistant to change.

CHARACTERISTICS OF PERSUASIVE TEXT

Aristotle introduced the study of persuasion with advice to orators (Cooper, 1932). Since, rhetoricians have turned to written persuasion as well. Kinneavey (1969) defines written persuasion as text in which an author focuses on the reader. Brooks and Warren (1972) in *Modern Rhetoric* describe persuasion as ". . . the art, primarily verbal, by which you get somebody to do [or believe] what you want and make him, at the same time, think that this is what he had wanted to do [or believe] all the time" (p. 176).

Calfee and I (Calfee & Chambliss, 1987; Chambliss & Calfee, in press) picture authors considering which content out of a whole universe of possibilities to include and how to organize it into a text by using one of a handful of possible structures. Ideally, in persuasive texts authors make their choices based on a single purpose—to change the mind of the reader. Authors structure well-designed persuasive texts to counter current beliefs of typical readers as well as to present new beliefs. They choose content that capitalizes on what the typical reader already knows and values.

Philosophers have concentrated on argument, a type of reasoning that writers frequently use to persuade and readers presumably use to be persuaded. Logicians assume that effective reasoning is *orderly* with an identifiable structure. A system of logic, quantified according to the logical calculus, has evolved to represent the formal relations among propositions (Alexander, 1969). Philosopher, Stephen Toulmin (1958), notes that as logic has become more mathematical, it has moved away from the real world of arguments. He suggests a structure to represent real world arguments regardless of particular content based on the relationship between proof and assertion used in jurisprudence. Following sections of the chapter present a framework for understanding persuasive text according to its structure, as suggested by Toulmin, and content, as specified by Aristotle.

The Structure of Persuasive Texts

Recently a newspaper editorial claimed that the high cost of [legal] drugs is caused by the profit seeking of large pharmaceutical companies (Drake & Uhlman, 1993). The $55 billion-a year pharmaceutical industry is the most profitable in America. Most drug companies increase their sales and profits year after year. Once a group of business managers joined the industry, prices started increasing at twice the rate of other consumer prices. Pharmaceutical sales reps are everywhere, one for every 12 doctors.

The synopsis of this editorial exhibits two of the three argument parts in the Toulmin (1958) model: the claim and its evidence. According to the model, the *claim* is an assertion exacting a reader's attention or belief (e.g., Drug costs are caused by the profit seeking of the pharmaceutical industry.) The *evidence* are the facts or examples offered as support for the claim (e.g., The pharmaceutical industry is the most profitable in America.) The third part of the model, the *warrant*, links the claim and evidence and either makes or breaks the argument. The warrant is the underlying reason or premise in the argument and is analogous to the major premise in a syllogism. *Pharmaceuticals* does not state the warrant per se, but a following section of this chapter discusses its role more fully. Figure 5.1 shows how the model can be used to depict the overall argument structure in *Pharmaceuticals.*

Claims and Evidence. Claims are invariably superordinate to evidence, which are at a basic level where they are more easily perceivable and verifiable than the claim. For example, whether the pharmaceutical industry is the most profitable in America is a matter of record that could be verified. Terms in the claim are superordinate and not observable. A reader cannot directly perceive the effects of profit seeking on the cost of drugs. This distinction between a claim and evidence is crucial. Competent readers use relationships of super and subordination to identify an argument's claim and distinguish it from the evidence (Chambliss, 1989). They are highly accurate at recognizing the two even in a lengthy text and explain that the claim is more general and "summarizes" all of the evidence.

The Special Role of the Warrant. Warrants turn subordinate facts and examples into *support* for the claim. Figure 5.1 displays a different warrant for each instance of evidence in *Pharmaceuticals* (e.g., For an industry to become the most profitable in America, it must engage in profit-seeking

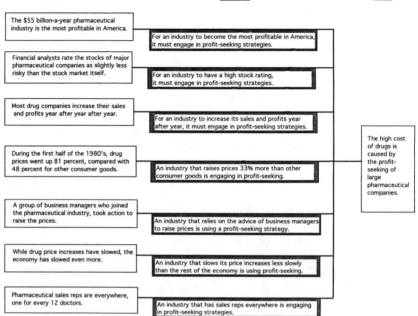

FIG. 5.1. Toulmin's model applied to a newspaper editorial.

strategies). Imagine another editorial with the same evidence, but a different claim: "The high cost of drugs is caused by the high demand of Americans for life-preserving wonder drugs." The first three warrants for this argument would be: "In order for an industry to become the most profitable in America, it must produce a product that is in high demand," "In order for an industry to be healthy enough to receive a high stock rating it must sell a product that is in high demand," and "Costs for consumer goods that increase 33 percent more than costs for other consumer goods, result from high consumer demand for the goods." In each case the warrant turns the same set of facts into support for a different claim.

As in *Pharmaceuticals*, warrants are typically implicit in text ("Everyone knows that. . . ."). Nonetheless, they are an important element in the Toulmin (1958) model. Stein and Miller (1991) have demonstrated that subjects of various ages offer different claims for the same evidence depending on the social understandings that they use as warrants. Likewise, I have suggested that the same evidence about the pharmaceutical industry could be used to support different claims depending on differences in the warrants.

Backing, Qualification, and Refutation. The reader, encountering the bare bones argument, might or might not be persuaded. Two important pieces of evidence are missing: the high cost of developing drugs and the high percentage of experimental drugs that never reach the market. Some readers may question the warrants. Is it true that for an industry to become the most profitable in America and receive a high stock rating, it must engage in profit-seeking strategies? In a persuasive text the author can anticipate reader objections by including additional structural features in the argument: backing, qualifying, and rebuttal (Toulmin, 1958).

Backing beefs up the basic argument by strengthening the claim, evidence, and warrant, typically through elaboration. An author may reword a claim several times or offer separate instances of support for different parts of the claim. To elaborate evidence, authors typically martial several related facts or examples for each instance, or category, of evidence. Toulmin (1958) suggests that authors may be more likely to present the backing for a warrant than the warrant itself. The bulk of *Pharmaceuticals* presents elaboration for the evidence. For example, to elaborate on the pervasiveness of sales reps the authors report on the size of the sales force, its role in giving doctors information about drugs, and its influence over all other medical personnel.

The author who still anticipates resistance from the reader can either qualify the initial claim or develop a rebuttal, presenting a claim related by a warrant to a whole new set of evidence that directly contradicts the primary argument. Over a third of *Pharmaceuticals* actually presents a counter argument for a counter claim: "Increased drug costs are necessary because of costs needed to develop new wonder drugs demanded by the public." Important pieces of evidence are martialled for this counter argument: the high cost of developing drugs, the public demand for new wonder drugs, and the significant proportion of new drugs that never reach the market. In order to convince the reader to accept the first argument in spite of the second, the author must either show the superiority of the first or qualify it in light of the second. The authors of this example chose the first alternative by repeatedly presenting part of the counter argument first (e.g., evidence on the high cost of drug development) followed by evidence to show the superiority of the author's claim (e.g., drug companies make huge profits anyway.)

Enthymemes and Maxims. Persuasive texts rarely follow Toulmin's model completely. Indeed, Aristotle in *The Rhetoric* (Cooper, 1932) recommended that orators present either claims and evidence or claims alone, relying on listeners to use prior beliefs and knowledge to infer missing parts. He explained that an audience could not keep an entire argument in mind easily. If orators and listeners share the same beliefs about how the world works in general, a persuasive speech could fruitfully present the evidence and claim under the assumption that the relationship between the two (the warrant) is obvious. Such an argument is classified by classical rhetoricians as an enthymeme (Cooper, 1932; Corbett, 1965). *Pharmaceuti-*

cals, with its missing warrants, is an enthymeme. If orators and audiences share not only the same general beliefs but also knowledge related to the beliefs, orators can omit evidence all together and present one claim after another. Aristotle referred to such claims as maxims (Cooper, 1932).

The Content of Persuasive Texts

The content characteristics of persuasive text are as important in persuading the reader as the text's structure. Aristotle (Cooper, 1932) proposed a taxonomy of content types for persuasion, which continues to influence the advice given to budding authors learning to design persuasive texts (e.g., Brooks & Warren, 1979).

Types of Proof. Content offered as evidence, what Aristotle called "the proof," has perhaps the most potent effect on the reader. Aristotle explained in *The Rhetoric* that proof comes in two forms: "artistic" proof that the speaker must create and "nonartistic" proof such as laws, witnesses, and contracts. He added that most persuasion uses artistic proof: by the character of the speaker, by the emotions in the hearer, or by demonstration of the truth of an idea.

Although *Pharmaceuticals* most strikingly uses facts to prove the truth of the claim, it also exemplifies proof by the character of the speaker. The authors quote several experts—an economist at the University of Minnesota, an internist, the head of surveillance and enforcement for the Food and Drug Administration's drug-marketing division, a professor of pharmacology at the University of Massachusetts Medical School, a professor at Harvard Medical School—who express opinions about the profit seeking of pharmaceutical companies. The authors also quote other experts—the president and the chairman of the Pharmaceutical Manufacturers Association and four presidents of pharmaceutical firms—who defend their industry. Presumably readers will be influenced positively by the knowledge of the former and negatively by the self-interest of the latter.

Reader Prior Knowledge and Beliefs. Authors also choose content for persuasion according to the knowledge and beliefs that they expect the typical reader to hold. Pollard (1982), reviewing the effects of subject background knowledge and beliefs on various reasoning tasks, suggests a rule of thumb: Use evidence that readers will either readily accept or already know about, and a warrant, or underlying premise, that they believe is true, to persuade them to accept an unknown or previously unaccepted claim. I suggest that the authors of *Pharmaceuticals* expect an audience with prior knowledge about economical causal relationships and a healthy respect both for statistics and the academic world.

Content that particular readers will find persuasive also may depend on the intellectual community to which they belong (Toulmin, 1958; Williams, 1991). Different domains have different standards. An economist preparing a manuscript for journal submission would choose different content to persuade his colleagues than the editorial writer intent on persuading the newspaper reading public. A writer for *The National Enquirer* would choose different content than the editor of a prestigious daily paper, and so on.

READERS CONFRONTING PERSUASIVE TEXT

Persuasive text, such as *Pharmaceuticals*, is predominately a presentation of evidence that can be characterized by the Toulmin (1958) argument model. Presumably, the authors assume that readers will carefully weigh the evidence and that some readers will change their beliefs after reading the text. However, studies of belief change, including a recent review on scientific beliefs (Chinn & Brewer, 1993), suggest that people, even trained scientists, may not carefully consider evidence. According to Nickerson (1991), an ideal thinker who is not subject to human constraints and limitations would systematically weigh evidence and retain or discard beliefs accordingly. Because of memory, reasoning, and knowledge limitations, people typically search for evidence to support what they already believe instead. Between these two extremes is the good thinker who is as reasonable as we can expect a person to be.

The remainder of this chapter focuses on readers as thinkers to begin to explain why their beliefs are so resistant to change even with text specially designed to change beliefs. Sections below (a) explore the ideal case and speculate on why it exceeds human limitations, (b) describe what typical readers seem to do instead, and (c) suggest prescriptions for how readers could process persuasive text based on what good readers appear to do.

The Ideal Reader

Kuhn (1992) suggests an ideal model whereby readers compare the evidence they have for their prior beliefs with the evidence in a persuasive text, consider the relative merits of the opposing evidence, and either retain or change their beliefs accordingly. This model, I propose, implies representations that match the Toulmin model. The beliefs of the ideal reader are stored in memory as claims with supportive evidence linked by warrants. When ideal readers read a persuasive text, they search for the claim and its evidence and use the warrants to construct a mental representation of the author's argument. Holding both representations in working memory, they compare the evidence point by point. If the two claims match, they add the new evidence to their representation and retain the same belief. If the two claims do not match, they choose the claim with the most meritorious evidence and either maintain their original representation or replace it with the new representation.

Picture the ideal reader of *Pharmaceuticals* who believes that high drug prices result from exorbitant amounts of money that the pharmaceutical industry must spend to develop the wonder drugs demanded by the public (the counter argument in the text). This belief and evidence for it are stored in the ideal reader's memory. Over the past two decades the industry has produced drugs that reduce cholesterol, protect organ transplants from rejection, heal ulcers, shrink prostate glands, ease depression, and bring heart attacks to a stop. During the same time period, the cost to bring one successful drug to market has increased from $54 million to $231 million (Drake & Uhlman, 1993). Linking the belief and its evidence are two warrants. Drugs to reduce cholesterol and so on are indeed wonder drugs that the public desires, and a dramatic increase in research and development costs will cause an increase in product prices. The reader comprehends the text by searching for the claim and evidence in the authors' argument and the counter claim and evidence in the counter argument, and inferring the warrants while constructing two parallel argument representations for the text.

At this point the ideal reader has three argument representations to compare: the original belief representation and the two text representations. To choose one representation over the others, the ideal reader compares the three representations item by item. If the text representation depicted in Fig. 5.1 seems to be more meritorious, the reader replaces the old belief and its evidence with the new claim-evidence-warrant representation. The text will have changed the reader's belief about high drug costs. Alternatively, if both the original belief representation and the counter argument seem of greater worth, the reader will reject the text's argument and will add any new evidence from the counter argument to the original representation. The text will have failed to change the reader's belief.

Keil (1991) proposes two types of human limitations that could affect this ideal model. People have information processing constraints that could make it impossible for them to construct two complete text representations in memory while storing the original belief representation and then to maintain in memory all three representations as they compare them simultaneously. Furthermore, it seems unlikely that people represent their beliefs in memory according to the Toulmin model.

The Typical Reader

Research results suggest that typical readers have not stored their beliefs in memory according to the Toulmin model, have trouble constructing an accurate text representation of persuasive text, and may fail to make a point-by-point comparison among belief and text representations. To explore whether persuasive text changes readers' beliefs, Garner and Alexander (1991) had 62 upper-division psychology students from the Pacific Northwest read a 5-page article on extermination of the ancient Pacific Northwest forest. The article blamed loggers, scientists, government officials, timber-industry executives, and environmental activists. As measured by pre- and post-reading tests, subjects varied on which of these participants they blamed. Two weeks after reading the article, subjects answered five questions asking for gist-level information that the author had offered as evidence. Subject recall for the information was poor. For example, only three subjects answered one of the items correctly. Apparently, subjects failed to store evidence from the article in long-term memory.

Kuhn (1992) focused on whether subjects could provide evidence to support their beliefs. The 160 subjects ranged from ninth graders to adults in their 60s and had already attained or were expected to attain either a college or high school education. Rather than genuine evidence, the majority of subjects offered plausible scenarios to support their beliefs. For example, Frank believed divorce causes children to fail in school.

> *Interviewer:*   How do you know that this is what causes children to fail in school?
>
> *Frank:*   Well, it's like mostly when the mother and father are divorced they can have psychological problems, you know, and they can't actually function in school.
>
> *Interviewer:*   Just to be sure I understand, can you explain exactly how this shows that problems at home are the cause?
>
> *Frank:*   Well, the kid, like, concentrates on how he's going to keep his mother and father together. He can't really concentrate on schoolwork. (p.161)

Even though subjects tended to rate themselves as sure or very sure of their beliefs, many of them seemed unable to provide evidence. Apparently they had not stored evidence with their beliefs.

Research results suggest that typical readers do not construct text representations that match the ideal model either. In a study to explore how subjects represent a persuasive text's claim and evidence, 20 upper-division college students rated their positions on Desert Storm from "strongly opposed" to "strongly supported" (Garner & Alexander, 1991). Thirteen of the subjects supported the war. All students read a short persuasive text with two claims opposing the war. One of the instances of evidence reported details about a U.S. soldier who had been killed during the fighting. Asked to recall the text's claim and evidence after reading, the majority of war proponents failed to recall either claim, but did recall the one instance of evidence, apparently identifying with the young soldier. In contrast, the majority of war opponents recalled both claims. Readers apparently selectively included in their representations claims and evidence that matched their beliefs. Even though this study had a small number of subjects, it supports earlier research on the biased processing of persuasive text (Lord et al., 1979).

My work (Chambliss, 1989) has focused on whether good readers have an argument schema analogous to the Toulmin model and, if so, how they use the schema to construct a mental representation of a text. Eighty twelfth graders in advanced placement English classes read six lengthy arguments from a possible 14 texts over the course of three experiments and completed either written comprehension tasks or think-aloud protocols. Eight of the 14 texts had a complex structure that presented separate instances of evidence for different parts of the claim, a common type of backing. The texts did not include other persuasive features such as counter argument or qualification and were actually simpler than *Pharmaceuticals.* Each subject read one complex text. The responses of some subjects suggested that typical readers may lack a text schema for complex arguments typically used in persuasive texts. Subjects accurately recalled the claims and evidence of the simple arguments, analogous to the simple structure in Fig. 5.1. In contrast, over one quarter of the subjects did not accurately recall the complex argument. Their recalls had a simple structure, either omitting part of the claim or some of the evidence. Since some subjects apparently had only a simple argument schema, which was inadequate for their comprehension of a complex argument, they did not construct an accurate representation of the complex case.

Kuhn (1989, 1992) concludes from a number of studies that particularly young and less well educated people cannot distinguish between a claim and its evidence. Readers with less expertise than the subjects in these two studies might construct text representations that are even more inaccurate.

Finally, research suggests that typical readers do not compare evidence point by point. Wineburg (1991) analyzed how historians and high school students examine historical evidence. He gave eight written and three pictorial documents about the Battle of Lexington to eight historians and eight high school students. Subjects completed think-aloud protocols, ranked the trustworthiness of the written texts, and chose the most accurate of the pictures. In contrast to the historians, the high school students failed to compare the documents, neglecting to recycle back through them to check for consistency in facts and reliability of the sources. They decided a textbook treatment, the type of document with which they are most familiar, was the most trustworthy and chose pictures based on artistic merit rather than consistency with written documents.

The Garner and Alexander (1991) work suggests two alternative rules that readers may use instead of evidence weighing: Ignore all evidence that does not match a prereading belief or accept all evidence in the text as true. In work described above, the adult readers who read the persuasive article on destruction of the ancient Pacific Northwest forest indicated who they believed was responsible before reading, three times during reading, and after reading. Most subjects (71%) seemingly ignored text evidence, consistently choosing the same group regardless of the text content. Other subjects (18%) appeared initially to accept all evidence as true, choosing groups depending on the evidence they had immediately read, but reverting to their original choice in the postreading task.

Typical readers apparently fail to store or retrieve their beliefs as arguments, construct accurate text representations, or make a point-by-point comparison of evidence. Instead, people may initially store virtually all beliefs as true (Gilbert, 1991), independently of any evidence to support them (Chinn & Brewer, 1993; Kuhn, 1989). Aristotle's notion of the *maxim* may actually be a better depiction of typical belief representations than Toulmin's model of claims and supportive evidence. In other words, strongly held beliefs may become part of a highly interconnected network of other beliefs, episodic memories, concepts, and facts (Chinn & Brewer, 1993). The plausible scenarios that people offer to justify their beliefs may be based on the contents of their particular network.

When readers encounter a belief in a persuasive text that refers to one they already represent as a true maxim, they have two possible alternatives. Some readers comprehend the text by searching for evidence that confirms their original belief, what Nickerson (1991) calls, "case building." These readers construct an inaccurate representation of the text. Other readers seem swayed by the text belief *while they are reading the text*, as Gilbert's (1991) notions suggest. On completing their reading, these readers briefly represent two conflicting beliefs as true. Because the initial belief is imbedded in an entire network, they choose it over the text claim. In either case, readers do not weigh evidence.

Imagine that the ideal reader pictured above is actually a typical reader. His belief that high drug prices result from exorbitant costs to develop drugs is connected in memory with episodes, other beliefs, and so on. The typical reader has a heart condition and has been told by the doctor that he would die without three very recently developed drugs. The monthly bill for these medicines is $150.00. The reader remembers reading somewhere that it can take years to develop a new drug. He also knows that drugs are developed by chemists who receive good salaries. The reader has a pharmacist friend who goes out of her way to help her customers. The reader believes that the pharmaceutical industry is humanitarian and trustworthy. The typical reader starts with the title, "Wonder Drugs, Windfall Profits," which reminds him of his belief. Because he disagrees with the title, he ignores it and begins to search the text for supportive content. The reader constructs one representation in working memory: his original belief, a scenario about John Forrest, Jr., whose heart attack was averted by a drug that dissolved a blood clot, and a trade group estimate that it costs $231 million to develop and market one successful drug. A month later, all he remembers is his original belief. Neither the scenario nor the dollar amount ends up in his long-term memory.

This depiction of typical readers takes into account human information processing constraints. Readers do not call up entire belief representations, construct complete text representations, or compare the two, conserving valuable working memory resources. Furthermore, all they need to store in long-term memory are the beliefs themselves. As Gilbert (1991) implies, this model probably is adaptive for many everyday situations. Just as people do not question what they see with their own eyes, they also may be prone to accept as true the beliefs they encounter and retain them tenaciously. Furthermore, storing the sorts of details that can serve as evidence in long-term memory is hard work. Remembering only the beliefs within a network of other knowledge saves valuable mental energy.

The Good Reader

Although not focusing on readers per se, both Nickerson (1991) and Kuhn (1992; Kuhn, Schauble, & Garcia-Mila, 1992) imply that readers can learn to do better. In contrast to typical readers, good readers come much closer to adhering to an ideal model. I suggest that they have evidence linked by warrants to some beliefs. They construct accurate gist representations of persuasive texts and can compare several sets of text representations. They seem to handle memory limitations through the use of a well-formed argument schema and strategies that rely heavily on the permanence of written text. According to the comprehension model proposed by van Dijk and Kintsch (1983), readers who can use a schema to link separate parts of a text into a whole and to access relevant knowledge conserve limited memory resources.

Research results suggest that good readers have an argument schema well represented by the Toulmin model that they can use to construct an accurate text representation (Chambliss, 1989). In work I have already described, students in advanced placement English classes pointed to the presence of claim/evidence structures to identify arguments and reproduced both argument parts when asked. Virtually all subjects accurately recalled texts with a simple argument structure and over half performed as well with complex texts.

Wineburg's (1991) work with historians and high school students examining history documents suggests that this argument schema can also have general content specifications for compelling evidence. The historians, but not the high school students, used three heuristics to consider evidence: corroboration (comparing the consistency of evidence across documents), sourcing (considering the source of a document before reading it), and context (placing the evidence in a time sequence and a geographical place). I suggest that the historian's argument schema specifies that compelling evidence must agree with other evidence, come from respected sources, and fit within a larger historical context.

Research has not directly addressed whether good readers store their beliefs according to the argument schema. Harman (1986) concludes that keeping track of the evidence for one's beliefs is more than "mere mortals" can do. I suggest, however, that experts can be distinguished (and are valued) because they know and can produce evidence for their beliefs. It seems plausible that people *can* store evidence for at least a relatively small number of important beliefs. Perhaps, within the network of episodes, facts, beliefs and so on, content experts have information linked by warrants as evidence for specific beliefs.

Good readers rely on the permanent record in the written text. The texts that the good readers in my study (Chambliss, 1989) read were several pages long. While reading, subjects would frequently refer back to text introductions and earlier paragraphs to verify the author's claim and evidence. Wineburg (1991) pictures historians rereading evidence to compare across documents. I suggest that good readers may also rely on the permanent record in text to store evidence for their own beliefs. Many of us in reading research have beliefs based on the work of others. We probably do not remember the exact tasks, measures, and outcomes for this work, but we have in our file cabinets or on our book shelves written records that we can use to refresh our memories when necessary. Our own writing may serve this function as well, a permanent record that renders unnecessary the difficult and sometimes tedious task of storing evidence in memory.

Imagine the *good* reader confronting *Pharmaceuticals*. This reader recently wrote a paper as part of her course work for a master's degree in public health. The paper presents support for her belief that high drug prices are the result of the high costs of developing wonder drugs. The good reader identifies the text's claim in the title of *Pharmaceuticals* and recognizes that she disagrees with it. She also identifies a counter claim in a side bar that matches her belief: "The $55 billion pharmaceutical industry insists that high prices they charge are essential to developing new medicines. But don't you believe it" (Drake & Uhlman, 1993). These two claims remind her of her belief and a few pieces of evidence that she remembers. She decides to find her paper in case she wants to refresh her memory further.

The good reader starts to read. The first few paragraphs in *Pharmaceuticals* present evidence for the counter argument. She begins to fill in her argument schema to construct an appropriate representation for the counter argument. With the sentence, "There is a difference, however, between financial risk and the R&D risks that the industry repeatedly cites" (Drake & Uhlman, 1993), the author switches to the main argument in the text. This switch confuses the good reader, and several paragraphs later she skims earlier paragraphs until she realizes the presence of a new argument. The good reader begins to fill in her schema for the second parallel argument in the text. As *Pharmaceuticals* repeatedly presents more of the counter argument refuted by the main argument, the good reader focuses on the claim and evidence in each, infers warrants linking the two, and uses her argument schema to construct a text representation with two arguments. She finds herself underlining evidence and making notes in the margins.

As the good reader comes to the end of the text, she applies her understanding of compelling evidence to compare the two text representations and her own belief representation as recorded in her paper. As she weighs the three representations, the good reader finds herself rereading evidence both from her own paper and *Pharmaceuticals.*

RETURNING TO THE ORIGINAL QUESTION

The final scenario suggests why persuasive texts typically fail to change reader beliefs. As Chinn and Brewer (1993) conclude from reviewing literature on theory change, belief change requires deep processing. The good reader model, while accounting for human memory constraints, requires a formal schema and the metacognitive skills to apply it. Kuhn (1992) implies that both the argument structure and the metacognitive skills must be learned. Even having the structure and skills may be insufficient. To be good thinkers, according to Nickerson (1991), good readers must also value evidence weighing and testing and be motivated to put in the necessary effort. It seems plausible that unless all of these features are present, readers process persuasion too superficially to bring about belief change.

REFERENCES

Alexander, P. (1969). *An introduction to logic: The criticisms of Arguments.* New York: Shocken Books.

Brooks, C., & Warren, R. P. (1972). *Modern rhetoric* (3rd ed.). New York: Harcourt Brace Jovanovich.

Calfee, R.C., & Chambliss, M.J. (1987). The structural design features of large texts. *Educational Psychologist, 22,* 357-378.

Chambliss, M. J. (1989). *Processes good readers use to construct the gist of texts with an argument structure.* Unpublished doctoral dissertation, Stanford University.

Chambliss, M. J., & Calfee, R. C. (in press). *Textbooks for learning: Nurturing children's minds.* Cambridge, MA: Blackwell Publishers.

Chinn, C. A., & Brewer, W. F. (1993). The role of anomalous data in knowledge acquistion: A theoretical framework and implications for science instruction. *Review of Educational Research, 63*, 1-49.

Cooper, L. (1932). *The rhetoric of Aristotle.* New York: Appleton-Century.

Corbett, E. P. J. (1965). *Classical rhetoric of the modern student.* New York: Oxford University Press.

Drake, D., & Uhlman, M. (1993, May 2). Wonder drugs, windfall profits. *The San Francisco Chronicle/World,* pp. 8-9, 13.

Garner, R., & Alexander, P. A. (1991, April). *Skill, will, and thrill: Factors in adults' text comprehension.* Paper presented at the meeting of the American Educational Research Association, Chicago, IL.

Garner, R., & Chambliss, M. J. (in press). Do adults change their minds after reading persuasive text? In A. J. Pace (Ed.), *Beyond prior knowledge: Issues in text processing and conceptual change.* Norwood, NJ: Ablex.

Gilbert, D. T. (1991). How mental systems believe. *American Psychologist, 46*, 107-119.

Harman, G. (1986). *Change in view: Principles of reasoning.* Cambridge, MA: MIT Press.

Keil, F. C. (1991). Intuitive belief systems and informal reasoning in cognitive development. In J. F. Voss, D. N. Perkins, & J. W. Segal (Eds.), *Informal reasoning and education* (pp. 291-309). Hillsdale, NJ: Lawrence Erlbaum Associates.

Kinneavy, J. E. (1969). The basic aims of discourse. *College Composition and Communication, 20*, 297-304.

Kuhn, D. (1989). Children and adults as intuitive scientists. *Psychological Review, 96*, 674-689.

Kuhn, D. (1992). Thinking as argument. *Harvard Educational Review, 62*, 155-178.

Kuhn, D., Schauble, L., & Garcia-Mila, M. (1992). Cross-domain development of scientific reasoning. *Cognition and Instruction, 9*, 285-327.

Lew, A. (1993, March 31). When a teacher's red pen can liberate. *Education Week*, p. 30.

Lord, C. G., Ross, L., & Lepper, M. R. (1979). Biased assimilation and attitude polarization: The effects of prior theories on subsequently considered evidence. *Journal of Personality and Social Psychology, 37*, 2098-2109.

Nickerson, R. S. (1991). Modes and models of informal reasoning: A commentary. In J. F. Voss, D. N. Perkins, & J. W. Segal (Eds.), *Informal reasoning and education* (pp. 291-309). Hillsdale, NJ: Lawrence Erlbaum Associates.

Pollard, P. (1982). Human reasoning: Some possible effects of availability. *Cognition, 12*, 65-96.

Spivey, N. N. (1990). Transforming texts: Constructive processes in reading and writing. *Written Communication, 7*, 256-287.

Stein, N. L., & Miller, C. A. (1991). I win-You lose: The development of argumentative thinking. In J. F. Voss, D. N. Perkins, & J. W. Segal (Eds.), *Informal reasoning and education* (pp. 265-290). Hillsdale, NJ: Lawrence Erlbaum Associates.

Toulmin, S. E. (1958). *The uses of argument.* Cambridge, England: Cambridge University Press.

van Dijk, T. A., & Kintsch, W. (1983). *Strategies of discourse comprehension.* New York: Academic Press.

Williams, J. M. (1991). Rhetoric and informal reasoning: Disentangling some confounded effects in good reasoning and good writing. In J. F. Voss, D. N. Perkins, & J. W. Segal (Eds.), *Informal reasoning and education* (pp. 225-346). Hillsdale, NJ: Lawrence Erlbaum Associates.

Wineburg, S. S. (1991). Historical problem solving: A study of the cognitive processes used in the evaluation of documentary and pictorial evidence. *Journal of Educational Psychology, 83*, 73-87.

PART TWO

TEACHERS' BELIEFS ABOUT TEXT AND INSTRUCTION WITH TEXT

Research Studies as Texts: Sites for Exploring the Beliefs and Learning of Researchers and Teachers

Penelope L. Peterson
Michigan State University, East Lansing

PROLOGUE

As participants in the community of educational researchers in our nation, we—the authors of chapters in this book—have spent most of our lives doing research. Over the years, we have conducted numerous research studies of teaching and learning; we have published extensive research reports, scores of scholarly articles and books on our "findings" from these studies. We have conversed and debated vehemently and continuously among ourselves about what we *know* and do not *know* as a result of our research. Throughout our scholarly work we have maintained a passionate concern for doing research that will lead to improved teaching practice in our nation's schools and ultimately, to improved student learning. Committed as we are to improving educational practice, we have frequently asked ourselves the question, "Why does our research often not make much difference in the practice of teachers in our nation's schools?" We sigh when our answers to this question come up short.

As a scholar who has conducted research on teaching for the last two decades, I am no exception. I wonder why my research has made so little difference in teachers' practice when I have worked so hard as a researcher.

I have conducted research in hundreds of teachers' classrooms, interviewing and observing them and their students in the practices of education. I have arrived at my own scholarly conclusions from these data and then published these in the form of scholarly texts to be read. All the while, I have never lost sight of my goal in the work—to improve the teaching and teaching in our schools.

All along the way, I have also been concerned about what I have learned. And one thing that I learned is that *I have learned.* I look back at the texts of my research and understand them differently than I understood them before, during, and after the research.

In this way, my thoughts echo the words of fellow researcher, Russell Hunt, who has written in 1992 in a refreshingly honest way about a research study of reading text that he did more than a decade earlier. In that study Hunt divided up a short story by an anonymous writer into nine pieces and presented each piece in order to individual readers who were either undergraduates or professors at the college where Hunt taught. After reading each piece, Hunt had the reader respond to questions about the piece of text the reader had just read. Hunt was surprised that his subjects—the readers—not only did not "understand the point of the story," but they also didn't see the "savage irony" that he saw in the story. Now a decade later, looking back on the text of his own research, and the reflecting on the changes in his own and his colleagues ideas reading, teaching and learning over the decade between 1977 and 1987, Hunt (1992) commented:

> . . . when you stop being embarrassed by what you used to believe, you've probably died and simply not noticed . . . So, it's no surprise to me that much about this study seems misconceived to me now, almost ten years after it was conducted. Most obviously, the ease with which I assumed that I knew what Graham Greene's story was "about" or "did" seems to me a very strikingly questionable assumption. Almost equally important is what I now see as my underestimation of the power of the reading situation, that is, the way my students and my colleagues understood the social situation of my study—their task and my purposes—to alter the stances readers take toward texts, and thus to affect central and important parts of the reading process. (p. 71)

In this chapter I explore my own learning and the changes in my own understanding of the texts of two different major research studies in which I have been involved. With my colleagues, I conducted these studies at two different points both in the development of the field of research on teaching and the development of my career as a researcher in teaching. Through my exploration, I examine researchers' beliefs about knowledge or text and discuss how these beliefs might influence not only the "findings" that they present, and also the way that the results of their research "are read" by others, including teachers. In this chapter I consider also teachers' assumptions and beliefs within studies of teaching.

THE FACTORIAL EXPERIMENT:
SCRIPTING TEACHING IN RESEARCH

The first real research study in which I was ever involved was a study that Christopher Clark, Ronald Marx, Nicholas Stayrook, Philip Winne, and I conducted with Dr. Nathaniel Gage when we were graduate students at Stanford University in the early 1970s. Gage was the Director of the research program that was funded by the Office of Education and was considered by many in the field to have fathered the field of research on teaching when he edited the first *Handbook of Research on Teaching* in 1963. Although Gage was clearly the expert, and we were the novices, each of us had a voice in designing the study. We met and designed the study together with Gage, and the graduate students conducted the study as a collaborative team. I recall this study as the first real collaborative research in which I was ever involved. In this study, known as the "factorial experiment," we attempted to manipulate levels of teacher structuring, soliciting, and reacting within a classroom recitation strategy to identify those teaching behaviors that enhance student achievement. Using a factorial design with high and low levels of structuring, soliciting, and reacting, respectively, we created 8 "treatments," as we called them:

high structuring, high soliciting, high reacting
high structuring, high soliciting, low reacting
high structuring, low soliciting, low reacting
high structuring, low soliciting, high reacting
low structuring, high soliciting, high reacting
low structuring, high soliciting, low reacting
low structuring, low soliciting, low reacting
low structuring, low soliciting, high reacting

We hired four teachers, each of whom administered each of the eight treatments. By so doing, we were trying to control for the effect of teacher. As we were designing the study, one of my colleagues came up with the metaphor that teachers would be like "memory drums." At the time, I thought this metaphor made perfect sense. As a psychologist, I was familiar with the traditional laboratory studies of learning in which psychologists used the memory drum to dispense the "treatment" which might be, for example, a list of paired words that the learner was to associate and remember. Just as psychologists always assumed that all memory drums were "the same," I agreed with my colleagues that it made sense to assume that with sufficient scripting and training, all teachers would be the same:

The teachers used lesson scripts—almost as specific as the scripts of plays—in teaching. These scripts controlled to a high degree the material actually presented to students and the teaching behaviors used during each lesson. Each script contained identical curriculum content regardless of the variations in structuring, soliciting, and reacting, called for in the experiment. The teachers were trained to follow these scripts verbatim when possible or to use equivalent phrases. (Clark, Gage, Marx, Peterson, Stayrook, & Winne, 1979, pp. 535-536)

As researchers working within a scientific empirical research tradition, we assumed that if we "operationally defined" our treatment variables, and we specified them in terms of low inference behaviors, then we could train teachers to implement this treatment with high consistency and agreement. In the high structuring variations, we specified that the teacher would review main ideas, state objectives of the lesson, indicate important points, and summarize and signal transitions throughout the lesson. In the low structuring variations, the teacher would do none of these things. In the high soliciting variations, the teacher would ask slightly more (60%) higher-level or thought questions than lower-level or fact questions (40%). In low soliciting, the teacher would ask mostly lower-order or fact questions (85%) and fewer higher-level questions (15%). In high reacting the teacher would consistently praise student's correct responses and prompt students by providing a hint when a student's response was incomplete or incorrect. In low reacting variations, the teacher would give neutral feedback (e.g., "OK") to a student's correct response and probe or repeat the question when a student's response was incomplete or incorrect.

We wanted to find out from this experiment which of these treatment combinations were most effective and led to the best student achievement. Knowing this, we assumed that we could prescribe effective teaching and teacher educators might use this knowledge to train elementary teachers.

The six of us who designed and conducted this factorial experiment were not alone in believing as we did that it was feasible to specify teachers' behavior and to script teaching. As participants in a community of researchers, our beliefs and assumptions reflected those of the community and the guiding assumptions of the process-product research program developed by Gage (1972, 1978) and others (Dunkin & Biddle, 1974). Also, this program of research was situated within other strong research traditions (Darling-Hammond & Snyder, 1992; Shulman, 1986). As Shulman (1986) later described this kind of research: "process-product research was consistent with a strong existing research tradition—applied behaviorist psychology and its task-analytic, training tradition wherein the decomposition of complex tasks into their components followed by the assessment and retraining of individuals on the components themselves had a demonstrably successful track record" (e.g., Gagne, 1970; Glaser, 1962). Following this behaviorist tradition, researchers on teaching assumed that if such approaches worked for radar technicians and aircraft mechanics, then they would work for teachers.

Teachers Are Like Memory Drums, Aren't They?

Although 20 years later, I wonder how we could have assumed that "teachers were like memory drums," when we designed the study, we, as researchers, believed that we could consider teachers "to be interchangeable owing to their rigorous training" (Clark et al., 1979, p. 539). In carrying out our research, I found evidence that led me to question our assumption. I read our data as saying that although we had scripted teachers' behavior, and we had trained the teachers and practiced them to perfection, we still found important differences among the teachers. In the published text of our study, we described our findings this way:

> Despite the rigorous control of content and teacher behavior, there were still noticeable differences in the effectiveness of individual teachers [i.e., a significant main effect of teacher] as measured by the subscales of the multiple-choice posttest of achievement . . . The highest adjusted mean achievement was attained by students of Teacher 1, and the lowest by students of Teacher 3 . . . the effect size of Teacher 1 as compared with Teacher 3 was only .40sc . . . Teacher 1's average student [50th percentile achievement] was only at the 66th percentile of Teacher 3's students. (Clark et al., 1979, pp. 546-547)

How could this be? We had thought that teachers were interchangeable. We had thought of teachers as "implementers." Now, come to find out we had obtained significant effects of teacher even when we had rigorously trained teachers and scripted their behavior. I was shocked. I was puzzled. How could we explain these findings?

Looking back at the published text of our research study from the vantage point of many years, I am surprised to see that we minimized the importance of this finding by asserting that "although this teacher effect was statistically significant, it was small" (Clark et al., 1979, p. 547). Possibly, we thought we were just restating what Cohen (1977) had given as general guidelines when he referred to an effect size of less than half a standard deviation as "small." At the time we failed to see what others later did. Several years after he wrote these words, Cohen's guidelines were contested by other methodologists who cautioned that for "effects sizes to have practical meaning, we need some basis to judge them" (Light & Pillemer, 1984, p. 80). Glass, McGaw and Smith (1981) put it even more strongly when they wrote:

There is no wisdom whatsoever in attempting to associate regions of the effect-size metric with descriptive adjectives such as "small," "moderate," "large," and the like. Disassociated from a context of decision and comparative value, there is no inherent value to an effect size of 3.5 or .2. (p. 104)

Alternatively, perhaps the reference to the teacher effect as *small* originated with one of the authors whose voice dominated those of the other authors of our text. Indeed, the words and the written text of this article were not co-constructed by all six authors, but rather written mainly by N. L. Gage with the help of Christopher Clark. While the other four authors of the text, read, edited, and approved the written "hard copy," this text was written before the age of intensive word processing, writing, revising, and editing on computers which has so changed the way I now write and revise text and also the way I collaborate with my research collaborators in writing text.

Gage's perspective and voice also comes through strongly at the conclusion of the article when we suggest that "future research workers would do well to study differences in teacher style, intensity, and similar dimensions unobserved in the present study. Wider ranging observation instruments should be employed to track down these variables" (Clark et al., 1979, p. 551). The writer of these words assumes that the important missing variables that account for the teacher effects *can* be observed, and as researchers, we simply did not *observe* the "right" behaviors that would explain the remarkable influence of teacher.

Some of us Revise Our Thinking: Developing a Cognitive View of Teaching

As one of the "other authors," I was developing a different perspective from Gage's on why these significant effects of teacher occurred and how we might understand them better. For example, 20 years later, I still recall very clearly two of the teachers whom I saw as very different people and teachers. One teacher, Nancy, had been a primary teacher for many years. She was young, bubbly, and blonde. When she implemented the "high reacting treatment," she squealed "fantastic" in response to her students' correct answers. In contrast, Tanya was a young, African-American, with a calmly competent manner. She typically taught the upper elementary grades, and she seemed more low-key than Nancy even when she was supposed to be implementing the "high reacting" treatment. Tanya would use words like "good" and "right" in response to students' correct answers. These two teachers enacted all the treatments differently in their own ways. Tanya was consistently more structured, academically oriented, focused on, and knowledgeable about the subject matter than Nancy. By comparison, Nancy was consistently more enthusiastic and focused on teaching children than on teaching the subject matter. Although these qualitative differences seemed important even then, we never attempted to describe them or explore them at the time. As we did not construe these attempts at sense making to be *data*, we did not deem them worthy to appear in the text of the report of the study that we wrote.

In addition to mulling over the results of this study, my ideas were developing within the context of the small community of researchers on teaching. Between the time that we conducted the factorial experiment in 1973 and the time it was published in 1979, some of the authors of this volume (Clark, Marx, and Peterson) had begun meeting with Dr. Lee Shulman who was on sabbatical at the Center for Advanced Study in the Behavioral Sciences for the year and with Dr. Bruce Joyce who took over directing Dr. Gage's research program for a 1974-1975 school year while Gage was in Washington, D.C. Marx, Clark, and I were influenced by the conversations we had with Shulman and Joyce about the importance of getting inside teachers' heads and probing teachers' thinking and decision making in order to understand teachers' practice.

What did I learn from what happened in our factorial experiment on teacher structuring, soliciting, and reacting and from the subsequent conversations that I had with my colleagues? For me, this knowledge of "teacher effects" in our experiment and our subsequent conversations were transformative. I began to question whether a "behavioral" view of teaching and teachers' actions was sufficient to explain what goes on among learners and the teacher. Conversations among Christopher Clark, Ronald Marx, and me resulted in our embarking on extensive research on teachers' planning and decision making during our next several years together as graduate students. Christopher Clark and I later received the Palmer O. Johnson Award from the American Educational Research Association (AERA) for a study we did while we were still graduate students at Stanford (Peterson & Clark, 1978). The study focused on teachers' reports of their cognitive processes during classroom teaching, and although it was deemed ground-breaking research at the time, Clark and I later significantly revised our thinking about that particular research study, and we wrote:

> We would suggest that neither Peterson and Clark's (1978) nor Shavelson and Stern's (1981) models of [teachers'] interactive decision making are sufficient. Both models need to be revised . . . Indeed, we now argue that these models may have led research on interactive decision making in the wrong direction because they assumed that student behavior was the only antecedent condition for teachers' interactive decisions and that teachers consider several possible alternatives, strategies, or courses of action when making an interactive decision. (Clark & Peterson, 1986, p. 277-278)[1]

---

[1]Although this article was co-authored, this text was actually written by me and the ideas were *not* coconstructed. Having said that, I realize that the statements about revising our earlier model reflects a revision of my own thinking but not necessarily that of my coauthor.

After we left Stanford University with our doctorates, my colleagues from the factorial experiment—Christopher Clark, Ron Marx, Philip Winne—and I spent the next decade studying teaching from a cognitive "mediational" perspective. In our research, we tried to consider teachers' thinking as well as their actions and performance, and we also attempted to explore students' cognitive processes as mediators of the effects of teachers on learners' achievement (see, for example, Clark & Peterson, 1986; Shulman, 1986; Winne & Marx, 1982). For example, in my own research program in the Wisconsin Center for Education Research, I conducted a series of studies in the early 1980s in which I interviewed students before, after, and during classroom teaching to try to understand how their cognitive processing, thinking, and own assessments of attention and understanding might account for and predict their achievement as a result of classroom teaching (see, Peterson, 1990).

"CGI": TEACHING FROM A RESEARCH-BASED "SCRIPT" FOR STUDENTS' KNOWLEDGE

In 1985, more than a decade after my involvement with the factorial experiment, my thinking had advanced, along with that of the field and my own professional career. I had moved from being a graduate student at Stanford University to a full professor with tenure at the University of Wisconsin—Madison, and thus, I had moved from a novice to an expert in the community of educational researchers. Yet in many ways I continued to frame the problem as the same. I still saw my goal as a researcher as one of finding research-based knowledge or frameworks that might be used by teachers in their teaching to improve their practice and student learning. In this way, I was still framing the problem of one of researchers coming up with the knowledge to give teachers in as a "script" for understanding. In the case of the Factorial Experiment, it was a framework for thinking of teaching in terms of high versus low levels of structuring, soliciting, or reacting by the teacher. In the case of Cognitively-Guided Instruction (CGI), it was a framework for thinking about students' understanding of addition and subtraction word problems.

The Researchers Invent Cognitively Guided Instruction

In 1984 Elizabeth Fennema, Thomas Carpenter, and I began conversations about writing a proposal to the National Science Foundation to conduct a research study together. We felt we had much to learn from each other, because we represented different research communities and each of us brought different kinds of knowledge and expertise to the conversation (see

Romberg & Carpenter, 1986). As an educational psychologist studying mathematics teaching, I learned from our conversations much about what mathematics education researchers studying mathematics learning had been learning about the development of children's problem-solving knowledge in addition and subtraction (Carpenter, Moser, & Romberg 1982; Riley, Greeno, & Heller 1983). Tom Carpenter talked a lot about how "children construct mathematics knowledge." From his own research and interviews with young children, he had learned that children really know much about arithmetic before they enter school than most teachers and other adults had assumed. Most children know how to count—they know the numbers and typically know how to count objects up to ten. Tom talked about how Rochelle Gelman and her colleagues had discovered that a 2- or 3-year-old child who can count three objects with one-to-one correspondence, can solve the word problem: "If there is one bunny eating carrots in the field, and another bunny hops to join it how many bunnies are there?" (see Starkey & Gelman, 1982). He talked about how researchers on mathematics learning were amazed when they discovered that children could solve story problems without knowing the number facts because previously they had assumed that the child had to know the facts first (1 + 1 = 2) in order to solve a story problem using the facts. As someone who had worked a lot with preservice and inservice teachers, Elizabeth Fennema kept pressing Tom on what these research findings would mean for teachers. I added that we knew from research on teaching that teachers' beliefs and knowledge would influence significantly what teachers would make of such findings. So, what would research finding on children's mathematics learning mean for teachers?

Like All Learners, Teachers Construct Their Own Meanings, Don't They?

Through our conversations together, Carpenter, Fennema, and I came to realize that just as we were thinking of children as constructing mathematical knowledge, so too we needed to think of teachers that way. Rather than telling teachers what to do, we decided to share with them Carpenter's (1985) findings from his interviews with children about addition and subtraction problem solving. We took this stance in our National Science Foundation-funded research project, which we began in 1985. In a month-long workshop during the summer of 1986, we presented 20 first-grade teachers with the actual data from Carpenter's study in the form of videotaped cases of 5-year-old children solving various types of addition and subtraction word problems, including those types that most adults have believed young children incapable of solving. We also presented teachers with two frameworks or sets of ideas constructed by Carpenter (1985) from these data. One framework described 11 addition/subtraction word problem types that represented Tom's categorization of the way children think about these problems; the other framework labeled and categorized the several kinds and sequence of strategies that children tend to develop to solve these problems (e.g., direct modeling; counting all; counting on; using derived facts; recalling facts). As we described our work with teachers, we asserted that:

> We did not tell teachers what to do with the knowledge they had gained. We discussed the importance of a teacher's knowledge of how each child solves problems; the place of drill on number facts; and the necessity for children to think and talk about their own problem solutions to each other and to the teacher. We talked about adapting the problems (by type of problem or size of number in the problem) given to a child depending on what the child understands and can do. We discussed writing problems around themes related to children's lives and classroom activities. We gave the teachers time to plan how they would use their new knowledge in their classrooms during the following year. Teachers talked extensively with us and with other teachers about possible implications of the knowledge about addition and subtraction. Most teachers wrote examples of all of the problem types to use in their classrooms, and tentatively planned one unit that they would teach sometime during the school year. (Peterson, Fennema, & Carpenter, 1991, pp. 75-76)

The CGI study differed from the Factorial Experiment, in that we did not tell the teachers what to do or how to behave. In addition, while we paid no attention to teachers' knowledge and beliefs in the Factorial Experiment, in the CGI study we attempted to directly influence teachers' knowledge and beliefs about children's mathematics learning, and about mathematics problem solving. Yet like the Factorial Experiment, we conceptualized the CGI study within an experimental research paradigm. We recruited first-grade teachers who were assigned randomly to either an experimental group who participated in the summer workshop or to a control group who did not. We then compared the knowledge, beliefs, practices of the teachers and the mathematics achievement of their students for each of these groups at the end of the 1986–1987 school year.

We found that compared to control teachers, teachers in the experimental (CGI) group, came to agree more strongly on a written survey with these ideas (Carpenter et al., 1989):

—children construct rather than receive mathematical knowledge;
—mathematics instruction should facilitate children's construction of knowledge rather than teachers' presentation of knowledge;
—mathematics instruction should build on children's knowledge and understanding and the development of mathematical ideas in children should provide the basis for sequencing topics for instruction;
—number facts should be learned within the context of problem solving and as interrelated with understanding.

Another way of construing our findings is to say that compared to the control group, the experimental group of teachers came to share many of the beliefs that we, as researchers, had. We assumed that children construct rather than receive mathematical knowledge. We also assumed that there were specific strategies that children used to solve word problems and these followed a developmental sequence. We found that CGI teachers had learned what we wanted them to know about these specific strategies that children use to solve word problems, and these teachers had learned the 11 different problem types. One way of summarizing these findings is to say that we were successful as good teachers or teacher educators. We had taught our students—the CGI teachers—what we wanted them to know.

We also found that, although we thought that we had not told teachers what to do, CGI teachers had constructed some similar practices. CGI teachers spent significantly more class time on word problem solving than did control teachers, and they spent significantly less time drilling on addition and subtraction number facts. CGI teachers encouraged their students to solve problems in many different ways; they listened to their students' verbalizations of ways they solved problems; and they knew more about their individual student's mathematical thinking than did control teachers. Most significantly, at the end of the 1986-1987 school year, students in CGI teachers' classes did better than students in control teachers' classes on written and interview measures of problem solving and number fact knowledge.

Like All Learners, Teachers Construct *Different* Meanings, Don't They?

As a researcher interested in improving teachers' practice and having research make a difference in teachers practice, I was ecstatic.[2] Why? I think it was because as Russell Hunt (1992) has said: ". . . I was at least as much a teacher as a researcher, and . . . my need to know was fueled by an more immediate need to do . . . as a teacher, it seemed clear to me that in justice I could only design a study from which I believed my students could learn something" (pp. 71-72). And our teachers *had* learned something or had they? And what had they learned? These questions were to occupy the next several years of my life.

Take 1: Beginning to "Unpack Teachers' Understanding." Although our initial pass through our data using quantitative methods suggested that

---

[2]Program officers at the National Science Foundation were ecstatic too. At the end of our 4-year grant, Fennema and Carpenter reapplied to the National Science Foundation to extend the research and development of Cognitively-Guided Instruction up through the third grade, and they were awarded several million dollars to do so.

our teachers had "constructed" what we wanted them to know (Carpenter et al., 1989) and they had developed more effective mathematics teaching practices, upon closer inspection and with deeper qualitative exploration, I began to wonder. In a further study (Peterson, Carpenter, & Fennema, 1989), we conducted case analyses of two teachers who were both in the CGI group. We read and reread the texts of the interviews we had done with each of the two teachers, and we analyzed the descriptive fieldnotes that Elizabeth Fennema and I had written when we had visited each teacher's class during the spring of the 1986–1987 school year. Through reading these texts, I began to see not only important similarities between these two teachers, but also important differences. Both teachers introduced word problems to their first graders at the beginning of the year and used them throughout the year to teach addition and subtraction; and both encouraged and expected students to use a wide variety of strategies to solve the problems. In contrast to Ms. Hardy, however, Ms. Miller also had her children model and work problems aloud in class so the children could see and hear the kinds of thinking used by others to solve problems. Ms. Miller had her first graders create their own word problems and pose them to teach other, and she actively listened to her students talking and thinking aloud, using this information to keep track of students' problem solving knowledge and strategies in an ongoing way. As a consequence, Ms. Miller was the most knowledgeable of all the CGI teachers about her own students' problem-solving knowledge and strategies. In an interview, she accurately predicted individual target student's performances on a number of specific mathematics problems. Ms. Miller also used her understanding of her children's mathematical knowledge in planning and creating her mathematics instruction. Ms. Miller's teaching seemed to reflect her beliefs about the role of the learner as an active one and the role of the teacher as one of actively facilitating children's construction of knowledge.

From this study, I learned different things than I had from our initial analysis in which we compared the experimental and control group of teachers (Carpenter et al., 1989). This study represented the first time I had ever really attempted to go beyond quantitative data and to use qualitative data to try to understand what was going on "beneath the numbers" and with individual teachers. I began to think that CGI teachers had learned different things, and the sense they had made of the research based knowledge was different for teach of them.

Take 2: Digging Deeper Into Teachers' Understanding and Use of CGI. I had moved from the University of Wisconsin to Michigan State University, and I wanted to continue to explore CGI teachers' learning. In 1990 I initiated with a graduate student a follow-up study of 20 of the original teachers, either 3 or 4 years after they had completed the initial CGI workshop. (The "control" teachers participated in the CGI workshop the summer following the experimental group workshop.) Because most research-based interventions have not had substantial long-term influences on teaching practice (Clark & Peterson, 1986), I was curious to learn what teachers thought of CGI 4 years later and whether or not they were still using CGI. Having just read Jerome Bruner's (1990) *Acts of Meaning,* I was intrigued by Bruner's words about the need for a psychology of teaching and learning "based not only upon what people actually *do,* but what they *say* they do, and what they *say* caused them to do what they did" (p. 16; emphasis in original).

To explore further the CGI teachers' interpretations of CGI, Nancy Knapp and I decided to interview 20 teachers who, 3 or 4 years earlier, had participated in inservice workshops on CGI. All interviews were done by phone and were recorded, transcribed verbatim, and analyzed. (See Knapp and Peterson, in press, for a complete description of this study and the results.)

We learned that 19 of the 20 teachers reported still using CGI to teach mathematics. All 19 teachers were focusing on problem solving and using manipulatives—watchwords not only of CGI but also of the current mathematics education reform. On going deeper beneath these watchwords, however, we discovered that teachers varied widely in how they thought about and describe their use of CGI. Some teachers used CGI occasionally or supplementally; others used CGI mainly or solely. We found teachers' use to be significantly related to their ideas about what it meant for them to "know" mathematics, how they believed students learned mathematics, and what they thought about the responsibilities and roles that teachers and students have in learning mathematics.

We read our data as showing three distinct patterns of use of CGI, and these patterns of use were related to the meanings that teachers had constructed for CGI. The first pattern consisted of 10 teachers who reported a steady, gradual increase to reach their current main or sole use of CGI. These teachers' created their mathematics practice from several key CGI ideas—the major one being that children have a lot of mathematical knowledge and understandings from which the teacher should build and develop mathematics instruction. These teachers' mathematics practices were dynamic, changing, and growing as they learned from their children and as they learned by using CGI. For example, Ms. Taylor talked about the meaning of CGI as "working with what children know—with their current understanding, and then providing experiences in a facilitating way that allows them to explore and build a greater understanding. . . ." For these teachers who used CGI as their main or only program, the relationship between their substantive knowledge and beliefs about these ideas and their mathematics practice seemed to be conceptual and interactive. Gradually over 3 or 4 years, their knowledge, beliefs, and mathematics practice had been transformed.

We came to realize that these teachers—for whom CGI involves substantive ideas and assumptions from which they develop their mathematics practice—formed one important group of teachers using CGI. These 10 teachers showed a continuous, developing pattern of use in their mathematics teaching, as well as some use of CGI ideas in their teaching of other subjects (e.g., asking students more "Why?" and "How do you know?" questions; finding out what students know and understand about a subject and then building on that in practice).

The second pattern involved four teachers who thought of CGI as a set of procedures such as using manipulatives or doing word problems. They reported having never used CGI more than supplementally or occasionally and were now settled in that use. These teachers' knowledge of CGI seemed static. For example, one of the four teachers in this study was Ms. Hardy whom had been the focus of our case analysis in the earlier study. Hardy's procedural stance toward CGI was representative of this group. Furthermore, Ms. Hardy's thinking and practice seemed substantially unchanged from what we had observed 3 years earlier (Peterson et al., 1989). In contrast to the way that Ms. Hardy and these three teachers construed CGI, Carpenter, Fennema, and I had intended CGI to be not a set of procedures, but rather as a set of working ideas developed from research on young children's mathematics problem solving. Also, we thought we had made a special attempt to present CGI to teachers *not* as a program or set of procedures but rather as research-based knowledge from which teachers might draw their own implications for their practice and construct their own ways of using CGI in their mathematics teaching. I learned later that researchers in literacy, who have made similar attempt to ours, have also reported similar proceduralization by teachers of ideas that the researchers themselves regard as substantive rather than prescriptive (Brown, 1992; Florio-Ruane & Lensmire, 1990).

Now, I began to wonder whether the way we had presented the research-based knowledge of the 11 problem types and the types of children's strategies had led teachers to think of these as static, uncontested, and unchanging. We had given CGI teachers a framework or script of categories of students' knowledge (strategies) and types of addition and subtraction word problems. We said that these represented research-based knowledge of the way actually thought about addition and subtraction word problems. Another way of thinking about these frameworks is that they represent one researcher's (Tom Carpenter's) constructions or "readings" of how young children interpret word problems. We presented this as a framework that was not subject to debate, even though alternative frameworks to Carpenter's had actually been proposed by researchers in the community of research on mathematics education, and these frameworks for children's understanding of addition and subtraction were being actively debated (De Corte & Verschaffel, 1985; Resnick, 1983; Riley, Greeno, & Heller, 1983).

Knapp and I found that the remaining six teachers reported using CGI in earlier years, but now only occasionally or not at all. These teachers showed what seemed to us to be a marked inconsistency between their espoused beliefs and espoused practices. For three of the teachers, we saw this inconsistency, but they did not. For the other three teachers though, this incongruity between what they believed and what they actually did in their classrooms was evident and troubling to them. For example, Kathy Pirelli was unusually honest in sharing her feelings of conflict with us. Kathy Pirelli described, almost wistfully, how she would like her mathematics teaching to be:

> I guess I get into this thing where I'm asking questions and they're simply reciting, and I sometimes stop, and I think, "I know that answer; I know that student knows that answer. I want something more. I want to ask a deeper type of a question" . . . I'm trying to ask more questions that don't have a right answer, "Explain that to me. Why do you feel that way?" or whatever, instead of always just going to the easy one. I think I do that many times during the day, as far as just [going for] the right answer. But somewhere in the back of my head, [I know] that it's so important to ask them, "How did you get that?" I saw those videotapes of students doing things, and it was always "How did you get that?" That relates to everything.

I found the case of Kathy Pirelli and these other five teachers to be particularly distressing. My research colleagues—Fennema and Carpenter—and I had thought to empower first-grade teachers by giving them access to research-based knowledge of first-grade children's mathematics learning and encouraging them to use, develop and transform the knowledge in ways that fit with their own beliefs, values, and context. Yet Kathy Pirelli and some of her colleagues felt either disempowered or disinclined to do so. Indeed, these six teachers frequently mentioned "barriers" that constrained them from teaching the way they would like. These constraints included lack of planning time and class time; the type of students they had; the expectations that the next teacher would have for these students; standardized tests that their students would take that would assess computational skills in mathematics; and the fact that there was no "packaged" curriculum for CGI. One teacher who was teaching second and third-grade volunteered that she felt particularly powerless and frustrated because "they" (the researchers) had not made a framework for CGI in second and third grade, and she felt insecure about trying CGI on her own without such a framework. What CGI meant for her was defined rather narrowly in terms of the children's strategies for solving addition/subtraction word problems and the addition/subtraction problems types. She did not seem to have a broader conceptual understanding of CGI as related to ideas of children's construction of mathematical knowledge, students as sources of mathematical knowledge, or children as responsible for their own learning. Further, this teacher did not see herself as having the authority and responsibility and knowledge to develop her own ideas and use of CGI on her own. She was still waiting for her researchers to do it.

This teacher's dilemma raised an interesting question for me as a researcher: What role can or should "research-based" knowledge play in transforming learning and teaching? In what ways might "research-based" knowledge (such as the addition/subtraction problem types and children's strategies) be illuminating? In what ways might research-based knowledge such as this become constraining? I explored this dilemma further by more deeply examining the case of one CGI teacher—Annie Keith (see Peterson, 1993).

Take 3: Reciprocal Learning and Transformation.   Annie Keith was among the teachers assigned randomly to the experimental (CGI) group so she participated in the month-long CGI workshop in summer, 1986. As she had just completed her first year of teaching, Annie was the most novice teacher in a group of experienced first-grade teachers. Up until the workshop that year and throughout her own schooling, Annie hated mathematics, and she thought of herself as math "phobic." In her preservice teacher education at the University of Wisconsin-Madison, Annie took two courses on mathematics for elementary teachers. When she began teaching in 1985, she still did not feel comfortable with mathematics. According to her, the turning point was when she became involved with the CGI project. One of the things that she learned during her first year of involvement with the CGI project was that in mathematics it was OK to ask "Why?" and "How come?" A second thing that she learned was that a teacher needs to become a better listener to children's thinking. As Annie put it:

> I think I was always a good listener to kids. I think a teacher needs to know some things to listen for. I found that CGI set up a kind of framework or grid in my mind so I started to think of things to listen for. When I would hear things being said by the kids, it would fit in somewhere, and it would make sense to me.

At the end of the first year Annie was asked whether she had changed her mathematics teaching and if so, how. She reported that she "put more stress and more time on oral story problems and talking—a lot more time on talking about how you are doing something and talking about, 'How are you getting the answer?' "

Annie Keith became more involved with the CGI project with each passing year. After the initial year, Annie became one of six teachers who were case study teachers and were the focus of continued study by Fennema and Carpenter. As part of this research, Annie Keith got to know well and met together frequently with the five other case study teachers including Sue Gehn and Mazie Jenkins. Annie also began giving workshop on CGI to other teachers in the Madison, WI, school district. When Nancy Knapp and I interviewed teachers in 1990, Annie Keith was one of the ten teachers whom we thought fit the first pattern. These teachers created their mathematics practice from several key CGI ideas and from these ideas they had transformed their knowledge, beliefs, and mathematics practice.

In 1991, Cathy Brown and I were asked by Tom Carpenter, Elizabeth Fennema, and Megan Loef Franke to conduct a study of the teachers at John Muir Elementary School in Madison, WI, in which the researchers and teachers were working to "extend the principles of CGI to the primary mathematics curriculum" (kindergarten through third grade) (Carpenter, Fennema, & Franke, 1992). Annie Keith was then serving as the mentor teacher on the CGI Project in that school, teaching full-time in the school and working with the other teachers there.

Although Fennema, Carpenter, and I have written that "each CGI teacher creates her own unique practice" we also have suggested that "CGI classrooms have been characterized typically by a focus on problem solving, particularly the solving of word problems; students' sharing of their diverse strategies for solving the problems; and teachers' and students' listening hard to students' solutions and ideas for solving problems" (Peterson, Fennema, & Carpenter, 1991). When I observed Annie Keith's first-grade classroom in May, 1991, I observed that these were important aspects of her mathematics teaching. Annie's first graders wrote their own word problems and posed them to each other. Children solved word problems and shared their solution strategies with one another. These characteristics of CGI classrooms were typical not only of Annie Keith's classroom, but also of the classrooms of all the other six first- and second-grade teachers at Muir school. But I began to notice some differences in the discourse, in the mathematics, and in the way in which knowledge was represented and conceived in Annie's classroom compared with other CGI teachers. These new "wrinkles" or transformations in CGI became more apparent in Annie's teaching when I observed her classroom during the following year in March, 1992.

Annie Keith's Classroom: A Teacher "Reinvents" CGI

Every day, Annie Keith teaches mathematics to her first-grade class from about 8:30 to 10:30 in the morning. The class starts the day with a meeting or whole class conversation with students sitting on the rug. On this particular day, a Thursday morning in March, 1992, the children gathered on the rug in the meeting area. Twenty students were present: 13 of the children were Caucasian, 5 were Afro-American; 1 was Hispanic; and 1 was Egyptian. Twelve were boys, and 8 were girls. After taking attendance and the lunch count, Annie asked one of the students to count the sticks representing students who were going to eat hot lunch. One of the boys counted the hot lunch sticks and concluded that there were seven. Annie asked, "How do you know it's seven?" The boy then counted the sticks one at a time, counting aloud as he did so. Turning to the class, Annie asked the children if they thought it was seven, and the class counted aloud together as the boy put the sticks down on the rug one at a time. At that point, Peter piped up and said that they would need one more to make eight, " 'Cuz after the seven comes eight. You have to have two fours to make eight."

In reply, Annie queried: "Does it help sometimes to know some of these facts—some of these doubles about some numbers to help you solve other things?" The class responded, "Yes." And when Annie asked, "What do you mean, Erica?" Erica suggested that "Two is an even number, and this is an even number (She showed two fingers on her right hand) so if you put two together (She showed two more fingers on her right hand) that would make four, so this would be an even number. And eight would be an even number if you put another four again. (She showed four fingers on each hand)."

Erica's remark opened up the door for a conversation that lasted nearly 40 minutes, and in which the students and their teacher traversed territory that included odd and even numbers, positive and negative numbers, zero and negative zero, and "touchpoints" on numbers.[3] The following selection came midway through the conversation when Erica returned the conversation to the question of whether there was a negative zero or not by piping up, "On the number chart there's not a zero negative." (Here Erica was referring to the number line on the wall that extended from −20 to 100.)

Following up on Erica's remark and realizing that she was responding to an idea that Daniel put forth earlier, Annie queried, "Daniel, did you hear what Erica's first comment was because I think that is kinda aimed at you?" Annie asked Erica to tell Daniel what she meant, and Erica did this. Then Annie asked "Daniel, what are you thinking about that?"[4]

---

[3] I use this metaphor of "mathematical territory" because Magdalene Lampert has her teaching as traversing mathematical territory with her students, and this metaphor seems apropos to Keith's teaching as well. See, for example, Lampert, 1990.

[4] I was doing fieldwork at Muir School this week, but I observed Annie's class on the day previous to this one. This transcription comes from my analysis of a videotape of Keith's class that was done by Susan Baker, a CGI project staff person and sent to me by Tom Carpenter. This videotape constitutes data being collected by the CGI researchers as part of their NSF-funded project. My analysis is in no way intended to substitute for or supplant their own analysis of these data.

Conversing About Zero—Is There a Negative Zero?

Annie: Hmmm. What about that idea of zero? She doesn't agree. She says there is just zero, not zero and negative zero. What do you think about her comment?

Daniel: I think I agree with Alex—because it's if zero is odd, then one would be even. There has to be a starting for negatives too.

Annie: So you're thinking that zero is an even number? So you're thinking there's a zero and a negative zero?

Daniel: Yeh, I would say that.

Annie: Do you think there's a zero and a negative zero?

Peter: Yeh. Before we didn't know about the negatives, zero was really like a starting. But now that we know about them there has to be a starting point for negatives too.

Alex: But then we'd have to keep on counting zeros and negative zeros.

Peter: No, there is only going to be one of each.

Annie: Erica. I think you need to come and listen to this 'cuz I think we need you in on this conversation.

Annie: Let me recap this: Peter you think there is a zero and a negative zero. Erica, you don't think there is a negative zero. Why not?

Erica: Because there's not.

Annie (to another girl who shook her head "no"): You don't think there's a negative zero.

Other students: Me either.

Annie: Let's listen to some of what you guys are thinking about it.

Erica: Because it doesn't go "negative zero, zero, one, two, three."

Annie: What does it do?

Erica: It just goes "one, two, three, four, five, six, seven, eight, nine."

Annie: So going up on the positive side it goes like this. Then what happens on the negative side?

Erica: It goes negative one, negative two, negative three. Maybe the number chart on the negative side isn't right, but I still don't think there is a negative zero.

Annie drew the following number line on the board as Erica explained it:

<————————————>
−3 −2 −1 0 1 2 3

Annie: So you don't think it goes zero, negative zero, negative one? Hmmm. Somebody else, what do you think about this idea right here about zero or negative zero?

Hannah: I don't think there is a negative zero because if it went zero negative zero, there would just be like two zeroes in a row

Alex: And the ones there would have to be two rows, the two would have to be two rows . . .

Annie: So you're thinking if it went like this (drew a new number line on board) and like this (drew on board) and this would be a negative one and a positive one, two. So you're thinking that wouldn't . . . ?

Annie drew the number line on the board as she thought Alex saw it:

<----------------------------->

−3 −2 −1 −0 0 1 2 3 4

Alex: Yeh, that might be it because there would be one zero for each set. One zero for that set (pointed to negative numbers) and one zero for that set (pointed to positive numbers).

Annie: Erica, you made a comment, you thought that zero was a ——(pause)?

Erica: A divider.

Annie: A divider. Can you elaborate on that a little more on that? What do you mean?

Erica: If you had ten numbers, then you put a zero, then you would need one more in order to make ten. And then if you need another one, you would need two more to make ten. If you count the zeros in it, you would have to have to count the other ones to get the other zeros. (While Erica spoke, Annie interspersed with "OK" and "Hmmm.")

Annie: So how does this zero act as a divider. What does it divide?

Erica: It divides the negatives right here and the positive numbers. (Erica went to the board and pointed to show this.)

Annie: Oh, you're thinking zero is kinda like a . . .

Heather: Which are the positives?

Annie: Which are the positive numbers?

Erica (pointed as she said this):   This is a positive number because it doesn't have this (pointed to a negative sign of one of the numbers on the number line) or else it would be not really a positive number, a negative number. Then if you had a negative zero, then this wouldn't be a divider, and this would be a positive and this would be a negative.

Annie: Hmmm.

Is "Negative Zero" in the "Script"?

The case of Annie Keith presents a puzzle for researchers on teaching for Annie's teaching has gone well beyond the original frameworks and knowledge she was given about addition and subtraction word problems and children's strategies. Annie has transformed the knowledge, yet she continues to develop students' understanding and to help her children understand how and why mathematician developed the numbers and symbols that they did. If one takes the latter view of the need for children to develop number sense and the idea of numbers as representations, then Annie's 6-year-olds are dealing with important mathematical issues in their discussion of whether or not "negative zero" exist and why or why not it might exist, and the evidence for their conjectures.

In reading an earlier draft of this paper, noted psychometrician and educational psychology professor, Lee J. Cronbach, was intrigued by this discussion of these six-year-old's discussion of the possibility of the existence of negative zero. Cronbach recalled an instance in which he actually got "−0" on a computer print-out due to the procedure that the computer used to round numbers. Another university professor, Susan Luks, read this episode and recalled a recent instance in which her adult computer science students had vigorously debated the existence of negative zero as they were learning to program in the computer language "C." In computer language one of the "bits" indicates whether the number is positive or negative. Luks' adult students puzzled about how then to represent zero in computer language. They proposed the idea of "negative zero" and "positive zero" to try to solve their problem of how to represent zero in computer language.

Mathematician and cognitive scientist, Alan Schoenfeld, had the following to say about the example of Annie Keith's students wrestling with the possibility of negative zero:

> When Annie Keith teaches in this new way, she has a lot more flexibility, and her students explore a lot of interesting mathematics. The example of a student rediscovering Pythagorean notions was a nice case in point. But it's not true that there's no "can't" in mathematics, at least not literally—once definitions are made, some things can be done, and some can't. In moving from teacher as dispenser of (a very narrow slice of) truth to teacher as facilitator of sense-making, Annie Keith and others take on a much greater burden than before. They have to negotiate between the students' current understandings and (a paraphrase of Kitcher) "what the mathematics allows them to do." (Alan Schoenfeld, personal communication, Sept. 28, 1992)

Perhaps Annie also has to negotiate between her students and the community of mathematicians and mathematics education researchers. And, Annie Keith is in a unique position to do so as we later found out.

Researchers and Teachers Learning From Each Other

One way in which Annie Keith is different from most other teachers is that Annie now participates is the community of researchers and university professors. On her days off, Annie feels free to go to the CGI offices at the university and to spend the afternoon talking about her teaching with CGI project leaders Elizabeth Fennema, Tom Carpenter, and Megan Loef Franke and with the graduate students there. By doing so, she has access to the on-line thinking, knowledge, and understandings of leading-edge scholars that most teachers would not have access to except through reading research articles or through attending a national conference and hearing a researcher give an invited address. Through these conversations with Annie Keith, the researchers also have on-line access to the knowledge, thinking, and understandings of a first-grade teacher, fresh from the challenges of learning and teaching a new mathematics in new ways to a diverse group of wriggling, laughing, boisterous young learners.

Another way that Annie differs from other CGI teachers is that Annie feels comfortable in challenging a researcher's thinking just as she might challenge her first graders and ask them to provide evidence for their thinking. An example was when Annie Keith and Tom Carpenter disagreed about "discovering" what Tom took to be a social convention in mathematics and Annie took to represent something deeper.

Tom Carpenter recalls vividly when he was in Annie's classroom, and the children discussed "a million." Annie had written the number "10,000" on the board. The students all agreed that it could be ten thousand. The question was, "Could it also be called a million?" One child said that "That's ten thousand so it can't be a million." Another child argued that the same number can have different names. The example was that "1200" might be called "twelve hundred" or "one thousand two hundred." From Tom's perspective, Annie had been "very open and tried to let the kids resolve it." Annie had made the point to Tom that a good discussion would ensue. Tom realized that Annie wanted her children to engage in "authentic discourse," and she wanted to avoid having her children see her as the arbiter of information.

But how do you discover social convention? Tom thought there was no way to discover a social convention. Tom explained to me that by social convention, he meant, "a million is a name for a particular number." As Tom explained it: For the British 1,000,000,000,000—a million is a billion (1 followed by 12 zeroes) and for us, 1 followed by 9 zeroes is a billion. Tom thought that the children were seeing it like this—Ones, tens, hundreds, thousands—every digit was getting a new name. Tom said that the children thought that a million should be the next named digit. "That's what Daniel seemed to be saying because we don't say ten hundred which we could."

But Tom admitted that Annie had been right—a wonderful discussion ensued. So, as a researcher, Tom Carpenter learned from this experience and the discourse he had with Annie and the discourse that occurred among Annie and her students.

After observing Annie Keith, Tom is thinking about the relationship between knowledge and CGI teachers' practice. Tom has been comparing the practices of the two CGI teachers they are doing case studies of this year—Annie Keith and Sue Gehn. For example, he noted that in CGI classrooms a lot of common things occur. Students solve problems, and teachers and students listen to children's solution strategies. But then he noted that there are many differences. For example, in her mathematics teaching Annie Keith seems to him to be more like Deborah Ball than she is like the other CGI teacher they have been following.[5] Moreover, Tom thinks that he could never teach like Annie. He thinks that, for a lot of people, Gehn's teaching will be the easier model to follow—her routines look pretty well established. For a beginning teacher, there is so much going on in Annie's class, it is so hard to figure out how she got it that way. In Annie's class there are many different things happening—a lot more open-ended discourse and discussion of affect. Although both teachers have established warm, accepting relationships with their students, Annie has more ongoing conversations in her class.

Tom says that Annie and the other CGI teacher provide contrasting styles in the way they have used the information they have been given in the CGI workshops. But ultimately for Tom, implementing CGI means "building on students' knowledge and extending that" and by students' knowledge he means the problems students can solve, the formal and informal knowledge they have.

The question with which Tom is wrestling most seriously is: To what degree does CGI reflect the extension of very particular research-based knowledge? And a related question then is: Is Deborah Ball a CGI teacher?

Tom's perspective is that there is a broad conception of teaching that encompasses the basic principles of CGI: the idea of attending to children's thinking and knowledge and attempting to build upon that. Deborah Ball would be a teacher that falls under this conception. CGI is embedded within

---

[5]Tom came to know Deborah Ball's work and teaching in her classroom because she participated in a conference that he and Fennema organized as part of the work of the Mathematical Sciences Education Research Center at the University of Wisconsin. Out of that conference came a paper which Ball has published in their edited book, entitled, *Rational numbers: An integration of research* (in press). In another paper entitled, "With an eye to the mathematical horizon" (Ball, 1993), Ball gives specific examples of mathematics tasks and discourse from her elementary teaching and also talks about her third-grade students' discussions of odd and even numbers and negative numbers and the representations that she and the students construct to understand these kinds of numbers.

this larger conception as a way of instantiating this principle. The analysis of children's thinking is at the core, but as you get away from the core, it gets "fuzzy." People interpret this core knowledge in different ways—they construct their own meanings and interpretations. The fundamental dilemma is this: On the one hand, you want to provide the latitude for teachers to take the broader conception, but on the other hand, as researchers and developers, Elizabeth Fennema and he have taken a particular analysis of children's thinking. Where do you draw the line when someone has adopted this broader perspective on teaching?

The case of Annie Keith presents a puzzle for researchers on teaching. On the one hand, the researchers who conducted the Factorial Experiment would see Annie Keith's thinking and practice as representing a lack of "fidelity of treatment implementation," and they would view Annie Keith as a real problem. On the other hand, researchers who see Annie's thinking and practice as knowledge transforming, would ask, "If we want to create teachers who think for themselves and who teach and encourage students to think for themselves, do we not want teachers like Anne Keith?" But if the answer to this question is, "yes," then what does that mean for researchers who strive to generate research knowledge that will improve classroom practice?

EPILOGUE

I began this chapter by considering the reflections of Russell Hunt on the text of his own research. Hunt wrote honestly about his own learning as a researcher since he conducted a study of reading text nearly a decade before. In reading Hunt's text—both his original one and his reconstruction—I was moved to write my own story, which has become this chapter. The only piece of Russell's text with which I cannot identify is when he says that he is embarrassed by what he wrote and by what he used to believe a decade before. I am not embarrassed by what I used to believe or by anything I have written earlier. I see myself as much like the learners I study—the teachers and their students in the public schools. Teachers can not be expected to "know" the latest research findings if they are not looking at the world through the same lenses as the researcher, or if they haven't had an opportunity to share the same experiences as the researcher, or if they haven't participated in the discourse of the community of researchers. So too, what I didn't understand ten years ago was not for lack of trying. I could not see it then from where I was then, but then most of the colleagues in my research community were in the same place, and they could not see either what we now see. Why are we as researchers embarrassed to admit that we revise our thinking when that is exactly what we continuously asking teachers to do? Why are we as researchers always asserting that we "know" when really we only discover more questions?

Is it not problematic to treat the text of research and our research findings of research as a set of indisputable truths when they shift over time as we revise them? Research is a human creation. Research occurs in a social and temporal context and emerges through debate, discussion and discourse. Like the teachers whom they study, researchers on teaching also have beliefs that influence how they design their research and how they construe the "findings" of their research.

Why do researchers not make their own beliefs more explicit and why do we not more openly admit when we revise our thinking? Researchers have beliefs that are often "invisible," but yet these influence the research that we create and the texts of our research. Our beliefs are situated within the context of our personal and professional lives as researchers and within the professional discourse of the time. As researchers, our ideas shift over time and develop as they as individuals "learn" but also as the field "learns." As researchers on teaching, our beliefs reflect our assumptions about knowing, learning, and teaching, as well as their assumptions about their relationship to those who "read" and use their research.

Why do researchers continue to assume that teachers will "implement" or "use" the findings of our research? Even when researchers on teaching shifted from a behavioral view of teaching in the 1970s to a cognitive view of teaching in the 1980s, we still assumed that much of the thinking and research would be done by the researchers who would give the research findings to the teacher all "figured out." Yet teachers *do* have beliefs about the text of research, which will influence how they make sense of the research findings. They will transform them in the classroom, or will they? Many contemporary researchers on teaching are coming to believe that learning and teaching involve transformation. Why do we not think of the relationship between research and practice as also a transformational one? It is encouraging that this issue has surfaced and become a subject of debate among researchers in the community of researchers on teaching and even within the smaller community of researchers on teaching here in the College of Education at Michigan State University (see Floden & Klinzing, 1990; Lampert & Clark, 1990). In this debate, one side believes that researchers seek and find the "truth" regarding teaching, and that teachers should simply receive this knowledge and alter their practices because of it. The other side argues that teachers like researchers, are thoughtful, intelligent beings who have valuable insights into teaching and learning, and that teachers might be considered as viable collaborators in research and in learning about teaching.

At the beginning of this chapter, I indicated that we researchers frequently ask ourselves the question, "Why do our research findings often not make much difference in the practice of teachers in our nation's schools?" But maybe we have been asking the wrong question. Maybe we need to revise our question. For example, how might we, as researchers on teaching, invent new ways of doing research? How might we work with teachers in ways that lead to reciprocal learning by researchers and teachers and to research and knowledge that has meaning for teachers as well as researchers?

Reinventing the ways we, as researchers, conduct research with teachers is not easy; and we have few images and examples. Such research changes the roles of researchers and teachers; makes roles ambiguous; and makes more negotiation necessary. The distances between researcher and practitioner are decreased and personal and professional issues come to the fore along with need to wrestle with different ideas about the subject matter and about what constitutes learning and teaching (see Ball & Rundquist, 1993; Wilson et al., 1993). As a research community, we are asking teachers to be reflective about and critical of their own beliefs and practices. So too, we need to think about these questions and work to become more reflective and critical of our own beliefs and practices as researchers.

REFERENCES

Ball, D. L. (1993). With an eye on the mathematical horizon: Dilemmas of teaching elementary school mathematics, *Elementary School Journal, 93*(4), 373-397.

Ball, D. L. (i1993). Halves, pieces, and twoths: Constructing representational contexts in teaching fractions. In T. Carpenter, E. Fennema, & T. Romberg (Eds.), *Rational numbers: An integration of research* (pp. 157-196). Hillsdale, NJ: Lawrence Erlbaum Associates.

Ball, D. B., & Rundquist, S. S. (1993). Collaboration as a context for joining teacher learning with learning about teaching. In D. K. Cohen, M. W. McLaughlin, & J. E. Talbert (Eds.), *Teaching for understanding: Challenges for policy and practice* (pp. 13-42). San Francisco, CA: Jossey-Bass.

Brown, A. (1992, April). *The cognitive basis of school restructuring.* Invited address presented at the annual meeting of the American Educational Research Association, San Francisco, CA.

Bruner, J. (1990). *Acts of meaning.* Cambridge, MA: Harvard University Press.

Carpenter, T. P. (1985). Learning to add and subtract: An exercise in problem solving. In E. A. Silver (Ed.), *Teaching and learning mathematical problem solving: Multiple research perspectives* (pp. 17-40). Hillsdale, NJ: Lawrence Erlbaum Associates.

Carpenter, T. P., Fennema, E., & Franke, M. L. (1992, April). *Cognitively-Guided Instruction: Building the primary mathematics curriculum on children's informal mathematical knowledge.* Paper presented at the annual meeting of the American Educational Research Association, San Francisco, CA.

Carpenter, T. P., Fennema, E., Peterson, P. L., Chiang, C., & Loef, M. (1989). Using children's mathematics thinking in classroom teaching: An experimental study. *American Educational Research Journal, 26,* 499-531.

Carpenter, T. P., Moser, J., & Romberg, T. (Eds.). (1982). *Addition and subtraction: A cognitive perspective.* Hillsdale, NJ: Lawrence Erlbaum Associates.

Clark, C. M., Gage, N. L., Marx, R. W., Peterson, P. L., Stayrook, N. G., & Winne, P. H. (1979). A factorial experiment on teacher structuring, soliciting, and reacting. *Journal of Educational Psychology, 71*, 534-552.

Clark, C. M., & Peterson, P. L. (1986). Teachers' thought processes. In M. C. Wittrock (Ed.), *Handbook of research on teaching* (Third edition), (pp. 255-296). New York: Macmillan.

Cohen, J. (1977). *Statistical power analysis for the behavioral sciences* (Revised edition). New York: Academic Press.

Darling-Hammond, L., & Snyder, J. (1992). Curriculum studies and the traditions of inquiry: The scientific tradition. In P. W. Jackson (Ed.), *Handbook of research on curriculum* (pp. 3-40). New York: Macmillan.

De Corte, E., & Verschaffel, L. (1985). Beginning first graders' initial representation of arithmetic word problems. *Journal of Mathematical Behavior, 1*, 3-21.

Dunkin, M. J., & Biddle, B. J. (1974). *The study of teaching.* New York: Holt, Rinehart and Winston.

Floden, R. E., & Klinzing, H. G. (1990). What can research on teacher thinking contribute to teacher preparation: A second opinion. *Educational Researcher, 19*(4), 15-20

Florio-Ruane, S., & Lensmire, T. J. (1990). Transforming future teachers' ideas about writing instruction. *Journal of Curriculum Studies, 22*, 277-289.

Gage, N. L. (1972). *Teacher effectiveness and teacher education: The search for a scientific basis.* Palo Alto, CA: Pacific Books.

Gage, N. L. (1978). *The scientific basis of the art of teaching.* New York: Teachers College Press.

Gagne, R. M. (1970). *The conditions of learning* (2nd edition). New York: Holt, Rinehart, and Winston.

Glass, G. V., McGaw, B., & Smith, M. L. (1981). *Meta-analysis in social research.* Beverly Hills, CA: Sage.

Glaser, R. (Ed.). (1962). *Training research and education.* Pittsburgh: University of Pittsburgh Press.

Hunt, R. A. (1992) Reading literature. What happens when our students read and what can we do about it? In J. R. Hayes, R. E. Young, M. L., Matchett, M. McCaffrey, C. Cochran, T. Hajduk (Eds.), *Reading empirical research studies: The rhetoric of research* (pp. 43-74). Hillsdale, NJ: Lawrence Erlbaum Associates.

Knapp, N. F., & Peterson, P. L. (in press). Meanings and practices: Teachers' interpretations of "CGI" after four years. *Journal for Research in Mathematics Education.*

Lampert, M. (1990). When the problem is not the question and the solution is not the answer: Mathematical knowing and teaching. *American Educational Research Journal, 27*, 29-64.

Lampert, M., & Clark, C. (1990). Expert knowledge and expert thinking in teaching: A response to Floden and Klinzing. *Educational Researcher, 19*(4), 21-29.

Light, R. J., & Pillemer, D. B. (1984) *Summing up: The science of reviewing research.* Cambridge, MA: Harvard University Press.

Peterson, P. L. (1990). Knowledge-generating educational research: Penelope L. Peterson. In H. J. Klausmeier (Ed.), *The Wisconsin Center for Education Research: Twenty-five years of knowledge generation and educational improvement* (pp. 96-99). Madison, WI: Wisconsin Center for Education Research.

Peterson, P. L. (1993). Knowledge transforming: Teachers, students, and researchers as learners in a community. In J. Mangieri & C. Block (Eds.), *Creating powerful thinking in teachers and students.* New York: Holt, Rinehart, and Winston.

Peterson, P. L., & Clark, C. M. (1978). Teachers' reports of their cognitive processes during teaching. *American Educational Research Journal, 15*(4), 555-565.

Peterson, P. L., Carpenter, T., & Fennema, E. (1989). Teachers' knowledge of students' knowledge in mathematics problem solving: Correlational and case analyses. *Journal of Educational Psychology, 81*, 558-569.

Peterson, P. L., Fennema, E., & Carpenter, T. (1991). Using children's mathematical knowledge. In B. Means, C. Chelemer, & M. S. Knapp (Eds.), *Teaching advanced skills to at-risk children* (pp. 68-101). San Francisco: Jossey-Bass.

Resnick, L. B. (1983). A developmental theory of number understanding. In H. Ginsburg (Ed.), *The development of mathematical thinking* (pp. 109-151). New York: Academic Press.

Riley, M. S., Greeno, J. G., & Heller, J. I. (1983). Development of children's problem solving ability in arithmetic. In H. Ginsburg (Ed.), *The development of mathematical thinking* (pp. 153-200). New York: Academic Press.

Romberg, T. A., & Carpenter, T. P. (1986). Research on teaching and learning mathematics: Two disciplines of scientific inquiry. In M. C. Wittrock (Ed.), *Handbook of research on teaching* (3rd ed., pp. 850-873). New York: Macmillan.

Shavelson, R. J., & Stern, P. (1981). Research on teachers' pedagogical thoughts, judgments, decisions and behavior. *Review of Educational Research, 51,* 455-498.

Shulman, L. S. (1986). Paradigms and research programs in the study of teaching: A contemporary perspective. In M. C. Wittrock (Ed.), *Handbook of research on teaching* (3rd ed., pp. 3-36). New York: Macmillan.

Starkey, P., & Gelman, R. (1982). The development of addition and subtraction abilities prior to formal schooling in arithmetic. In T. P. Carpenter , J. M. Moser, & T. A. Romberg (Eds.), *Addition and subtraction: A cognitive perspective* (pp. 99-116). Hillsdale, NJ: Lawrence Erlbaum Associates.

Wilson, S. M., Miller, C., & Yerkes, C. (1993). Deeply rooted change: A tale of learning to teach adventurously. In D. K. Cohen, M. W. McLaughlin, & J. E. Talbert (Eds.), *Teaching for understanding: Challenges for policy and practice* (pp. 13-42.). San Francisco, CA: Jossey-Bass.

Winne, P. H., & Marx, R. W. (1982). Students' and teachers' views of thinking processes for classroom learning. *Elementary School Journal, 82*(5), 493-518.

CHAPTER SEVEN

Emerging Epistemologies of Text: Learning to Treat Texts as Human Creations in a "Writing Classroom"

Emily Hutton
Jan Spiesman
Vay Bott
Washington State University, Vancouver

Diane is a 6-year-old in a "writing classroom," a first-second multiage classroom in a primary school in Washington state. Her responses, as part of the study described in this chapter, show us how young children, who are authors themselves, know that authors make decisions about text. Diane was presented with two versions of *The Ugly Duckling*. The first was a traditional retelling adapted by Katharine Ross. Before she heard the Ross version, Diane asked, "What does *adapted* mean?" When the term was explained to her, she said, "I am going to try to adapt a book, too!" The second version was a parody of the traditional story written by Jon Scieszka and Lane Smith. Before she listened to this version, Diane said:

> It's by two people. Because one should have . . . One did the drawing and one did the writing . . . and they would . . . they might be able to help each other on how to, like, put it into words.

June is the teacher in Diane's classroom. June believes that writing is an integral part of becoming literate. Her classroom environment and pedagogy are whole language—integrating writing, reading, speaking, and listening into the process of learning. June reads to the children, asks them to share their writing, and encourages reading and writing for peer audiences. The atmosphere in her room allows the students to use their skills while still in the process of acquiring them. Her classroom is like a learning laboratory, where others can observe as students demonstrate development of literacy skills as they read, write, and communicate in a real setting.

This chapter investigates the influence of a "writing environment" on young children's emerging epistemologies of text. Three elements are discussed: (a) students, with a focus on children's concept of authorship; (b) teacher beliefs concerning children's emerging understanding of text; and (c) classroom environments that foster or limit young children's emerging literacy.

RELATED LITERATURE

Recent research on literacy has focused on a developmental, constructivist view of literacy acquisition in young children. Sulzby and Teale (1991) define the term *emergent literacy* as the process young children go through when they acquire reading and writing skills. Emergent literacy research tells us that reading, writing, and oral language develop concurrently and interrelatedly in literate environments. Children bring prior knowledge in oral language skills, vocabulary, and life experience to the tasks of learning to read and write. They use their prior knowledge to construct meaning from text.

Sulzby and Teale also cite research which indicates that the language and social activity surrounding the text are as important to its meaning as the text itself. Reading books aloud to children is a social interaction and an act of construction. Heath (1983) describes the almost universal experience that young children bring to the process of acquiring literacy: being read to aloud by an adult from storybooks.

Teachers have developed instructional strategies to accommodate young children's need for integrating oral language, reading and writing in a social context. Goodman (1989) describes the "whole language" classroom as a place where real literature by real authors is used as a basis for children to practice their emerging literacy skills in a literate environment. The whole-language classroom gives students a contextual frame upon which to build their skills.

Writing in the classroom, as a means of enhancing literacy among school children, has become the topic of many articles about literacy and application of literacy instruction. In their article, "The Author's Chair," Graves and Hansen (1983) describe how children's concept of authorship develops when they are exposed to a literate environment like the whole language classroom. They list three phases in children's growing understanding of authorship: (a) Replication Phase—children recognize that authors write books; (b) Transition Phase—the concept of author becomes real as children publish their own books, and (c) Opinion-awareness Phase—children realize that the author controls what a book says and how it is said.

Brown and Briggs (1991) describe how children use composing as a springboard for literacy development, within the social context of a writing, whole-language classroom. Scardamalia and Bereiter (1985) describe how students who compose develop from "knowledge telling" to "knowledge transforming" in their writing. Their writing process develops from direct retelling of experience to transforming their experience through setting goals for their writing, and organizing, revising, and interconnecting ideas.

However, research also tells us that not all teachers or classrooms subscribe to the principles of emergent literacy and whole-language instruction. A study by Bridge and Hiebert (1985) showed that teachers who claimed to be providing children with rich writing opportunities were not having them write composition as described by Graves, Hansen, and others. Writing in most of the six elementary classrooms they studied consisted primarily of copying or paraphrasing someone else's ideas. Also, a study done by Wineburg (1991) of secondary students' perceptions of history textbook information showed that students looked at the textbook information as infallible truth. They had no experience in viewing text as a human creation, with an author whose views they could question or examine.

The authors of this chapter share the concern about the level of literacy among our school children. We subscribe to the developmental, constructivist, and whole-language views of literacy acquisition. Two of us are student teachers in our final semester of teacher preparation, in primary whole language classrooms, and one of us (the second author) is a primary teacher in practice for more than 20 years. We decided to investigate both the developmental and instructional influences on literacy acquisition in young children by comparing children in composition-oriented classrooms to children in more traditional classrooms. Specifically, for this chapter, we decided to investigate what factors influence young children's acquisition of the concept of authorship. We used observation, interviews, and an oral reading activity with the children to collect data for our study.

Is there a developmental difference among first- through fourth-graders in their concept of authorship? What develops? Do young children in a "writing classroom" have a greater awareness of the author as creator of the text than would children in a more traditional classroom? Do young children in a writing classroom, who are authors themselves, and who share their reading and writing among their peers, show literacy behaviors that are different from the behaviors of children in more traditional classrooms?

ASKING CHILDREN ABOUT AUTHORSHIP

We chose four classrooms in two schools in the same district for our study of developing ideas about authorship. We categorized the classrooms using Moffett's (1979) hierarchy of writing activity. Moffett lists 5 levels of writing that can occur in classrooms: (a) handwriting—creating symbols on paper; (b) transcribing—copying someone else's writing; (c) paraphrasing—restating someone else's writing; (d) crafting—composing using a prescribed form or topic; and (e) revising inner speech—composing from inside oneself.

Two of the classrooms were *writing classrooms:* June's first-second multiage classroom and Penny's third-fourth multiage room. Eighty-five percent of the writing going on in these classrooms was independent, creative, and shared with peers. The other two classrooms were more traditional: Nellie's second-grade and Pete's fourth-grade. Writing in the latter two classrooms focused on filling in worksheets, penmanship, conventional spelling and rules of phonics, and writing for one audience, the teacher. Composing as defined by Moffett's levels 4 and 5 occurred less than 5% of the time in these classrooms. We randomly selected 20 children from each of the classrooms for our study. Boys and girls were about equally represented in each group. The population represented by the children is from a middle income, semirural economy.

We used what Revelle, Wellman, and Karabenick (1985) have called a "quasi-naturalistic" method of study to examine children's perception of authorship. Task (responding to questions), stimuli (narratives), and situation (listening to two stories read aloud by an adult and then talking about them) were simple and familiar to the children. We read the same two stories to each child, and asked them the same three questions in an invariant order after the reading. All the children seemed eager to listen to the stories, and seemed to enjoy the one-on-one participation. As the literature points out (Heath, 1983), young children are familiar and comfortable with a scenario where the adult reads or tells a narrative, and they respond. We videotaped each session, which lasted about 5-10 minutes.

The two stories we read were two versions of Hans Christian Andersen's *The Ugly Duckling.* The first was an adapted version (Ross, 1991), which told the traditional tale of how an ugly duckling is hatched, shunned by all he meets, then grows up to discover that he is a beautiful swan! The second was a parody of the tale, by Jon Scieszka and Lane Smith (1992). In this story, the really ugly duck grows up, but remains a really ugly duck—and is no swan! After reading these two stories out loud to the children, we asked them the following questions:

1. What do you think about the two stories?
2. Why do the versions end differently?
3. Who decides how a story ends?

Students who talked about authorship at or before the first undirected question were considered to have the most developed sense of authorship of text. Those who did not mention authorship until cued by the second question were considered to have a moderately developed sense of authorship. Students who did not talk about authors until prompted by the third question were considered to have a beginning concept of authorship. Students who did not mention authorship in response to any of the questions were considered not to have a concept of authorship when presented with text.

We assigned scores according to the student's indicated concept of authorship. Those who talked about author at or before question one scored 3 points; those who mentioned author at question two scored 2 points; those who mentioned author in answering question three received 1 point; and if authorship was not mentioned at all, the student scored 0 points.

Each of us viewed the videotaped record of our work with the children, scored responses, and transcribed the children's comments. Then, a second researcher independently viewed the videotapes and scored all responses. Interrater agreement on scoring was high (90% for data from both June's and Nellie's classes, 92% for data from Penny's class, and 95% for data from Pete's class). Disagreements were resolved in conference.

YOUNG CHILDREN'S CONCEPT OF AUTHORSHIP

The data from our study of children's concept of authorship were analyzed in two ways. First, we did a statistical analysis of the differences in scores. Then we examined patterns found in the children's transcribed comments and did a qualitative analysis.

Our initial analysis of variance revealed a significant effect for instructional setting (classroom), $F(3, 76) = 6.95$, $p < .001$. Post hoc Tukey tests indicated that all comparisons involving Penny's third-fourth multiage class yielded significant differences favoring Penny's room. That is, scores in June's classroom ($M = 1.10$, $SD = 0.79$) and in Nellie's classroom ($M = 0.95$, $SD = 0.69$) and in Pete's classroom ($M = 1.25$, $SD = 0.55$) all differed significantly ($p < .01$, $p < .001$, $p < .05$ respectively) from the scores in Penny's classroom ($M = 1.9$, $SD = 0.79$). All other comparisons failed to reach conventional significance levels.

We interpreted the results as having both developmental and instructional components. A purely developmental effect should have favored both upper-grade classrooms (i.e., Penny's and Pete's). However, students in Penny's room not only achieved significantly higher scores than the students in the first- and second-grade rooms, they also scored significantly higher than students in Pete's fourth-grade room. If the influence had been purely instructional, scores from the composing classrooms (Penny and June) would have been significantly higher than scores from the noncomposing classrooms (Nellie and Pete). Statistical analysis shows that the differences between Penny's and Pete's rooms were significant, but differences between June's and Nellie's rooms were not.

Further support for the developmental influence of children's concept of authorship appeared in a comparison of the third and fourth graders within Penny's classroom. Although the subsamples were too small to produce statistically significant differences, the 9 third graders averaged 1.67 (SD = 0.87), while the 11 fourth graders averaged 2.09 (SD = 0.70).

The instructional influence indicated by the statistical difference between Penny's writing classroom and Pete's traditional classroom was profound. Sixteen of the 20 students (80%) in Pete's classroom did not mention author until the most directed question, "Who decides how a story ends?" Over half of the 20 from Penny's room talked about authorship before the third direct question.

Qualitative analysis of the transcribed comments of the children to the three questions also revealed developmental and instructional influences on their concept of authorship. Developmental differences were apparent in comparing comments of first- and second-graders to comments of third- and fourth-graders. Typical responses of first- and second-graders focused on narrative elements: characters, setting, and plot. Many retold portions of the two stories in response to questions one and two. The concept of authorship was at a beginning level for most first- and second-graders, with over 80%, scoring 1. Comments such as the following were typical from this age level:

(to Q2) That one turned out to be a swan. That one turns out to be the same.

(to Q1) This one thought he was going to grow up like this one turned out to be. But he really turned out ugly. The other thought he'd be ugly forever, but he turned out to be like that [swan].

(to Q1) That story had a gray duck and that one had a really really ugly duck. That one had big feet, and this one had small feet. He didn't believe the animals that he was so ugly.

Responses such as these show that first- and second-graders can recognize narrative elements of a story and compare differences in different versions. Also, about half of the first- and second-grade respondents showed a developmental phenomenon that Flavell, Miller, and Miller (1993) call appearance-reality errors, when they talked about the ugly duckling in the first version turning into a swan. Young children at this age are just beginning to acquire an understanding that an object may not be what it appears to be. Children who still could not make the distinction between appearance and reality didn't understand that the ugly duckling was really a baby swan all along. However, some of the children did understand, as is evidenced by these speculative comments:

Maybe the mother or father dropped the egg in the duck's nest to keep it from getting eaten by another animal.

and:

> When a swan was hatching an egg, one probably rolled down into the duck's nest.

Comments of the third- and fourth-graders were more critical and analytical. There was no confusion expressed about the ugly duckling in the first version really being a swan. The older children talked about humor, morals, author's intentions, theme, and about the responses the stories evoked. Typical responses of the older children were:

> (to Q1) *The Ugly Duckling* has a moral, and in the other book, the author writes really weird stories!
>
> (to Q2) The first one was more like a children's story and children like happy endings. The second one is more sophisticated.
>
> (to Q1) I don't think you can judge people by how they look.
>
> (to Q1) The first one is sad. I felt sad.

Some third and fourth graders retold parts of the versions like the first and second graders did. But they expressed more familiarity with both versions, and they talked about authorship at a higher level of understanding than the younger children:

> (to Q1) I've read stupid tales before, and it's true—they are really stupid! And I don't know, but I think the original author of *The Ugly Duckling* is Hans Christian Andersen.
>
> (before Q1) He [Scieszka] also wrote *The True Story of the Three Little Pigs*.
>
> (to Q1) I liked the *Stinky Cheese Man* one. The first one is just a little different from the original. The *Stinky Cheese Man* is interesting.

While there was a statistically significant difference between the scores of the children in the older grades, according to instruction (classroom), and not in the scores of the children in the younger grades, qualitative differences were apparent when we compared the comments from the writing classrooms and the traditional classrooms of both ages. The writing classrooms both included younger children (first- and third-graders, respectively) in comparison with the traditional second- and fourth-grade classrooms, and yet their mean scores were higher. Although all the children from all the classes seemed enthusiastic and eager to be a part of the reading activity, and expressed enjoyment after the stories were read, responses from students in the traditional classrooms were generally less verbal and more tentative. Responses to question 3, "Who decides how a story ends?" were often put into question form by students from the non-composing classrooms: "The person who wrote it?" or, "(pause) . . . the author?" Students from the composing classrooms were more certain of their responses, and made statements like, "They're different because they have different authors" or "the writer decides how the story will end." Responses such as the following were more typical of the students from the writing classrooms:

> (First grader) Both of these stories were nice. He solved his problem, but this guy is just ugly.

> (Second grader) I think that the ugly duckling was not very ugly, but everyone thought he was ugly because he was different.

> (Second grader) If he would copy the same idea out of this story, then he would want the same amount of money as this author!

> (Fourth grader) Because this one was from the *Fairly Stupid Tales*, it was changed . . . it was weird. . .

A particularly engaged student from Penny's third-fourth multiage room was a blind third-grade boy. He listened attentively as one of us read the stories and described the pictures to him orally. He asked questions for clarification, and commented that he had read other stories by Jon Scieszka, as soon as he heard his name. When the graphic illustration of the really ugly duck, drawn by Lane Smith, was described to him, he laughed and said, "He sounds like he's an owl!"

TEACHER BELIEFS AND CHILDREN'S CONCEPT OF AUTHORSHIP

Our study shows that there is a developmental progression from a more concrete, literal view of text (focused on narrative, with a beginning sense that "the person who writes the story" decides how it ends) to a more critical, analytical view of text (with a more sophisticated sense of author control over narrative, style, and theme).

However, a strong instructional influence on children's perception of authorship is also indicated by the statistically significant difference in the scores of the students from Penny's composing third-fourth class compared to those of the students from Pete's traditional fourth-grade classroom. Instructional influence also explains the qualitative differences in the responses of the students from both first-second and third-fourth writing classrooms to the students from the traditional second- and fourth-grade rooms respectively.

What are the instructional differences among the four classrooms in our study? What do the classroom environments resulting from these instructional differences look like? What are the teachers' beliefs and attitudes towards children's interaction with text and experience with authorship? Research literature points out a strong correlation between teacher beliefs and their instructional practices. A recent study by Richardson, Anders, Tidwell, and Lloyd (1991) demonstrated that of the teachers they studied, teacher beliefs related directly to classroom practices in the teaching of reading comprehension. In our observations for our study, we saw striking contrasts among the four classrooms in environment and instructional methods. We suspected that the teachers' underlying beliefs would be as variant as the environments they created.

As student teachers in the two multiage classrooms, we observed and participated extensively. We also observed in the other two more traditional classrooms. We interviewed each of the four teachers, using the following questions to elicit their beliefs about children's emerging literacy:

1. Please outline your beliefs about the classroom environment and young children's emerging understanding of text.
2. Please give three or four examples of your pedagogy in helping children develop reading and writing skills.
3. Please give your assessment of the reading and writing skills of the following students. (Here we listed specific students in the teacher's classroom who had scored either above or below the median score for the classroom in our study.)

We assumed that answers to questions 1 and 2 would provide us with straightforward responses from the teachers concerning their beliefs and examples of instruction, in relation to reading and writing. In question 3, we wanted to see how closely teachers' assessment of particular students' reading and writing skills correlated to our scores of the students' developing sense of authorship. We hypothesized that the assessment of students by teachers in the writing classrooms would more accurately match the level of student perception of authorship as reflected in their scores.

All four teachers in our study had Master's degrees, and 15- to 20-years of teaching experience. All were nurturing, caring teachers who believed that they were offering the best they had to their students.

Nellie's Room

Nellie team-taught with the teacher in the second-grade class next to hers. Her classroom environment and pedagogy were similar to those of the traditional classrooms described by Bridge and Hiebert (1985). There was a large shelf of trade books ("our library") in the other teacher's room, but they were stored inside Princeton files for use during teacher directed reading groups and were not accessible for student browsing. A smaller shelf in Nellie's room, accessible to the students, held basal readers, and multiple copies of dictionaries. No samples of children's work were displayed. One Princeton file contained the books the children wrote themselves: not quite one per student by midyear.

Nellie's beliefs about classroom environment and children's emerging literacy were in evidence in her response to our first question. She said, "You're asking two different questions. I'll answer them one at a time. First, I will tell you about our classroom environment." Organization and neatness were the concept behind Nellie's classroom environment. Children were seated in rows side by side, so that student interaction was minimal. Assigned daily clean-up activities were emphasized. The few posters on the walls were lists of directions and procedures. The classroom environment reflected Nellie's belief that there was no relationship between environment and the children's emerging literacy.

Nellie went on to explain her beliefs about children's emerging under-standing of text. She believed that writing was the basis for all understanding and that reading was enhanced by writing. However, the writing she was alluding to was at Moffett's first three levels. Ninety percent of the writing activity in Nellie's room was handwriting, copying, and paraphrasing. Nellie believed that children needed to learn phonics rules in order to be able to read. She felt that the whole language approach was too "hit and miss" for phonics instruction. The focus of the writing in Nellie's classroom was on mechanics; content was teacher directed, and context was not addressed. As they wrote, Nellie reminded them several times to use "perfect" handwriting, and "perfect" spelling and punctuation. Children were not encouraged to collaborate or share their reading or writing with other children. The audience for the students' work was the teacher.

Nellie believed that reading aloud to children was very important, but she relegated oral reading to "spare time." She expressed that in her experience, children of this age are hesitant to choose new books to read on their own. They seem to choose only books they've heard before.

Of the six students in her classroom who scored higher or lower than the median, Nellie's assessment matched only two. Nellie assessed the student who scored a 3 as being very low in reading and writing skills. She said that the student had no concept of the flow of a story. Her comments were in contrast to the student's response to our read-aloud activity: The student spontaneously and fluently retold the first version of *The Ugly Duckling* after hearing it. Three of the children whom Nellie considers highly skilled in reading and writing scored 0 in their response to the questions in our study. Our hypothesis is that although these children have acquired good decoding skills, and can copy and paraphrase neatly, their lack of experience in composing as real authors themselves, and their lack of being exposed to literature where the author's influence is talked about, makes them unable to answer the question, "Who decides how a story ends?"

June's Room

The writing environment in June's first-second multiage classroom closely modeled her beliefs and instructional practices. The room was arranged into learning centers for language arts, math, science, and art. Print covered the walls, and hung from the ceiling; children's writing was displayed everywhere in the room and out in the hallway. One end of June's room was devoted to a writing center and library. Two computers were used in this area for book publishing. Hundreds of trade books were on a long shelf at the children's level. Pillows and beanbag chairs accommodated young readers. Unlike the students in Nellie's room, the students in June's room were not at all hesitant about selecting reading material. They eagerly went through the shelves, shared reading with each other, and talked about what they read with each other.

Eighty-five percent of the writing activity of these students was at Moffett's two highest levels: crafting and revising inner speech. Children published an average of 8-10 books each per year. Children shared their reading and writing daily, and collaborated by responding to each other's literary products. Children's desks were arranged in groups of four, facing and touching each other. This arrangement facilitated oral communication and cooperative learning.

June's instructional practices closely followed those outlined by Dole, Duffy, Roehler, and Pearson (1991) in their article on reading comprehension instruction. The teacher is seen as "a facilitator who helps students construct understandings about: (a) the content of the text itself; (b) strategies that aid in interpreting the text; and (c) the nature of the reading process itself" (p. 252). Instruction from the teacher would come in the forms of modeling, planning, selecting academic work, providing information, and restructuring student understanding (Dole et al., 1991).

June's beliefs about the relationship between her classroom environment and her students' emerging literacy reflected the whole language concept described by Goodman (1989). According to June, a traditional classroom was considered an important place to learn. However, the multiage classroom was not only considered an important place to learn, but the classroom itself became a teaching tool. It was not just a room to be placed in for learning, but a rich environment with functional literacy opportunities placed for children to use as they become real readers and writers. In June's multiage classroom, the environment was print-rich and there was evidence of functional communication going on in every area.

June believed that in order for children to become readers and writers, they must at the emerging stages be free to take risks and make mistakes.

She believed in a child-centered classroom which allows children to develop at their own rate and accepts approximations in both reading and writing, encouraging and celebrating accomplishments. In June's classroom, the goal for reading and writing was meaning and context, rather than mechanics. Students compared versions of stories and themes. They studied character, setting, and plot; examined authors' intentions; and made predictions. They used commercially published books as springboards for student and class published books. They wrote real letters, notes, books, magazine articles, and lists for real audiences, rather than only for the teacher.

June's perceptions of the stages of literate development of the students in her classroom matched the scores they received in our study of their percep-tions of authorship. The four children in her room who scored 0 she identified as being in the early emergent reading stage, still acquiring decoding skills. Such children would be using much of their cognitive energy to decode the text, and would not be ready to focus on where text comes from (Graves & Hansen, 1983). The four children who scored 2 in her classroom June identified as fluent early readers moving quickly into consolidation in their reading and writing skills. June described Diane, the first-grader who scored 3 in our study, as a child who often explained her way of thinking and learning, because she had a metacognitive awareness of the skills that she is acquiring. There was room for children at all stages of development in June's room.

Pete's Room

Pete's room was a traditional fourth-grade room similar to those described by Bridge and Hiebert (1985). Like Nellie's room, the focus of Pete's environment was on neatness and organization. The atmosphere in Pete's room was stark. There was a total absence of student work on display. A few commercially produced posters were on some bulletin boards, but most of the walls were bare. In contrast to June's and Penny's rooms, the desks in Pete's room were arranged in rows with lots of space between each desk in the row, creating an impression of isolation.

Seventy-five percent of the writing in Pete's classroom was at the first three levels of Moffett's (1979) hierarchy. Twenty-five percent of their writing was at level four (crafting) where topic and form were chosen by the teacher. Pete stressed copying and recopying until the product was "acceptable." Pete talked about the high frustration level of students during these "writing activities."

Even though Pete believed that his methods reflected whole language, there was little resemblance between his classroom and Goodman's (1989) description. Choice of reading material was absent. The only shelf of books was located behind the teacher's desk, inaccessible to the students. The entire class read the same "fourth-grade level" children's novel at the same time. Oral reading consisted of rereading portions of the novel. Students did two worksheets per week related to the novel. One half hour per day was scheduled for oral reading by the teacher, but like in Nellie's room, students worked on recopying assignments during this time. Also like Nellie, Pete stressed phonics, workbook activities, and practicing skills isolated from context. His environment and instruction kept student cooperation or interaction to a minimum. The teacher was the sole audience for all written and oral communication.

Pete's belief about writing, like Nellie's, was very different from June's, or Penny's. His concept of writing focused on mechanics: penmanship, grammar, conventional spelling, and not on content or meaning. Pete's philosophy of literacy, like Nellie's, lacked the idea of the classroom as a literate environment made up of a community of writers.

Pete's perception of his student who scored 3 in our study did not correlate with the child's score. He attributed the student's low performance in reading and writing in his classroom to behavior and attitude problems.

Penny's Room

Penny's third-fourth multiage classroom reflected her belief in a whole-language, integrated learning environment as an inviting place for young children to practice their literacy skills. There were two large, 10-foot display bookcases holding trade books and students' published books, readily accessible to students. There were two more bookcases in other parts of the room, one containing encyclopedias, dictionaries, and sets of trade books for literature study groups. The few basal readers in Penny's room were being used to press flowers. Penny believed that to talk about literature, trade books, not textbooks, needed to be used.

Penny's room, like June's, was arranged in areas for special student-directed activities. There was a reading corner with pillows and beanbag chairs, and a rocker that doubled as an author's chair during sharing times. One bulletin board was devoted to decorated folders that held students' published books, for access and reading at all times. Two tables of varying size were for small group and project work. A large open space was maintained for student literature presentations, literature study groups, and class meetings. Two computers on a table at the back of the room were in constant use for integrating literacy with science and social studies in small group and individual projects. Student art and written work covered the room.

Eighty-five percent of the writing in Penny's classroom was at Moffett's (1979) fifth (creative) level. Penny believed that the classroom environment was crucial for providing a common vocabulary for children to discuss text. Students conferred, worked together, shared ideas, and talked about all aspects of their work. They collaborated in writing several volumes of one story (for example, *Space Police 2000* by Jon, and *Space Police 2003* by

David). They wrote plays and produced them for the class, as expressions of their intimate involvement in a writing community.

Penny believed that the school environment is as important as the classroom environment in fostering literacy. Her students loved to share their published works with students from other classrooms. They met once a week with students from a kindergarten class to act as tutors and peer editors for books being published by the kindergartners. They had free access to the school library at any time. She believed that when the students came to her classroom, they had already obtained a background knowledge to talk about literature.

Penny shared June's belief that the teacher's role was as a facilitator. She felt that her job was to help students grow from where they were developmentally and cognitively as individuals, and provide them with an environment that excites their innate desire to learn.

Penny's daily routine included creative writing during all activities of the day. Writing skills practice was integrated into the children's individual daily writing activities. Students wrote in response to the literature they read individually, in small groups, and in response to Penny's daily oral reading. Penny shared June's belief that reading and writing should be real. Like June, she modeled giving credit to the author, talking about authors' ideas and putting the authors' ideas into context. She believed that as children experience being authors themselves, they will gain an appreciation for authors of commercially published works, and for the writing process. They will understand the importance of giving credit to the authors of the books they read, including other authors in their classroom.

Penny's comments about the students in her room who scored above or below the median showed that she is cognizant of their developmental level in literacy. Three of the four students who scored 3, and have an advanced concept of authorship, have physical limitations which slow them down mechanically (blindness, mild CP, poor fine-motor skills), but Penny feels that their participation in a literate environment enables them to have advanced knowledge and conversation about the meaning of text and authorship. The fourth student who scored 3 Penny described as highly gifted and capable, an excellent reader, and good at any activity she decides to put effort into. The child who scored 0 is a third grader with learning disability who's positive attitude helps her perform above her ability level. There is room for all ability levels in Penny's classroom.

SUMMARY

In this chapter we have discussed the results of our investigation concerning the influence of a writing environment on young children's emerging literacy, specifically, on their emerging concept of text as a human creation. We examined the teacher beliefs that foster an environment conducive to young children's literacy acquisition.

Our results support the research of other investigators in whole language, composing classrooms (Crismore, 1983; Graves & Hansen, 1983; Lehr, 1988; Monteith, 1991; Sulzby & Teale, 1991). Young children's concept of authorship is developmental and it is also influenced profoundly by instructional setting. Whole-language, composing classroom environments have a positive impact on students' abilities to conceptualize authors as creators of text, and as decision makers in meaning, setting, characters, and style. Students who are a part of a writing community, such as those in Penny's and June's classrooms, are free to choose topics of interest and to share their writing with authentic audiences. As authors themselves, they view text in a different way, and exhibit different literate behaviors, from students in traditional, noncomposing classrooms.

Our study also indicates that the instructional approaches used in writing classrooms are more sensitive to the developmental aspects of children's acquisition of literacy. The whole-language, integrated environments of June and Penny's classrooms allow for all developmental stages and ability levels. If indeed, third and fourth graders are ready developmentally to view authorship as a proactive element in text construction, style, and interpretation, these students should be allowed an environment where they can actively engage in the process of authorship, comparison, criticism, and collaboration, which characterize a vital literate community.

Students like Diane, the first-grader in June's classroom, had little trouble viewing text as human creation, rather than as infallible truth. Diane's comments reflected the kind of student-directed learning that is fostered in a multiage, whole language, composing classroom. In this classroom, the students, as well as the teacher, create and interpret text. Diane would often say, "Something is happening in my brain!" and go on to explain the strategies for acquiring literacy which she and all members of her writing community were experiencing.

REFERENCES

Bridge, C. A., & Hiebert, E. H. (1985). A comparison of classroom writing practices, teachers' perceptions of their writing instruction, and textbook recommendations on writing practices. *Elementary School Journal, 86,* 155-172.

Brown, D. L. & Briggs, L. D. (1991). The composing process: A springboard for literacy development. *Reading Horizons, 31,* 332-340.

Crismore, A. (1983, November). *The roles of interpretive communities for reading and writing at Atkinson Academy.* Paper presented at the 33rd Annual Meeting of the National Reading Conference, Austin, TX.

Dole, J. A., Duffy, G. G., Roehler, L. R., & Pearson, P. D. (1991). Moving from the old to the new: Research on reading comprehension instruction. *Review of Educational Research, 61,* 239-264.

Flavell, J. H., Miller, P. H., & Miller, S. A. (1993). *Cognitive development* (3rd ed.). Englewood Cliffs, NJ: Prentice-Hall.

Goodman, K. S. (1989). Whole-language research: Foundations and development. *Elementary School Journal, 90,* 207-225.

Graves, D., & Hansen, J. (1983). The author's chair. *Language Arts, 60,* 176-183.

Heath, S. B. (1983). *Ways with words.* Cambridge, England: Cambridge University Press.

Lehr, S. (1988). The child's developing sense of theme as a response to literature. *Reading Research Quarterly, 8,* 337-357.

Moffett, J. (1979). Integrity in the teaching of writing. *Phi Delta Kappan, 61,* 276-279.

Monteith, S. K. (1991, November). *Writing process versus traditional writing classrooms: Writing ability and attitudes of second grade students.* Paper presented at the Annual Meeting of the Mid-South Educational Research Association, Lexington, KY.

Revelle, G. L., Wellman, H. M., & Karabenick, J. D. (1985). Comprehension monitoring in preschool children. *Child Development, 56,* 654-663.

Richardson, V., Anders, P., Tidwell, D., & Lloyd, C. (1991). The relationship between teachers' beliefs and practices in reading comprehension instruction. *American Educational Research Journal, 28,* 559-586.

Ross, K. (1991). *The ugly duckling.* New York: Random House.

Scardamalia, M., & Bereiter, C. (1985). Helping students become better writers. *The School Administrator, 42*(16), 26.

Scieszka, J., & Smith, L. (1992). *The stinky cheese man and other fairly stupid tales.* New York: Viking.

Sulzby, E., & Teale, W. (1991). Emergent literacy. In R. Barr, M. L. Kamil, P. B. Mosenthal, & P. D. Pearson (Eds.), *Handbook of reading research* (Vol. 2, pp. 727-757). New York: Longman.

Wineburg, S. S. (1991). On the reading of historical texts: Notes on the breach between school and academy. *American Educational Research Journal, 28,* 495-519.

CHAPTER EIGHT

Relationship Between Teachers' Beliefs and Their Instructional Practice in Reading

Patricia L. Anders
Karen S. Evans
University of Arizona, Tucson

This chapter is a record of our interpretations of fourth, fifth, and sixth grade teachers as they considered the teaching of reading comprehension. It traces changes in their beliefs about reading comprehension and text, and also changes in their teaching of reading comprehension and use of text. We were accorded access to these teachers due to their agreement to participate in two studies. The first, the Reading Instruction Study (RIS),[1] was designed to discover the barriers to teachers' use of research based practices. The second, a follow-up study,[2] was designed to learn about teachers' continued change with regard to their teaching of reading comprehension. A major theme that emerged from these two studies and is the focus of this chapter is that of teachers' beliefs about text and their instruction of text—in terms of both the role of text in teaching reading comprehension and the role of text in content area instruction.

RELATED LITERATURE

We conceptualize this chapter as related to two broad categories of literature. The first is the literature regarding teacher beliefs, particularly with regard

---

[1]The Reading Instruction Study (RIS) was funded by the Office of Educational Research and Improvement (OERI), U.S. Office of Education, Grant # G008710014. The co-principal investigators were Patricia L. Anders and Virginia Richardson.

[2]A Study of Long-Term Changes in Teachers' Beliefs and Practices was funded by OERI, U.S. Department of Education in the Field Initiated Studies program, January 1991. The principal investigator was Virginia Richardson.

to beliefs about teaching reading comprehension. The second is the literature regarding text, especially as related to the teaching of reading and also the role of reading in the content areas.

Teacher Beliefs

Interest in teacher beliefs and the relationship of those beliefs to instructional practices has mushroomed, as evidenced by this book and by major conference programs of the last few years. Harste and Burke (1977) may have signaled interest in this topic for the reading field by describing their research-in-progress which predicted that "despite atheoretical statements, teachers are theoretical in their instructional approach to reading" (p. 32). A dissertation by DeFord (1985), and supervised by Harste and Burke, confirmed this prediction. She developed a multiple-choice instrument (TORP) to differentiate among teachers on the basis of theoretical orientation toward reading (phonics, skills, or whole language), and compared teachers' theoretical orientation with practices observed in their classroom. She found a strong relationship between the TORP scores and what teachers actually did. Further, Mitchell, Konopak, and Readance (1991) found a high degree of consistency between Chapter One teachers' beliefs about reading and their instructional decision making.

In contrast, Duffy (1981) and Hoffman and Kugle (1982) were unable to find a strong relationship between teachers' theoretical orientations and specific classroom behaviors. To attempt a resolution to this apparent contradiction in the literature, O'Brien and Norton (1991) conducted case studies of 10 elementary school teachers who were obtaining their M. A. degree in reading. They found a limited one-to-one correspondence between reading theories and reading practices because considerations other than theoretical influence a teacher's decisions and practices in the classroom. For example, they found that teachers' pedagogical beliefs and theoretical beliefs are complex and not necessarily consistent, that both available materials and expectations from administrators and peers sometimes constrain their instructional decisions, and, despite theoretical orientations, a practice has to be "successful" to be used.

This leads us to a question of the definition of beliefs. Other chapters in this book have reviewed and discussed definitions of beliefs and have contrasted those definitions with definitions of knowledge. Richardson and Anders (1990; Richardson, in press) turned to the anthropologists, social psychologists, and philosophers for perspectives on the notion of what beliefs might be. Goodenough (1963) describes beliefs as propositions that are held as true, and are "accepted as guides for assessing the future, are cited in support of decisions, or are referred to in passing judgment on the behavior of others" (p. 151).

In the psychological literature, knowledge and beliefs are often used synonymously, but not in the philosophical literature. For example, Alexander, Schallert, and Hare (1991) equate knowledge with belief: "knowledge encompasses all that a person knows or believes to be true, whether or not it is verified as true in some sort of objective or external way" (p. 317). Kagan (1990) also uses the terms interchangeably because ". . . mounting evidence that much of what a teacher knows of his or her craft appears to be defined in highly subjective terms" (p. 421). Philosophers, however, do not consider knowledge and beliefs as synonyms. For philosophers, knowledge is not a psychological process because it depends on a "truth condition" that is outside the individual with the particular thought (Green, 1971; Leher, 1990). Hence, for Green, an evidential belief could, under certain conditions, be based on knowledge. Critical among these conditions are whether there is rigorous evidence for the proposition, whether the procedures for developing the argument are consistent with philosophical conventions, and whether the conclusions are agreed upon by a community of scholars, scientists or other professionals. In this view, the proposition as held by the individual is a belief.

In the work represented in this chapter, then, beliefs were defined as "a set of conceptual representations which signify to its holder a reality or given state of affairs of sufficient validity, truth and/or trustworthiness to warrant reliance upon it as a guide to personal thought and action" (Harvey, 1986 p. 660). Hence, beliefs were considered as a set of assertions held by informants and realized in the natural language as declarative sentences.

Notions of Text

Like beliefs, text is difficult to define. A detailed review or even synthesis of what has been written is not possible or appropriate here. We mention, however, literature that we have found to be relevant to the presentation of our findings.

The common-sense notion of text, probably notions held by most educators, is that text is a compilation of graphic symbols written to convey a message or to entertain. Textbooks fall into this category, i.e., those materials that are used in schools, usually by mandate but sometimes by teacher choice. Within the category of textbooks are basal materials, including the reading, social studies, science, and math books that are purchased for teachers to use in the elementary school.

Recent definitions of text, however, indicate that it is far more than mere graphic symbols on the page. Short (1986) expanded the definition of text to refer to "any chunk of unified meaning that could be shared with others" (p. 227). Hence, other sign systems such as music, art, spoken language (such as discussions), can be considered text. Another indication of the varying perspectives on the meaning of text, was exemplified by Jackson and Haroutunian-Gordon's (1989) decision to include the ways that teachers are portrayed in classical literature as "texts within texts" (p. ix). This abstract and generalized notion of text suggests that most any construct that has a sense of structure and coherence, and is subject to interpretation, is thought of as a text. Two examples include teachers and students forming a text as they develop a community of learners, and colleagues sharing bibliographies and common academic experiences. This perspective of text is intriguing because it sheds a different light on what has been commonly thought to be "text," and suggests possibilities for reconstructing our traditional, common sense notions of "text."

The literature related to text(books) is of three types: critical theory, the analysis of the quality of textbooks, and the use of textbooks in schools. A theme running through the critical theory literature is that the textbook represents authority in the classroom. Teachers are provided a Teacher's Manual with varying degrees of instructional guidelines. For example, some materials provide a script for the teacher to follow, but others only provide general suggestions as to the ways a lesson might go. Students also are inclined to perceive the text as authority because their lessons tend to center on "getting the meaning" from the text and on "comprehension checks" encouraging them to repeat the author's words when asked.

Critical theorists argue that this authoritative stance is a form of hegemony. Lankshear and Lawler (1987) elaborate on this point considerably:

> As well as communicating the general message of resigned quiescence, school texts can be viewed as inducting children from subordinate groups into a view of the world that positively reflects the ideas, beliefs, values, ways of seeing and being, and (thus) the very interests of those who dominate them. (p. 156)

Lankshear and Lawler are not alone in their criticism; Apple (1992) has echoed and expanded elaborately on this idea of texts as agents of dominate cultural reproduction.

Analysts of text from the field of reading usually draw from psychology, curriculum, or literary theory to portray their descriptions. Stodolsky (1989) synthesizes this literature pointing to, for example, Armbruster's and her colleagues' (1984) research that characterized texts as being on a continuum from "considerate" to "inconsiderate."

Critical curriculum theorists evaluate the literature that is available for children to read. Taxel (1991) points out that the political and ideological functions of children's literature are often dismissed; however, many researchers argue that literature cannot be divorced from social, cultural, political, and economic contexts (Harris, 1990, 1992, 1993; Shannon, 1986;

Zipes, 1982). For instance, Christian-Smith (1991) found that working class girls were attracted to a model of femininity portrayed in girls' romance novels that is rooted in material culture, patriarchal values, individualism and female competitiveness.

Also of interest, is the actual use teachers make of textbooks. Some argue that the textbook dominates teachers' instruction, with the teacher slavishly following the textbook from page to page and from activity to activity. Stodolsky (1989) searched the literature for evidence of this assumption. She found that reading researchers (Barr & Dreeben, 1983; Durkin, 1978) tended to believe that such was the case, especially in classrooms where the basal series dominated the instruction. In other content areas, however, the data are less conclusive. It seems that teachers perceive much more autonomy in the use of materials and the shape of the curriculum in areas other than reading (Stodolsky, 1989).

Experts in reader response theory have also demonstrated interest in the nature of text. Rosenblatt's (1978) theory is interesting because she accounts for differing types of material and readers' appropriate response to that material. She describes "aesthetic" reading, the reading of text for a personal, aesthetic-type response and "efferent" reading, the reading of text for information. Notice, she is not suggesting that the form of the text is the driving force; rather, she is crediting the reader with the responsibility to read in a way that is describable as efferent, aesthetic, or somewhere on a continuum between.

Another perspective, one related to both reading and curriculum, is the role of text in the content areas. Herber and Herber (1993) perhaps best exemplify this view, although several of their colleagues and students share their perspective. That is the perspective that reading and writing are "tools" used to discover meaning in the disciplines. Herber and Herber (1993) use the tool metaphor in their chapter on texts. The organizing principle for that chapter is "Workers know their tools and understand how to use them well" (p. 55). This principle epitomizes the notion of text (and reading and writing) as a tool. One interpretation of the use of this metaphor goes like this: if we want to get somewhere we need a map and the text is analogous to a map, it traces the paths of the great thinkers in a particular content area and by reading the map we can become familiar with the discipline (Herber & Herber, 1993, p. 56). Interesting, perhaps true. Problem is, according to philosophers and critical theorists, truth does not lie in that map, truth cannot be found there; rather, the truth must be constructed. At best, the map might help on the journey, but it can also hinder and so it needs to be used carefully and critically. And sometimes the pilgrim needs to make a new map.

A surprising lack in the literature, given the abundant attention recently paid to beliefs, is the nature of teachers' beliefs about text and the subsequent use of that text. The discussion of the findings from the RIS and follow-up study attempt to speak to that issue.

THE READING INSTRUCTION STUDY
AND THE FOLLOW-UP STUDY

This work began in response to a call for proposals (U. S. Department of Education, 1986) that asked for an examination of the degree to which teachers use current research knowledge of reading and literacy and the factors that prevent their doing so. We responded by designing a study that was open-ended, collaborative, and descriptive. Richardson (cf.2) designed and carried out a follow-up study, similar in certain respects to the RIS Project and one in which we participated, to investigate changes in teachers' beliefs and practices over five years.

During our investigation, we learned of teachers' beliefs about and practices of teaching reading comprehension. Recent studies (Hollingsworth, 1989; Munby, 1984; Richardson, 1990) led us to assume that teachers' beliefs related to their practices. These studies suggested that the way teachers adapt or adopt new practices relate to whether their premises or beliefs match the assumptions inherent in the new programs or methods. We conducted two activities three times to understand these teachers' instructional beliefs and practices.

One activity was the conduct of an interview at the beginning of our project, at the conclusion of a staff development program a year later, and four years later for the follow-up study. The interview lasted between three-quarters of an hour to two hours, was tape-recorded, and transcribed. The interview protocol was designed to elicit beliefs about reading comprehension in two different ways. The first set of questions was designed to elicit teachers' "declared" beliefs about reading comprehension—i.e., propositions given by a person in public behavior and speech, cited in argument, or used to justify actions to others (Goodenough, 1971). The second set was designed to elicit more private beliefs by asking teachers to talk about specific students. A constant comparative method (Glaser & Strauss, 1967) was used on six randomly selected interviews to develop categories by which the interviews were coded. One category was "Teaching Reading" and comments made about text were included in this category.

The second activity, also conducted three times as with the interview, was "practical argument" (Fenstermacher, 1986) sessions with each teacher. These sessions consisted of the teacher and two researchers viewing a video-tape of the teacher teaching a reading comprehension lesson. The practical arguments were tape-recorded and transcribed. During the viewing of the video, the teacher and researchers discussed the reasons for the teaching being observed

(Richardson-Koehler & Fenstermacher, 1988; Hamilton & Richardson, in press). These sessions lasted about one hour, were conducted in a relaxed and conversational manner, and were intense but rewarding experiences (Hamilton & Richardson, in press). We used the same categories as those from the interviews to gather perspectives from the teachers. Some of the practical arguments revealed little because of the direction the argument took; others however, were closely related to the interviews, usually confirming or elaborating on points made in the interviews.

Over the course of the research, 39 teachers of grades 4, 5, and 6 from five schools were involved. Some of our results include all 39 teachers, some reflect what we learned from 17 teachers, and others reflect the reports of 10 teachers. Three of the five schools were designated as "experimental;" that is, 17 teachers from those schools participated in the interview, practical argument and group staff development sessions. Twenty-two teachers were in two "contrast" schools and were interviewed, but did not participate in the practical argument and received a different sort of "staff development." Then, due to transfers, illness, and retirement 10 teachers remained for the follow-up study.

From these discussions, four themes related to teachers' beliefs about and use of texts emerged: (1) beliefs, as revealed by the teachers during the interviews, were predictive of their classroom practices; (2) perspectives and concerns were voiced by teachers as to the similarities and differences between fiction and nonfiction; (3) teachers' understanding of knowledge, teaching, and learning changed over the course of the study; and (4) challenges and inherent contradictions related to assessment were dealt with throughout the study.

Beliefs as Predictors of Practice

Richardson, Anders, Tidwell, and Lloyd (1991) investigated the reliability of using certain beliefs to predict classroom practices. That is, based on the analysis of the belief interviews, could teachers' practices be predicted? The selected categories of practice included the following: use of the basal reader, either flexibly or inflexibly; use of oral or silent reading, and if reading orally, whether the teacher interrupted the student if an error was made in pronunciation; consideration of students' background knowledge; and, whether vocabulary was taught in or out of context.

Not coincidentally, these categories of practice are related to two different theories of the reading process: one theory that assumes meaning lies in the text and that accurate decoding enables the reader to "get the meaning;" and alternatively, a theory that assumes reading is a transaction between the reader and the author, that miscues occur naturally, and that the reader constructs meaning.

All 39 teachers from the original RIS study were included in this investigation. The data sources for this study were the same as described above and also observations of classroom instruction. In each of the categories of practice, the percentage of agreement between beliefs and practices ranged from 66% to 92%. The least amount of agreement occurred in the flexible/inflexible use of basals category, with many more teachers indicating flexible use in their interview than were observed in their classrooms.

Overall, the percentage of agreement between beliefs and practices is high, but why isn't it perfect? One reason might be that from the researchers' perspective, some of the teachers' beliefs seem contradictory. Consider the case study of Susan:

> The one thing I try to do more than anything else, in teaching reading, is find some experience that they have in their life to relate to the story . . . I do that purely because I've read the research that proves that's how children comprehend. . . If they can't relate anything to this story, I don't know if it's going to have any meaning for them.
>
> At the same time, she indicated that social studies is quite different from the stories. "It's hard to give social studies meaning . . . in social studies, there are correct answers, and these come directly out of the text." (Richardson et. al., 1991, pp. 576-577)

This quote exemplifies contradictions that may exist between beliefs and practices. Richardson et. al. acknowledged these contradictions, but speculated that perhaps these seeming contradictions were in fact indicative of confusion or points of potential change. The findings from the post-staff development data collection and from the follow-up confirm this speculation. At the beginning of the RIS study, most of the teachers described learning to read as "understanding the words." For example, Marsha said:

> You have to be able to start with the basics and have the background to be exposed to different words so that when you see a word in print, its not necessarily the first time you have heard that word. So its understanding the words, understanding the words that are put together in a sentence.

This view of reading changed considerably for most teachers, as indicated by Marsha's definition of reading after the RIS staff development:

> Well, understanding what you have read is I guess the very top layer, you know. Besides that I think is understanding, not understanding but how you feel about the book. You know, what is between the lines . . . When people read different things that the author has written down they each feel differently about it and how do you feel about it and what does it make you think about and what does it mean to you. You know how the characters are feeling and

how does that relate to anything that you have, that happened to you. Can you, do you understand that or is it something that is so foreign to you . . .

These changing theoretical orientations toward reading comprehension continued after the staff development and were evident in the follow-up interviews and practical arguments. Teachers' changing beliefs regarding comprehension led to a distinct change in their instructional practices. At the beginning of the RIS study all but one of the teachers were using the district selected and recommended basal to teach reading. The follow-up study indicated that 6 of the 10 teachers were no longer using basals and relied solely on literature for their reading program. One teacher was using a combination of basal and literature, one teacher was using the district selected basal, and two teachers had no clear reading program, but relied heavily on informational reading in the content areas.

Fiction and Nonfiction

As indicated by Richardson and Anders (1990), the teachers' orientation toward the teaching of reading and beliefs about the reading process, did, indeed change considerably from the first data collection to the second. Whereas, most teachers held a skills view of the reading process when they agreed to participate in RIS, that view changed to acknowledge the importance of text for teaching reading.

Stan's interview represents the change in beliefs. In response to the question, How do you see reading comprehension now? Stan said:

> Well, I see it on different levels. I see it as facts, reading facts and coming back with answers to specific questions and I see it as a different . . . its different in different subjects. And I see right now I think, literature is more a feeling you get from the literature, an overall feeling whereas comprehension in social studies or science is more facts. And yet as I say that, I've gotten away from that into more reporting and more studying of other specific areas. Like the reading of the Civil War in the social studies book is so hard to do; its boring and there are so many facts paragraphed and its very difficult. So some of those facts we need to know in certain areas so I'll have them read that and they'll have a facts answer sheet. But general feeling about the war, the feeling about the slavery, the feeling about fighting. I'll teach that differently.

The follow-up interviews and practical arguments showed further teacher change in terms of valuing literature. Many of the beliefs expressed by the teachers reflected response theory (Rosenblatt, 1978). Kevin provided a good example of this way of thinking when he said:

. . . right now I'm just asking for their reaction on an emotional level to what
they read. Which we, we do a lot to avoid them just regurgitating you know,
giving a plot summary, or you know . . . we want them to respond to the
literature on an emotional level.

Teachers focused on the affective, or aesthetic (Rosenblatt, 1978) response
to literature and frequently mentioned that they were most interested in
having students talk about their feelings about a book rather than give plot
summaries. Many teachers expressed that comprehension was the result of
a personal interaction with a book and emphasized the importance of being
able to relate a book to your own life. When talking about reading comprehension, teachers often discussed empirical premises such as activating
prior knowledge, the importance of relevance for learning to be meaningful,
the need to apply understanding, viewing comprehension as a personal
construction, and validating aesthetic responses to reading (Anders & Evans,
1993).

Reading in the content areas was markedly different in each of the three
data gathering events. In the beginning, very few beliefs or practices related
to content area reading. One teacher of the 10 discussed content area reading
at some length during her initial interview. In response to an interview
question that asked "as students exit grade 4, what would you like them to
be able to do?" she responded:

During that period they gain a lot of skills in well, for instance, our social
studies adoption requires a lot of reading, and a lot of picking out of literal
things, they ask them questions that don't really require too much other
thinking skills, just being able to go back through the book and they learn
that in fourth grade. They really do, to survive or to pass social studies, it's
totally an experience of being able to pick an answer out of a book . . . they
needed to do that to get through fifth and sixth grades.

Later, in the same interview and in response to a question about the
differences between teaching reading and social studies, she said:

It's a lot easier to teach reading because we can discuss things that have
happened in real life. In doing social studies they are just reading about the
past, it's real hard to give them concrete ideas or to give it meaning. I don't
think it's that easy to give social studies meaning. That they do as well as
they do is amazing to me because it's nothing that has to do with their
experience, really. A lot of kids don't like social studies, but I have a lot of
achievers . . . it's like they are in training or something.

As suggested by Susan's quote, most teachers believed originally that the
process of reading narrative and exposition were different. In the first

interviews and practical arguments, stories were read to "get the basic skills." In contrast, in the post staff development interviews and practical arguments, reading of stories was for an aesthetic response, and in the follow-up study, many teachers were using literature (fiction) to teach reading and to enhance their content area studies. Stan, who originally described the "boring and difficult text presentation of the Civil War," became involved in reading Civil War literature and relating it to the "facts." His class read five novels while reading to answer student-generated questions about the Civil War. The novels provided opportunities for an "aesthetic response" and the facts and details subsequently came to life for his students.

Views of Knowledge and Teaching and Learning

This theme is indicative of changes in perspective regarding what teaching, content and learning are. Originally, nearly all the teachers believed they were teaching the basal (in terms of reading and also other subject areas). In terms of epistemology, these teachers viewed the teaching of school subjects as transmitting knowledge and skills to the students. The follow-up data, however, suggest a very different picture. A major change among these teachers was the idea that they no longer taught subjects; rather, for all but 2 of the 10 teachers in the follow-up study, they were actively, aggressively, and purposefully working to integrate the subject areas and to include reading and writing as tools to study what was of interest. Hence, some teachers didn't think they were teaching "subjects" any longer—they talked of units and themes that integrated the various curricular areas. For example, Margaret explained during her follow-up interview, "I don't think the kids think we're studying subjects . . . its all integrated."

This new view of teaching and learning resulted in our identifying many of the teachers as conceptualizing "teaching as a composing process." This conceptualization occurred to us as we pondered Maria's practical argument. She said "When I am starting off a lesson I end up completely opposite of where I thought I was going to be and then I think 'well, oh well' you know, and take it from there because I can't go back and start over and control it the way I used to want to." At least 4 of the 10 teachers explicitly said that they carefully plan and organize, but once they get in the room with the kids they can never predict what is actually going to happen—it's going to be created (or composed) as the class works.

The follow-up data also suggested that these teachers dismissed any reading instruction that wasn't connected to life or didn't have a meaningful purpose. All but one of the teachers elaborated considerably on the importance of a meaningful purpose for comprehension to take place. This is in stark contrast to the teachers' beliefs at the beginning of our project. The reasons for needing a meaningful purpose included motivation, connecting prior knowledge to new information, and both taking advantage of students' interests and developing new student interests. These teachers spoke with conviction, it is difficult to imagine they would ever expect students to read for the sake of answering comprehension questions at the end of the chapter. For example, Margaret said:

> I want what we are doing to be so rich that kids want to be here, I want stuff to make sense . . . it's not monolithic . . . I want kids to be involved in content and to be excited . . . I want kids to get a strong sense of who they are and their interests.

Hence, it seems that 8 of the 10 teachers changed their conceptualization of teaching from one of transmitting knowledge to students to helping students construct knowledge. This is indicative in the sorts of units and themes they were doing with their students. For example, Mary described her science program as being extensive and that reading and writing occurred because it is natural for scientists to write their observations in notebooks, to read what other scientists have discovered, and to write reports for others to read. Hence, a science textbook was used as a resource to answer student's questions rather than to answer teacher's questions. Margaret taught angles by building solar cookers and studying the effects of the angle of the sun on the cooking of food. Students read about building solar cookers, observed, measured, experimented, and wrote their results for others to read.

Assessment

In our initial data gathering, teachers seemed confident that what they were to do was follow their basals, teach the skills that were listed there, and assess using the tests provided by the basal publisher and the mandated tests provided by the State and the District. Grading was viewed as a response to outside demands for accountability rather than a means of providing teachers, parents, and students with information that would help them in the instruction and learning process (Anders & Richardson, 1992). As teachers changed their beliefs about reading comprehension and their instructional practices, however, new ways to assess comprehension were needed.

In the follow-up study, teachers talked about assessment in relation to "quality control," that is, are students really constructing a deeper understanding of the book or are they simply getting the plot? Since many teachers viewed comprehension as a personal construction of meaning, there was not one right answer to comprehension questions. Consequently, teachers' original practice of collecting grades on numerous comprehension worksheets to be averaged for an overall grade was no longer an appropriate means of assessment. Several teachers were using portfolios and students' writing to assess comprehension and there was a greater emphasis on informal assessment measures such as observations, field notes, talking with students, and listening to discussion groups.

Moreover, as many teachers were concerned with students' aesthetic response to books, they tended to focus their assessment on students' describing their feelings about the book and justifying their opinions rather than answering comprehension questions and giving plot summaries. Kevin's response to an interview question regarding assessment reflects this changing perception toward assessment:

> I used to love it [if] kids could summarize a plot. Now I can't stand it . . . now I don't want them to just summarize cause I want to get, I want to know what, how they are feeling about the book. What they are thinking.

DISCUSSION

Emerging from the literature on teacher beliefs and practices is the issue of whether beliefs influence practice or practice influences beliefs (Richardson, 1990). On the basis of our studies, we think this is analogous to a modern-day chicken and egg problem (Evans & Anders, 1993). As we talked with teachers over the five years of the study we came to realize that determining which is the catalyst in facilitating change, beliefs or practices, is perhaps not a productive question to pose nor attempt to answer. When teachers spoke of their beliefs and instructional practices, the two were closely intertwined and dependent on one another. When a contradiction existed between the two, it was indicative of uncertainty and potential change. The process of reflection contributed to sorting out the issue and increased the possibilities for change. Hence, it became clear to us that rather than viewing beliefs and practices as two separate entities, it was necessary to consider both of them as mutually dependent and equally important to the change process.

When we first interviewed and observed the teachers with whom we worked, we found their beliefs about reading comprehension and their teaching of reading comprehension to be "basal based." They behaved much as Durkin (1978) described—teachers followed the instructional guidelines that were found in the teacher's manual. When we conducted the second interviews and practical arguments, teachers talked of wanting to incorporate more literature into their instruction. At the follow-up, 8 of the 10 teachers were regularly using literature across the curriculum through integrated units. This change indicates that the use of fiction and nonfiction is not a matter of choosing either efferent or aesthetic reading; rather, it is a matter of choosing a particular stance toward multiple texts to construct meaning.

Strategies were adopted and adapted by the teachers as the students needed them in the context of the classroom inquiry being conducted.

The constraints of the basals were discarded as teachers' developed their own theory of the reading process and as they became reflective about their practices. They were drawn to the importance of constructing knowledge rather than transmitting information and skills. When we revisited for the follow-up study we found that the power of story—those stories written by "authorities," the stories written by students, and the text constructed in the classroom community—had overtaken their instruction.

This change in belief and practice also affected teachers' views of themselves professionally. Half the teachers in this study began to talk about themselves as learners and as researchers. One teacher said, "I have to admit, sometimes I get so involved and excited about what we are doing, that I forget I'm teaching." The overwhelming consensus seemed to be that teaching is fun—learning is exciting for them and for their students when all are involved in constructing meaning. None of our teachers reported that these changes in practice were easy; nonetheless, they found the hard work to be necessary and valuable because of their beliefs about teaching and learning.

Just as textbooks and basals often constrained teachers' adoption of new beliefs and practices, so did perceived assessment requirements. Teachers' concern with accountability to external sources is consonant with notions of "high stakes" assessment (Shepard, 1989). Moreover, teachers were convinced that they were not capable of being objective (Anders & Richardson, 1992). Reflection about and discussion of the constraints imposed by these perceptions of assessment challenged the teachers to conceptualize and create alternative forms of assessment.

When viewed from this perspective, assessment is a form of hegemony. Teachers' concerns with accountability and objectivity made them fearful of changing the instructional status quo. Moreover, standardized tests did not assess the knowledge students were constructing as they engaged in self-selected inquiries. Teachers became disillusioned with standardized tests and sought alternative assessment measures to provide meaningful evaluations of student learning.

A long line of progressive educators have called for making reflective inquiry part of teacher education and part of the profession. The research represented in this chapter echoes that call. As teachers reflected on their beliefs and practices, they changed their understanding of teaching and learning, challenged their previous instructional stances, and became constructors of knowledge with their students. In short, these teachers became excited about teaching and learning and continued over a five year period to elaborate on their goals for the future. This way of teaching has a heart, it is rich, and it is full of possibility.

REFERENCES

Alexander, P. A., Schallert, D. L., & Hare V. C. (1991). Coming to terms: How researchers in learning and literacy talk about knowledge. *Review of Educational Research, 61*(3), pp. 315-344.

Anders, P., & Richardson, V. (1992). Teacher as game-show host, bookkeeper, or judge: Challenges, contradictions, and consequences of accountability. *Teachers College Record, 94*(2), 382-396.

Anders, P. L., & Evans K. S. (1993, April). Changing conversations about content area reading instruction. In V. Richardson (Chair), *Continuity and change in teaching reading comprehension.* A symposium at the American Educational Research Association, Atlanta.

Apple, M. W. (1992). The text and cultural politics. *Educational Researcher, 21*(7), 4-11, 19.

Armbruster, B. (1984). The problem of inconsiderate text. In G. Duffy, L. R. Roehler, & J. Mason (Eds.), *Comprehension instruction: Perspectives and suggestions* (pp. 202-317). New York: Longman Inc.

Barr, R., & Dreeben, R. (1983). *How schools work.* Chicago: University of Chicago Press.

Christian-Smith, L. (1991). *Love makes the world go 'round: Generating gender in adolescent romance fiction.* Unpublished manuscript.

DeFord, D. (1985). Validating the construct of theoretical orientation in reading instruction. *Reading Research Quarterly, 20,* 351-367.

Duffy, G. (1981). *Theory to practice: How does it work in real classrooms?* Research Series #98. East Lansing, MI: Institute for Research on Teaching, College of Education.

Durkin, D. (1978). What classroom observations reveal about reading comprehension instruction. *Reading Research Quarterly, XIV*(4), 483-533.

Evans, K. S., & Anders, P. L. (1993, April). Continuity and change in reading comprehension instruction. In V. Richardson (Chair), *Continuity and change in teaching reading comprehension.* Symposium conducted at the meeting of the American Educational Research Association, Atlanta.

Fenstermacher, G. D (1986). A philosophy of research on teaching: Three aspects. In M. C. Wittrock (Ed.), *Handbook of research on teaching* (3rd. ed., pp. 37-49). New York: Macmillan.

Glaser, B., & Strauss, A. L. (1967). *The discovery of grounded theory: Strategies for qualitative research.* Chicago: Aldine.

Goodenough, W. H. (1963). *Cooperation in change.* New York: Russell Sage Foundation.

Goodenough, W. H. (1971). Culture, language, and society. *Addison-Wesley module in anthropology* (No. 7). Reading, MA: Addison-Wesley.

Green, T. (1971). *The activities of teaching.* New York: McGraw-Hill.

Hamilton, M. L., & Richardson, V. (in press). Staff development: The practical argument process. In V. Richardson (Ed.), *A theory of teacher change and the practice of staff development: A case in reading instruction.* New York: Teachers College Press.

Harste, J., & Burke, C. (1977). A new hypothesis for reading teacher research: Both the teaching and learning of reading are theoretically based. In P. D. Pearson (Ed.), *Reading: Theory research and practice* (Twenty-sixth Yearbook of the National Reading Conference, pp. 32-40). Chicago: The National Reading Conference.

Harris, V. J. (1990). African American children's literature: The first one hundred years. *Journal of Negro Education, 59,* 540-555.

Harris, V. J. (Ed.). (1992). *Teaching multicultural literature in grades K-8.* Norwood, MA: Christoper-Gordon.

Harris, V. J. (1993). Literature-based approaches to reading instruction. In L. Darling-Hammond (Ed.), *Review of Research in Education, 19,* Washington D.C.: American Educational Research Association (pp. 269-301).

Harvey, O. J. (1986). Belief systems and attitudes toward the death penalty and other punishments. *Journal of Personality, 54,* 143-159.

Herber, H. L., & Herber, J. N. (1993). *Teaching in content areas with reading, writing, and reasoning.* Boston: Allyn and Bacon.

Hoffman, J. V., & Kugle, C. (1982). A study of theoretical orientation to reading and its relationship to teacher verbal feedback during reading instruction. *Journal of Classroom Interaction, 18,* 2-7.

Hollingsworth, S. (1989). Prior beliefs and cognitive change in learning to teach. *American Educational Research Journal, 54,* 143-159.

Jackson, P. W., & Haroutunian-Gordon, S. (1989). *From Socrates to software: The teacher as text and the text as teacher* (Eighty-ninth Yearbook of the National Society for the Study of Education, pp. ix-xi). Chicago: The University of Chicago Press.

Kagan, D. (1990). Ways of evaluating teacher cognition: Inferences concerning the Goldilocks principle. *Review of Educational Research, 60*(3) 419-469.

Lankshear, C., & Lawler, M. (1987). *Literacy, schooling and revolution.* New York: The Falmer Press.

Leher, K. (1990). *Theory of knowledge.* San Francisco: Westview Press.

Mitchell, M., Konopak, B., & Readence, J. (1991). The consistency between Chapter I teachers' beliefs about reading and their instructional decision-making and interactions. In J. Zutell & S. McCormick (Eds.), *Learner factors/teacher factors: Issues in literacy research and instruction* (Fortieth Yearbook of the National Reading Conference, pp. 377-384). Chicago: National Reading Conference, Inc.

Munby, H. (1984). A qualitative study of teachers' beliefs and principles. *Journal of Research in Science Teaching, 21*(1), 27-38.

O'Brien, K., & Norton, R. (1991). Beliefs, practices and constraints: Influences on teacher decision-making processes. *Teacher Education Quarterly, 18,* 29-38.

Richardson, V. (in press). The consideration of beliefs in staff development. In V. Richardson (Ed.), *A theory of teacher change and the practice of staff development: A case in reading instruction.* New York: Teachers College Press.

Richardson, V. (1990). Significant and worthwhile change in teaching practice. *Educational Researcher, 19,* 10-18.

Richardson, V., & Anders, P. L. (1990). *Final report of the reading instruction study.* Report submitted to OERI, Department of Education. Tucson, AZ: College of Education, University of Arizona. ERIC Document Number: ED 312 359

Richardson, V., Anders, P. L., Tidwell, D., & Lloyd, C. V. (1991). The relationship between teachers' beliefs and practices in reading comprehension instruction. *American Educational Research Journal, 28,* 559-586.

Richardson-Koehler, V., & Fenstermacher, G. D (1988). *The use of practical arguments in teacher education.* Paper presented at the annual meeting of the American Association of Colleges of Teacher Education, New Orleans, 1988. ERIC Document number SP 030 047

Rosenblatt, L. (1978). *The reader, the text, the poem.* Carbondale: Southern Illinois Press.

Shannon, P. (1986). Hidden within the pages: A study of social perspective in young children's favorite books. *The Reading Teacher, 39,* 656-663.

Shephard, L. (1989, April). Why we need better assessments. *Educational Leadership, 46,* 4.

Short, K. G. (1986). Literacy as a collaborative experience: The role of intertextuality. In J. A. Niles & R. V. Lalik (Eds.), *Solving problems in literacy: Learners, teachers, and researchers* Thirty-fifth Yearbook of the National Reading Conference (pp. 227-232). Rochester, NY: The National Reading Conference, Inc.

Stodolsky, S. (1989). Is teaching really by the book? (Eighty-ninth Yearbook of the National Society for the Study of Education, pp. 159-184). Chicago, IL: The University of Chicago Press.

Taxel, J. (1991). On the politics of children's literature. *The New Advocate, 5,* 7-12.

U. S. Department of Education. (1986). *Application for grants under the educational research grant program: Research grants on reading and literacy*. Washington D. C.: Office of Educational Research and Improvement.

Zipes, J. (1982). Second thoughts on socialization through literature for children. *The lion and the unicorn, 5*, 19-32.

CHAPTER NINE

Teachers' Knowledge and Beliefs About Summary as a Component of Reading

Hilda Borko
Kathryn H. Davinroy
Maurene D. Flory
Elfrieda H. Hiebert
University of Colorado, Boulder

This chapter describes the knowledge, beliefs, and practices of a group of third-grade teachers related to the use of summaries in reading instruction. In particular, we describe and examine the teachers' knowledge and beliefs about what constitutes a good summary, how to teach children to write summaries, and the use of summaries for assessment purposes. We also examine the nature and extent of changes in teachers' ideas and practices related to summary, during the first semester of a year-long staff development program designed to help participants develop performance assessments in reading and mathematics, the Alternative Assessments in Reading and Mathematics (AARM) project.[1]

BACKGROUND

Members of the project team worked as both staff developers and researchers. Our perspectives on teacher change and on summary as a component of

---

[1]The Alternative Assessments in Reading and Mathematics project is part of a larger research project, Studies in Improving Classroom and Local Assessments. It is supported in part by the Office of Educational Research and Improvement, through the National Center for Research on Evaluation, Standards, and Student Testing (CRESST). All members of the AARM project's research team contributed to the conceptualization of staff development and data collection for this study. Any opinions, findings, and conclusions or recommendations expressed in this publication are those of the authors and do not necessarily reflect the views of other project team members, CRESST, or the Office of Educational Research and Improvement.

literacy instruction provide important lenses for the analyses we report in this chapter. We begin the chapter by describing these perspectives.

Working With Teachers to Change Their Practice: A Cognitive Perspective

The AARM project has as its stated purpose to help participating teachers design classroom-based performance assessments compatible with their instructional goals. The project fits Richardson's (1992) characterization of a "new generation of staff development . . . which attempts to introduce new ways of thinking and practices within a context that attends to what we know about how and why teachers change their practices" (p. 287). These staff development programs tend to be cognitively framed and to focus on helping teachers examine their knowledge and beliefs and alter their practices. Cognitive psychology identifies several characteristics of knowledge and learning (cf. Borko & Putnam, in press) that have informed many cognitively-framed staff development efforts, including our own.

According to cognitive psychology, knowledge and beliefs play a central role in thinking, acting, and learning. Teachers' knowledge and beliefs about teaching, learning, learners, and subject matter are critical determinants of whether and how they implement new ideas to which they are introduced. For teachers to change their classroom practices, they must have the knowledge necessary to implement the changes and the beliefs to support them. Thus, efforts to help teachers make significant changes in their teaching practice often must help them to acquire new knowledge and beliefs. At the same time, it is through their existing knowledge and beliefs that teachers come to understand new practices. The same knowledge and beliefs that are critical targets of change also function as filters through which change takes place (Cohen & Ball, 1990; Putnam, Heaton, Prawat, & Remillard, 1992). This dual role of knowledge and beliefs can make the achievement of fundamental changes in teaching practices difficult.

An important characteristic of knowledge and learning, from the perspective of staff development, is that they are situated in contexts and cultures. Knowledge does not exist in the minds of individuals as abstract bits of information, detached from the external world. Rather, there are close connections between knowledge and its physical and cultural contexts. For teachers to learn to teach in new ways, the knowledge they acquire must be grounded in the classroom contexts in which it will be used.

We also found the ideas of social constructivism to be particularly helpful in informing our thinking about the learning that occurs in the context of staff development programs. Group settings such as staff development programs function as learning communities in which individual and social processes of knowledge construction occur concurrently and interactively

(Cobb, Yackel, & Wood, 1992; Simon & Schifter, 1991). The process of learning in a group situation can be characterized as individuals' construction of personally meaningful ideas as they participate in learning communities where "taken-as-shared" meanings (i.e., meanings and interpretations which members of a learning community assume to be shared; Cobb et al., 1992) are developed. Individuals actively construct their own understandings based, in part, on their existing knowledge and beliefs. At the same time, as members of a learning community, they work together to develop taken-as-shared meanings through negotiation and consensus-building. Throughout these processes, the constructions of individuals and of the group mutually contribute to and constrain one another.

Cobb et al. (1992) suggest that there is a third point of reference that must be considered in the picture of knowledge construction—the taken-as-shared knowledge and practices of the wider community. A constructivist view of learning does not imply that any individual or learning community is free to construct their own private truths, or that any interpretation is as good as any other. Using mathematics teaching as an example, Cobb et al. argue that "the goal is still that students eventually construct correct or true mathematical understandings [i.e., mathematical meanings and practices institutionalized by wider society] with the teacher's guidance" (p. 16). Applied to staff development, this perspective suggests an important role for staff developers—that they provide the guidance that will enable participating teachers to construct taken-as-shared meanings and practices that are compatible with those advocated by wider society. In the case of summary, the researchers/staff developers in our project considered the wider society to be the literacy community.

Summary as a Component of Reading:
The Literacy Community's Perspective

An examination of the professional literature (e.g., Anderson, Hiebert, Scott, & Wilkinson, 1985; Barr, Kamil, Mosenthal, & Pearson, 1991) and of curriculum frameworks of states ranging from Hawaii to Maryland (e.g., Au, 1994; Kapinus, Collier, & Kruglanski, 1994) shows that, while stances on word-level processes and instruction may be divergent, there is agreement on the central role of construction and sharing of meaning in literacy (Barr et al., 1991). Perspectives on what it means to make meaning have been elaborated substantially over the past 2 decades, as documented by Pearson and Fielding's (1991) review of comprehension research. The view of meaning making outlined in *Becoming a Nation of Readers* (Anderson et al., 1985), for example, emphasized building on prior knowledge of experiences relevant to the text and elaborating on inferences from texts. More recently, the role of literary response and of connections across texts in readers' constructions of meaning have been integrated more fully in the literacy community's discussions of meaning making (Beach & Hynds, 1991; Hartman, 1990).

Although Pearson and Fielding (1991) do not define what does and does not constitute comprehension, they do identify processes that characterize comprehension. One of the primary processes they identify as fostering comprehension is summarizing. This conclusion draws on research of the 1980s, where proficient readers were shown to engage in summarizing (Palincsar & Brown, 1984; Paris, Wasik, & Turner, 1991), or at least to be superior to poorer readers when asked to engage in this process (Paris et al., 1991). Meaning making goes much beyond summarizing as readers bring prior life and textual experiences to a text. However, summarizing consistently appears in descriptions of the critical processes of meaning making.

Summarizing was one of four processes that Palincsar and Brown (1984) identified in their Reciprocal Teaching model as central to instruction for poor readers. Relative to the other three processes of Reciprocal Teaching (predicting, questioning, and clarifying confusing parts of text), summarizing results in a construction of meaning. Palincsar and David (1991) state that the aim of summarizing is to "identify the gist of what has been read and discussed." They argue that summarizing takes a very different form within a social-constructivist perspective than within a reductionist perspective. From the latter perspective it involves children in underlining the main idea in a short piece of text; from the former, it is a process of exchange and discussion to create a representation of what has been read. The view of summarizing within the literacy community, then, has moved considerably from the research of the early 1980s where students were taught a set of five rules for summarizing text that included deleting trivial and redundant information and providing superordinate terms and main ideas (Brown & Day, 1983).

When summarizing is defined more as identifying the "gist of a passage," it becomes a process that can be applied by the reader to any passage. Expository or narrative, paragraph or novel, a passage can be expected to have a gist that readers can construct. As performance assessment efforts in states (Weiss, 1994) and at the national level (Resnick & Resnick, 1992) have moved to open-ended responses to texts, the generalizability of summarizing has made it a focal task on performance assessments. Summaries as a representation of constructing meaning can be found on classroom-based or teacher-based assessments as well. For example, when Valencia and Place (1994) worked with a group of teachers over a 3-year period, summaries were identified by teachers as a common way of representing the goal of construction of meaning across different grade levels.

The curriculum framework for the district in which this assessment project was implemented shares the emphasis on constructing meaning with the broader literacy community. The first of three outcomes for language arts pertains to the construction and production of meaning. The seven outcomes that flesh out the construction and production of meaning in reading contain many of the processes that can be found in recent reviews of comprehension and strategic reading (Dole, Duffy, Roehler, & Pearson, 1991; Paris et al., 1991; Pearson & Fielding, 1991): predicting, self-monitoring, reading with fluency and automaticity, literal comprehension, applied and interpretive comprehension, appreciation/enjoyment, and self-assessment. Although the process of summarizing was not stated explicitly in the district's curriculum framework, the researchers interpreted terms like *meaning making* and *interpretive comprehension* as including (although not limited to) summarizing.

Summary, then, is regarded in the literacy community as the "gist" of a passage and as one representation of a reader's construction of meaning. Within this social-constructivist perspective, the process of summarizing is seen as an interactive one in the sense that children construct meaning through interaction with one another and their teacher, and in the sense that an individual's summary of a text can be expected to change as new insights are gained through these interactions and through rereadings and writing. This perspective on the process of summarizing and on summary as a representation of meaning making fits with the district's curriculum framework.

Considerations in the Design and Study of Staff Development

These perspectives from cognitive psychology and literacy have several implications for the design and study of staff development efforts. To facilitate meaningful change in teachers' classroom practices, staff development programs must encourage and support participants' efforts to examine and change their knowledge and beliefs, and support their attempts to incorporate new ideas into their ongoing classroom practices. And staff developers must take into account individuals' personal ways of knowing, the learning community's taken-as-shared knowledge and practices, and the knowledge and practices institutionalized by the wider society.

Further, these perspectives suggest that the process of making fundamental changes in one's knowledge, beliefs, and practices is hard work. For teachers to actively engage in meaningful change, they must have a commitment to the experiences and outcomes of the staff development effort. This situation implies another important consideration in designing and studying staff development programs, a consideration that Richardson (1992) has labeled the "agenda-setting dilemma" (p. 287). This dilemma, which staff developers in all cognitively framed programs may face, relates to the dual goals of introducing participants to new content and creating an environment that facilitates their ownership of the content and processes of staff development. It arises because teachers are likely to see predetermined content as belonging to the staff developers, thus making it difficult for them to have a sense of ownership or empowerment with respect to the staff development process. Yet if staff developers allow teachers to control the program, it may be difficult to introduce the content to which we are committed.

In this chapter, we examine the knowledge, beliefs, and practices of 5 third-grade teachers related to summary as a component of their reading program. Our examination is guided by the considerations about staff development presented earlier. It is organized around the following questions:

1. What were the teachers' knowledge, beliefs, and practices related to summary as a component of the reading program, at the beginning of the school year?
2. What were the teachers' knowledge, beliefs, and practices related to summary at the end of the fall semester?
3. What were the patterns of stability and change in the teachers' knowledge, beliefs, and practices related to summary?
4. What characteristics of the staff development process in which these teachers participated help to explain these patterns of stability and change?

THE STUDY

The present study, conducted in the 1992–1993 academic year, is part of the AARM staff development/research project. The major staff development purpose during the 1992–1993 academic year was to work with third-grade teachers at three schools to develop classroom performance assessments in reading and mathematics. The major research focus was to study the effects of the staff development process and performance assessments on the teachers' knowledge, beliefs, and practices concerning teaching, learning, and assessment, and in turn to study the effects of instructional and assessment practices on student learning. The staff development/research team met with teachers at each school on a weekly basis throughout the year to provide support and guidance in the development of classroom performance assessments. Our intention in these weekly workshops was to facilitate changes in the teachers' assessment practices by helping them to think about their instructional goals and the relationships among goals, instruction and assessment; to develop or select assessment tasks appropriate to their goals; and to articulate scoring criteria for the assessment tasks. We expected that each team of teachers (i.e., the group of third-grade teachers within a school) would design a shared set of assessments that captured key goals of the school and district in reading and mathematics, and that individual teachers would adapt assessments to their particular classroom contexts. Because the district curriculum framework is consistent with views of the wider literacy community as well as our views about instruction, and because all teachers participating in the project were volunteers, we expected the teachers' ideas about instruction to be compatible with our own. Thus, our intention was not to challenge the teachers' instructional goals, but to help them develop new assessment practices compatible with those goals.

Participants and Setting

Primary participants in the project are the third-grade teachers at three elementary schools in a school district on the outskirts of Denver. Schools wishing to be considered for the project submitted a short proposal and documentation of approval by the principal, all third-grade teachers, and the parent accountability committee. Participating schools were selected to represent a range of socioeconomic levels and student achievement.

For purposes of this investigation, we decided to study teachers at one of the schools in depth. Because each school team met separately with the staff developers/researchers, a case study approach seemed most appropriate to our interest in carefully examining individual and social construction of knowledge within the context of a learning community. We selected Pine Elementary School (Pine is a pseudonym, as are all names used in reference to the project except those of the staff developers/researchers) as the focus of the investigation because, as we explain next, an initial reading of a sample of interview and workshop transcripts, coupled with our own (admittedly biased) impressions of the three schools, suggested that it would be an interesting case for in-depth analysis.

The 1992-1993 third-grade team at Pine consisted of 5 teachers, each with several years of teaching experience including at least 1 year prior to the study as a member of the third-grade team. At the beginning of the study, the teachers did not comprise a cohesive team. In addition to the isolation that is fairly typical of elementary buildings, several teachers on the previous year's third-grade team differed in their beliefs about teaching. Some of their interactions around teaching left the teachers agreeing to disagree and collaborating very little. By the end of the study year, in contrast, Pine's third-grade teachers had developed a strong sense of community, and they had come to use the workshop setting to develop ideas and to negotiate shared understandings. These features of the team's working relationship were one reason for our selection of Pine as the focus of our investigation; we felt that it would provide a rich opportunity to study the development of a learning community and social and individual construction of meaning within that community.

As a group, Pine's third-grade teachers were generally enthusiastic about trying out innovative educational ideas. At the same time, they were comfortable with their current reading program. This combination of interest in change and comfort with existing practices was another feature of the school that influenced its selection for analysis; we felt that it would enable us to examine the dual roles of knowledge and beliefs both as targets of change and as filters for change.

Data Sources

Data sources for this chapter are two sets of teacher interviews and fall workshops with the third-grade teachers at Pine Elementary School. The first set of interviews was conducted before we began our weekly workshops (September, 1992); the second set was conducted at the end of the fall semester (January, 1993). Teachers were interviewed by members of the research team, at their schools, during the school day. All interviews were audiotaped and transcribed. Semistructured questions focused on teachers' knowledge, beliefs, and practices related to assessment, instruction, and the relationship between assessment and instruction. Because the AARM project focuses on literacy and mathematics, parallel sets of questions were asked about knowledge, beliefs, and practices related to the two subject areas. Only the questions about literacy were analyzed for this study.

Weekly workshops with school teams alternated in focus between the literacy and mathematics subject areas. The literacy educator (Elfrieda Hiebert), one other principal investigator (Hilda Borko or Lorrie Shepard), and one graduate research assistant were present at each literacy workshop. (Staff developer/researcher participation in mathematics workshops was parallel, with the mathematics educator [Roberta Flexer] present at each session.) Workshop sessions were audiotaped. In addition, written notes were taken by the graduate research assistant to record nonverbal communication as well as descriptions of materials to which participants referred. When possible, artifacts (e.g., samples of assessment materials and student work) were collected. The audiotapes, written notes, and artifacts were used to prepare detailed field notes of the workshop sessions. The entire set of fall literacy workshops for Pine (a total of 7 workshops) was analyzed for this study. One additional source of data—a preparatory meeting in May, 1992 intended for teachers' sharing of their existing classroom reading and mathematics assessments—was also considered.

Data Analysis

There is no easy way to analyze data produced in conversations among people—talk tends to shift focus, turn back on itself, work forward, return to earlier topics, remind a speaker of a similar situation. Such is the nature of communication. This paper focuses on what many people said about summary in the context of workshop and interview conversations, in an effort to understand the individual and social processes of knowledge construction and to identify patterns in teachers' views of summary that grew out of their participation in these processes.

Our analyses began with a careful reading of a sample of interview transcripts and workshop field notes by three of the chapter's authors. Based on this reading, and keeping in mind our research questions, we developed a tentative coding system. This system went through several iterations of experimentation (i.e., use in coding other transcripts and field notes), discussion, and revision. Our final coding system consisted of the following categories: definition of summary, purpose for learning and teaching summary, strategies for teaching summary, strategies for assessment related to summary, and expectations for students.

We used this system to code and sort information in the three data sets. For each data set, we identified major patterns related to each of the research questions and wrote a summary of the patterns. We then looked across the analyses to trace issues related to the themes from cognitive psychology that were outlined earlier: the relationship between knowledge, beliefs, and practices; the situated nature of knowledge and learning; and learning as an active, constructive process. This chapter presents patterns of teacher change and stability and discusses them in terms of these themes.

TEACHERS' EVOLVING IDEAS ABOUT SUMMARY

Our presentation of findings is organized chronologically in order to provide a sense of the teachers' evolving ideas and practices. We begin by examining the teachers' thoughts about the project as expressed in a meeting late in the 1991-1992 academic year.

Introduction: Getting to Summaries

In the preparatory meeting held in May 1992, the year preceding the biweekly workshops on literacy, the third-grade teachers involved in the project voiced a desire to work within the district's curriculum framework in selecting goals and assessments for the project. As part of developing portfolio assessments that year (AY 1991–1992), Pine school had selected two district goals from the language arts "significant learnings": "Summary of a chapter or a summary of a novel that demonstrates writing skills and comprehension skills and spelling skills, and then cursive writing, those were the two things that we picked . . . to be in our third-grade portfolio." When asked to select a third-grade literacy goal for our project, the teachers felt they had spent time and energy developing summaries for the portfolios and that, given their choice, they would prefer to continue with summaries. A connection between summaries and specific goals for third-grade literacy was not explicitly articulated during the meeting. This was the Pine teachers' first mention of using summaries as assessment for the AARM project.

Teachers' Ideas and Practices About Summary at the Beginning of the Project

Defining Summary. Not surprisingly given the previous year's work, all of the teachers shared a similar definition of a summary in their fall Reading interviews. For these teachers, a summary is a written document that contains the character(s), the setting, and three or four (rarely more) key events which define the "problem" that is addressed in the story and its resolution. It is not a written retelling of the story and does not contain any details that were not pertinent to the story. Most teachers added that a summary should be presented in a manner that is "interesting" and "flows well." In her fall interview, Karen was hesitant but was willing to allow for an oral summary. The other teachers, however, were consistent in defining summaries as written products. Their definitions seemed to be compatible with the reductionist view of summary characteristic of the literacy community in the early 1980s.

The teachers' definition of summary matched well with their beliefs about the purpose of teaching summarizing. During the interview the teachers were asked, "What do you think is important for students to learn about summarizing?" Their answers were, for the most part, vague. The teachers typically said that summarizing is important because it is a good skill and it means students can "organize their thoughts." Lena added that summaries are important because they show that her students can identify different events in the story. Only Sara said that they are important because they show comprehension. At this point in the year, the teachers saw summarizing as a skill that results in a written product that must contain the "essential elements" and just enough details to make the summary itself enjoyable to read.

In the fall, the teachers' talk about summary was interspersed with talk about story maps. Because story maps were what the third-grade teachers worked on the previous year to fulfill the summary requirement for students' portfolios, their talk about story maps and summaries was often one and the same. For Pine teachers, story maps contain the "five key elements": characters, setting, problem, plot (important events leading up to the solution), and solution. Story maps differ in definition from summaries only in that there is no expectation that they be interesting. And while summaries are expected to appear in paragraph form, story maps can be written as single word answers to questions, a list of words or phrases after a prompt (e.g., characters:), or complete but unconnected sentences (e.g., "The characters are _. The setting is _.").

With few exceptions, the teachers mentioned summarizing during fall interviews only when prompted by a question specifically about the topic. In contrast, they referred to story maps in response to several interview questions such as "What would I expect to see if I came into your class during reading time?", "What do you think is important for students to learn about summarizing?", and "How do you know what your students know and can do in the subject area of reading?"

Teaching Summary. The teachers were most concrete when they talked about how they teach summarizing. At what point in the school year they begin working on summaries, what the final product looks like, and their expectations for the final product vary, but there is a high degree of similarity in the teaching progression. Most of the teachers begin teaching summarizing by reading a book to the whole class and then modeling a summary. Some model the summary orally and others in written form. This teacher-constructed summary is often followed by a self-critique and then a student critique. Next, the students are grouped, and each group writes a summary. Finally, students write individual summaries. Except in Lena's case where story maps and summaries seem to be taught as two different skills, story maps are an integral part of the summary teaching/learning progression. The overall process seems to include teaching the students how to identify the "key elements" using the story map, and then putting all the information down on paper in paragraph form. The teachers did not include much detail outside of this basic outline when they described how they teach summarizing.

Assessing Summary. The teachers had a difficult time articulating how they assess summaries and the role that summaries play in the assessment of their students as readers. When the teachers model summaries and when the class critiques them, they talk about the components of a good summary: It contains the key elements (character, first event . . .); the events are in the order that they occurred in the story; and the final product is interesting to read. There was a lot of ambiguity and uncertainty, however, when the teachers talked about grading final products. Cindy wondered aloud "how comprehensive people mean for them [summaries] to be." Sara commented that the grading of summaries is "subjective." Elly reported looking to see if they have the pertinent details that show the progress of the plot. Karen, the most articulate on this point, said, "I would say a child was on the right track when they left my class if they were able to . . . well, if I asked them to read a book and then give me a summary on it, they would be able to pick out some of the points and say it so that it kind of flowed." Lena reported looking for the "key elements" but was thankful that she only has to give Hs, Ss, and Ns (i.e., high, satisfactory, needs improvement) on the students' report cards, because she finds summaries difficult to grade. The teachers talked about preferring story maps to summaries because story maps are well defined and thus easy to grade. As these comments suggest, the teachers' shared definition of summary was not a definition that guided them in assessment.

The teachers seemed hesitant to use summaries *for* assessment of reading. Their major concern seemed to be an uncertainty about the appropriateness of using writing to evaluate reading skills. Lena noted that students are often capable of picking out good summaries and know in their minds what is important, but they find it difficult to put their ideas on paper. She emphasized that including all the components in a written summary is often difficult for students, but knowing the components and recognizing them when they see them is not. Sara made a similar point, that some good readers "freeze" when it comes to the actual writing. "They can tell you anything about a story but the writing is hard for them." In contrast, although Cindy did not say it is appropriate to evaluate reading skills using writing, she did comment that good readers are also good writers "because it translates." The teachers' discussion and exploration of these concerns continues throughout the fall reading workshops.

Working Through Ideas About Summary:
The Fall Reading Workshops

Selecting Goals for the Workshops. The teachers and researchers met on September 15, 1992, for a half-day workshop to initiate the year's activities. For the first half of the workshop, project researchers/staff developers presented key ideas about performance assessment, from the perspectives of the assessment, literacy, and mathematics education communities. The literacy expert presented a scheme she had developed, that matched types of assessments with the district's goals. That scheme included summaries and the process of summarizing as a means of gaining insight into children's construction of meaning. In addition, it included other types of assessments related to district goals—for example, literature logs as sources for information on appreciation and enjoyment, annotations for self-assessment, and running records for fluency and automaticity. The literacy expert also provided each teacher with a binder of resource materials. The workshop and binder included ideas about the ways in which process (summarizing) and product (summaries) can be assessed, and different response modes along dimensions of oral/written and open-ended/forced choice. Thus, the theoretical scheme that the research/staff development team presented to the teachers as a resource included summaries, along with several other tools, as a means of capturing critical district language arts/reading outcomes.

Following the overview session, individual school teams met to discuss literacy and mathematics goals for the first quarter. When pressed to discuss specific literacy goals at this initial session and other early workshops, teachers at Pine relied rather heavily on their reading specialist who attended several early workshops with them. The reading specialist suggested, and the teachers quickly agreed, that they select comprehension or meaning making of text as the goal of the third-grade curriculum for which they would develop and implement a performance assessment. Teachers returned the conversation to their interest in using last year's summary work as the basis for their work on the project. And without examining an explicit link with the goal of text comprehension, they chose summaries to develop as a literacy assessment. "We chose the goal of summary for our portfolio last year and then [for this project] we need a goal for first quarter"; "[the goal is] summarizing stories that includes important details." It seems safe to say that the teachers chose summaries (or agreed to the choice) mainly because of their work the previous year.

Throughout this goal selection process, little was said explicitly about summary as assessment of reading comprehension or meaning making. In the closing minutes of the September 15 workshop, the teachers agreed to "ultimately work toward summaries, using the story maps and story frames going toward our end result of a 9-to-15 sentence [written summary]." Thus, the teachers, in selecting a goal, shifted the assessment focus from summary as assessment *of meaning making* (a literacy goal; a goal of the literacy community) to assessment *of summaries* (a curricular goal; a goal derived from Pine's curriculum framework). During this discussion, Karen helped maintain the workshop focus on the curricular framework by looking in the curriculum binder and referring to it frequently: "So is that [summarizing] from within a 3.5, or is that one of the little [subheadings]: 'summarizing stories that includes important details'?" Although the literacy expert asked questions about the teachers' "vision for the end of the quarter," seemingly as a way to probe the link between summary and comprehension, discussion on this topic was not forthcoming. Thus, it appears that the teachers had not taken ownership of the theoretical scheme presented by Hiebert during the initial session. Their work on summary as assessment proceeded without explicitly addressing the connection between summary and a literacy goal like comprehension, thus avoiding a potential conflict between the theoretical scheme and the teachers' concern about the appropriateness of using writing to evaluate reading skills.

Transcripts of early workshops show that teachers brought with them their individual ideas of summary as they described them in the fall interviews. The four major themes evident in interviews were present in the workshops as well: establishing a working definition of summary for the assessment project; discussing and sharing strategies for instructing summaries; unraveling the complexities of assessing summaries; and exploring their own difficulties in understanding, teaching, and using summaries. Most workshop conversations were dominated by two of the categories: instructing and assessing summaries. The other themes, summary definition and teacher expectations, were less objects of entire conversations, and more scattered throughout the workshops.

What follows describes teacher talk in workshops about summary, loosely organized around the four themes. The reader should be aware that definitions established early in the year were not cast in stone, and that teachers returned to defining summary frequently throughout the fall. In addition, conversations about the four themes naturally overlapped as teachers recognized the need to instruct what they were assessing, and to modify their operational definition of summary in light of instructional and assessment problems they encountered.

Defining Summary: What Does Summary Mean? When the concept of summary initially was considered for the assessment project, Pine teachers provided vague definitions, although they could offer a rich repertoire of instructional activities. The definitions were very similar to those offered in the interviews: "main ideas, story elements." Workshops enabled the teachers to scaffold each other as, early on, they asked for clarification of ideas, extended their own ideas into another's ideas, summarized each other's perspectives, built on one another's knowledge, and arrived at a consensus for understanding summary. The workshop context, in which teachers worked with one another to derive common knowledge, facilitated questioning and reflection on their individual pedagogical understandings of summary. In this process of defining summary, researchers remained relatively hands-off, permitting the teachers to sort out and create a working knowledge of summary among themselves.

Three aspects of defining summary emerged in our analyses of interview and workshop data: (a) summary as important ideas in a text; (b) summary as a component of the reading program; and (c) summary with the purpose of assessing comprehension. The first—summary as main ideas in a text— dominated workshop conversations. The infrequency of conversation around the other two aspects of summary suggests that the teachers did not consider them to be integral parts of their definition of summary for this project. Perhaps not surprisingly, later conversations about assessment focused on the question, "What makes a good summary?" rather than "What are the qualities of a summary that show good reading comprehension?"

In the initial workshop, teachers discussed their individual views and came to realize that though they shared a common vocabulary and a number of common ideas, each had a particular view of summary. Sara began by defining summary as "story frames, and there's a blank, and it is very obvious that a name of a character . . . needs to be in that blank"; Elly followed with "later, the story frame needs more than one word, we expect a sentence at least"; and Lena extended this description by saying "It's [story frame] the introduction to summaries." In a later September workshop, the teachers became explicit about how their individual ideas fit together into a continuum. They negotiated their individual views and arrived at a compromise, or a new idea about summary: Summaries of text fall on a continuum that ranges from highly directed story maps and frames to more loosely structured written products. In several of these conversations, as teachers came to share knowledge of summary, they practically finished one another's sentences.

In some conversations, the teachers refined their idea of summary further by distinguishing between summaries and other types of written responses to text. For example, Cindy noted, "I think lit logs and responses assure showing more on how you enjoy and appreciate rather than 'Can I get some meaning?'" The group agreed that for this project's assessment purposes, they would include the meaning of text in their definition of summary, but exclude personal responses to literature and demonstrations of reading appreciation. At this initial stage in the process, then, the teachers seem to have agreed upon a definition of summary as a continuum of products, each containing the features common to fictional text: characters, setting, major events, problem, and solution. At one end of the continuum was the story map consisting of one-word entries; at the other was the 9-to-15 sentence paragraph.

Pine teachers revisited their definition of summary in later workshops as they discussed instructional activities to support student progress toward a good summary and attempted to identify criteria for scoring student products. Throughout this process, they worked hard to operationalize the definition in ways that would provide guidance for teaching and assessment purposes. Their efforts required ongoing questioning and negotiation as difficult issues arose.

The definition of summary evolved as teachers collected and evaluated students' work. The earliest summaries they collected tended to mirror the formulaic steps outlined in the story frames. These list-like summaries elicited some consternation from the teachers as a group. Lena commented, "My summaries right now are 'the characters are ____, the story takes place ____ the problem ____. the solution ____ . . .' It's so rote, grocery list. It doesn't flow." The teachers recognized and noted the inadequacy of the story frame as a summary. Working together, they agreed that the summaries needed to be more than a comprehensive list of story elements. "Interesting" writing "that flows" became critical criteria for a good summary.

This conversation seemed to lead to a reconceptualization of the summary continuum as an *instructional* continuum (i.e., a continuum to guide instructional activities) rather than a definitional one. It also shifted the emphasis away from using summaries to assess reading toward defining them in a more traditional way as a writing exercise. In the course of these shifting ideas, the notion that summaries "show comprehension"—present to a limited extent in early workshops—seemed to disappear from the teachers' conversations.

Throughout the workshop conversations about defining summary, participation by the researchers/staff developers was characterized primarily by occasional questions. They encouraged the teachers to discuss their ideas of summary and to come to a consensus about a working definition.

Teaching Summary: The Instructional Continuum.   Because of their past experiences with summary, Pine teachers had much to say about instructional issues, and conversations frequently turned spiritedly to teaching. In these conversations, the teachers developed a shared general progression for summary instruction that began with the class summary, moved through small groups, then pairs, and finally to independent work. They shared instructional activities for each component of the progression, borrowed from one another, and incorporated new ideas from each other. Instructional activities for the class summary, for example, included collective writing of a summary, a class critique of a teacher-written summary, and a summary written and critiqued collectively by the class.

All of the teachers at Pine used modeling as a major instructional strategy. Lena's comment at a workshop in late September is illustrative, "I have a bunch of samples . . . I'm just a believer that the more modeling the quicker they catch on." The other teachers enthusiastically agreed. One purpose for modeling was to provide instruction regarding the important issue of writing quality. As Lena explained in a mid-November workshop, "I'm sharing the adult [written] summaries strictly for the writing quality. To get away from 'the characters are, the setting is.' . . . first it [summary writing] begins with just a list—a grocery list, then it becomes a list of sentences in paragraph form."

Teachers discussed adapting classroom management, organization, and assignments to address the goals of summary instruction. They described classrooms where children were scaffolded by the teacher and by one another, socially constructing "good summaries." As teachers shared their strategies for instructing summary, the researchers listened. On several occasions, the literacy expert made efforts to shift the conversation to assessment, urging the teachers to explicitly consider criteria they might use to assess their students' summaries. Thus, conversations about teaching strategies and assessment criteria overlapped.

Assessing Summary: The Scoring Rubric. Because the overall project was about assessment, developing methods for scoring summaries and attaining consistency in scoring were important components of the later workshops. One entire session was devoted to scoring summaries. In an earlier workshop, before the teachers actually sat and scored as a group, the literacy specialist introduced four terms that the teachers could use to describe or rate the quality of their students' summaries: thorough, solid, some and little/inaccurate. She guided the teachers in setting up a scoring rubric, suggesting that they collect samples of student work and agree upon particular examples to anchor the ratings. In subsequent workshops, teachers fleshed out the ratings with criteria, and they assigned anchors to the scoring rubric.

In these assessment conversations, the teachers worked out a number of issues concerning scoring. In one discussion, they arrived at the consensus that the scoring rubrics should reflect a criterion standard, rather than a comparative standard:

Karen: I have a question. Does, will this [scoring rubric], maybe . . . change throughout the process? I mean we might, I might get a Thorough tomorrow when I have them do individual summaries that, from that group it's the most Thorough, but then as time goes on somebody might [do better]. . . . Or is Thorough going to be set for the whole time?

Lorrie: I think it should be changeable as you get new insights, but the first way you said it I want to argue against. It shouldn't be normative or comparative, that is, it shouldn't be Thorough because that's the best that got done. You do want to be able to tell kids even if nobody can do it to start with, what makes (interrupted by Karen). . .

Karen: What a good summary is. Okay.

. . .

Karen: So the reason you (talking to Lena) choose a, you know, like on the way you're teaching it, you choose a Thorough because it had all the elements and it was written the way you knew a summary should be written. Not because that was one of the best ones out of the class.

Lena: Yes.

Group scoring sessions enabled teachers to probe each other's reasons for assigning particular scores to particular summaries. As they worked to understand each other's views, and to agree upon student prototypes of Thorough, Solid, Some, and Little/Inaccurate summaries, they continued to elaborate their taken-as-shared understanding of summary. These conversations, like most that occurred in the workshops, were grounded in the teachers' classroom practice. In this case, they were based on an examination of actual samples of student work.

Elly: OK, Solid is . . . (interrupted by Sara)

Sara: But if they were missing a setting, I don't know that I would knock them down to Some understanding, 'cause sometimes that's real critical on it but I don't think that's always

Cindy: No, we've been holding to that as we went through it.

Elly: That you have to have all the parts?

Cindy: There's a difference in your writing skills between the Solid and the Thorough is what we've—how descriptive you are—

Elly: But a Solid would have to have all the parts?

Cindy: All of them is what we've been saying.

Elly: OK.

Group scoring sessions thus enabled the teachers to test out their ideas of a "good" summary in a public forum. Assessment conversations focused on achieving agreement among themselves and applying the agreed-upon criteria consistently. As Pine teachers participated in these conversations, they revisited the definition of summary and raised a number of troublesome issues.

Using Writing to Assess Reading: An Unresolved Dilemma.   In their fall interviews, teachers noted that summary was a hard skill for them to teach and for students to learn. Though this theme did not dominate any one workshop, it did influence conversations as teachers worked out a satisfactory definition, instructional progression, and assessment practices. Arriving at a shared definition of summary helped the teachers decide how to teach. Teaching summaries incrementally from story maps to paragraphs, from whole class to individual efforts, grew out of the early work they did in defining summary. The idea of an instructional continuum allowed teachers to accommodate students of varying ability and to address individual students' understanding of summary writing. As the workshop conversations shifted to assessment, however, other more persistent difficulties arose. Primary among these was the issue of using writing to assess reading.

In the initial fall workshop, teachers voiced a concern that students with limited writing ability would be unjustly penalized if writing were used to assess their reading comprehension. Comments by Lena and Elly capture that concern:

Lena: Now Elly is concerned about the writing skill. I did have those two boys in my room last year that were great readers, and had those terrible writing skills . . . their writing skills were so poor that they would have to get a bad grade [in reading].

Elly: Are those reading goals? See, I have a hard time sometimes, evaluating . . . because I think we are evaluating writing. . . Is that reading?

The issue of using writing for reading assessment reappeared in conversations throughout the fall workshops. It became more problematic when writing quality was included in the definition of summary and as an explicit scoring criterion. Student difficulty with writing summaries led the teachers to another consensus: Once they had agreed upon the scoring rubric and criteria, they would share their expectations with their students and have the students score their own and peers' summaries. Sharing of the scoring rubric and criteria, and having students use them to score summaries, represented an attempt to resolve the "writing/reading dilemma." Lena likened these activities to "the teaching to the test" she did for standardized tests:

> If they don't know how to use those papers [summary papers], I can't ever assess them . . . teaching kids how to do CTBS because we've found that they were not failing the test because they did not know that knowledge, but instead they were not test-wise. I feel the same way with a lot of these strategies [using summary as assessment]. It is not that they are not showing us what they know, they don't know how to do these activities.

In a later workshop, Elly took up this point, saying "the fact is, that kids before they start, need to know the criteria."

Throughout most of the workshops, conversation about summary focused on understanding summary, instructing summary, and assessing summary—not on summary as a strategy for teaching reading comprehension or for determining a student's ability to construct meaning from text. By focusing on instruction and assessment of summary, teachers avoided, for the most part, explicitly addressing the writing/reading dilemma. The dilemma did appear periodically in their conversations, however. And, Pine teachers' decision to share scoring rubrics with their students, and to involve them in scoring their own and peers' summaries, represented initial attempts to seek a resolution to this complex issue. Researchers did not make strong attempts to redirect these conversations—either by explicitly encouraging attention to summaries for the purpose of assessing reading comprehension or by suggesting ways of thinking about the writing/reading dilemma and its resolution.

Change and Consistency in Teachers' Ideas and Practices: Winter Interview Data

Defining Summary. After 7 workshops, in their winter interviews the teachers articulated a shared definition of summary similar to the one they shared in the fall. All of the teachers agree that a summary still has to contain the "five key elements" and be interesting to read. It must be written using complete sentences in paragraph form and ". . . it needs to be concise, but have details . . . it needs to be well written, not a grocery list." Although they shared this common definition, each teacher stressed particular elements. For example, Cindy was concerned that her students' summaries be more detailed than story maps and more interesting; Lena did not want her students to include unimportant events; and Elly wanted summaries to capture "the big picture." Each teacher owned the group's definition, but was able to choose to emphasize different aspects of the definition.

Their shared definition differed from the one in the fall in that interesting was as important a component of summary as the key elements—it had become a criterion instead of a desirable characteristic. Story maps were now differentiated from summaries and were considered a good exercise to teach students about the key elements. Two of the teachers talked about alternative definitions of summary that might be acceptable in other situations. They dismissed them, however, because the team had settled on this other definition. For example, Elly talked about having her students "tell me what happened . . . in what you just read today. But that's not a real summary, it's a summary of what happened in those five pages, but it's not a summary how we talked about what a summary is."

All of the teachers said that summarizing was an important component of their reading program, with only one teacher saying that summaries were "a major part of my program before." Unlike in the fall interviews, they mentioned summaries when they responded to general questions about their reading program such as, "Is reading time different than it was at this time last year?", "If you were planning now for next year's reading program, what key ideas would you incorporate into your plans?", and a request to ". . . describe what I [the interviewer] would expect to see during reading time at this point in the school year." However, the purpose of teaching and learning summarizing was still not clear in the interview data. For the most part, the teachers believed that their students were learning more because of the concentration on summaries; however, it was difficult to articulate what these additional learnings were. For example, Cindy reported that her students were "learning more" and that they could write better, but she could not be more specific about *more* or *better.*

Teaching Summary.   Although each teacher's personality and personal style were evident in her teaching of summarizing, all of the teachers followed a similar path, one developed in the workshops. Despite more detail in the winter responses, the way the teachers said they taught summarizing during the fall was similar to the way they said they would teach it in their initial interviews and mirrored workshop discussions of teaching strategies. In general, they began with a whole class summary of a teacher-read book, moved to small group summaries of a single text, and then on to individual summaries. There were some new elements in their teaching of summary, such as extensive teacher modeling, class discussions about criteria for good summaries, and student participation in scoring. All of the teachers were pleased that the modeling and class discussion resulted in the students being more aware of what the teacher looked for in a written summary.

Assessing Summary. When the teachers talked about assessment and summaries, they talked about the assessment *of* a summary—what makes a good summary, and (less often) about using summaries *for* assessment purposes—what a summary tells them about what their student knows and can do in the subject area of reading. The interview included a specific question about how the teachers knew if their students knew how to summarize (assessment *of*). There was not a parallel question to elicit their use of summarizing to assess other skills or levels of knowledge (assessment *for*).

There was a lot of talk about how to evaluate a summary. The teachers seemed to agree that summaries were easier to grade than they had been the previous year because of the scoring rubric and their knowledge about what it takes for a summary to receive a Solid, a Thorough, and so on. However, they were still not comfortable grading summaries. Most of the teachers reported not being completely satisfied with the amount of "subjectivity" in grading that accompanied the nonspecific "interesting with details" component of their definition. Although it was not a completely satisfying resolution, the heavy amount of modeling that they did was their way of teaching their students the boundaries of this subjectivity.

In contrast, the teachers had relatively little to say about using summaries as assessment tools (i.e., assessment *for*). Each teacher was asked general questions about her assessment practices such as how she determined ". . . what your students know and can do in the subject area of reading" and what evidence she considered when assigning a reading grade. Given their responses to these and other general assessment questions, it is not clear to what extent these teachers gathered information about their students' reading using summaries. One teacher did not mention using summaries as assessments for reading at all. Though another reported using summaries as assessment tools, she quickly backed away from this stance when asked what she learned about her students when she looked at their summaries. Only one teacher said that it is possible to gather information about her students such as how well they spell or construct sentences. She gave no indication, however, that she actually used summaries in that way.

There was some agreement among the teachers that summaries are better assessments of reading skills—including comprehension—than the multiple choice, fill in the blank, short answer assessments they had used in the past because summaries are "more related to real reading." Nonetheless, all of the teachers explicitly mentioned a number of other ways, such as comprehension questions, that they gathered information about their students' comprehension levels. And a couple of the teachers said they would like the project to show them more "analytic" ways to measure comprehension.

CONCLUSIONS

As a result of participating in the AARM project, Pine teachers made several significant changes in their teaching and assessment of summary. With respect to teaching, for example, they developed a continuum of instructional activities designed to guide students' progress from 5-word story maps to well-written, interesting paragraphs. One instructional strategy that figured prominently in this continuum was modeling, and teachers reported using modeling much more than they had in previous years.

With the guidance of the research/staff development team, the teachers also developed a scoring rubric for assessing the quality of summaries. From early in the school year, they involved students in the assessment process by having them use this rubric to evaluate summaries written by the teacher, groups of students, and eventually individuals. This peer- and self-assessment component exemplifies the connection between instruction and assessment that was prominent in the teachers' work on summary. It also is important in the literature of the larger literacy assessment community (Tierney, Carter, & Desai, 1991) and is one of the seven reading-specific outcomes of the district framework. The "taken-as-shared" notion of self-assessment in these two broader communities relevant to the teachers' professional lives was one that the teachers at Pine came to own. That is, through their participation in project workshops, they socially constructed a set of instructional and assessment activities that were taken-as-shared within their own learning community as well as connected to the broader pedagogical and literacy communities.

In addition to providing a context for the teachers' social construction of a definition of summary and instructional and assessment practices, participation in the AARM project created an opportunity for individual teachers to make their own unique adaptations of the group's ideas. For example, the teachers stressed different aspects of the definition of summary and had their own variants of story frames or story maps to guide instruction. These changes, and others that Pine teachers made during the 3 months examined in this chapter, were substantial. In retrospect, however, they seem to represent extensions or elaborations of practices that were in place prior to participation in the project, compatible with the teachers' preexisting beliefs, rather than fundamental shifts in their beliefs and practices. As one example, teachers' interpretations of summary remained where they were at the beginning of the project—closely tied to story structure (Pearson & Fielding, 1991)—rather than moving toward the view of summary as "gist of a passage" (Palincsar & David, 1991).

In addition, teachers did not shift their views regarding the role of summary within their own reading programs. They continued to view summary as an activity of value in and of itself, and to focus on instruction and assessment of summary. They did not come to consider summarizing as a critical process for meaning making or fostering comprehension. Thus, with respect to instruction, they did not focus their attention on teaching summary for the purpose of enhancing students' ability to construct meaning. Similarly, with respect to assessment, they rarely considered assessment of summary for meaning making—that is, summary as an indicator of students' ability to construct meaning from text. This pattern of consistency with preexisting beliefs supports the idea that the teachers' beliefs served as filters for interpreting new ideas that were presented during the workshops (Borko & Putnam, in press).

In retrospect, our finding of changes consistent with preexisting beliefs is not surprising, given that the purpose of the AARM project was to help participating teachers develop performance assessments compatible with their instructional goals, not to have them confront these goals or other beliefs about reading instruction. Nonetheless, given that the district curriculum framework—adopted by the teachers as a basis for their instructional goals—did stress reading for meaning making, and given that the teachers expressed some concerns about using summaries to assess reading—a dilemma that they were unable to resolve—it seems reasonable to ask what it would have taken for Pine teachers to make more fundamental changes in their beliefs and practices regarding instruction as well as assessment. For example, how might the researchers/staff developers have helped the teachers to move toward an understanding of summary as "gist," and toward the use of summaries for teaching and assessing the construction of meaning from text?

One immediate response to these questions is that the project needed more time. The patterns reported here reflect the first phase of a staff development program that extended over a year. The research/staff development team met with Pine teachers in seven literacy-focused workshop sessions during the 3 month period examined. During that time, we asked teachers to examine and implement practices related to instruction and assessment in both reading and mathematics. The literature on teacher change suggests that this is NOT a long time. The Cognitively Guided Instruction (CGI) project, a multiyear research/staff development project focused on helping first-grade teachers to change their mathematics instruction, provides evidence of the long-term nature of teacher change. In that project, during an intensive summer workshop teachers acquired knowledge of children's strategies for solving addition and subtraction problems and were encouraged to listen to how their students solve problems. By the end of the first year following the workshop, participating teachers were using the taxonomy of problem types and solution strategies and were asking students to describe the processes they used to solve problems. However, they were most influenced by details of the program. It was not until well into the second year following the workshop that teachers began to really listen to students, assess their understanding, and plan instruction to build upon and extend their knowledge (Carpenter & Fennema, 1992). We are currently analyzing data from the second semester of the AARM staff development, and our preliminary analyses suggest that additional changes did occur in the teachers' ideas and practices concerning summary. We also plan to follow a group of the teachers during the 1993–1994 academic year to see whether and how they continue to incorporate ideas from the project into their reading and mathematics programs.

The histories and contexts of individual schools also enter into the responses of teachers to staff development. A previous analysis of the dilemmas within sessions with this particular school team and the two other schools in the project, revealed the strength of Pine teachers' interest in concrete and specific activities (Hiebert & Davinroy, 1993). Pine teachers' adoption of a reading textbook series the year prior to the project, in a district that encouraged trade book use, further illustrates their push for making instruction concrete and specific. This orientation to concrete and specific activities was evident in the emphasis on story structure and the continuum of activities in their use of summaries. Their need to "nail things down" also meant that Pine teachers moved quickly in implementing assessments at the beginning of the project and in developing a scoring rubric. We expect case studies of the other two schools, with their different histories and contexts, to demonstrate patterns compatible with the orientations and contexts of those schools.

Although time is a necessary ingredient for change, and school contexts and histories can be expected to influence the change process, further reflection on the content and process of the AARM staff development is warranted to determine if other directions might have resulted in more of the types of shifts in ideas and practices advocated by the literacy community. As was outlined in the introductory section of this chapter, our staff development effort had the dual goals of introducing participants to new content about assessment and creating an environment that facilitates teachers' ownership of the staff development program. The research team had a conceptual framework for classroom-based assessment which was introduced at the initial workshop and referred to frequently over the course of the semester. The general progression of topics in sessions—identification of goals, identification of tools, and development of scoring rubrics—derived from this conceptual framework. While providing this framework and introducing these topics, however, the researchers were intent on encouraging teacher expression and ownership of goals, tools, and scoring rubrics. Therefore, we typically did not attempt to redirect conversations when teachers moved to emphasize instructional activities rather than interpretations of students' comprehension processes, despite the fact that such shifts in the conversations moved them away from our conceptual framework. The balance between presenting new information and encouraging teacher ownership is a delicate one and one with which the research team continually struggled.

For the most part, we also did not push teachers to confront their preexisting beliefs about summary, or about the teaching and learning of reading more generally. One reason for our decision not to confront these beliefs relates to the original intention of the project—to help teachers develop performance assessments compatible with their instructional goals. As the workshops progressed, we came to realize that there were discrepancies between the teachers' instructional goals and our ideas about reading instruction, despite the compatibility between our ideas and the district curriculum framework. Although we realized these problems and their potential impact on the development of performance assessments, we were hesitant to confront the teachers' beliefs about reading instruction to a great extent, given our initial agreements about the nature of the project. This was particularly true at Pine because the teachers were already annoyed with some aspects of the project such as the work load within and outside the classroom. Given this hesitation on our part, it is not surprising that the teachers' beliefs changed relatively little. As we noted at the beginning of the chapter, the literature on learning to teach suggests that teachers typically do not confront beliefs on their own. Rather, the process seems to require systematic attention and guidance over time by teacher educators/staff developers (for a review, see Borko & Putnam, in press).

The practical-argument-based staff development program used by Richardson and Anders (in press; Anders & Richardson, 1992) in the Reading Instruction Study provides one empirically supported approach to helping teachers confront their ideas about teaching and learning and consider alternative premises and practices. In a semester-long staff development program Richardson and Anders encouraged teachers to examine their explanations for reading instructional practices in relation to theoretical and empirical evidence drawn from the literature on reading comprehension. The program included individual elements such as each teacher viewing a videotape of the teacher's reading comprehension instruction with staff developers and exploring premises behind various instructional practices, and group elements such as workshop sessions in which participants discussed their beliefs about teaching and shared ideas about reading comprehension that they were trying out in their classrooms. Participating teachers exhibited changes in their theories of reading, learning to read, and teaching reading; their beliefs about reading comprehension; and their reading instructional practices.

The program by Richardson and Anders is but one approach. And it is one that has been used to foster changes in instruction rather than assessment. Teachers, however, generally have more experience and expertise related to instruction than assessment. In fact, members of the assessment community such as Stiggins (1991) warn that many teachers lack the "assessment literacy" necessary to implement performance assessments. As a result, it may be more difficult, and require somewhat different staff development approaches, to help teachers change their assessment practices.

A lack of experience explains only part of what may be unique about the staff development on assessment in comparison to instruction. Assessment is not a neutral topic for teachers (Anders & Richardson, 1992). Rather, it is an arena in which external mandates to teachers have been many and teachers' voices have been silenced. For teachers to take ownership of a domain in which their ideas have been ignored can be expected to be a long process. Teachers are likely to gravitate to the area in which they are more familiar and confident—instructional practice. This, in turn, may lead them away from making the substantial efforts that are required to develop classroom-based assessment. For this particular group of teachers—as with the entire field, greater use and ownership of classroom-based assessment can be expected to require considerable effort and reflection over an extended period of time.

REFERENCES

Anders, P., & Richardson, V. (1992). Teacher as game-show host, bookkeeper, or judge? Challenges, contradictions, and consequences of accountability. *Teachers College Record, 94*, 382-396.

Anderson, R. C., Hiebert, E. H., Scott, J. A., & Wilkinson, I. A. G. (1985). *Becoming a Nation of Readers: The Report of the Commission on Reading.* Champaign, IL: The Center for the Study of Reading & National Academy of Education.

Au, K. H. (1994). Portfolio assessment: Experiences at the Kamehameha Elementary Education Program. In S. W. Valencia, E. H. Hiebert, & P. Afflerbach (Eds.), *Authentic reading assessment: Practices and possibilities* (pp. 103-126). Newark, DE: International Reading Association.

Barr, R., Kamil, M. L., Mosenthal, P. B., & Pearson, P. D. (Eds.). (1991). *Handbook of Reading Research* (Vol. 2). New York: Longman.

Beach, R., & Hynds, S. (1991). Research on response to literature. In R. Barr, M. L. Kamil, P. B. Mosenthal, & P. D. Pearson (Eds.), *Handbook of Reading Research* (Vol. 2, pp. 453-489). New York: Longman.

Borko, H., & Putnam, R. (in press). Learning to teach. In R. Calfee & D. Berliner (Eds.), *Handbook of Educational Psychology*. New York: Macmillan.

Brown, A., & Day, J. (1983). Macrorules for summarizing texts: The development of expertise. *Journal of verbal learning and verbal behavior, 22,* 1-14.

Carpenter, T. P., & Fennema, E. (1992). Cognitively Guided Instruction: Building on the knowledge of students and teachers. In W. Secada (Ed.), *Curriculum reform: The case of mathematics in the United States* (pp. 457-470). Special issue of the International Journal of Educational Research. Elmsford, NY: Pergamon Press.

Cobb, P., Yackel, E., & Wood, T. (1992). A constructivist alternative to the representational view of mind in mathematics education. *Journal for Research in Mathematics Education, 23,* 2-33.

Cohen, D. K., & Ball, D. L. (1990). Relations between policy and practice: A commentary. *Educational Evaluation and Policy Analysis, 12,* 330-338.

Dole, J. A., Duffy, G. G., Roehler, L. R., & Pearson, P. D. (1991). Moving from the old to the new: Research on reading comprehension instruction. *Review of Educational Research, 61,* 239-264.

Hartman, D. K. (1990). *Eight readers reading: The intertextual links of able readers using multiple passages.* Unpublished dissertation, University of Illinois, Urbana-Champaign.

Hiebert, E. H., & Davinroy, K. H. (1993, April). *Dilemmas and issues in implementing classroom-based assessments for literacy.* Paper presented at the annual meeting of the American Educational Research Association, Atlanta, GA.

Kapinus, B. A., Collier, G. V., & Kruglanski, H. (1994). Maryland School Performance Assessment: A new view of assessment. In S. W. Valencia, E. H. Hiebert, & P. Afflerbach (Eds.), *Authentic reading assessment: Practices and possibilities* (pp.42-63). Newark, DE: International Reading Association.

Palincsar, A. S., & Brown, A. L. (1984). Reciprocal teaching of comprehension-fostering and monitoring strategies. *Cognition and Instruction, 1*(2), 117-175.

Palincsar, A. S., & David, Y. (1991). Promoting literacy through classroom dialogue. In E. H. Hiebert (Ed.), *Literacy for a diverse society: Perspectives, practices, and policies* (pp. 122-140). New York: Teachers College Press.

Paris, S. G., Wasik, B. A., & Turner, J. C. (1991). The development of strategic readers. In R. Barr, M. L. Kamil, P. B. Mosenthal, & P. D. Pearson (Eds.), *Handbook of Reading Research* (Vol. 2, pp. 609-640). New York: Longman.

Pearson, P. D., & Fielding, L. (1991). Comprehension instruction. In R. Barr, M. L. Kamil, P. B. Mosenthal, & P. D. Pearson (Eds.), *Handbook of Reading Research* (Vol. 2, pp. 815-860). New York: Longman.

Putnam, R. T., Heaton, R. M., Prawat, R. S., & Remillard, J. (1992). Teaching mathematics for understanding: Discussing case studies of four fifth-grade teachers. *Elementary School Journal, 93,* 213-228.

Resnick, L. B., & Resnick, D. P. (1992). Assessing the thinking curriculum: New tools for educational reform. In B. R. Gifford & M. C. O'Connor (Eds.), *Changing assessments: Alternative views of aptitude, achievement, and instruction* (pp. 37-75). Boston, MA: Kluwer, Academic.

Richardson, V. (1992). The agenda-setting dilemma in a constructivist staff development process. *Teaching and Teacher Education, 8,* 287-300.

Richardson, V., & Anders, P. (in press). Staff development and the study of teacher change. In V. Richardson (Ed.), *A theory of teacher change and the practice of staff development: A case in reading instruction.* New York: Teachers College Press.

Simon, M. A., & Schifter, D. (1991). Towards a constructivist perspective: An intervention study of mathematics teacher development. *Educational Studies in Mathematics, 22,* 309-331.

Stiggins, R. (1991). Assessment literacy. *Phi Delta Kappan, 72,* 534-539.

Tierney, R. J., Carter, M. A., & Desai, L. (1991). *Portfolio assessment in the reading-writing classroom.* Norwood, MA: Christopher-Gordon.

Valencia, S. W., & Place, N. (1994). Literacy portfolios for teaching, learning, and accountability: The Bellevue Literacy Assessment Project. In S. W. Valencia, E. H. Hiebert, & P. Afflerbach (Eds.), *Authentic reading assessment: Practices and possibilities* (pp. 141-163). Newark, DE: International Reading Association.

Weiss, B. (1994). California's New English-Language Arts Assessment. In S. W. Valencia, E. H. Hiebert, & P. Afflerbach (Eds.), *Authentic reading assessment: Practices and possibilities* (pp. 72-93). Newark, DE: International Reading Association.

CHAPTER TEN

Gender, Text, and Discussion: Expanding the Possibilities

Donna E. Alvermann
Michelle Commeyras
University of Georgia, Athens

It seems that in these postmodern times, we are experiencing a renaissance that embraces the possibilities of new ways of thinking about knowing, being, and believing. This renaissance has the potential to affect profoundly the ways of doing and researching text-based classroom discussions. But it is a renaissance that extends beyond academic concerns. Consider the 1993 Public Broadcasting System's series titled "Healing and the Mind" with Bill Moyers. Moyers reported on new insights into mind-body connections and ways in which healing is a matter of meaning, not mechanics. The move in medical circles away from dichotomizing the mind and the body echoes Derrida's deconstruction of Western philosophical thought, which has framed our understanding of the world in two-term oppositions: for example, male/female, rational/irrational (Orr, 1991).

We find this renaissance challenging and compelling. It is a challenge to read the polyphony of texts on postmodernism, poststructuralism, feminisms, critical and feminist pedagogies, and more. We feel compelled to accept the challenge to explore new ways of thinking that run counter to our own rooted ways of thinking. In particular, we see many windows of opportunity for moving beyond the ingrained dominance of a male Western philosophical mode of thinking. Thus, we have begun a quest to find, construct, and articulate new ways of thinking about research and instruction that better represent our intuitions about what it means to view text-based classroom discussions from feminist postmodernist perspectives. This chapter provides a forum for sharing the beginnings of our quest. Our goal is to explore possibilities for expanding current discursive practices so as to deal more equitably with gender-related issues in classroom talk about texts.

In this chapter we argue that classroom discussions are important sites of investigation, not for the purpose of identifying and prescribing effective discussion strategies, but for understanding why particular discursive practices tend to dominate classroom talk and what might be done to alter such practices. In particular, we examine discursive practices that construct one's sense of self and "other" for the purpose of exploring ways teachers, students, and researchers can begin to "interrupt" (Brodkey, 1992, p. 310) those practices that are counterproductive to learning from and about text-based classroom talk. We ground our remarks in feminist postmodernist thinking, which seeks to continue the struggle against sexism while developing new paradigms of social criticism—paradigms that speak to possibilities and not just to givens (Nicholson, 1990).

The chapter is divided into three major sections. In the first section, we explain what we mean by discursive practices and then identify predominant discursive practices currently associated with classroom discussions of texts. In the second section, we examine our own work on text-based classroom discussion for instances of how ingrained, gendered ways of thinking have perpetuated particular discursive practices. The third section explores ways of expanding possibilities—of moving beyond currently accepted discursive practices—so as to understand more fully the complexities of learning from and about text-based classroom talk.

PREDOMINANT DISCURSIVE PRACTICES
IN CLASSROOM DISCUSSION

In laying the groundwork for what we mean by discursive practices, it is important to draw distinctions between what Gee (1990) refers to as discourses with a lowercase *d*, which include "connected stretches of language that make sense, like conversations, stories, reports, arguments" (p. 142) and Discourses with an uppercase *D*, which are:

> ways of being in the world, or forms of life which integrate words, acts, beliefs, attitudes, social identities, as well as gestures, glances, body positions and clothes. . . . A Discourse is a sort of "identity kit" which comes complete with the appropriate costume and instructions on how to act, talk, and often write, so as to take on a particular social role that others will recognize. (p. 142)

Still another way to conceive of Discourses, Gee suggests, "is as 'clubs' with (tacit) rules about who is a member and who is not, and (tacit) rules about how members ought to behave (if they wish to continue being accepted as members)" (p. 143).

Thus, it is clear from Gee's use of the term, a Discourse involves more than just talk. It involves all the discursive practices that signal one's membership in a particular group. For example, having been educated as teachers means we have learned to think, act, and speak like teachers; it also means we recognize (and are recognized by) others who have been similarly educated into the teaching profession. Other Discourses that we have learned include (but are not limited to) how to be graduate students, women, daughters, and U.S. citizens.

In the 1960s, Foucault asserted that social institutions construct themselves through their discursive practices (Orr, 1991). Since that time discursive practices have been studied in connection with peace activists (Blain, 1991), academic conferences (Morton, 1987), organizational management (Mumby & Stohl, 1991), patient-centered medicine (Silverman & Bloor, 1990), honor in an Arab community (Gilsenan, 1989), and many other areas. Smith (1987) proposed that a closer focus on the discursive practices of schools would lead to theories that better account for the complexities of schooling.

Most relevant to our focus on discursive practices in this chapter is the work of Bronwyn Davies (1989), who has written about the discursive production of the male/female dualism in classroom settings and the power differentials this dualism engenders. Davies (1989, 1990a, 1990b) has examined some of the ways in which discursive practices position young children, such that beliefs about the male/female dualism embedded in the usual stories that children hear and read become a lived reality in the classroom. Based on this research, Davies has written on why primary school children have difficulty seeing the princess, Elizabeth, as a hero in *The paper bag princess* (Munsch & Marchenko, 1980), despite the fact that Elizabeth rescues the prince, Ronald, from the dragon. She suggests that the predominance of other narratives about males rescuing females precludes a feminist hearing of the text by even the youngest of children.

Davies' (1990a, 1993) research on how some texts tend to perpetuate the male/female dualism ties in with Gilbert's (1989) concern that privileging the personal in child-centered pedagogies may "encourage the construction of stereotypical female subject positions which limit [females'] understanding of their textual inscription and encourage them to see such inscription as 'natural' and 'normal' " (p. 263). One implication to be drawn from Gilbert's work is that classroom discussions need to include opportunities for students to question textual inscriptions that define or relegate women and men to particular gendered positions.

The discursive practices that are of interest to us in this chapter are those associated with the Discourse of text-based classroom discussion. Of particular interest is how gendered discursive practices are manifested in the language of the classroom and the language of the text.

Language of the Classroom

In class discussions there are tacit language conventions for holding the floor, interrupting, and introducing new topics. These conventions are bound up with power relationships among participants in a discussion, such as *who* speaks *when* and to *whom* (Fowler, 1985). They are also representative of discursive practices that reproduce gender inequalities based on power differentials emanating from society at large. In illustrating how tacit language conventions can operate in classroom discussions to unwittingly perpetuate gender inequalities, we draw upon the research of Alton-Lee, Nuthall, and Patrick (1993) and their analyses of sixth graders' public and private statements. In an excerpt from their analyses, we learn how a male teacher's perceptions of a female student, Ann, are colored by discursive practices that have become all but invisible to both teacher and student.

> Ann's style of participation in the lesson indicated almost total continuous involvement in the tasks or with the content. Of all the case-study children, she was most often observed to be focused on the teacher or on a relevant resource. Ann received no positive feedback from the teacher for her two publicly nominated responses, and she appeared frustrated in her desire to participate publicly more frequently. Of the four [case-study] children, she was least likely to elicit teacher nomination with her hand raises: her fifteen hand raises during the lesson only elicited two teacher nominations. Ann responded by calling out her answers five times and by talking privately at a rate of two or three utterances per minute. A third of these utterances involved cooperative interactions with her friend, Julia. This private peer interaction appeared to play an important, mutually supportive role in both girls' management of the evaluative climate during the lesson. Julia sought Ann's help with strategies to remember the dates presented by the teacher. Ann shared her misconceptions with Julia. This talk was hidden, enabling Ann to give and receive peer support during the lesson, yet allowing her to avoid being seen by the teacher as contravening the rules of order. Her management (masking) of her contravention of the rules of order was so effective that even when the teacher reviewed the video (long after the unit), Ann's private utterances were hidden, and he commented that "Ann doesn't offer as much as some of the others in terms of an active type of learning. . . . She learns just sitting and soaking it up." (p. 67)

We believe that certain discursive practices emanating from differential gender expectations for students may account for why Ann's teacher saw her as a passive learner. One of those practices involves allowing boys to talk more than girls in classroom discussions (American Association of University Women, 1992). According to the AAUW report, titled *How schools shortchange girls* (1992), females are called on less frequently than males, and they are rewarded more often for compliance than for critical thinking. LaFrance's (1991) review of research suggests that teachers believe girls talk more than boys, when in fact the reverse has been documented. Ann's teacher may have unconsciously decided that Ann's two public responses were sufficient. This would fit with LaFrance's (1991) finding that cultural cliches about females' proclivity for talk influence who is called on and who is ignored. Another discursive practice that may have been operating in Ann's class is the expectation that female students are just naturally good listeners. LaFrance (1991) suggests that verbal participation by female students may be regarded as less valuable than listening. Thus, the teacher's comment that Ann "learns just sitting and soaking it up" may have been his way of saying that he values the listening ability of females.

LaFrance (1991) also reviewed research that shows females are interrupted more often than males. Individuals who interrupt others' speech can be viewed as exerting power over and/or controlling those whom they interrupt. The extent to which controlling or collaborative language occurs in classroom discussions may be related to the sex of participants. In a study of 5- and 7-year-old children, Leaper (1991) found that 7-year-old girls used more collaborative speech acts than did boys and younger girls. Although collaborative speech increased with age among the girls playing with puppets in female dyads, this was not the case for girls in mixed dyads.

What constitutes an interruption is a complex issue (Murray, 1985). However, for purposes of this chapter we use the term to refer to those instances when speakers are cut off before they have made their points. Interestingly enough, interruptions are not limited to school-age females; even a world leader like Margaret Thatcher is known to have been interrupted by interviewers more frequently than was the case for her male counterparts (Beattie, Cutler, & Pearson, 1982).

Language of the Text

Just as there are power differentials present in the discursive practices found in classroom discussion, so too are they manifested in the language of texts. Power differentials related to the social and cultural meanings attributed to being male or female are evident in the language used in texts. Attributing meaning to the sex of individuals reveals the social construction of gender. Reading texts where language is used to constitute gender dichotomies demands a certain amount of complicity on the part of the reader. If readers are not encouraged to discuss how the language of a text socially constructs gender, it is likely that gender stereotypes will go unexamined and thereby be reconstituted in each reading.

Penelope (1988) provides many examples in her work on characterizing genderization of how the language of a text can legitimize stereotypes by assuming complicitous readers. Notice, for example, the female attributions we are asked to call up in comprehending Stephen King's use of the term *womanish shriek* to characterize the wind in the following excerpt from *The Shining*:

> It snowed every day now, . . . sometimes for real, the low whistle of the wind cranking up to a womanish shriek that made the old hotel rock and groan alarmingly. (Penelope, 1988, p. 260)

In pointing out how the author of a text can reinforce deeply entrenched gender stereotypes through the use of sex-biased language, Penelope (1988) asks us to consider whether or not Stephen King could just as easily have used the term *mannish shriek* to describe the wind.

Christian-Smith's (1991) research on adolescent fiction provides an example of how the language of texts can foster complicitous readings and lead to young females' construction of stereotypical femininity. In describing how the language of romance novels shaped female adolescent readers' gender subjectivities in her study, Christian-Smith (1991) reported:

> Through romance reading, readers transform gender relations so that men cherish and nurture women rather [than] the other way around. This, together with readers' collective rejection of a macho masculinity, represents their partial overturning of one aspect of current traditional gender sentiments. However, readers' final acceptance of romantic love and its power structure undercuts the political potential of these insights. Romance reading in no way altered the young women's present and future circumstances, but rather was deeply implicated in reconciling them to their place in the world. (p. 207)

The roots of complicity in reading may lie in part in our history as readers and the books we have read. As Segal (1986) has noted, for generations parents and teachers have channeled books to or away from children according to their sex. Education textbooks over the years have advised teachers to use more "boy books" than "girl books" based on the notion that boys are *not* interested in reading about girls, but girls *are* interested in reading about boys. Gendered experiences in reading at home and in school shape our attitudes toward appropriate gender-role behaviors and influence what we choose to read throughout our lives.

Concerns regarding sex bias and a male-dominated reading curriculum have produced numerous studies on the portrayal of male and female characters in children's literature and other school materials (Barnett, 1986;

McDonald, 1989) Authors concerned with sex bias have written books where male and female characters are portrayed in ways intended to break down stereotypes (Fox, 1993). Taking a somewhat different tack, publishers of commercial reading programs have attempted to avoid sex bias by creating neutered characters, such as talking trees and animals, or by featuring both a male and a female as primary characters (Hitchcock & Tompkins, 1987).

However, efforts to create sex-equitable literature has not seriously challenged students' gendered views of themselves and the world. As Purcell-Gates (1993) has noted in her exploration of research related to the complexity of gender issues, real-life experiences seem to be the key to whether or not children accept nontraditional roles in literature. It is real-life experiences that prepare the complicitous reader to imagine a "wind cranking up to a womanish shriek." Merely changing the language of texts to include phrases like "mannish shriek" or to create stories about boys who want to study ballet or girls who are baseball umpires will not change our gendered view of the world.

Awakening an awareness in students of ways in which they engage in complicitous reading will depend largely on teachers who see for themselves a role in altering power relations and in challenging the subordination of women. This role will involve exploring with students through class discussion how gender is socially constructed in a multiplicity of ways—only one of which is the language of texts.

INFLUENCES OF GENDERED THINKING
IN OUR OWN RESEARCH

We view the term gendered thinking not as a synonym for stereotyped thinking about gender but as a cultural artifact that shapes the way we interpret the world. Each of us experiences the world through filters that are colored by our own personal histories. Gender is but one of those filters; race, ethnicity, class, and culture are others. Thus, it should not be assumed that gendered thinking always carries a negative connotation. Only when such thinking is used to stereotype individuals simply on the basis of their membership in a group is it problematic.

Our own work on text-based classroom discussion reflects a variety of ways in which ingrained, gendered ways of thinking influenced some of the research studies we have conducted in the past. For example, the inclination to cater to boys by avoiding books about girls is something Michelle vividly recalls doing:

> In 1990, while conducting a research project on dialogical-thinking reading lessons (Commeyras, 1991), I rewrote one of the stories used in the lessons so that the main characters were boys instead of girls. I took the story *I wish*

Laura's mother was my mommy by Barbara Power (1979) and changed the female protagonists, Leslie and Laura, into Jack and Bob. My rationale for taking this liberty was to provide stories that I thought might be engaging to seven fifth-grade boys who were considered "learning-disabled." I assumed these boys would be more interested in reading about boys than girls, and I thought it vitally important to pick stories that were easy to read and potentially appealing to 11- and 12-year-old boys who had experienced many years of academic discouragement. However, in light of my recent readings on feminisms, I agree with Segal (1986) that the boy-book/girl-book dualism depreciates the female experience and severely limits boys' reading experiences. Furthermore, this dualism probably serves to perpetuate the genderization of human experience. In retrospect, I think it would have been far more interesting to find out how the seven boys would have responded to *I wish Laura's mother was my mommy.*

Like Michelle, Donna also can recall instances in her own research that demonstrate how some gendered discursive practices become so commonplace that they are accepted as "natural" or "normal"—or at the very least, dismissed as being outside a study's purpose and thus not analyzed. For example, in one study (Alvermann, 1989), Donna remembers sitting quietly by as a participant observer in an eleventh-grade English class where the following discussion took place in response to a group worksheet exercise titled, *Who should survive?*:

I observed students, working in groups of four, discuss among themselves the solution to this problem: The world has undergone total nuclear destruction. To avoid death from fallout, 16 survivors must take refuge in a shelter for an extended period of time. However, due to limited provisions, only 8 people can survive; the others must be left outside to face certain death. Once you have compiled your personal list of 8 survivors, work toward group consensus in arriving at a final list of 8. Be prepared to defend your choices from among the 16 people listed on your worksheet. [Note: The list included among others a 30-year-old White Roman Catholic priest, a 55-year-old Black male concert violinist, a 28-year-old Black mother on welfare with no job skills and her 2-year-old son, a 55-year-old White male university professor, a 48-year-old Black male Lt. Colonel with two purple hearts from the Vietnam conflict, and a 28-year-old White female high school English teacher.]

John: Keep the priest. What you got Kessia? How come you pick the concert violinist? (Kessia acts as though she does not hear John's question.)

Marilyn: I picked the violinist, too, but don't ask me why.

Kessia: (looking toward John) He could make money. Why *you* pick the Black mother on welfare? You want to keep the child and ditch the mother?

Marilyn: Who gonna take care of her child while she out prostitutin'?

Kessia: She can have child care.

Marilyn: People on poverty—they don't get child care.

John: (looking toward Kessia) Why you pick the university professor?

Kessia: He has a good reputation—he a professor, he know alot.

Marilyn: He could build a school.

Exzavior: Don't we need an English teacher?

Kessia: Yeah, we need an English teacher if we gonna have schools again.

Marilyn: We got 1, 2, 3, 4, 5 . . . we need 3 more.

Kessia: Why keep the Black welfare mother? She ain't got no money.

[Note: This discussion, which was part of a thematic unit on survival, lasted the entire class period. Transcripts of other groups suggest that the talk represented in this excerpt was also representative of the class at large.]

In retrospect, certainly there is much more going on in this discussion than merely the stereotyping of Black women on welfare. The remarks directed toward the woman on welfare by the two females in the group send a strong message about what these young women have come to "accept" about personal worth and who is at risk in society. Their remarks also demonstrate how the language of a text (in this case, the worksheet descriptor assigned to a 28-year-old Black mother) can legitimize stereotypes in class discussions by assuming complicitous readers.

However, the point I am making here is that I did not find the dialogue between Kessia and Marilyn particularly informative, nor even that disturbing at the time. I did nothing with this information in my original analysis of the data. I was intent on studying eleventh graders' understanding of literacy and what it means to be labeled "at risk" of dropping out. Perhaps like these two young women, my own history as a woman has been so inscribed with female stereotypical positioning that I noted nothing out of the ordinary in their talk—a personally disturbing thought and one of several reasons for my interest in writing this chapter.

EXPANDING THE POSSIBILITIES

As historically and broadly defined, the discursive practices commonly associated with classroom discussion have derived from Discourses of social regulation. At a time in history when circumstances gave rise to the beginning of schools as we now know them, pedagogy was institutionalized "out of practical needs to cure (ignorance and moral depravity), to reform, to discipline, and to educate the social body. . . . The school . . . became the site of . . . a discourse of both repression and formation" (Luke, 1989, pp. 145-146). At the same time that teaching school took on more and more socially regulative functions, classroom discussions typically became teacher-centered events aimed at legitimizing the authority of the text and the teacher's superior knowledge (Alvermann, O'Brien, & Dillon, 1990; De-lamont, 1983; Goodlad, 1984). Not surprisingly, as Cohen (1993) noted in a recent symposium on classroom discussion presented at the annual meeting of the American Educational Research Association (AERA), "traditional school learning has had no room for difference, promoting instead a uni-reading— one text, one reading" (p. 3).

However, feminist postmodernist theories offer some different ways of thinking about pedagogy and research, particularly as these theories relate to text-based classroom discussion. In this last section of the chapter, we explore some possibilities or ways of moving beyond currently accepted discursive practices in learning from and learning about classroom talk.

Learning From Classroom Talk: Feminist Pedagogies

The power differentials described in the first part of this chapter are part of the empowerment issue Gore (1992) problematizes in her writings on discursive practices embedded within feminist pedagogies. To understand Gore's thinking, it is necessary to know how she defines *pedagogy*. Drawing on the work of Lusted (1986), Gore views *pedagogy* as concerned with "the processes of teaching that demand that attention be drawn to the politics of those processes and to the broader political contexts within which they are situated . . . that is, . . . [a] concern for how and in whose interests knowledge is produced and reproduced" (Gore, 1993, p. 5).

Through her interpretations of Foucault's analyses of power and knowledge, Gore (1992) has identified the need to be somewhat cautious (and critical) about engaging in discursive practices that attempt to empower "others." For example, by drawing upon Foucault's argument that "power is exercised or practiced, rather than possessed," Gore (1993, p. 52) raises questions about power as a commodity, as transferrable property. In Gore's (1992) words:

> Theoretically, Foucault's analysis of power raises questions about the possibility of empowering. First, it refutes the idea that one can give power to (can *em*power) another. Thus, to accept a view of one's work as giving power (as property) to others . . . is to overly simplify the operation of power in our society. Given Foucault's conception of power as "circulating," "exercised" and existing "only in action," empowerment cannot mean the giving of power. It could, however, mean the exercise of power in an attempt (that might not be successful) to help others to exercise power. That is, Foucault's analysis of power doesn't preclude purposeful or politically

motivated action; it does point out the rather strong possibility that our purposes might not be attained.

Second, conceiving of power *as exercised* points immediately to the need for empowerment to be context-specific and related to practices. . . . Understanding power as exercised, rather than as possessed, requires more attention to the microdynamics of the operation of power as it is exercised in particular sites. (Foucault cited in Gore, 1992, pp. 58-59)

We believe this interpretation of power and the limitations it spells for empowering others is useful in understanding the precautions that must be taken in attempting to devise ways of enabling teachers and students to interrupt the discursive practices currently embedded in text-based classroom discussions. We also believe there are several ongoing projects in feminist pedagogies for involving teachers and students in class discussions that do not violate Gore's concerns about empowerment. One of these projects is in its fifth year in an urban high school in Philadelphia (Cohen, 1993).

In presenting her project at the AERA symposium on classroom discussion, Cohen (1993) focused on describing how "adolescents constitute their (multiple) identities by trying out different positions in relation to others" (p. 2). However, we also found in the students' talk (excerpted below) several examples of how they exercised their authority as readers. These examples, which bear on Foucault's notion of power being exercised and circulating, are captured in a discussion following the reading of a controversial text.

Cohen (1993) sets the scene for the excerpts and commentaries that follow:[1]

Cohen: *We are in the second year of a school within-a-school program in a urban high school where 90% of the families receive AFDC [Aid to Families of Dependent Children]. One set of English classes has read an article in a news magazine about the alleged rape committed by boxing champion Mike Tyson. A group of young women debate the purpose and merit of this reading in the classroom [during a discussion in which] assumptions about male aggression and female victimization are thrown open. . . . Nina, whose class didn't read the article, questions what is gained by a strategy of taking on serious differences in school.*

Nina: I feel as though [the teacher] shouldn't have talked about Mike Tyson's case because that happened out in the street and if you bring it into school there's gonna be a lot of conflict . . . when we

[1]Reprinted by permission of the publisher from Fine, Michelle, Ed., *Chartering Urban School Reform: Reflections on High Schools in the Midst of Change.* (New York: Teachers College Press, copyright © 1994 by Teachers College, Columbia University. All rights reserved.) " 'Now Everybody Want to Dance': Making Change in a Urban Charter" by Jody Cohen.

was in advisory everybody was arguing—I'm saying this doesn't have nothing to do with school really, to me.

Pam: [The teacher] trying to make us learn comprehension with the article. I think she wants us to think about it, be interested.

Kimberley: She likes us to argue though.

Pam: She don't like us to argue, she like us to learn how to say what we wanna say without arguing.

Kimberley: It's okay to talk about it but not to get into it too much. You know it could start something big, cause we was talking about it in [math] class and it was Lisa—Ms. B. threw her out cause she started getting into a discussion with everybody. Everybody just arguing, everybody not worried about the math work!

Cohen: *When readings invite into the open radically different perspectives on issues young people care about, monolithic, dominant and often unspoken narratives are interrupted. . . . Still, Pam insists on the value of reading this text in school.*

Pam: With our class [the teacher] was asking, Well y'all read the article, how do y'all feel about the article? And the way we did it, she would ask me and if you had a rebuttal you raised your hand. And if you ain't had nothing to say she'll go on and read the next line. She wanted to know what the person wrote on the paper [and] what did you get from what they feel.

Chantelle: And what did people get from that article?

Pam: What the people got was that the article was not about some particular rape; we thought it was about how boxing, how like Mike Tyson he was brought up like, go for what you want and fight for what you believe in.

Cohen: *Making accepted meanings problematic unleashes "unpopular" readings (Britzman, 1992) . . . [and] a set of assumptions about race, gender, sexuality, and aggression are destabilized. (pp. 9-10)*

By entertaining a Discourse of differences, the teacher in the example above made it possible for students to explore multiple perspectives on a text that destabilized and blurred their thinking on aggression and victimization. In doing this, she interrupted counterproductive discourse practices that often serve to silence students in the face of teachers' authoritative voices. She also revealed something of her own epistemology, namely that students can be "knowers" in the fullest sense and that reading the world always precedes reading the word (Freire, 1991).

As Cohen (1993) suggests, discursive practices for making it safe to share multiple readings of a controversial text and to negotiate rather than suppress differences related to the text are rarely found in traditional teacher-centered discussions. "In the talk excerpted here," Cohen notes, "students from different classes [began] to sound like a community reading a text to read itself—asking, Who are we individually and collectively as we read this text, what groups do we belong to, and how can we negotiate meanings with others of same/different affinities?" (p. 11) We submit that the teacher in Cohen's study knew it was not enough to create safe spaces. She also recognized the need for intentional problematizing (in this instance problematizing the circumstances surrounding the Mike Tyson case), for honoring students' voices (Oldfather, 1993), and for really listening to what students say (Newkirk & McLure, 1992; Paley, 1986).

One further observation we have on how students learned from classroom talk in the project just described has to do with Gore's (1992) interpretation of Foucault's thinking on the rhetoric of empowerment. If we read Cohen (1993) correctly, the English teacher who assigned the news magazine article on Mike Tyson did not hold an overly omnipotent view of agency. That is, she did not view herself as empowering students; instead, she created sufficiently safe spaces for students to exercise their own authority as readers. Nina exercised this authority in her pronouncements on the inappropriateness of the text the teacher assigned for class discussion. Pam and others in the class exercised their authority as readers by coming up with a collective reading that could be seen as broadening traditional views on what constitutes male aggression.

Learning About Classroom Talk: Feminist Perspectives on Research.

Ways of interrupting some of the gendered discursive practices that were invisible to us in the past, as we designed and analyzed our own research on text-based classroom discussion, are becoming evident as we continue to read the literature on feminist research. We see a need to interrupt women's tendencies to take care and make nice. In particular, we see ourselves growing in our understanding of the need to critique the power and stereotypical positioning that adversely affect students' participation in classroom discussions. To choose not to critique such abuses is to ensure that the discursive practices embedded (and largely invisible) in our research will go unexamined and unchanged.

Fine (1992) has described activist, feminist research projects as firmly planted in the political and strongly committed to the study of change. In her words:

> Activist research projects seek to unearth, interrupt, and open new frames for intellectual and political theory and change. Researchers critique what seems natural, spin images of what's possible, and engage in questions of how to move from here to there. In such work, researchers are clearly positioned within the domain of a political question or stance, representing a space within which inquiry is pried open, inviting intellectual surprises to flourish. (p. 220)

Drawing on the work of Lather (1986), Fine (1992) has attempted to capture what she describes as "some images of activist scholarship, all of which share three distinctions" (pp. 220-221). One distinction, as suggested earlier, is that feminist researchers are explicit about their political and theoretical stances, even though such stances may be multiple and shifting. A second distinction is that research narratives of activist projects reflect the current social order and are openly ideological inasmuch as "the people who identify and define scientific problems leave their social fingerprints on the problems and their favored solutions to them" (Harding, 1987, p. 184). This is not an unusual state of affairs, for as Neilsen (1993) has noted, we live values first and describe them later. A third distinction is that the texts of these narratives "[unhook] the past, present, and future from traditional, taken-for-granted notions" (Fine, 1992, p. 227).

By pressing us to imagine the possibilities of feminist research, Lather (1990), like Fine, invites us to "begin to understand how we are caught up in power situations of which we are, ourselves, the bearers" (p. 25). This invitation has particular meaning for us in relation to how we plan to design, carry out, and interpret our research on class discussions in the future. No longer willing to collude in reproducing the gendered discursive practices that have dominated our thinking about research in the past, we now recognize the need to put aside claims to neutrality (see Alvermann, 1993) and join in the struggle for what Harding (1987) claims is a necessary condition for generating knowledge claims in a postmodern world:

> [F]eminist politics is not just a tolerable companion of feminist research but a necessary condition for generating less partial and perverse descriptions and explanations. In a socially stratified society, the objectivity of the results of research is increased by political activism by and on behalf of oppressed, exploited and dominated groups. Only through such struggles can we begin to see beneath the appearances created by an unjust social order to the reality of how this social order is in fact constructed and maintained. (p. 127)

SUMMARY

We believe Gee's (1990) two metaphors for Discourses—"identity kits" and "clubs"—work well, for they underscore how our thoughts, actions, words, and beliefs are influenced by normative social practices that eventually (through repetition) become all but invisible to us. When discursive practices embedded in learning from and about texts through discussion become so routine that we never think to question their existence, we tend to perpetuate *givens* and risk forfeiting *possibilities*.

In this chapter we have argued for the need to include such possibilities through opportunities for students to question textual inscriptions that define or relegate women and men to particular gendered positions. We have also argued for revealing through feminist pedagogies and feminist research the asymmetrical power relationships between males and females and between adults and children that serve to perpetuate inequalities in classroom talk about texts. Like Brodkey (1992), we are interested in "devising ways for teachers and students and researchers to 'interrupt' those discursive practices that, for one reason or another, appear counterproductive to teaching and learning" (p. 310). In particular, we are interested in creating spaces for students and teachers to explore and discuss multiple perspectives based on multiple readings of texts. Finally, we have found ourselves agreeing with Fine (1992) that researchers who are committed to feminist inquiry have little choice but to adopt an activist stance in their work. For us, that involves researching classroom discussions in ways that create opportunities to explore and question textual inscriptions of gendered positions.

REFERENCES

Alton-Lee, A., Nuthall, G., & Patrick, J. (1993). Reframing classroom research: A lesson from the private world of children. *Harvard Educational Review 63*, 50-84.

Alvermann, D. E. (1993). Researching the literal: Of muted voices, second texts, and cultural representations. In C. K. Kinzer & D. J. Leu (Eds.), *Examining central issues in literacy research, theory, and practice* (pp. 1-11). Chicago, IL: National Reading Conference.

Alvermann, D. E. (1989). *What it means to be "at risk" of dropping out: Through the eyes of the 11th-grade class in room 102.* Unpublished manuscript, University of Georgia, Athens, GA.

Alvermann, D. E., O'Brien, D. G., & Dillon, D. R. (1990). What teachers do when they say they're having discussions following content reading assignments: A qualitative analysis. *Reading Research Quarterly, 25,* 296-322.

American Association of University Women. (1992). *How schools shortchange girls: the AAUW report: A study of major findings on girls and education.* Washington, DC.

Barnett, M. A. (1986). Sex bias in the helping behavior presented in children's picture books. *The Journal of Genetic Psychology 147,* 343-351.

Beattie, G., Cutler, A., & Pearson, M. (1982). Why is Mrs. Thatcher interrupted so often? *Nature, 300,* 744-747.

Blain, M. (1991). Rhetorical practice in an anti-nuclear weapons campaign. *Peace and change 16,* 355-378.

Britzman, D. (1992). What schools can do: Critical pedagogy in practice. In K. Weiler & C. Mitchell (Eds.), *Decentering discourses in teacher education: Or, the unleashing of unpopular things* (pp. 9-10). Albany, NY: State University of New York Press.

Brodkey, L. (1992). Articulating poststructural theory in research on literacy. In R. Beach, J. L. Green, M. L. Kamil, & T. Shanahan (Eds.), *Multidisciplinary perspectives on literacy research* (pp. 293-318). Urbana, IL: National Conference on Research in English/National Council of Teachers of English.

Cazden, C. B. (1988). *Classroom discourse.* Portsmouth, NH: Heinemann.

Christian-Smith, L. K. (1991). Readers, texts, and contexts: Adolescent romance fiction in schools. In M. W. Apple & L. K. Christian-Smith (Eds.), *The politics of the textbook* (pp. 191-212). New York: Routledge.

Cohen, J. C. (1993, April). *Trashfires and the text: Readings in urban classrooms.* Paper presented at the annual meeting of the American Educational Research Association, Atlanta, GA.

Commeyras, M. (1991). *Dialogical-thinking reading lessons: Promoting critical thinking among "learning-disabled" students.* Unpublished doctoral dissertation, University of Illinois, Champaign-Urbana.

Davies, B. (1993). Beyond dualism and towards multiple subjectivities. In L. K. Christian-Smith (Ed.), *Texts of desire: Essays on fiction, femininity and schooling* (pp. 145-173). London: The Falmer Press.

Davies, B. (1990a). Agency as a form of discursive practice: A classroom scene observed. *British Journal of Sociology of Education, 11,* 341-361

Davies, B. (1990b). The problem of desire. *Social Problems, 37,* 501-516.

Davies, B. (1989). The discursive production of the male/female dualism in school settings. *Oxford Review of Education 15,* 229-241.

Delamont, S. (1983). *Interaction in the classroom* (2nd ed.). London: Methuen.

Fine, M. (1992). Passions, politics, and power: Feminist research possibilities. In M. Fine (Ed.), *Disruptive voices* (pp. 205-231). Ann Arbor: University of Michigan Press.

Fowler, R. (1985). Power. In T. A. Van Dijk (Ed.), *Handbook of discourse analysis* (pp. 61-82). London: Academic Press.

Fox, M. (1993). Men who weep, boys who dance: The gender agenda between the lines in children's literature. *Language Arts. 70*(2), 84-93.

Freire, P. (1991). The importance of the act of reading. In C. Mitchell & K. Weiler (Eds.), *Rewriting literacy: Culture and the discourse of the other* (pp. 139-145). New York: Bergin & Garvey. (Translated by Loretta Slover)

Gee, J. P. (1990). *Social linguistics and literacies: Ideology in discourses.* London: The Falmer Press.

Gilbert, P. (1989). Personally (and passively) yours: Girls, literacy and education. *Oxford Review of Education, 15,* pp. 257-265.

Gilsenan, M. (1989). Word of honour. *Sociological Review Monograph, 36,* 193-221.

Goffman, E. (1971). *Relations in public: Microstudies of the public order.* New York: Harper and Row.

Goodlad, J. I. (1984). *A place called school.* New York: McGraw-Hill.

Gore, J. (1993). *The struggle for pedagogies.* New York: Routledge.

Gore, J. (1992). What we can do for you! What *can* "we" do for "you"?: Struggling over empowerment in critical and feminist pedagogy. In C. Luke & J. Gore (Eds.), *Feminisms and critical pedagogy* (pp. 54-73). New York: Routledge.

Harding, S. (1987). *Feminism and methodology: Social science issues.* Bloomington, IN: Indiana University Press.

Hitchcock, M. E., & Tompkins, G. E. (1987). Are they still sexist? *The Reading Teacher, 41,* 288-292.

LaFrance, M. (1991). School for scandal: Different educational experiences. *Gender and Education, 3*(1), pp. 3-13.

Lather, P. (1990, April). *Staying dumb? Student resistance to liberatory curriculum.* Paper presented at the annual meeting of the American Educational Research Association, Boston, MA.

Lather, P. (1986). Research as praxis. *Harvard Educational Review, 56,* 257-277.

Leaper, C. (1991). Influence and involvement in children's discourse: Age, gender, and partner effects. *Child Development, 62,* 797-811.

Luke, C. (1989). *Pedagogy, printing and protestantism.* Albany, NY: State University of New York Press.

Lusted, D. (1986). "Why pedagogy?" *Screen, 27*(5), 2-14.

MacDonald, S. M. (1989). Sex bias in the representation of male and female characters in children's picture books. *Journal of Genetic Psychology, 150,* 389-401.

Morton, D. E. (1987). The politics of the margin: Theory, pleasure, and the postmodern conference. *American Journal of Semiotics, 5*(1), 95-114.

Mumby, D. K., & Stohl, C. (1991). Power and discourse in organization studies: Absence and the dialectic of control. *Discourses and society, 2*(3), 313-332.

Munsch, R., & Marchenko, M. (1980). *The paper bag princess.* Toronto: Annick Press.

Murray, S. O. (1985). Toward a model of members' methods for recognizing interruptions. *Language and Society, 14,* 31-40.

Neilsen, L. (1993, April). *Women, literacy, and agency: Beyond the master narratives.* Paper presented at the annual meeting of the American Educational Research Association, Atlanta, GA.

Newkirk, T., & McLure, P. (1992). *Listening in.* Portsmouth, NH: Heinemann.

Nicholson, L. J. (Ed.). (1990). *Feminism/postmodernism.* New York: Routledge.

Oldfather, P. (1993). What students say about motivating experiences in a whole language classroom. *The Reading Teacher, 46,* 172-181.

Orr, L. (1991). *A dictionary of critical theory.* New York: Greenwood Press.

Paley, V. G. (1986). On listening to what the children say. *Harvard Educational Review, 56,* 122-131.

Penelope, J. (1988). Interpretive strategies and sex-marked comparative constructions. In A. D. Todd & S. Fisher (Eds.), *Gender and discourse: The power of talk* (pp. 255-275). Norwood, NJ: Ablex.

Power, B. (1979). *I wish Laura's mother was my mommy.* New York: J. B. Lippincott.

Purcell-Gates, V. (1993). Focus on research: Complexity and gender. *Language Arts, 70,* 124-125.

Segal, E. (1986). "As the twig is bent . . .": Gender and childhood reading. In E. A. Flynn & P. P. Schweickart (Eds.), *Gender and reading—Essays on readers, texts, and contexts* (pp. 165-186). Baltimore: The Johns Hopkins University Press.

Silverman, D. & Bloor, M. (1990). Patient-centered medicine: Some sociological observations on its constitution, penetration, and cultural assonance. *Advances in Medical Sociology 1,* 3-25.

Smith, R. (1987). "Process" and educational analysis. *British Journal of Sociology of Education, 8,* 391-405.

CHAPTER ELEVEN

Do Teachers Consider Nonlinear Text to Be Text?

Mark G. Gillingham
Washington State University, Vancouver

Michael F. Young
Jonna M. Kulikowich
University of Connecticut, Storrs

Mechanisms are being devised which allow direct machine-supported references from one textual chunk to another; new interfaces provide the user with the ability to interact directly with these chunks and to establish new relationships between them. These extensions of the traditional text fall under the general category of hypertext *(also known as* nonlinear *text).*

—Conklin (1987, p. 17)

Teachers in the same building with the same years of experience can have different notions about using text in their classrooms. Imagine the following two teachers: Pat is standing before his fourth-grade classroom giving directions to read the next chapter in the science textbook. The following day, Pat gives his students a publisher's test on the text. The next week, after having read other chapters in the textbook, Pat gives the publisher's unit test. Pat's students see no alternative texts on science or any other subject. Another teacher, Patti, is helping a small group of children in her multiage classroom of third- and fourth-graders find a way to determine the amount of pollution in a local stream. The group has several ideas. Patti suggests that the group split up and check their ideas using various textual resources. One child goes to the classroom's bookshelf, another goes to the building's library, a third checks a multimedia encyclopedia on CD-ROM, and the fourth signs onto the Internet to find Environmental Protection Agency documents using *Veronica*—a search system for documents on the Internet. Pat relies solely on a textbook for *the* text while Patti has children reading a variety of textual sources including nonlinear hypermedia and original documents on the Internet. These two teachers have different notions about text and how texts function in educational settings.

In our example, Patti is fluent at using distributed knowledge—knowledge stored "out in the environment" in books, computers, other people, and many varied sources (Pea, 1988). This stored knowledge can be viewed as a literature, a system of interconnected writings, or a web of topically related and interconnected information (Yankelovich, Meyrowitz, & van Dam, 1985). In particular, Patti is encouraging her students to engage these webs of information by using nonlinear hypermedia—what we call here nonlinear text. Perhaps, Patti's notions of nonlinear text, arising from her own experiences, have been instrumental in enabling her to become fluent in using the web of information available in the real world (i.e., in her classroom, school building, and beyond the boundaries of the school).

Nonlinear text is uniquely appropriate to traverse complex webs of ill-defined and complex real-world knowledge (Spiro & Jehng, 1990). Because it can use multiple media, nonlinear text can model the effective coordination of information from various sources. These properties of nonlinear text are properties that lead directly to a different, more constructivist, approach to teaching. We thought that even novice teachers would perceive the uniqueness of nonlinear text and would not judge it to be like other forms of text (e.g., a textbook).

In this chapter we explore the meaning of text from the viewpoints of teachers and text scholars by using a repertory grid analysis to tease out meanings that teachers and text experts give to various types of text. We did so to understand the various ways teachers could view nonlinear text in the context of other textual materials they might use in their environment. We speculate that teachers may not expand their notions of text unless they are willing to see information as distributed more broadly: beyond textbooks, outside their classroom, in multiple media, and including writing as well as reading.

CHARACTERISTICS OF NONLINEAR TEXTS

Notions of text have historically followed the development of technology to read and write texts: Storytelling in preliterate societies gave way to storytelling based on texts held by a special member of the society (e.g., shaman or priest). Scribes' handwriting gave way to printing presses, and finally, to the variety of ways to place text on paper that we have today. New technologies allow texts to be read and written in a variety of electronic ways. Some of these techniques allow readers, rather than authors, to select the order of the text and digressions that are taken. In this chapter, we refer to these texts as nonlinear texts.

Well-structured expository text has an ideal form that many agree upon, but that is seldom complete in extant texts. Well-structured texts have topic sentences that most often appear at the beginning of each paragraph (Meyer, Brandt, & Bluth, 1980). Topics introduced by topic sentences are continued to the close of a paragraph or section (Williams, Taylor, & Ganger, 1981). Cohesion between and among sentences and larger chunks of text are created through lexical and graphical ties (Taylor & Samuels, 1983). Authors of well-structured text take pains to make their text easy to read—at least for those readers who hold a schema for the structure and have sufficient prior knowledge in the domain. For novel text structures (e.g., nonlinear texts), this model would predict that readers would experience difficulty comprehending (e.g., miss the gist or fail to apply appropriate strategies).

Most teachers are not scholars of text and, therefore, do not hold their model of text to the standards of well-structured text. As Anders and Evans (this volume) explain, most teachers think that "text is a compilation of graphic symbols written to convey a message or to entertain." This definition fits well with the teachers most common text, the textbook. Anders and Evans go on to describe expansions of this definition that include any sign system that provides meaning including graphical, musical, and oral systems. This definition could include students editing each others work, the electronic messages and responses of an electronic mail (e-mail) conversation, or a multimedia report of an ecosystem under a rock.

Nonlinear text is not structured in the same way as traditional well-structured text. In fact, a main characteristic of nonlinear text is the "hidden" or "implied" structure that it may contain. We use the term *nonlinear text* to include *hypertext* and *hypermedia*. Hypertext is the way the texts are linked and hypermedia is the apparatus that allows the linkage of texts. As the term implies, nonlinear texts are those that may be read in a variety of orders and paths. Some of the paths may be constrained by the hypermedium (i.e., the equipment and software of the text), depending on how the database of texts, definitions, maps, or other material are linked.

Definitions of Nonlinear Text

There is no single agreed upon definition of nonlinear text, but at the core of all definitions is the linking of textual nodes (Barrett, 1989; Burnett, 1993; Conklin, 1987; Hirmes, 1993; Landow, 1992; Vitali, 1992). When "hypertext" was coined by Ted Nelson, it meant any nonsequential text regardless of medium, but now assumes some form of computer control. This definition of hypertext is close to our definition of nonlinear text. The distinguishing concept that sets nonlinear text apart from other text or media has not been agreed upon. Nonlinear text differs from linear text in its structure or lack of it (Burnett, 1993; Landow, 1992), readers' responsibility to internally construct the text (Barrett, 1989; Landow, 1992), its ability to integrate texts (Vitali, 1992), and its ability to help readers and authors communicate with each other (Barrett, 1989).

Typical definitions of nonlinear text include phrases like "non-sequential writing" (Hirmes, 1993), "electronic linking" (Landow, 1992), "navigational apparatus of links and nodes" (Burnett, 1993), "unstructured exploration" (McLellan, 1992), and "connections" (Vitali, 1992). Most scholars agree that nonlinear text need not be electronic, but usually is, and this electronic form can vary by computing machinery, text, and reader or writer purpose. Linear texts become nonlinear (or "hyper") when they are linked to other texts for some purpose. The "texts" that are linked are sometimes whole and complete manuscripts or volumes, but may be something less than a paragraph (e.g., definition or reference citation) or may be visual or auditory information (e.g., graphic, or movie). Thus, to many, nonlinear text is linking objects that are not text at all.

We will concentrate on five constructs we have identified that clarify the similarities and distinctions between linear and nonlinear text: They are structure, effort, medium, audience, and purpose.

Structure of Nonlinear Texts

The structure of nonlinear text is a function of the web of links to nodes within the bounds of a particular domain or across domains (links to other hypertext documents) and of the various structures of individual nodes themselves. Individual nodes may be all or part of a traditional linear text or be nontextual (e.g., a video clip). For Burnett (1993), the main difference between text and hypertext is its web-like structure: neither linear nor hierarchical. The following describes hypermedia (as have defined nonlinear text) as a mode of information with no structure:

> What distinguishes hypermedia from other modes of information is not that it is computer-driven—after all, the browsing and retrieval mechanisms of Vannevar Bush's Memex were non-electronic—nor that it is interactive, since the entire history of oral communication, whether electronically mediated or not, might be characterized as interactive; nor even that it includes navigational apparatus such as links and nodes, which might better be thought of as symptoms than causes, or buttresses rather than groundwork. What distinguishes hypermedia is that it posits an information structure so dissimilar to any other in human experience that it is difficult to describe as a structure at all. It is nonlinear, and therefore may seem an alien wrapping of language when compared to the historical path written communication has traversed; it is explicitly non-sequential, neither hierarchical nor "rooted" in its organizational structure, and therefore may appear chaotic and entropic. (par. 1)

Burnett sees nonlinear text as an organic form—a rhizome. The rhizome is an extended web where some portions are thin and others thick. The rhizome metaphor fits with a multiplicity of inconsistent nodes that are linked (sometimes multiply, which makes them thick) in nonlinear texts. But because nonlinear text has little structure of its own, the reader must supply the structure—or at least a strategy for navigation. Burnett suggests that the reader is an explorer who is seeking a destination. On the way the explorer travels to familiar, well traveled (thick) nodes and creates paths (links) to new destinations (nodes). Landow (1992) suggests that the nonlinear-text reader must provide entry and exit points that, unlike a topic sentence or topical relatedness in ideal-linear texts, become the focus or topic of the text. The reader, rather than the writer, supplies the topical relatedness of the nonlinear text.

In addition to the internal structure of elements in a particular nonlinear text, various hypertext documents may be linked to cross traditional topic domains. Vitali (1992) suggests that the texts linked in nonlinear text must be *integrated* by whatever hypermedium is used for this purpose. Texts must include previously written literature as well as newly written texts. This virtual space would integrate all of the texts in a domain to one hypermedium or connectivity web. Nonlinearity, according to Vitali, is just a small feature of nonlinear text. Reading a well thought-out linear argument is still very important and should not be interrupted by taking alternate paths. However, when one wants to go deeper or step back, the nonlinear features help to integrate all of the related texts for the reader. In Vitali's description of integrated texts, lack of local structure is minimal because each text has a traditional text structure and even these texts are linked by traditional references. The difference is that the references are available immediately as complete manuscripts, books, and other documents.

Because of the web-like structure of nonlinear texts, they have no organized focus or center to give the reader a familiar structure. It is up to readers to create their own "focus or organizing principle" (Landow, 1992) as they traverse the nonlinear text. Nonlinear text requires a reader with all of the skills needed to read linear text, plus the ability to organize and reorganize the focus of the text.

Unfortunately, this lack of organized focus (structure) can wreak havoc on readers' comprehension. Various studies have reported that readers, especially poor readers, of nonlinear text get confused or lost in the labyrinth of nodes (Gillingham, 1993; Gray & Shasha, 1989; McGrath, 1992). Readers have reported being afraid of getting lost and therefore not pursuing promising links or not using special nonlinear text tools (Gray & Shasha, 1989). In a task of answering three questions by reading a nonlinear text, 37% of the readers scored zero and only 23% received over half of the points allowed (Gillingham, 1993). Those who did poorly on the questions could not adequately form a strategy or could not operate the hypermedium well enough to traverse the nonlinear text. Those who could form a strategy (organizing principle) were rewarded with higher scores. Reasoning that one's ability to create an organizing principle to read a nonlinear text depends in part on spatial ability, McGrath (1992) had high- and low-spatial ability undergraduates read a nonlinear text. "Low Spatial Nonlinear text subjects made the most nonsequential choices—nearly five times as many as High Spatial subjects in the same group" (p. 529). In most cases, making many nonsequential choices does not help organize or focus the nonlinear text. These studies demonstrate the effort required to read structure-poor nonlinear texts.

Effort of Reading Nonlinear Texts

Effort can be viewed as the cognitive energy required to construct meaning from text. In both psychology and literature, it is common to assume that readers spend their effort constructing a personal textbase from the words on the page (or screen). In a sense, this is the reader as compiler, editor, sampler, and writer of the possible texts. Kintsch (1989) described learning from text as an act of construction mediated by the reader's construction of a "textbase" using their declarative knowledge and a "situation model" that integrates pictorial, spatial, and/or episodic knowledge. Personal knowledge and elements of the situation model can act in combination to affect a reader's effort.

Kintsch's model assumes that a reader is actively constructing a textbase while reading, but the bounds of this construction are unclear. How large is the personal textbase of a typical linear text? Should one stop constructing the textbase with the gist of succeeding paragraphs or should it include references to other texts? Should it include whole other works? Any text has a relationship to those texts that have come before, various contemporary texts, and texts that have not been written, but the relationship is typically *implicit* and dependent upon the knowledge and effort of the reader. Nonlinear text can make this intertextuality *explicit* through direct links to sources, references, notes, communications, and other means. For instance, the typical reference notes of a manuscript lead the reader to a citation, but in nonlinear text would lead to the full text of the cited work itself. This linking is common in all definitions of nonlinear text.

Young children probably understand sources, especially multimedia ones, better than they understand scholarly citations. Patti's students (from our initial example) are reaching out to various known media to find information on water pollution. They are neither constrained by academic precedent for scholarly citations nor limited to writing, but are willing to use a variety of media sources including video, drama, and song to make their point (Daiute, 1992). Daiute argues that media are familiar to children and help them to communicate. Although children may not spontaneously cite their sources when writing a traditional report, they would have to in a nonlinear-text environment because linking is citing. To take this idea a step further, children may be more knowledgeable about media structures than traditional text structures. Therefore, even though nonlinear-text structure may be unfamiliar, nonlinear text that includes other media may be more familiar to children than traditional text.

Nonetheless, nonlinear texts may require extra effort for other reasons. For instance, nonlinear texts speak in multiple voices because both authors and audiences may be different from node to node. Multiple voices of multiple texts with little organizing focus make it difficult for readers. It requires effort to understand where one is reading within a connectivity web. Readers may experience confusion and the feeling of being lost. Creators of hypermedia attempt to decrease the effort and confusion while increasing the structure of nonlinear texts through the electronic medium (Conklin, 1987). These same hypermedia innovations allow audiences of nonlinear text to become authors within the nonlinear text. Landow (1992), for instance, sees personal textual construction as a major component in his definition of nonlinear text. Landow's English students may respond to texts in marginal notes, references, even complete other texts. Although this is possible with paper-based texts, a big difference in computer-based nonlinear text is that others may immediately see the newly created text and, in turn, comment on it. Allowing readers of nonlinear text to write back to it is a wonderful innovation, but may make the burden on readers even more effortful.

Medium

Most scholars agree that nonlinear text need not be electronic, but usually is and this electronic form can vary by computing machinery, text, and reader or writer purpose (Burnett, 1993; Conklin, 1987; Landow, 1992). Nonlinear text can be quite elaborate in its use of computer linking, with several texts "open" in computer-screen windows simultaneously, and each linked to hundreds of other electronic sources (Yankelovich, et al, 1985). Such complex instantiations of nonlinear text typically require electronic aids as well. These navigation aids allow a reader to move from one node to another as well as keep their place within the broader "space" of the text (Conklin, 1987). Conklin's (1987) list of advantages of nonlinear text is filled with those that are only possible with a computer (e.g., forward and backward reference tracing, multiple accesses to a text, multiple organizations of texts). Unfortunately, the very fact that nonlinear texts usually require a computer may make the task more effortful for many readers who are uncomfortable with them. In short, while the medium need not be electronic, typically it is and for more complex hypertexts, computer support is nearly always required.

Audience and Purpose

Traditional linear and nonlinear texts have an audience that can be personal and private (as with a personal letter posted to a friend) or public (as the readers of a novel). This sense of audience is important in many text forms (e.g., argument and novel). Unlike linear texts, nonlinear texts allow a reader, as a member of the audience, to become a writer to comembers of the virtual audience by either entering text or making new links among existing linked documents. For Barrett (1989), the links in a nonlinear text are a "communication function" that point to ideas, arguments, and other interpersonal communications. In this framework, nonlinear text is the embodiment of socially constructed knowledge implying a *purpose* of communication to an audience.

> If by text we mean not only words in some rhetorical format, but also *any kind of work*: a discussion of alternatives, the attempt at understanding something, the development of an agenda for a meeting, as well as the drafting of a report. At other times we reconstruct a text for the purpose of changing someone else's understanding of something—in other words, we are asserting control over another's text, deconstructing it in order to recompose it. At the core of all of these different manipulations of text is a *communicative function*, between ourselves and others, or within the private arena of the self. Language is being used to construct meaning, and that meaning is being communicated to others or back to the individual. (p. xiii)

The communicative purpose of nonlinear text is a means of understanding complex ill-structured knowledge domains (Spiro & Jehng, 1990). Barrett's conception of nonlinear text nodes being "any kind of work" is very close to how nonlinear text actually appears in practice. Typical nodes in a nonlinear text are not simply (or simple) texts, but include pictures, phrases, audio, tables, icons, and other forms for multiple public and private purposes.

We have presented nonlinear text as a novel form of text of which teachers may have little knowledge and experience, but do teachers consider nonlinear text to be a form of text? In an attempt to answer this question, we asked teachers and text experts (authors of this book) to generate lists of text types. We used these text types to generate a repertory grid consisting of five text constructs and 10 specific texts, which we showed to a class of inservice teachers.

EXPLORATION OF TEACHERS' BELIEFS ABOUT TEXT

We conducted our study in three steps: We asked teachers to generate lists of text-type elements, we asked authors of this book to generate lists of characteristics of text (text constructs), and then we used this information to create tasks for another group of teachers. The tasks consisted of writing a definition of text, generating a list of text types, and rating triads of text types on five characteristics of text. The triad ratings were analyzed using a repertory grid technique that is described next.

Repertory grid analysis is a technique based on Personal Construct Psychology (Kelly, 1955) and used in a variety of contexts in which constructs are created from individuals interaction with one another or their environment. Dillon and McKnight (1990) used repertory grid analysis to classify the types of texts used in their workplace (a research institute) by asking their colleagues to compare and contrast texts found in their environment. Our analysis is similar: Individuals created personal meaning of characteristics of text (constructs) through comparison with examples of various text types (elements). The text-type comparison entails making decisions about how two text types are similar and contrast with a third on a given characteristic of text. For instance, for the three text types shown in Fig. 11.1, newspapers, advertisements, and fiction; one might judge each text type against the other two on whether its purpose (a characteristic of text) was more to inform or to entertain (see Fig. 11.1). One might reason that the first text type, newspapers, are mostly to inform, but not exclusively since style and comic sections are usually part of a newspaper. Likewise, advertisements are to inform, but must be highly entertaining in order to capture a potential customer's attention. Fiction, on the other hand, is almost exclusively entertaining. On a Likert-type scale of the text characteristic "Purpose," where 1 is the "Inform" pole and 5 is the "Entertain" pole, one might assign 2 to newspapers, 3 to advertisements, and 5 to fiction (see Fig. 11.1). The specific text types provide a context in which one can make comparisons regarding one or more characteristics of text. When multiple characteristics are applied to the same triad of text types, a web of meaning can be developed for the group of characteristics (Lehrer & Franke, 1992).

Typically, one would show subjects text types and have them create their own characteristics of text on which the elements could be compared (e.g., Dillon & McKnight, 1990). An obvious problem with this technique is how to show a nonlinear-text element. We chose to circumvent this problem by designing a computer-based presentation that could show triads of text types and allow subjects to rate characteristics of text pertaining to each triad in a group using a standard paper-based form (Fig. 11.1). To get to this point, we had to develop a list of text types and characteristics of text.

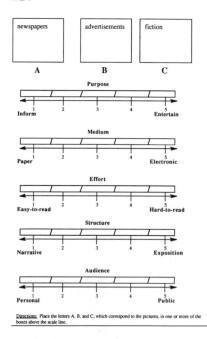

FIG. 11.1. Response form for triad task.

To begin, we asked two groups of teachers (one group in Washington and the other in Connecticut) to generate a list of at least 10 text types with an example of a member of that type for each. For example, for the text type "newspaper" an example is *The Hartford Courant.* We received responses from nine teachers. These responses were used to analyze what teachers thought text was as well as to generate a list of 10 text types for use in a repertory grid analysis. For comparison, we asked the editors of this book to do this task also. Selecting the most frequent text types resulted in a list of 10 text types: manuscript, magazine, newspaper, advertisement, fiction, nonlinear text, personal letter, information, nonfiction, and memo.

Next we asked the authors of this book to create characteristics of text based on these text types grouped in triads. The authors looked for ways that two text types were similar and contrasted with the third. Based on this analysis, the five most common characteristics of text were selected for use in the final repertory grid. By analyzing the examples provided by authors, we chose poles for each construct based on emergent themes. Table 11.1 displays the five characteristics of text and their poles.

Finally, we created stimuli based on ten triads of randomly ordered text types and the five characteristics of text. Each text type was represented by a picture of a collection of like texts (e.g., three newspapers) and a series of pictures of one of the texts (e.g., title, lead story, interior follow-up to lead story, related story, graphic companion to story, and picture related to story). Pictures were taken of the elements using a videocamera (e.g., a

TABLE 11.1
Five Characteristics of Text and Their Poles

Pole A	Construct	Pole B
(Inform)	Purpose	(Entertain)
(Paper)	Medium	(Electronic)
(Easy-to-read)	Effort	(Hard-to-read)
(Narrative)	Structure	(Exposition)
(Personal)	Audience	(Public)

picture of the cover of the *New York Times*). Each picture was digitized and saved as a color-still picture so that specially created software could show the element triads all at once along with a series of pictures depicting a single element. For instance, the opening display included three pictures of text types—one each of newspapers, advertisements, and fiction. Each of these pictures represented the first of a series of examples that were shown to give the viewer an extended representation of the text type.

Our participants were 23 teachers enrolled in an instructional computing course, which was one of their final classes in a 3-year Master's degree program. As part of the course, the participants had access to electronic mail (e-mail) and were required to use it for 2 weeks to discuss a book. The students had seen examples of nonlinear text as a part of their course (e.g., children's books on CD-ROM and computer-controlled videodiscs), but had little experience with them. Given that our participants had relatively more teacher's knowledge than computer-technology knowledge, we wanted to determine if they had a definition of text that included nonlinear text. To observe this, we ask each participant to define text in a "few phrases or sentences." We reasoned that some participants might change their definition after performing the task, so we asked them a similar question following the task. We also asked them to "describe any changes you think you have made in the definition." This question was asked in order to determine participants' metacognitive knowledge about a possible change in their definition of text.

Because we selected the text types used in the task a priori, we wanted to know if participants would generate similar lists of text elements as did our sample teachers and book editors. We asked each participant to list "five examples of text." To determine if participants had modified their conception of text because of the task, we asked this question following the task also.

Treatment of Data

Data were in written form for the *text-definition* and *text-type* tasks and a numeric vector (distance from the pole of a scale) for the *triad* task. For the text-definition task, responses were recorded verbatim. These responses were analyzed to extract idea units, which were sorted alphabetically and analyzed for change from before to after the triad task. Any mention of changing one's answer was also noted.

The text-type task asked participants to list five types of text and an example of each. Responses for the text-type task were compared with the text types used in the triad task to determine their similarity. We employed a scoring scheme that added a point when an item in a participant's list matched a triad-task text type and subtracted a point when no match occurred. For instance, if a participant's list were; newspaper, letters, fiction, memos, and photographs; then 4 items would match with the text-types used in the triad task and 1 would not (i.e., photographs), which would lead to a match-minus-mismatch score of 3 (i.e., 4 matches − 1 mismatch = 3). Each participant received a pre- and posttext type score (before and after the triad task) that could range from 0 to 5.

Participants rated triads of elements using a Likert-type scale (from 1 to 5) for each of the five constructs (Fig. 11.1 is a sample response sheet). These data were arranged in a grid with five rows corresponding to each characteristic of text and 10 columns corresponding to each text-element triad. This grid can be analyzed for various patterns, which are represented as distances among elements in the grid. Because of the small number of participants (22 completed the triad task) and large number of ratings each would give ($n =$ 150), we chose to analyze the proximity grid using multidimensional scaling techniques (du Toit, Steyn, & Stumpf, 1986; McDonald, 1985). Multidimensional scaling serves as a convenient graphical description of patterns in a grid and a summary of the grid data (Tversky & Gati, 1982).

Because we chose the characteristics of text and the text types a priori, which is not standard for repertory-grid analyses, it was important to test that our participants' personal constructions of characteristics of text were similar to those of our samples from teachers, authors, and editors. The results demonstrated that the participants' constructions of characteristics of text matched the a priori ones well. Low stress values between .05 and .11 indicated that the proximity solutions for characteristics of text were not far from perfect (Olson & Biolsi, 1991). High *R-square* values between .94 and .96 indicated that the proximity solutions for characteristics of text explained much of the variance (du Toit et al., 1986). In addition, proximity solutions for characteristics of text were resolved in a small number of dimensions. For four of the five characteristics, text types were best depicted in two-dimensions. Only the text types of audience were depicted better in three dimensions. For each characteristic of text, one dimension appeared to represent the text types as specified by our text experts (e.g., the text types used in the triad task). For instance, near one pole of the characteristic purpose were fiction, magazine, and nonlinear text and near the far pole were informational book, nonfiction, manuscript, newspaper, and memo. These data have a good fit to the poles of entertain and inform from the triad task.

Making meaning of second or third dimensions was relatively more speculative. Fewer instances of relatively large positive or negative values of text-type distances were found. For instance, the characteristic "purpose" had a second dimension with personal letter being far from nonlinear text. If one relaxed the strict requirement of distance, other text types that were close to personal letter were magazine, advertisement, and memo. and to nonlinear text were informational book and nonfiction. It is not too much of a speculation to imagine that this dimension describes relatively short texts (e.g., personal letter) versus longer texts (e.g., nonfiction). This solution is adequate, but not perfect, because participants saw fiction as being neither short nor long rather than relatively long. One may consider that even short stories are relatively longer than advertisements or personal letters.

We concluded that the strong first dimension of each of the characteristics of text was important and adequate to allow us to view individual participant's clusters of text types on each of these characteristics. The second and third dimensions of each characteristic of text were less interpretable than the first dimension. In the section that follows, we describe the results of the text-definition task, text-type task, and triad task.

WHAT TEACHERS BELIEVE

Teachers' Definitions of Text

Our participants were asked to define text before and after the triad task. We expected a variety of responses including those definitions that were tied to their classroom uses of textbooks, but we were mostly interested in whether they would consider nonlinear text as a form of text and whether the triad task would help to change any definitions in the direction of nonlinear text.

In general, out participants defined text as teachers might; concentrating on practical classroom features of text. Nearly all participants mentioned that text had a communication function (e.g., written language or symbols to communicate thoughts) and could take a variety of forms and purposes (e.g., exposition, procedure, entertainment). Of the 23 participants, 13 changed their definition after the triad task. Eight participants mentioned that text might be electronic or conveyed by various media. Most of these ($n = 5$) mentioned this after the triad task. For instance, Participant 5 thought that text might include nonlinear text before the text task: Text "can be linear (like a book) or nonlinear (like a computer)." Other participants expanded their notion of text after the triad task. Before the triad task, Participant 6 reflected the "teacher notion of text" described by Anders and Evans (this volume): "Text can be the written portion of an assignment, paper, book, etc. It carries meaning via words." After the triad task,

Participant 6 expanded the definition to: "Just about any medium for conveying an idea be it informational or entertaining, personal or private, electronic or paper, easy or difficult to read, narrative or exposition. Can contain both words, pictures . . . and maybe sound???" This expansion of the notion of text is in keeping with newer definitions of text (e.g., Barrett, 1989; Landow, 1992). Participant 1 appeared to have a grasp of the multimedia nature of text even before the text task. Participant 1 explained that "the printed material does not necessarily mean printed on paper—it includes anything that can be read or interpreted and meaning drawn from it. I would include some art forms in this." After the triad task, this participant added; "Still any medium (better word) that conveys an author's intent." Our participants seemed to have a conventional and practical definition of text that served them well in their classrooms. Few of them included nonlinear text, alternative media, or multimedia in either their initial or final definitions.

We were also interested in whether or not participants' text types were similar to those chosen for the triad task so we asked them to generate a list of five examples of text both before and after the triad task. The 10 elements generated for the triad task were: informational books, nonfiction, memos, fiction, nonlinear text, personal letters, magazines, newspapers, advertisements, and manuscripts. In analyzing the text types generated by our participants for matches, we had to make decisions about synonyms for category membership. We decided that textbooks would count as "nonfiction," resource books would count as "informational books," and computer messages would count as "personal letters." Before the triad task, participants generated on average 3.29 matches, 1.52 mismatches for a hits-minus-misses score of 1.95. After the triad task, there were 3.37 matches and 0.89 misses for a score of 2.47. The increase in the hits-minus-misses score was 0.52. Most of the participants generated text types similar to the ones that our experts did. Sixteen of 21 participants had 3 or more matches before and after the triad task. Most of the participants also generated a text type or two that was different from our list. Seventeen of 21 participants had 1 or more mismatches, but only 4 had more than 2 mismatches before the triad task. After the triad task, 13 participants had 1 or more mismatches and none had more than 2 mismatches. These data give credibility to the text types used in the triad task because a majority of them were also chosen by our participants. These data also show that the triad task helped to shape the participants' responses in favor of the text types used in the triad task.

Teachers' Notions of Nonlinear Text as Seen by Repertory Grid Analysis

The triad task is described in terms of how each individual constructed relationships among the characteristics of text and text types with special emphasis on the place of nonlinear text in those relationships. These relationships can be depicted graphically through hierarchical clustering analyses based on a grid data with five rows representing each characteristic of text and 10 columns representing each text-type triad (Olson & Biolsi, 1991). A grid for each participant was analyzed using Johnson hierarchical clustering (Johnson, 1967), which is an algorithm that creates a hierarchical representation of the elements (Olson & Biolsi, 1991). The results of these cluster analyses can be depicted using tree diagrams that portray the history of the joining of the various elements and their clusters. Clusters may combine with previously constructed clusters during this process until all clusters and elements have been combined. Figure 11.2 shows a tree diagram that represents a cluster analysis of one individual. Longer horizontal lines in the tree represent text types that joined another text type or cluster of text types later in the process. Text types that are near each other were seen as relatively similar by the individual.

Students' notions of the text types were best described by one, two, or three main clusters. As shown in Table 11.2, of 22 participants 2 had a one-cluster solution, 15 had a two-cluster solution, and 5 had a three-cluster solution. The number of clusters was determined by inspecting the size of eigenvalues (i.e., explained variance) associated with each cluster using a cut-off value of 1.00. Our analyses showed cumulative proportions of variance that ranged from 62% to 93%. Notice in Table 11.2 that the two participants with the least *R-square* values had one-cluster solutions. Participant 10 had a reduced data grid because of several errors responding to the triad task. Participant 19 did not differentiate text-types in a typical manner. For instance, manuscript and magazine are clustered together.

Nonlinear text is seen by most of the participants as being much different than other text types. Table 11.2 shows the 16 participants (marked with an asterisk) who clustered nonlinear text relatively late in the procedure. Of

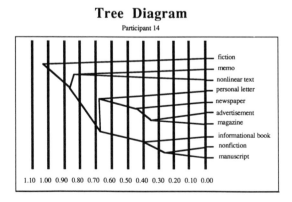

Tree Diagram

Participant 14

1.10 1.00 0.90 0.80 0.70 0.60 0.50 0.40 0.30 0.20 0.10 0.00

FIG. 11.2. Additive tree of Participant 14 depicting three clusters and nonlinear text entering the clustering late in the process.

TABLE 11.2
Proportion of Variance Explained by Clusters Sorted by Increasing Number of Clusters

Participant	No. of Clusters	Proportion of Variance Explained by Clusters
10	1	.72*
19	1	.62*
1	2	.78*
2	2	.86*
5	2	.89*
6	2	.92
7	2	.84*
8	2	.86*
9	2	.82*
11	2	.85*
12	2	.91*
13	2	.93*
16	2	.85*
17	2	.80
20	2	.74
21	2	.88
23	2	.87
3	3	.92*
4	3	.92*
14	3	.87*
15	3	.89
29	3	.93*

Note. Asterisks denote where nonlinear text entered the procedure late.

these 16 cases, nonlinear text was alone (e.g., not clustered with any other text type) 9 times and clustered with memo 6 times. Figure 11.2 displays a representative tree diagram of this most common pattern. Based on this tree diagram, one can see that Participant 14 has constructed three main clusters of text types. For instance, nonlinear text (clustered together with memo and fiction) is viewed as being different from newspaper (clustered together with magazine, advertisement, and personal letter). Figure 11.2 also suggests that nonlinear text is not closely linked to most of the other text types as can be seen by the length of the lines before nonlinear text is joined to other clusters. If one asked the participants about nonlinear text, a majority might say; "Nonlinear text is different, but we are not sure how."

WHAT DOES THIS TELL US ABOUT TEACHERS AND TEXT?

We set out to determine teachers' notions of nonlinear text—whether teachers distinguish nonlinear text among texts in their environment. Nonlinear text represents a web of connected knowledge similar to the distributed knowledge that Patti's students are using from our initial example. Teachers who see texts as woven throughout their environment and existing in a variety of media may be better able to direct students to the web of connected knowledge in the world. We discovered that teachers have a common-sense definition of text that does not include many formal components and that they see nonlinear text as something different from other texts.

The teachers who participated in this study viewed text as a "compilation of graphic symbols written to convey a message or to entertain" (Anders & Evans, this volume). In the words of our participants, text was defined as: "script or pictorial which describes language," "group of words put together for the purpose of informing or entertain," "symbols that represent thoughts," and "words, symbols, some representation of language communicated for info., enjoyment, etc." None of the participants mentioned topical related-ness, superordination, or cohesion—ideal qualities of text thought important by those who study text. Most participants thought text is on paper. Only two before our triad task and eight following thought text could be electronic or nonlinear. Also, the notion the participants held was something less than a "web of connectivity." Five participants did mention electronic mail as an example of text, a form of communication used in the class they were attending. Although one participant mentioned nonlinear text by name, it was not clear how embellished the concept was.

Data from the repertory grid analyses corroborated the participants' written text definitions and text examples—participants did not think nonlinear text was like other texts. In the cluster analyses, nonlinear text generally entered a cluster late, which signifies that it is unlike the text elements entering earlier in the procedure. Although the repertory grid analyses could not tell us what the participants thought nonlinear text was, the written data leave us with the impression that not much was known about it and that the triad task did not add much information to their limited knowledge. Only a few participants changed their text definitions or text examples based on the triad task. Our small dose of text types was not enough to change many participants' notions of text. This is essentially an issue of transfer, which is often difficult or impossible to observe (Detterman & Sternberg, 1993). We believe that teachers who gain some knowledge of and experience with nonlinear text, will be cued to the distributed sources of knowledge that such texts embody. This is similar to Spiro and Jehng's (1990) "Cognitive Flexibility Theory" in which they contend readers of nonlinear text are cued to the cognitive strategies (flexibility) required to navigate and learn from such a text. However, since teachers have such a practical definition of texts in general, it will not be easy for them to transfer their notions of traditional texts to include nonlinear text. They may have very little worth transferring in their common-sense definitions of text. We speculate that it would take a teacher like Patti, who is open to various knowledge sources and who has access to various nonlinear texts before changes in notions of text would occur.

We have other questions regarding how the constructs of text generated for this study affect readers of nonlinear text. We assume that the lack of structure inherent in nonlinear text will make it difficult for most readers to find a focus within the nonlinear text. However, we wonder if the multimedia nature of nonlinear text might offset some of this difficulty, especially with young media-smart readers. We also wonder if increased effort in the form of writing to nonlinear text might lead to better readers of and thinkers with nonlinear text. Would the act of making links to nodes through the hypermedium improve associative thinking in other distributed-knowledge contexts like classrooms? Is this link causal; that is, can we expand teachers use of distributed knowledge by expanding their notions of nonlinear text? In addition, might readers and writers of nonlinear text improve their sense of audience and author through the multiple exposures in the text? Finally, if nonlinear text became a common form, would its purpose for knowledge storage and creation take a prominent place in classrooms? If so, students' reports, essays, and journals could have common links, which could, when reinspected, help writers reorganize their knowledge and help readers create knowledge. The social context of knowledge creation in a classroom could have a nonlinear-text repository; always accessible by teachers and students for reading, writing, and arranging other media. But for teachers like Pat, this would be a long step outside of the comfort zone of the familiar textbook.

REFERENCES

Barrett, E. (1989). Introduction: Thought and language in a virtual environment. In E. Barrett, *The society of text* (p. xiii). Cambridge, MA: MIT Press.

Burnett, K. (1993, January). Toward a theory of hypertextual design. *The Arachnet Electronic Journal of Virtual Culture, 3*(2). (Available by anonymous ftp to byrd.mu.wvnet.edu, cd /pub/ejvc, get BURNETT V1N2)

Conklin, J. (1987). Hypertext: An introduction and survey. *Computer, 20*(9), 17-41.

Daiute, C. (1992). Multimedia composing: Extending the resources of kindergarten to writers across the grades. *Language Arts, 69,* 250-260.

Detterman, D. K., & Sternberg, R. J. (1993). *Transfer on trial: Intelligence, cognition, and instruction.* Norwood, NJ: Ablex.

Dillon, A., & McKnight, C. (1990). Towards a classification of text types: A repertory grid approach. *International Journal of Man-Machine Studies, 33,* 623-636.

du Toit, S. H. C., Steyn, A. G. W., & Stumpf, R. H. (1986). *Graphical exploratory data analysis.* New York: Springer-Verlag.

Gillingham, M. G. (1993). Effects of question complexity and reader strategies on adults' hypertext comprehension. *Journal of Research on Computing in Education, 26,* 1–15.

Gray, S. H., & Shasha, D. (1989). To link or not to link? Empirical guidance for the design of nonlinear text systems. *Behavioral Research Methods, Instruments and Computers, 21,* 326-333.

Hirmes, D. (1993, January). Frequently asked questions (FAQ) file for alt.hypertext (version 0.9). (Available from Gopher searching on the keyword "hypertext")

Johnson, S. C. (1967). Hierarchical clustering schemes. *Psychometrika, 32,* 241-254.

Kelly, G. A. (1955). *The psychology of personal constructs* (Vol. 1). New York: W. W. Norton.

Kintsch, W. (1989). Learning from text. In L. B. Resnick (Ed.), *Knowing, learning, and Instruction: Essays in honor of Robert Glaser* (pp. 25-46.). Hillsdale, NJ: Lawrence Erlbaum Associates.

Landow, G. P. (1992). *Hypertext: The convergence of contemporary critical theory and technology.* Baltimore, MD: Johns Hopkins University Press.

Lehrer, R., & Franke, M. L. (1992). Applying personal construct psychology to the study of teachers' knowledge of fractions. *Journal for Research in Mathematics Education, 23*, 223-241.

McDonald, R. P. (1985). *Factor analysis and related methods.* Hillsdale, NJ: Lawrence Erlbaum Associates.

McGrath, D. (1992). Hypertext, CAI, paper, or program control: Do learners benefit from choices? *Journal of Research on Computing in Education, 24*(4), 513-532.

McLellan, H. (1992). Hyper stories: Some guidelines for instructional designers. *Journal of Research on Computing in Education, 25*, 28-49.

Meyer, B. J. G., Brandt, D. M., & Bluth, G. J. (1980). Use of top-level structure in text: Key for reading comprehension of ninth-grade students. *Reading Research Quarterly, 16*, 72-103.

Olson, J. R., & Biolsi, K. J. (1991). Techniques for representing expert knowledge. In K. A. Ericsson & J. Smith (Eds.), *Toward a general theory of expertise: Prospects and limits* (pp. 240-285). Cambridge, England: Cambridge University Press.

Pea, R. D. (1988, August). *Distributed intelligence in learning and reasoning processes.* Paper presented at the meeting of the Cognitive Science Society, Montreal.

Spiro, R. J., & Jehng, J. (1990). Cognitive flexibility and hypertext: Theory and technology for the nonlinear and multidimensional traversal of complex subject matter. In D. Nix & R. Spiro (Eds.), *Cognition, education, multimedia: Exploring ideas in high technology* (pp. 163-205). Hillsdale, NJ: Lawrence Erlbaum Associates.

Taylor, B. M., & Samuels, S. J. (1983). Children's use of text structure in the recall of expository material. *American Educational Research Journal, 20*, 517-528.

Tversky, A., & Gati, I. (1982). Similarity, separability, and the triangle inequality. *Psychological Review, 89*, 123-154.

Vitali, F. (1992). Response to Vaninni and Spinelli. *Links Forum, 1*(4). (Available from listserver Links at Pascal.ACM.Org).

Williams, J. P., Taylor, M. B., & Ganger, S. (1981). Text variations at the level of the individual sentence and the comprehension of simple expository paragraphs. *Journal of Educational Psychology, 73*, 851-865.

Yankelovich, N., Meyrowitz, N., & van Dam, A. (1985). Reading and writing the electronic book. *Computer, 18*(10), 15-29.

PART THREE

ISSUES IN RESEARCH ON BELIEFS ABOUT TEXT

CHAPTER TWELVE

Adults' Views About Knowing and Believing

Patricia A. Alexander
Texas A&M University, College Station

Filip J. R. C. Dochy
Open University, Heerlen, Netherlands

> *The beginning of philosophy is to know the condition of one's own mind.*
>
> —Epictetus (1st century AD)

Since the time of Plato and Aristotle, from Spinoza to Kant, philosophers have wrestled with the boundaries between knowledge and beliefs. What does it mean when we say that something is *known* or *believed?* How do evidence and certainty relate to *knowing* and *believing?* How is *true* knowledge distinguished from *mere* beliefs? What separates strongly held from weakly held beliefs? Such provocative epistemological questions have long troubled the greatest philosophical minds. Despite the centuries of contemplation, however, philosophers have left the puzzle of the relationship between knowledge and beliefs unresolved.

There are those epistemologists who would say that knowledge signifies complete conviction, whereas beliefs are guarded or tentative assertions:

> . . . in common language, when beliefs and knowledge are distinguished, knowledge is understood to mean complete conviction, belief a conviction somewhat short of complete. Mills (1865/1979, p. 63)

Reciprocally, there are those who endow beliefs, rather than knowledge, with the power of certainty or assurance (Laird, 1972).

Beyond the attributes of *conviction* or *assurance*, other terms are commonly used in philosophical literature to distinguish knowing from believing, among them *truth, objectivity,* and *detachment* (e.g., Frye, 1967; Goldman, 1986; Thagard, 1991). Further, there are those philosophers, like Dewey, who consider beliefs to be dimensions of knowing. Just as there are those, like Kierkegaard and Sartre, who would argue that believing *is* knowing. For instance, in his treatise on *How We Think,* Dewey (1910), in the tradition of William James, characterized beliefs as hypotheses to be acted upon and knowledge as the product or articulation of the inquiry process. For one to move from the state of belief to the state of knowing requires the intermediate state of *doubt,* that is, a questioning of the pragmatic value (i.e., *truth*) of one's beliefs.

Regardless of the outcome of the on going debate, it is evident that the relationship between knowledge and beliefs has occupied the minds of philosophers both past and present. It is further apparent that within the community of philosophers neither *knowledge* nor *beliefs* is univocal. Each term evokes a cadre of meanings; meanings that are at times oppositional and conflicting.

Yet, thoughts about knowledge and beliefs are not the exclusive domain of renowned philosophers. All adults, we would argue, operate under, at least, tacit understandings when they elect the words *knowledge* or *beliefs* to communicate their ideas or intentions to others. Outside the realm of philosophy, it is likely that particular communities of adults (e.g., under-graduates or educational researchers) share certain views of knowing and believing, views that arise from similar cultural or social backgrounds or educational experiences. Our goal in this chapter is to raise these often tacit conceptions to more explicit levels so that they can be surveyed and scrutinized.

Of course, not all views on knowledge and beliefs are unconscious or implied. For instance, we were encouraged to find that Chinn and Brewer (1993), in their review on responses to anomalous data, articulated their stance in the knowledge and beliefs debate. As they stated:

> In philosophy, the term *knowledge* has traditionally been taken to be justified true belief. However, we will use the word in a more general way to refer to the total set of beliefs held by an individual. We use the term *belief* to refer to any piece of knowledge with the knowledge base. (p. 39)

Still, few researchers, even those engaging in the study of knowledge and beliefs, provide us with such clear statements as to their perspective in this knowledge/beliefs dialectic.

It should be noted that we have no desire to offer a philosophical treatise on the relationship of knowledge and beliefs in this chapter or to review the relevant psychological literature. Our interests lie in the views of adults who, though well educated, would not be called authorities in epistemology.

As with Olson and Astington (1993), we value the words that these individuals select when they make their views public on complex constructs, like knowing and believing. We hold that such words are critical markers of the implicit theories that guide individuals' interactions with the world.

Specifically, we collected the thoughts of university students and faculty on their personal interpretations of the terms *knowledge* and *beliefs*. We also sought the opinions of educational researchers who have engaged in the study of either construct. We hoped that having these communities of adults share their thoughts on knowing and believing would allow us to explore the conceptual boundaries that they traverse in their informal or formal communications with others.

It was important to us, as contributors to a volume on beliefs, to have some guiding notions about what students, educators, and educational researchers mean when they speak about knowing and believing. Certainly, educational researchers, ourselves included, have investigated the enigmatic nature of knowledge and beliefs. Studies, for example, have shown that beliefs influence researchers' areas of inquiry, methodologies, and interpretations (e.g., Alexander & Judy, 1988; Dole & Sinatra, this volume), and that students' beliefs impact their learning activities and learning outcomes (e.g., Araudin & Mintzes, 1985; Clements, 1986; Marton, 1988; Palmer & Goetz, 1988). Few researchers, however, have explored the conceptual boundaries between these two fundamental constructs—the goal of this endeavor.

In the sections that follow, we first present the perspectives on knowing and believing that have guided our own research. As with Chinn and Brewer (1993), we feel that it is important to make our personal view of the relationship between knowledge and beliefs public so that its potential influence on the outcome of our study can be judged more readily. Next, we offer our summary of how the adults we surveyed articulated their notions of *knowledge* and *beliefs*. Finally, we consider the implications of these perspectives for future research and practice.

PERSONAL PERSPECTIVES ON THE RELATIONSHIP

Over the past several years, we have undertaken the study of prior knowledge in an attempt to map its various forms and types (Alexander, 1992; Alexander, Schallert, & Hare, 1991; Dochy, 1992; Dochy & Alexander, 1993) and to understand how domain-specific knowledge interacts with certain motivational and situational factors (Alexander, Jetton, & Kulikowich, 1993; Alexander & Judy, 1988; Alexander, Kulikowich, & Jetton, in press; Dochy, 1993). In the process of generating these conceptual maps and exploring various interactions, we have positioned ourselves with regard to the relationship of knowledge and beliefs. First, we have defined knowledge as the internalization of *all* one's experiences. Those experiences can be known both explicitly and tacitly. Further, that knowledge, in our judgment, can be both accurate (in terms of common convention or accepted wisdom) or inaccurate (as in the case of misconceptions). Consequently, for us, truthfulness and authenticity are not attributes that distinguish knowing from believing. "Knowledge encompasses all that a person knows or believes to be true, whether or not it is verified as true in some sort of objective or external way" (Alexander et al., 1991, p. 371).

Our mappings of prior knowledge recognize the incorporation of beliefs in other ways as well. First, beliefs are addressed within the component of metacognitive knowledge. (Flavell, 1987; Garner, 1987), and more specifically within its subcomponent, self-knowledge. Self-knowledge, according to Flavell (1987), entails all individuals' understandings or interpretations about themselves as learners and thinkers. It involves the plans and goals these individuals have internalized, as well as their needs, as influenced by affective understandings about themselves. Finally, our mappings of prior knowledge consider the individuals' beliefs and attitudes within the dimension of sociocultural knowledge (Alexander et al., 1991). This knowledge, operates as a filter through which all new experiences and information are shaded and interpreted.

Thus, on the basis of these aspects of our research, we would subsume beliefs within the all-encompassing construct of knowledge, since it would be impossible to believe anything that was not experienced and, therefore, not "known." As cognitive researchers, it is not surprising that we distinguish between knowledge or beliefs. Neither is it startling that our orientation in these activities stress the state of knowing over believing. According to Dole and Sinatra (this volume) and Anders and Evans (this volume), terms such as *knowledge* and *beliefs* are treated differently within the research community depending on one's theoretical orientation. As cognitive researchers, the nature and acquisition of knowledge has been a primary agenda—one that has situated beliefs in a more subordinate role. Fortunately, our examination of knowledge and beliefs included responses of researchers whose theoretical orientations are varied from our own, thus, offering us a diversity of perspectives.

EXTERNALIZING ADULTS' PERSPECTIVES: METHODOLOGICAL ISSUES

Respondents

In order to build a rich picture of adults' views of knowing and believing, we tapped the understandings of individuals with varied educational experiences who were differentially dedicated to the study of *knowledge* and *beliefs*. To be more specific, our sample consisted of 54 adults whose general education, experiences, and fields of study placed them in one of three educational communities. The first community included 18 undergraduate students from a large Southwestern university. These were all honor students enrolled in an honors section of introductory educational psychology taught by the first author. Our purpose in choosing this sample was to identify a community of well-educated and articulate young adults whose perspectives on knowing and believing had not been influenced by formal study in knowledge or beliefs.

Our second community of adults consisted of 21 graduate students and faculty members in educational psychology, many of whom were from the same institution as the undergraduates. The specializations of these graduate students and faculty ranged from tests and measurement and human learning/development to counseling psychology and school psychology. We took care to exclude any individuals who, according to their self-reports, had formally studied or researched knowledge or beliefs. Thus, our goal in identifying this second community was to locate adults with more education and more experience than the undergraduates, but who, like the undergraduates, did not possess any expertise in the areas of knowledge or beliefs.

Our final community of adults was composed of 15 educational researchers expressly engaged in the study of knowledge or beliefs (many of whom are contributors to this volume). As with the first author, a number of these researchers come from the field of text processing and have merged their interests in texts with the study of knowledge or beliefs. Further, these researchers operate from varied theoretical stances, including social cognition, information-processing theory, and social psychology. Thus, while the members of this community had much in common with those in the graduate student/faculty group, they differed in terms of their personal investment in the topics under study in this chapter—knowing and believing.

Experimental Task and Procedure

As a means of externalizing these individuals' personal theories about knowing and believing, we asked them to complete an experimental task. By *theory*, we mean one's way of seeing and interacting with the world. The first step of the task asked respondents to select from among various representations depicting possible relationships between knowledge and beliefs or allowed them to draw their own alternative. We developed these representations, shown in Fig. 12.1, from our examination of the literature. Therefore, one representation exemplifies the complete separation of knowledge and beliefs (#1), while another characterizes their complete infusion (#4). Representation #2, by contrast, subsumes knowledge within the construct of beliefs, whereas beliefs are subsumed within knowledge in

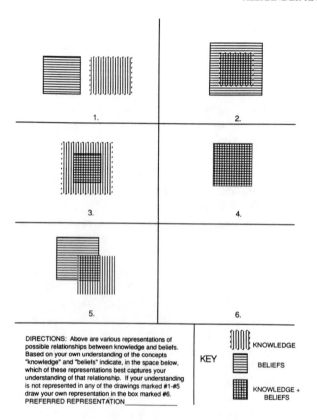

FIG. 12.1. Representations of various relationships between knowledge and beliefs.

Representation #3. In Representation #5, knowledge and beliefs are portrayed as overlapping with dimensions of each existing beyond the influence of the other. Finally, in the remaining space (#6), our respondents were allowed to present their own interpretation of the relationship between knowledge and beliefs. Whether they selected or generated a representation, we stressed to them that they should draw upon their own understanding of the concepts of *knowledge* and *beliefs*.

We followed this graphic task with a series of questions that elaborated upon each adult's selection. We first asked our respondents to define the terms *knowledge* and *beliefs*. Next, we asked them why their representation of the relationship between knowledge and beliefs was the best choice. In other words, we wanted them to defend their particular selection. In addition to defending their decision, we asked these adults to provide us with an example from their own experiences that supported their chosen representation. Lastly, we wanted to know if these adults felt that beliefs were changeable and, if so, under what conditions were such changes likely to occur. We explored these resulting data by examining descriptive statistics for all adults and for each of the three community of respondents. We also engaged in content analysis of the adults' responses in order to identifying emerging patterns that were suggested by the ideas that were shared.

HOW ADULTS TALK ABOUT KNOWING AND BELIEVING

To make sense of adults' views about knowing and believing, we explore responses to each question of our experimental task in turn. We first offer general observations gleaned from these responses, so as to build an overall framework for subsequent discussion. We then compare and contrast the responses given by the three communities of adults within our sample, so that potential influences of education, experience, and expertise can be better understood.

Selecting a Preferred Representation

With few exceptions, our respondents chose their representation of the relationship between knowledge and beliefs from among our five options. Of our 54 subjects, only 9% (5) elected to generate their own representation. We include several of these depictions in Fig. 12.2.

As seen in Fig. 12.2, dynamism was a characteristic that epitomized these creations. The stated goal of our respondents, who expressed concern for the static nature of our given representations, was to capture the fluid character of the relationship between knowledge and beliefs. Consider the comments of the graduate student who produced Fig. 12.2a:

> The diagram I constructed to portray the relationship between beliefs and knowledge is by far the best representation because it is the only model that depicts a dynamic rather than a static relationship. Knowledge and beliefs are not separate entities (figure 1), nor are they overlapping entities (figure 2-5). The relationship between beliefs and knowledge is one of interaction. To put it simply, the knowledge an individual holds is directly influenced by an individual's belief network and in turn, one's beliefs network is influenced by the knowledge one holds and acquires. The only way to depict such a model is through reciprocal movement from one entity to the other, as in the diagram I constructed.

In addition, as exemplified in Fig. 12.2b, several of the respondents wanted to interject a developmental dimension into the relationship. Again, to some of these adults, the changing nature of the relationship between knowledge and beliefs was not satisfactorily portrayed in the five options given them.

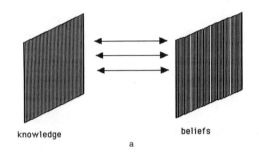

knowledge   beliefs

a

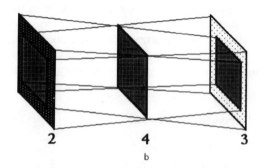

2   4   3

b

KNOWLEDGE/BELIEFS
I BELIEVE IT ALL STARTS WITH KNOWLEDGE

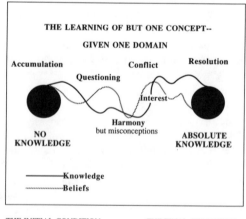

THE LEARNING OF BUT ONE CONCEPT--

GIVEN ONE DOMAIN

Accumulation   Conflict   Resolution

Questioning

Interest

Harmony
but misconceptions

NO
KNOWLEDGE   ABSOLUTE
                           KNOWLEDGE

———Knowledge
·············Beliefs

THE INITIAL CONDITION   THE FINAL CONDITION
IS "TRUTH"   IS "TRUTH"

FIG. 12.2. Samples (2a-2c) of representations generated by adults in the study.

Finally, a common aspect of several of these generated representations was their inclusion of additional forces acting upon the relationship of knowledge and beliefs (see Fig. 12.2c). To these individuals, the relationship between knowledge and beliefs could not be understood without the intervening influence of other factors, such as *questioning*—a variable possibly related to Dewey's intermediate state of *doubt*.

As it pertains to the given options, Representation #5 was clearly the favored choice of the respondents. Fifty-two percent of our subjects picked this particular representation. This suggests that the majority of the adults held that knowledge and beliefs interacted, although both could exist independent of the other. Nineteen percent of the respondents opted for Representation #3. Like the authors, these individuals apparently held to the view that beliefs are part of the overarching construct of knowledge. Almost as popular as this view, however, was option #2. Approximately 15% of the subjects selected this representation, which positions knowledge within beliefs. Thus, the adults in our sample were almost as likely to see knowledge as a facet of beliefs as they were to theorize the reverse. Only 6% of the adults chose Representation #4. As noted, this particular conceptualization blurs any distinction between knowledge and beliefs—an orientation Dole and Sinatra (this volume) describe as more common to social psychologists. Somewhat to our surprise, no one selected Representation #1 in which knowledge and beliefs are depicted as completely unrelated constructs. However, this representation was the least supported in the literature on epistemology that we reviewed in preparation for this chapter, so the lack of appeal is understandable.

Cross-Group Comparisons. When we compared the selections of the three communities of respondents (i.e., undergraduates, graduate students/faculty, and experts), several trends emerged. First, the preference for Representation #5 was consistent across all three groups. Fifty percent of the undergraduates opted for Representation #5, as compared to 52% of the educational psychology graduate students and faculty, and 47% of the experts. Clearly, the appeal of this particular representation was not constrained by educational level, experience, or expertise. Second, beyond Representation #5, the undergraduates in our sample were drawn only to Representations #2 (28%) and #3 (22%). Apparently, for these students, knowledge and beliefs are either overlapping or subsuming constructs. For none of these students was knowledge and beliefs viewed as separate or synonymous constructs. Within the expert community, there were no individuals who preferred Representation #2, and only a relative few who selected Representation #4 (13%) or #6 (13%). Based on their strong partiality for Representation #5 and their moderate preference for Representation #3 (27%), it would appear that these experts were more inclined than the other communities to view knowledge and beliefs as overlapping constructs or to conceptualize beliefs as a special case of knowledge.

Of all three groups, it was the graduate students and faculty who were most cohesive in their preferences. That is, only one representation garnered strong or even moderate support among community members. Beyond Representation #5, this group showed only a weak preference for Representations #2 (14%), #3 (10%), #4 (5%), and #6 (14%). This strong preference for Representation #5 is intriguing in light of the fact that it was also this community that displayed the greatest breadth of choices (i.e., selecting from all representations except #1). Further, it was only graduate students/faculty, along with experts, who elected to construct their own representations or viewed Representation #4 as a viable option. Overall, it would seem that advanced education and related experiences resulted in (a) greater diversity among adults, as evidenced by their willingness to consider different perspectives on the relationship between knowledge and beliefs (however weakly), (b) greater likelihood of seeing knowledge and beliefs as synonymous or inextricably related constructs, and (c) greater freedom to reach beyond the given alternatives, in order to create a representation more indicative of their personal theories about knowing and believing.

Defining Knowledge and Beliefs

On the basis of their selections or their creations, we have some conception of how the adults in our sample view the relationship between knowledge and beliefs. But, how do they define each construct and how do these definitions relate? To answer the first of these questions, we charted the key words included in each definition looking for patterns or keys to these adults' views. We did recognize several trends in these responses.

Not surprisingly, there was an wide array of concepts mentioned in the respondents' definitions. Yet, there was a great deal of shared meanings among these adults as well. As it relates to *knowledge*, there was a total of 194 concepts mentioned, which sorted into 49 categories. Five of these categories were predominant in these definitions: learned/taught (48%), facts (46%), information (39%), experience/environment (35%), and widely held (32%). Additionally, 19% of the respondents described knowledge as tangible or concrete. Only 9% of the adults specifically used the term *true* to distinguish knowledge, and four of these individuals were from the expert group. Like many of the classical (e.g., Locke, Hume) and contemporary philosophers (e.g., Leher, 1990; Pollock, 1986), the respondents generally equated knowledge with factual, externally verified, or widely accepted content. This content could either be acquired through formal instruction or from one's life experiences.

A similar number of concepts (184) and categories (50) surfaced in the definitions for beliefs as was documented for knowledge. Our general observation, however, was that *beliefs* was a more difficult concept for the respondents to define than was *knowledge*. This observation was based, in part, on the fact that there was less commonality in defining words for beliefs than for knowledge. However, patterns in responses did materialize. When explicating their theories, for example, these adults held that beliefs are inherently personal in nature (24%), strongly held (17%) and associated with feelings or emotions (28%), as well as with one's values and morals (24%).

When truth was mentioned in these definitions of beliefs, it was generally characterized as personal or idiosyncratic in nature (28%). That is, the truth allied with beliefs required no external validation. According to our respondents, beliefs were ideas or thoughts that individuals either perceived to be true or wanted to be true (19%) or claims that were subjective, for which truth or validity was essentially unimportant (31%). Despite their questionable validity and subjective nature, however, beliefs were also conceptualized as guiding principles that served as the basis for decision making (17%). Overall, these perspectives conflict somewhat with the views of various educational researchers (e.g., Harvey, 1986) who profess that beliefs must be of sufficient truth or validity to their holders if they truly are to guide one's actions. Finally, beliefs were described as either socially or culturally transmitted (13%) or acquired from one's experiences (15%).

How then did the conceptualizations of knowledge shared by the respondents compare to those of beliefs? Several distinctions were clearly evident in this content analysis. First, while knowledge was public in that it was widely accepted, beliefs were private in that they represented personal understandings or interpretations. Second, knowledge was objective, factual, or externally verifiable, whereas beliefs were subjective and demanded no such external validation. In addition, there was an affective dimension to beliefs that was absent in the definitions of knowledge. As with Frye (1967), many of our respondents associated detachment and objectivity with knowledge, but not with one's beliefs.

Another distinction between knowledge and beliefs pertained to their source. Whereas knowledge was frequently acquired through the educational process (i.e., formal learning), beliefs were passed down from one generation to the next as part of the individual's cultural or familial legacy. As a point of similarity, however, both knowledge and beliefs were viewed as arising from one's experiences; be they direct or vicarious. Finally, only in their definitions of beliefs did our respondents frequently speak about goals, intentions, or decision making. Thus for our respondents, it would seem that beliefs, regardless of their subjectivity or questionable validity, have greater power than knowledge to influence actions or behavior. Based on these differences, it is easy to see why beliefs are more resistant to change and why, as Abelson (1986) describes, beliefs as possessions that people hold dear.

Cross-Group Comparisons. To this point we have been describing the general patterns or trends manifested in the definitions of respondents. We would now like to offer some observations about the way our different communities of adults talked about knowing and believing. First, as would be expected, it was the experts whose definitions were the most elaborate and conceptually rich. The performance of the other two communities, however, were remarkably similar with regard to this attribute. Specifically, each expert used on the average of 4.67 concepts to define knowledge. This compares to 3.34 for the undergraduates and 3.00 for the educational psychology graduate student and faculty. A matching pattern was seen in the definitions for beliefs, with experts producing an average of 4.60 concepts per definition as contrasted to undergraduates (2.94) and graduate students/faculty (2.95).

As with the initial selection task, we were struck by the agreement among the undergraduates in terms of the concepts that were central to their definitions. Seventy percent of the undergraduates' coded descriptors fell within the five most popular categories of concepts for knowledge (i.e., learned, factual, information, experience-based, and widely held). This compares to 67% for the graduate students and faculty and 31% for the experts. This shared understanding among this community of young adults was again apparent in their definitions for beliefs. The five most frequently mentioned categories for beliefs (i.e., subjective, feelings, idiosyncratic, personal, and values) accounted for 58% of concepts listed by the undergraduates, as compared with 35% for the graduate student/faculty group and 29% for the community of experts.

In contrast to the foregoing pattern, it was the experts who manifested the greatest variety in their views of knowing and believing. That is, many of the concepts that these experts incorporated in their definitions were not shared by others, even from their own community (i.e., 20 for knowledge; 18 for beliefs). This is not to say that this community of experts did not have shared meanings of the terms *knowledge* and *beliefs*. Only experts (27%), for instance, defined knowledge as socially constructed or situated, and 47% characterized beliefs as strongly or deeply held. In addition, many of the words chosen by these experts to define knowledge and beliefs can best be described as "professional language" typical of a community of research scholars (e.g., encyclopedic, episodic, situated, inert, and cued). This pattern is due in part to the fact that this group occasionally supported their personal views with findings from their own and others' research. Further, the definitions of experts occasionally featured an apparent contradiction or cautionary statement. For example, beliefs were described as "both strongly-held and weakly-held" and simultaneously as "shapers of knowledge and shaped by knowledge." Overall, it was our conclusion that perspectives on knowing and believing become increasing more varied and conditional as adults continue their education and, particularly, as they engage in the study of epistemology.

Defending One's Views

Not only did we ask these adults to define knowledge and beliefs, but we also asked them to defend their choice of representation. Our purpose in posing this question was to look for consistency between choice and explanation and to explore the conviction with which such choices were made. We first looked at those individuals who chose Representation #2. In constructing this option, we intended to convey knowledge as an aspect of beliefs. Those selecting this option argued that "beliefs extend the boundaries of knowledge"; that "knowledge is the basic core of understanding and beliefs come from knowledge." Their defense of option #2 was also based on their view that beliefs have more impact on the individual's life than knowledge. By comparison, those who chose Representation #3, considered beliefs to be a special case of knowledge. As one individual noted, "You can't believe something you don't know." The selection of option #3 was also defended on the premise that "beliefs are born from knowledge, but are only a small part of one's cognitive experiences." One respondent felt that this was the most viable option since "beliefs constrain one's interaction within a given situation."

With Representation #4, selections were apparently predicated on the view that knowledge and beliefs are inseparable or so intricately meshed in memory that they cannot be thought of as independent. One respondent choosing option #4, for example, argued that "knowledge and beliefs lie on a continuum and are constantly interacting." It should be remembered that very few respondents (3) preferred this particular representation. Further, two of those individuals expressed some reservations in their decision. As one of these individuals put it, "The representation I chose does not fit very well with the definitions I've just provided." Thus, not only was Representation #4 a relatively unpopular selection, but it was also defended with somewhat less conviction than other options.

Arguments for Representation #5, the most popular option, centered around the view that aspects of knowledge and beliefs can exist independently, although they also overlap. In discussing their choice, respondents described how there were many things that they knew but did not believe. Likewise, there were things they believed, but for which they possessed no knowledge. Yet according to these respondents, beliefs and knowledge do, at times, converge. Others defended their selection of option

#5 on the premise that "knowledge can influence beliefs, but long-cherished beliefs cannot be swayed by knowledge." Because many of these individuals associated knowledge with factual information and beliefs with feelings and values, this defense seemed quite justified.

The variability in representations generated for option #6 led to different statements of support. As we noted earlier, several of these defenses established the need to address dynamic or a developmental change in the representation. One production, a modification of option #5, was justified on the basis that knowledge should be expanded since it represents a larger dimension than beliefs. In general, those creating their own representation of the knowledge/beliefs relationship gave rather elaborate justifications of these creations, describing most of the components within their productions.

Cross-Group Comparisons. One theme that was again evidenced in this cross-group comparison was that increased experience and training in the area of knowledge and beliefs resulted in more elaborate but more conditional statements. Surprisingly, it was the undergraduates who seemed most assured and less hesitant in their choices. It was also the undergraduates in our sample who offered the simplest explanations for personal selections. Indeed, these undergraduates wrote with great conviction about how much they had learned that they neither believed nor valued, and about how resistant their truly valued beliefs were to outside intervention. For these young adults, knowledge and beliefs may coincide, but such occurrences were not the rule. Such a statement speaks sadly about the nature of learning as experienced by these young people.

Overall, the defenses offered by the communities of graduate students/faculty and experts were detailed, rich explanations that afforded insights into their decision-making processes. Further, these individuals, particularly the experts, frequently prefaced their defense by describing how difficult the initial decision was for them. In addition, these two communities, especially the experts, occassionally remarked on the tentativeness of their decisions and the transition in their thinking that has occurred over time. Consider the words of the following two individuals (the first an educational psychology faculty member and the second a nationally recognized researcher in this field) in terms of the tentativeness and transition they convey.

> I'm not sure. I had a difficult time deciding between #2 and #3. Two may be a better example of where I am today because my beliefs are greater than my knowledge. However, I am moving toward #3. My beliefs become smaller and more based on knowledge the older and more experienced that I become.

> You do NOT ask easy questions! I've been struggling with the issue of the distinctions between knowledge and beliefs for several years, in the work I've been doing with various colleagues. And, I don't have very coherent

answers to the questions you pose. In fact, after hours of reading and discussion, the team of researchers on one project, Learning to Teach Mathematics, decided to use the word "claims" to include both knowledge and beliefs. We did not want to tackle the distinction in our writing: nor did we feel that the vast amounts of data we had on participating novice teachers enabled us to clearly determine the distinctions they made between knowledge and beliefs. With those caveats, I'll attempt to address your questions. These responses are best considered to be my current thinking, which does continue to evolve. . . My flippant response [to this particular question] is that I have chosen this representation on the basis of beliefs rather than knowledge.

It is likely that their extensive knowledge of the field made these individuals more aware of the numerous alternatives available to them and to the counterarguments that could be directed to any option that they may have chosen.

Providing Personal Evidence

Beyond justifying their individual choices, we asked the adults in our study to turn to their personal experiences as evidence of their views on the relationship between knowledge and beliefs. Before we tender our analysis of the types of experiences shared by these adults, we would like to discuss what we identified as the reasons these experiences were chosen. That is, what were the respondents' purposes for conveying particular experiences. Primarily for those who initially selected Representation #5, the choice of personal experience seemed intended to epitomize the separation between knowing and believing. Thus, these individuals frequently selected controversial and contemporary issues to establish a case for which something was known but not believed. For others, especially those preferring Representations #2 and #4, personal experiences were chosen to describe a situation where knowledge and beliefs were intricately interwined. In addition, there were several respondents who used past experiences to capture a dramatic change or shift in their beliefs. Several of those who generated their own representations shared this particular purpose. Finally, there were those adults, most of whom were researchers of knowledge or beliefs, who used instances from their own research or that of others to substantiate their views.

What types of experiences were shared by these individuals? As might be expected, many of the 79 experiences shared by these respondents pertained to religious convictions (29%), such as a belief in God, Jesus, the Bible, and the virgin birth. The next broad category of experiences that these adults conveyed were of a scientific nature (20%), although a number of those topics (e.g., origins of the universe) were confounded with religious beliefs. For example, four respondents discussed evolution (as opposed to creationism). Each of these respondents used this as a well-defined case of knowing but not believing. In other words, they reported that they knew about evolution but held strongly to the belief of creationism. The fact that evolution would be such a controversial subject for university-educated adults was surprising to us. Of course, evolution was not the only controversial topic described by our respondents. Other contentious and contemporary issues that served as personal evidence for these adults were homosexuality, multiculturalism, abortion, and the use of steroids. Fourteen percent of the responses fell into this category.

Two other categories of evidence deserve mention. One can broadly be classified as psychological since it dealt with such human conditions as prejudice, dishonesty, self-help skills, and criminal behavior. Thirteen percent of the adults' responses drew their personal evidence from such experiences. The other frequent category of personal evidence came more directly from individuals' educational or research experiences. Those adults drawing on these academic experiences (13%) talked about an array of topics, among them schema theory, computers, research, controversial texts, and literacy.

Cross-Group Comparisons. Unlike several of our previous comparisons, we found almost as much diversity in responses of the undergraduates as in those of the graduate/faculty and expert groups. All three communities of adults were well represented within most of the main categories of personal evidence (e.g., religious, scientific, or psychological). Notwithstanding, there were several distinctions among the adult communities that desire mention. For one, undergraduate students were much more likely than the other groups to draw upon experiences of a religious nature. Specifically, 41% of this community's 34 responses were within this one category, as compared to 22% for graduate students and faculty (27 responses) and 17% for experts (18 responses). As noted, this group even cast certain scientific (e.g., evolution) and contemporary subjects (e.g., homosexuality, abortion) within a religious framework. For another, it was these same undergraduates who wrote about the "valueless" knowledge they acquired in their schooling (e.g., Columbus or the circulatory system). Perhaps because of their very conservative, religious upbringing, these students judged much of what they learned (i.e., knew) against the religious dogma that they professed.

As might be expected, the graduate students/faculty and particularly the experts differed from the undergraduates in that they referenced professional and research experiences as the basis for their justification. For instance, one graduate student offered the following dismal account of his graduate school experiences as personal evidence of his representation of knowledge and beliefs:

> I believe graduate work is more of a series of hurdles rather than knowledge gained. I had heard this but now have personal knowledge and experiences that have validated this information.

One expert, by comparison, discussed her personal experiences as a researcher in literacy, while another discussed her research using controversial or pervasive texts and what that research had indicated about the relationship between knowing and believing:

> Our flier data show that non-controversial texts can persuade (e.g., one on fishing for steelhead and then releasing the fish), whereas controversial texts (e.g., abortion) are discarded by adult readers who report *not* changing their minds after reading them, we argue that belief systems are engaged by the abortion text, whereas knowledge systems ("I didn't know about catch and release programs") are engaged by the fish text.

Thus, for those adults immersed in the study of knowledge and beliefs, there was a convergence between the personal and the professional in the experiences that they shared.

Changing Beliefs

The final question that we posed to these adults was whether they thought that beliefs were changeable, and, if so, under what conditions such a change was apt to occur. All but one respondent stated that they felt that beliefs were, indeed, changeable, and even that one dissenting respondent went on to state that she did think that beliefs were modifiable. Apparently to this respondent, change and modification were distinct ideas. However, many of the respondents who wrote in favor of change went on to qualify their statements by declaring that beliefs were very difficult to change or modify. As shown in the following example from one of the experts, the respondents also occasionally provided evidence from personal experience or research to support that contention.

> Beliefs are changeable, if you can change the propositions with which the beliefs is entangled. So I am suggesting that they are not easily changed. For example, I can remember having strong religious beliefs as a young person. Then one day in an undergraduate class in which we studied other cultures, I learned that one tribe BELIEVED that there was no relationship between having sex and having babies. They believed that God made that decision. When the missionaries tried to prove this to them, the tribe refused to believe them. I thought to myself, if a religious belief could mis-guide this tribe that badly, what is my religion doing to me? Why have I not questioned the things I have been made to believe? Since that time my religious beliefs have changed tremendously.

Like Chinn and Brewer (1993), we classified the conditions presented by our respondents into factors that appeared to influence one's beliefs. Specifically, 101 factors were generated by the adults in our sample and classified into six broad categories: information/knowledge (32%), educa-tion/experience (31%), personality (21%), nature of beliefs (11%), and other (6%). As these data suggest, the prevailing factor that these adults referenced was new knowledge or information, particularly information that was convincing or contradictory to the belief held. Further, a number of individuals mentioned that experience, especially experiences that were of a crisis nature, could bring about a change in beliefs. One respondent shared a moving story about her long-held belief about the evils of homosexuality; a belief that was dramatically altered when she learned that a dear friend was gay and dying of AIDS. Within this category of education/experience, the adults also noted that changes in beliefs are contingent on the age or maturity of the believer. To a number of respondents, whether beliefs change or not has a great deal to do with the personality (e.g., emotional state, self-esteem, patience) of the holders, and whether they are willing to be open-minded and questioning about their beliefs. Only a relatively small number of respondents spoke about the nature of the beliefs as factors in their malleability. Those who did described such conditions as how entrenched or valued the beliefs were. Among the ideas that we sorted into the "other" category were such mentions as psychotherapy and perception.

Thus, as Chinn and Brewer (1993) also found, characteristics of the knowledge received, in addition to the nature of the holders' education and experiences, were seen to alter beliefs for the adults in our study. Although the nature of the beliefs held was also a category in both investigations, it received relatively little attention from the communities in this study. Yet, one category not addressed in the Chinn and Brewer review, but predominant in the responses of the adults in our study, dealt with the personality and character of the believer. According to the individuals with whom we interacted, whether beliefs will or will not be altered has much to do with the characteristics of the holder, irrespective of the knowledge acquired or one's personal or academic experiences.

Cross-Group Comparisons. In general, the emergent factors just described were fairly well distributed among the three groups. Several trends are worthy of note, however. First, it was the community of graduate students/faculty who, on the average, identified the greatest number of potential influences on one's beliefs (2.10). This compares to an average of 1.87 for the experts and 1.61 for the undergraduates. Second, although only 21% of *all* responses fell into the "personality" category, 38% of the undergraduates' 29 explanations were of this type, as contrasted with 16% for the graduate student/faculty community (44 explanations) and 11% for the experts (28 explanations). Thus, for the younger, less experienced adults in our study, it was the personality of the believer that was the most influential factor in changing beliefs. For graduate students and faculty, by comparison, it was one's educational background and life experiences (45%) that were more pivotal in changing beliefs. This contrasts markedly with the response patterns of the undergraduates (10%) and experts (29%). The most important factor in altering beliefs for the community of experts, on the other hand, was the nature of the knowledge or information that was acquired. Forty-six percent of the experts' responses to this question fell into this category, as compared to 21% for the undergraduate group and 30% for the graduate students and faculty.

To be frank, we were somewhat taken aback to find that a number of the undergraduate students felt that it was a sign of character to resist changes in beliefs. To these individuals, the better the person, the more apt he or she was to resist the temptations to alter or abandon a belief. Perhaps this situation is related to the fact that many of these undergraduates thought of beliefs in terms of "faith"; a faith that "should not be explored or doubted." Baron (1991) would say that these young adults have assumed an aggressive stance toward their beliefs, rather than a cooperative one. In an aggressive stance, one seeks to defend his or her beliefs, whereas in a cooperative stance those beliefs are opened up for examination by others. By contrast it was the graduate students, faculty, and experts who associated changes in beliefs with age and maturity (i.e., wisdom) or with compelling or convincing new information.

What is particularly troubling to us about this overall pattern in the undergraduates' responses is that these were honor students whom we believe to be bright and articulate on many measures of academic performance. Yet, a number of these students did not reach the *doubting* stage that Dewey (1910) regarded as essential to learning. Perhaps their unwillingness to explore or question their beliefs could be understood in terms of Kohlberg's (1981) conceptions of moral development. That is, the responses of many of these undergraduates suggests that, despite their general intellectual abilities and verbal proficiency, they may still be at a stage 4 of moral development, where one follows accepted rules and accepts authority without question. Given more education and experience, however, these students may progress to the stage where their beliefs can be opened to examination and exploration.

GENERAL DISCUSSION

It was our goal in this study to have adults share their thoughts on knowing and believing so that we could better understand the implicit theories that influence, if not guide, their behaviors. We hold that words are powerful markers of human reflection and that thoughts are the foundation for human action. In choosing college students, educators, and educational researchers as our respondents, we felt that our sample had the experience and the verbal proficiency to convert their thoughts on the difficult questions we asked about knowing and believing into meaningful and honest expressions of their personal understanding. Further, we hoped that posing these questions to individuals who are members of distinct educational communities would afford us the opportunity to explore differences in perspectives that might exist as part of community membership.

Overall, we feel that we did succeed at our goals. We learned much about the way adults in different communities view knowing and believing and we evidenced divergence in the responses across these communities. Some of what we learned reinforced expectations. Some of what we discovered surprised and dismayed us. For example, in analyzing the words individuals used in their definitions of knowledge and beliefs we recognized that, as with many in the community of philosophers, our respondents considered knowledge to be factual and verifiable. Though more difficult for them to define, these adults perceived beliefs to be personal and value-laden. In addition, what these adults told us was that beliefs can be changed and modified. Sometimes the catalyst for change is external, as in the form of new and compelling knowledge, education, and experience. Sometimes the stimulus for change is internal, as in the willingness of the believer to be open-minded, questioning, or doubting.

These latter summaries regarding change agents were mirrored in the differences we detected among the communities of respondents. As the more experienced and well-educated community, it was the experts, and to a lesser extent the graduate students/faculty, in our study who were more varied and tentative in their reactions, and more willing to recognize the limitations in their arguments. In comparison, it was our younger, less experienced respondents (i.e., the undergraduates) who conveyed their thoughts with more consistency and greater assurance. Thus, just as these adults stated, it was factors of education, age, and maturity that apparently contributed to greater flexibility in the one's beliefs—even when those beliefs were about beliefs, themselves.

One of the insights we garnered from this exploration had to do with undergraduates' perspectives on value of beliefs and the "valuelessness" of knowledge. That is, to many of the undergraduates in this study, school was a place where one learned information, like "Who is Christopher Columbus?" or "What is the circulatory system?" that had no meaning or value to them. As researchers who have studied learning and instruction for many years, this alone is neither a new nor shocking revelation. However, this view is compounded by two other insights.

First, these undergraduates not only do not value much of what they learn in schools but they also do not believe much of what their teachers think they are learning—information that many teachers would not consider controversial or contentious (e.g., evolution, depletion of the rain forests, the importance of multiculturalism). Second, among these same undergraduates there were a number who expressed the view that it is strength of character to resist doubt and to ignore information that is contradictory to one's beliefs.

Thus, as a collective, these observations about the undergraduate students in our study, all of whom were university honor students, suggests to us that beyond one's general intellectual ability or one's specific verbal or text-processing skills (see Chambliss, this volume), there are attributes of the human character that contribute to or constrain one's view about knowing and believing. Further, these observations leave us deeply concerned about the potential for future education and experiences to penetrate the barriers that these young adults have constructed between knowing and believing. It also helps to explain why so many misconceptions remain unaffected by learning and why so many "unschooled minds" (Gardner, 1991) continue to reside even within the ivory-covered walls of academia. Perhaps if we can provide avenues for adults, like these undergraduates, to externalize their views about knowing and believing, as we have done in this investigation, we can open them up for public scrutiny and examination. This may serve as the first step to the intermediate stage of doubt that Dewey claims is so essential to genuine knowledge. At the very least it affords the opportunity to "know the condition of one's own mind"—What Epictetus and we see as the beginning of philosophy.

ACKNOWLEDGMENTS

The authors wish to thank P. Karen Murphy for her helpful comments on an earlier draft of this chapter.

REFERENCES

Abelson, R. P. (1986). Beliefs are like possessions. *Journal for the Theory of Social Behavior, 16*, 223-250.

Alexander, P. A. (1992). Domain knowledge: Evolving issues and emerging concerns. *Educational Psychologist, 27*, 33-51.

Alexander, P. A., Jetton, T. L., & Kulikowich, J. M. (1993, April). Interdomain knowledge: A within-subject examination of comprehension and interest in the fields of human immunology and physics. In D. Shell (Chair), *Subject-matter knowledge: Interdomain, multidimensional analysis of individual differences.* Symposium presented at the annual meeting of the American Educational Research Association, Atlanta.

Alexander, P. A., & Judy, J. E. (1988). The interaction of domain-specific and strategic knowledge in academic performance. *Review of Educational Research, 58*, 375-404.

Alexander, P. A., Kulikowich, J. M., & Jetton, T. L. (in press). The role of subject-matter knowledge and interest in the processing of linear and nonlinear texts. *Review of Educational Research.*

Alexander, P. A., Schallert, D. L., & Hare, V. C. (1991). Coming to terms: How researchers in learning and literacy talk about knowledge. *Review of Educational Research, 61,* 315-343.

Arnaudin, M. W., & Mintzes, J. J. (1985). Students' alternative conceptions of the human circulatory system: A cross-age study. *Science Education, 69,* 721-733.

Baron, J. (1991). Beliefs about thinking. In J. F. Voss, D. N Perkins, & J. W. Segal (Eds.), *Informal reasoning and education* (pp. 169-186). Hillsdale, NJ: Lawrence Erlbaum Associates.

Chinn, C. A., & Brewer, W. F. (1993). The role of anomalous data in knowledge acquisition: A theoretical framework and implications for science instruction. *Review of Educational Research, 63,* 1-49.

Clements, J. (1986). Misconceptions in high school physics. *Cognitive Processes Research Group Newsletter, 1*(2), 2-3.

Dewey, J. (1910). *How we think.* Boston: D. C. Heath.

Dochy, F. J. R. C. (1992). *Assessment of prior knowledge as a determinant for future learning.* London: Jessica Kingsley Publishers.

Dochy, F. J. R. C. (1993, April). An alternative to the assessment of domain-specific knowledge: Profile analysis. In D. Shell (Chair), *Subject-matter knowledge: Interdomain, multidimensional analysis of individual differences.* Symposium presented at the annual meeting of the American Educational Research Association, Atlanta.

Dochy, F. J. R. C., & Alexander, P. A. (1993). *Mapping prior knowledge: A Euro-American approach.* Unpublished manuscript.

Flavell, J. H. (1987). Speculation about the nature and development of metacognition. In F. E. Weinert & R. H. Kluwe (Eds.), *Metacognition, motivation, and understanding* (pp. 21-29). Hillsdale, NJ: Lawrence Erlbaum Associates.

Frye, N. (1967). The knowledge of good and evil, In M. Black (Ed.), *Morality of scholarship* (pp. 3-28).

Gardner, H. (1991). *The unschooled mind.* New York: Basic Books.

Garner, R. (1987). *Metacognition and reading comprehension.* Norwood, NJ: Ablex.

Goldman, A. I. (1986). *Epistemology and cognition.* Cambridge, MA: Harvard University Press.

Harvey, O. J. (1986). Belief systems and attitudes toward the death penalty and other punishments. *Journal of Personality, 54,* 143-159.

Kohlberg, L. (1981). *The philosophy of moral development.* New York: Harper & Row.

Laird, J. (1972). *Knowledge, belief, and opinion.* Hamden, CT: Archon Books.

Leher, K. (1990). *Theory of knowledge.* San Francisco: Westview Press.

Marton, F. (1988). Describing and improving learning. In R. R. Schmeck (Ed.) *Learning strategies and learning styles* (pp. 339-348). New York: Plenum Press.

Mill, J. S. (1979). An examination of Sir William Hamilton's philosophy. In J. M. Robinson (Ed.), *Collected works of John Stuart Mill* (Vol. IX). Toronto: University of Toronto Press. (Original work published 1865)

Olson, D. R., & Astington, J. W. (1993). Thinking about thinking: Learning how to take statements and hold beliefs. *Educational Psychologist, 28,* 7-23.

Palmer, D. J., & Goetz, E. T. (1988). Selection and use of study strategies: The role of the studiers' beliefs about self and strategies. In C. E. Weinstein, E. T. Goetz, & P. A. Alexander (Eds.), *Learning and study strategies: Issues in assessment, instruction, and evaluation* (pp. 41-61). San Diego: Academic Press.

Pollock, J. L. (1986). *Contemporary theories of knowledge.* Totowa, NJ: Rowman & Littlefield.

Thagard, P. (1991). Concepts and conceptual change. In J. H. Fetzer (Ed.), *Epistemology and cognition* (pp. 101-120). Dordrecht, Netherlands: Kluwer.

CHAPTER THIRTEEN

Social Psychology Research on Beliefs and Attitudes: Implications for Research on Learning From Text

Janice A. Dole
Gale M. Sinatra
University of Utah

Recent research has extended our thinking about the many factors that influence what and how much students learn from the texts they read. Early research focused on isolated variables related to the text (for a review, see Meyer & Rice, 1984). More recent research focused on characteristics of readers, like their prior knowledge (Anderson, Reynolds, Schallert, & Goetz, 1977), and their perspective (Anderson & Pichert, 1978). Most recently, researchers have begun to focus on "hot cognition"—that is, affective factors within readers, like their motivation (Brown, 1988), their interest (Garner, Gillingham, & White, 1989; Hidi, 1990; Hidi & Baird, 1986; Wade, Schraw, Buxton, & Hayes, 1993), and their beliefs (Dole, Sinatra, & Reynolds, 1991; Otero & Kintsch, 1992).

This most recent interest in affective factors within readers arises from the central role that cognitive research has attributed to the construct of prior knowledge in comprehension and learning. Studies have demonstrated quite convincingly that students, even very young children, do not come to school as blank slates, but rather with extensive and often elaborate ideas about their world and how it works (McCloskey, 1983; Posner, Strike, Hewson, & Gertzog, 1982). Further, students do not necessarily give up this knowledge with instruction (Anderson & Smith, 1987). As a matter of fact, some knowledge appears to be highly resistant to change—students hold onto it despite substantial evidence to the contrary (West & Pines, 1985).

Research on the tenaciousness of some prior knowledge has led researchers to recognize that there are important *affective* as well as *cognitive* processes that influence learners as they struggle to make sense out of the instruction they receive. Of course, this makes intuitive sense, but up to now, educational researchers have not addressed these affective processes. At this point in time, researchers have not been able to differentiate affective factors from cognitive ones. Yet, researchers have begun to recognize that the affective ones count, perhaps in far more important ways than we had previously thought. Thus, affect has become a legitimate area of research exploration.

The field of social psychology has a long tradition of studying affect, especially beliefs and attitudes. Social psychologists have conducted literally hundreds of studies to determine how beliefs influence the processing of information. They have examined under what conditions information is most likely to be considered and under what conditions information is most likely to be ignored. And they have studied factors related to learners, specific contexts, and presenters that make learners more or less likely to consider and learn new information. This literature can be useful to cognitive psychologists and educational researchers who are interested in beliefs and their contributions to knowledge acquisition and restructuring.

For this reason, this chapter reviews the social psychology research on beliefs and attitudes. We begin with an orientation to social psychology theory and research and present a brief history of the field as it diverged from experimental psychology and then converged in recent years with cognitive psychology. We also discuss key differences in important terms used by social psychologists and cognitive psychologists. Next we discuss relevant social psychology research on the structure and functions of beliefs, and present two widely recognized theories of how beliefs change. Then we apply the social psychology research findings to educational research by summarizing what the social psychology research tells us about learning from text. We compare these findings to those from educational research. Lastly, we discuss the constructs of knowledge and beliefs in terms of the implications for research on learning from text.

ORIENTATION TO SOCIAL PSYCHOLOGY THEORY AND RESEARCH

To orient educational researchers operating within a cognitive psychology framework to the social psychology literature, it is useful to define the field and explain its historical roots within the field of psychology. Social psychology research focuses on how people make sense of their social environment (Fiske & Taylor, 1991). Social environment is broadly defined to include social issues and ideas as well as other people. For example, social psychologists study people's views on politics and politicians, nuclear war, prejudice, environmental issues, cigarette smoking, and alcoholism.

Further, and more importantly for education, social psychologists study how people acquire their views, how likely they are to change them, and under what conditions they do so.

Social psychologists have traditionally used the term *cognition* in a broad sense. They define cognition as *general mental processes,* which include affective, as well as what cognitive psychologists would call cognitive, constructs. Affective constructs such as beliefs, attitudes, motivation, drive, desire, and emotion have been studied by social psychologists for decades as part of their focus on cognition (e.g., general mental processes). Further, they studied these *cognitive* constructs even when cognition was excluded as a legitimate focus of research by behavioral and experimental psychologists who argued that only readily observable phenomena could be studied and understood. Social psychologists pride themselves in having a tradition of "unabashed commitment to mentalism (cognition)" (Fiske & Taylor, 1991, p. 14).

During the *cognitive revolution,* experimental psychology was transformed from a field that was predominantly behavioral to one that was predominantly cognitive (Eagly & Chaiken, 1993). During this time thinking was resurrected as a legitimate focus of research in the new cognitive psychology, but other affective constructs like beliefs, attitudes, and motivation were not. Eagly and Chaiken (1993) speculate that affective constructs were not considered to be a part of the study of cognition because they did not fit into the computer-analogy, information-processing approach adopted by cognitive psychology. Thus, cognitive psychology incorporated thought into its domain of study, but not affect. This has left cognitive psychology open to the criticism that it is the study of "cold cognition" (Zajonc, 1980).

Compared to cognitive psychology, though, the social psychology research has remained "hot" over the last several decades. A fundamental interest among social psychologists has continued to be the affective factors that influence how people perceive, organize and understand their world.

This is not to say, however, that social psychologists are clear about the construct of affect. For example, Eagly and Chaiken (1993) consider such concepts as "emotion, mood, affect, arousal, incentives, needs, [and] motives" as "affective" (p. 390). On the other hand, Zajonc (1980) considers preferences and feelings "affective processes," but not emotions such as anger and guilt. Still other researchers consider affect to be evaluation (Fishbein & Ajzen, 1975).

Further, social psychologists are not clear about whether affect is part of cognition, or whether it is a separate and distinct mental system (Lazarus, 1982, 1984; Zajonc,1980). This confusion becomes evident in the study of attitudes. Early work in the field differentiated cognitive from affective components of attitudes. Researchers identified three unique components of attitudes—what they called *cognitive, affective,* and *behavioral* (McGuire, 1969, 1985). They argued that all attitudes consisted of "thoughts and knowledge" about an object, "feelings and evaluations" of the object, and corresponding behavior towards that object (Eagly & Chaiken, 1993). For example, students' attitudes towards evolutionary theory may consist of specific knowledge and thoughts they have about the evolutionary process—such as natural selection and speciation, feelings about the theory—such as uncomfortable feelings and negative evaluations that occur when they read that humans evolved from animals, and behavior toward the theory—such as their unwillingness to study carefully the chapter on evolution in their biology textbooks.

Recent research in social psychology, however, has questioned the validity of this three-part model of attitudes (Tesser & Shaffer, 1990). Researchers have questioned how cognition and affect relate to one another and whether cognition, affect and behavior are all necessary components of attitudes (Eagly & Chaiken, 1993). Most recent theorists have rejected this three-part model of attitudes (Tesser & Shaffer, 1990) in part because there is no consensus about how cognition and affect relate to one another or just what each construct represents. Thus, social psychology, like cognitive psychology, has not clarified the nature of, nor difference between, cognition and affect.

Cognition, Knowledge, Beliefs, and Attitudes

Although cognition and affect remain unclear constructs for both social and cognitive psychology, other related constructs are more clearly delineated in social psychology. While social psychologists use the term *cognition* to refer to the general nature of what they study, they also use the term more specifically to mean *thoughts* and *knowledge*. We have found these terms scattered throughout the social psychology literature, but without clarification. The terms are frequently used, but we have never found them defined. We have concluded that social psychologists use the terms *thoughts* and *knowledge* to refer to unexamined or unevaluated information. On the other hand, in general they use the term *affect* to refer to feelings, emotion or evaluation associated with the information.

This distinction between knowledge and evaluation of the knowledge is evident in social psychologists' definition of beliefs and attitudes. Social psychologists consider beliefs to be positive or negative evaluations people have about objects (Fishbein & Ajzen, 1975). "Objects" can refer to anything from concrete objects, to people, to abstract ideas or positions or views about something. For example, an individual may have a belief that nuclear power plants are expensive and dangerous, a belief that there are alternative sources of power less potentially harmful to the environment, and a belief that nuclear power plants cannot be adequately monitored and regulated, and so forth. The unexamined statement, "There are alternative sources of power less potentially harmful to the environment" may be defined as a *thought* or *knowledge*, but the commitment to the truthfulness of that knowledge is defined as the *belief*.

Beliefs are considered to be the building blocks of attitudes (Eagly & Chaiken, 1993) in that a set of beliefs makes up one's attitudes about an object. Thus, an attitude is defined as a related and interconnected network of beliefs. An individual's attitude toward nuclear power plants consists of a related and interconnected set of beliefs about nuclear power and power plants. The individual who held the set of beliefs about nuclear power plants described earlier would be said to hold a negative attitude toward nuclear power plants.

Thus, social psychologists subsume beliefs under attitudes. The hallmark for both beliefs and attitudes, however, is that they have an evaluation component. In this chapter we use the term *beliefs* for what social psychologists usually refer to as *attitudes*. This is helpful for educational researchers working within a cognitive framework and unfamiliar with the construct of attitudes.

Beliefs as Schemata

Social psychologists conceptualize beliefs as memory representations consisting of networks of associations (Tesser & Shaffer, 1990). Beliefs, like *knowledge* in cognitive psychology, are conceptualized as *schemata*, with interconnected and interrelated sets of schemata about related beliefs. (Social psychologists use the term *schemata* in the plural to reflect the complex nature of beliefs.) More complex schemata reflect more complex beliefs, and less complex schemata reflect simpler beliefs. For example, a less complex schemata about slavery may contain beliefs about what slavery is and what it means to be a slave. A more complex schemata about slavery, however, would likely entail richer and more detailed ideas about slavery and its related concepts (e.g., the implications of slavery for the Civil War, early views about African-Americans, racial discrimination) as well as awareness of the arguments of both pro-and anti-slavery positions of the Civil War.

Cognitive psychologists use the singular term *schema* to describe the nature of knowledge storage and representation in memory (Anderson & Pearson, 1984) in much the same way. As a matter of fact, a central theme in cognition has been to describe the nature of memory representations as related schemata with associative networks (J. Anderson, 1983). A Civil War historian would have a rich schema with many knowledge nodes related to slavery and many connections to other related knowledge nodes, while a high school student studying the civil war period would have fewer knowledge nodes and fewer connections to other concepts.

This similarity between the way social psychologists and cognitive psychologists conceptualize schemata is more than coincidental. In the early to mid-1970s, social psychologists adopted some of the theory and methodology of cognitive psychology to understand the structure and functions of beliefs (Fiske & Taylor, 1991). As far as we can tell, there are no major differences in the way social psychologists and cognitive psychologists use and apply the term *schemata*. It does appear, however, that social psychologists include a full range of affective factors in their discussions of schemata. Although cognitive psychologists originally conceptualized schema in the same way (see, for example, Spiro, 1980), the affective components of schema were not carried through in further discussions.

Using schemata as a theoretical framework, social psychologists have spent the last 2 decades examining the structure of beliefs. They have found that beliefs about controversial issues—abortion, AIDS—and beliefs by individuals who are activists—nuclear war protesters, conservationists—are likely to contain detailed schemata about both sides of those issues. On the other hand, attitudes about less controversial issues and attitudes held by nonactivists are more likely to contain schemata with only supportive information about the issues. Thus, an individual is more likely to have only supportive information in a schemata about nutrition or exercise, but probably both supportive and nonsupportive information in a Vietnam War schemata. Likewise, activists are likely to have complex schemata about the issue they hold dear, and are likely to have both supportive and nonsupportive information about that issue.

Complex schemata, though, in and of themselves, are not always associated with more extreme beliefs. Sometimes they are associated with more moderate beliefs. Tesser and Shaffer (1990) argue that when individuals hold schemata *consistent* with one another, they are more likely to have extreme belief structures. So, for example, conservationists who have a set of beliefs consisting of only *negative* effects of logging operations in the Northwest are likely to have extreme belief structures or attitudes about logging. They may believe that all logging operations hurt the environment, that logging destroys delicate ecosystems, that loggers could easily get other jobs, and that the economy of logging towns is not a major problem. In this case there is consistency within the conservationists' beliefs, thereby producing more extreme beliefs structures or attitudes.

In contrast, when individuals have beliefs that are inconsistent with one another, they are likely to have more moderate belief structures. Thus, individuals who believe that logging operations destroy delicate ecosystems, but that putting loggers out of jobs would be harmful to them and their families would be more likely to hold a more moderate belief structure. Even though these individuals have complex belief structures, the beliefs are not consistent with each other, thereby producing more moderate attitudes.

RESEARCH ON HOW BELIEFS CHANGE

One topic of great interest to educational researchers is how affective factors such as beliefs influence knowledge acquisition and restructuring. This interest arises from the abundance of research evidence which shows that many students do not learn new information—presented through instruction or text—when that information conflicts with prior held knowledge. Studies conducted in science education (Eaton, Anderson, & Smith, 1984; West & Pines, 1985), and reading (Dole, Niederhauser, & Hayes, 1991) demonstrate the difficulty of "conceptual change learning," that is, learning that involves what Piaget calls accommodation or Vosniadou and Brewer (1987) call "radical restructuring." Such learning involves a major restructuring of knowledge, and involves deep and extensive rethinking and restructuring of concepts and how they relate to one another. Conceptual change learning would be said to occur when young children learn to conserve, and when they come to understand that the earth is shaped like a sphere rather than like a flat pancake. Conceptual change would be said to occur when older students or adults become convinced of the harmful effects of smoking after they have smoked for several years, or when they change their minds about the moral imperative of the Vietnam War. Such conceptual change obviously *can* occur, but it is difficult, and in some cases, not always successful.

Interestingly enough, these ideas are not new to social psychologists who have spent years studying what they call attitude change and persuasion. As a matter of fact, the social psychology research provides compelling, corroborating evidence that, when presented with information, learners are heavily influenced by what they already "know" or believe (Eagly & Chaiken, 1993). They have found that strong beliefs are highly accessible, easily activated and tend to bias information processing (Fazio, 1986, 1987, 1989). Further, individuals' beliefs about an issue are likely to influence their judgments, especially when a decision needs to be made quickly and expediently (Tesser & Shaffer, 1990). Abelson (1986) summarized by saying that beliefs are like possessions—we hold on to them, value them and can be resistant to letting them go.

Social psychology researchers have examined in detail the many factors involved in how beliefs change. The general framework for understanding the change process has been conceptualized through many different models and hundreds of studies. Two models that seem to be widely recognized

(Tesser & Shaffer, 1990) are summarized here and used as theoretical frameworks for presenting the research on factors influencing how beliefs change.

Two general models for belief change present a similar picture of what happens when individuals do change their beliefs based on receiving new information, or a "message" in social psychologists' terms. Petty and Cacioppo's (1986) "central route to persuasion" and Chaiken's (1987; Chaiken, Liberman, & Eagly, 1989) "systematic" processing both hypothesize that individuals differ in how *motivated* they are and how *able* they are to think about and evaluate a given message. When individuals are highly motivated and willing to think deeply and thoughtfully about a message, then the route to belief or attitude change, or what social psychologists refer to as *persuasion*, is "central" (Petty & Cacioppo, 1981, 1986) or "systematic" (Chaiken, 1987). This route requires individuals to want to spend the time and effort to examine new information and weigh both sides of an issue and to be intellectually capable of doing so. When they do so, then permanent belief change can occur.

However, belief change can also occur through what Petty and Cacioppo (1981, 1986) call the "peripheral" route, similar to what Chaiken (1987) calls "heuristic" processing. Sometimes, individuals are not interested in thinking deeply about a message, or they are not capable of doing so, or they have little knowledge about the issues related to the message. In these cases, a host of "peripheral" cues—such as an expert, an attractive source, a pleasant situational context like music or food accompanying the message, an easily comprehensible message—can cause individuals to change their beliefs. This route to persuasion involves other factors such as systematic thinking through and weighing arguments that cause change in individuals' beliefs.

The central or systematic processing route to belief change is very similar to "deep processing" theory in cognitive psychology (Craik & Lockhart, 1972). Cognitive psychologists studying memory and learning have found that elaborative, thoughtful processing of information results in the formation of a memory representation, or learning. The more active learners are, the more likely they are to process the information deeply and learn from it. On the other hand, when information is not meaningfully elaborated, as can occur through rote memorization, for example, learners tend to be passive, and the effects of the learning experience can be short-lived. This is similar to the peripheral route to belief change and results, over time, in no learning.

It appears that much of the work conducted in social psychology has examined peripheral routes, rather than central routes, to persuasion and belief change. This may be due, in part, to the extensive body of research conducted in the 1950s and 60s by Hovland and his colleagues at Yale (see, for example, Hovland, Janis, & Kelly, 1953). These researchers sorted out the multitude of variables that appeared to influence how individuals change their beliefs, but most often they did not examine long-term changes in beliefs by readministering dependent measures over time.

Social psychologists have studied various forms of peripheral cues that can cause individuals to change their beliefs. One peripheral cue that has been extensively studied is the communicator. Certain characteristics of communicators—physical attractiveness, likeableness, credibility, trustworthiness, and similarity to the audience—have all been shown to influence individuals' willingness to listen to and believe a message (Fiske & Taylor, 1991). In general, communicators who are attractive and likeable are more persuasive in their message (Eagly & Chaiken, 1975). This is a general and well-established finding in social psychology (Fiske & Taylor, 1991) which makes intuitive sense educationally. We all are aware of our own experiences in school where we have been influenced by the views of a teacher or someone else whom we liked or admired.

Another common finding in the social psychology research is that communicators who are seen as having a vested interest in a particular position are regarded more suspiciously and less believably than communicators who appear to have no vested interest (Eagly & Chaiken, 1993). Thus, we are likely to regard a CEO for an oil company with suspicion and skepticism when he advocates an anticonservationist position because we see that person as having a vested interest in his position. But when a spokesperson for an environmental group advocates the same anticonservationist position, we are likely to view her as unbiased and fair because that position is considered to be *against* her vested interest. Thus, when communicators advocate a position that is considered to be against their vested interest, they are regarded as objective and fair (Eagly & Chaiken, 1993).

Likewise, communicators who are similar to the individuals receiving a message are more believable and trustworthy. These communicators are often regarded as objective and fair-minded (Fiske & Taylor, 1991). Thus, it makes sense that teachers who advocate good nutrition and exercise might be less credible to students than peers who advocate these positions. Peers are more similar to each other and therefore they will often listen to each other more carefully than they would to a teacher. The advantages of having students learn together in cooperative learning groups is clear through the social psychology research and corroborates what many educators have seen—students are often more willing to listen and learn from their peers than from adults.

On the other hand, the social psychology research also indicates that communicators who argue positions dissimilar to one's own tend to be regarded as biased and subjective (Fiske & Taylor, 1991). Thus, even though it might be better for students to present information about the benefits of exercise to their peers than for adults to do so, it will still be likely that those students who never exercise will tend to view the students who discuss the benefits of exercising as being biased and subjective.

It must be remembered, though, that these findings that show this important influence of communicators are predicated on the assumption that the individuals receiving the message are relatively uninterested in it or do not have a stake in the outcome of the message. In these cases, individuals tend to be unwilling or unable to think carefully about the message. Therefore, they may respond to superficial cues, including the likeability, or similarity of the communicators, to change their beliefs.

Extending these findings to education, it is easy to see the potential influence of the teacher and students in the educational setting, especially as students try to understand the textbooks they read. It will often be the case that, in fact, students are unwilling to think about the information presented in the text, process it deeply and to critically weigh the issues they read about. In these cases, they may be persuaded to change their minds not by the evidence presented in the text but by the influence of the teacher or their peers. However, social psychology research provides a cautionary note for us here. There is clear evidence that change that comes about through these peripheral cues only—without accompanying deep processing of the information—is often temporary.

The communicator is only one of several peripheral cues that can influence change in individuals' beliefs. Other peripheral cues include certain kinds of message effects. The most obvious one that has been researched extensively is *message repetition*, or "mere exposure." Numerous studies have shown that merely exposing individuals to a message can affect their belief about that message (Fiske & Taylor, 1991). Advertisers use this peripheral visual cue frequently when they expose individuals to a particular logo—for example, Nike, Coca-Cola—and succeed in having individuals show a preference for the brand based on repetitive exposure to it. Researchers argue that such exposure effects occur when individuals are "lazy" processors (McGuire, 1969) who do not think about or cognitively process the message.

On the other hand, research has shown that message repetition does not seem to affect persuasion when the message involves linguistic as opposed to visual cues. Simply repeating a verbal message is not effective in changing individuals' beliefs, unless individuals are willing to take the time to think deeply and process the information. Otherwise, individuals apparently do not even notice the repetition, and the effect is negligible (McGuire, 1969).

In education, teachers sometimes repeat information or have students do repetitive tasks in the hopes that they will learn new information. Yet, repetition alone can result in rote learning or *peripheral* change rather than deep understanding or *central* change. Thus, having something repeated over and over is unlikely to result in deep processing and learning, as evidenced by a new memory representation or knowledge restructuring. We would note, however, that repetition is not the same as practice, which can, when there is active student engagement and processing, result in new learning and knowledge restructuring.

Another message effect is the content of the message itself. Difficult messages are harder to understand, and therefore take more cognitive processing. Such processing takes effort, time, and energy, and individuals are limited in how much they want to do such effortful processing. Further, the more difficult the message, the less willing individuals are to try to understand it (Eagly & Chaiken, 1993). Uninvolved individuals will be most affected by message difficulty, in that these individuals will probably ignore the message completely because they would have to think about the material to process it.

Eagly (1974) and Chaiken and Eagly (1976, 1983) argue that message difficulty can do more than result in nonlearning. Individuals can hear a difficult message that produces for them a negative affect that may then become associated with the message. When this happens, individuals will then associate the message with the opposite of the desired intention of the communicator. In this case, then, the communicator not only failed to produce learning, but produced, instead, a negative association with the message.

Students have been known to express dislike for subjects traditionally considered difficult, like math and science. The research in social psychology suggests that this negative affect may be a result of the perceived difficulty in learning the material. This is not a finding that would surprise many teachers who teach these subjects, but cognitive psychology has not addressed these issues or explored ways to deal with them.

An issue related to that of difficulty is comprehensibility. The comprehensibility of a message is an important determiner of whether a message will be learned or not. The easier the message is to understand, the more likely it is to be effective (Eagly, 1974). In general, when individuals comprehend a message, they are more likely to be persuaded by it—so long as the arguments are good (Eagly & Himmelfarb, 1978). If individuals understand a message, they can repeat it to themselves and can think about supporting arguments for the position advocated in the message (Fiske & Taylor, 1991). Thus, they are more likely to agree with the message.

Another issue relating to the message is the structure of the message when it involves an issue having two sides. Pratkanis (1989) found that, for individuals who are not knowledgeable about a subject, a message containing only supportive information about the subject is more likely to foster new knowledge and learning than a message containing both supportive and nonsupportive information. He reasoned that once individuals have a belief about an issue and they know both supportive and attacking arguments about the issue, they are more resistant to changing their beliefs than when they know only one side of the issue. Eagly and Chaiken (1993) suggest that the knowledge about critical arguments against an issue provide individuals with a kind of screen or defense that wards off attacks on their beliefs, making it harder to learn new material related to that belief.

This finding is similar to that of Garner and Chambliss (in press) on beliefs about the Pacific forests. They gave readers a text presenting both sides of the effects of logging operations in the Northwest. They found that most readers did not change their beliefs after reading the text. To the contrary, readers only became more certain of their own positions. Thus, Garner and Chambliss's readers appeared to use their initial beliefs as a filter for understanding what they read about in the text. Further, they used that filter to reinforce what they already believed rather than to examine and possibly rethink their positions. What is especially interesting about this study is that, when asked to support their positions after reading, readers used the same segments of texts as evidence to support their very different positions. These readers were able to modify arguments in the text to support their positions even when those arguments did not. Thus, the power of beliefs as a distorter of information is clear.

Sherif and Hovland's work (1961) extends these findings to provide a framework for understanding when belief change is most likely. They argued that messages that are similar to one's initial position will be viewed as the same, with little or no change taking place. Messages with a very different position will be viewed as even more different, with little or no change taking place. The most likely change will arise out of messages that are perceived as moderately different (Milburn, 1991).

There are at least two factors which mediate these findings, however. First, when there is ego-involvement, as when one has a high personal stake in one's belief, then there will be less likelihood of change (Krosnick, 1988). Second, when individuals have extreme positions, they will perceive a moderate message as more opposed to their own positions than the message actually is (Hovland, Harvey, & Sherif, 1957).

In sum, the different routes to persuasion suggest that individuals must think deeply and thoroughly as they process a message for belief change to occur. Change can also occur through peripheral cues, but such change is not likely to be permanent.

DISCUSSION

Throughout this review we have noted the similarities between the findings from the social psychology literature and the literature from cognitive and educational psychology. Our goal is to understand the implications of the social psychology literature and how it relates to learning from texts. We now summarize these implications.

At times, students' beliefs may conflict with information they read or hear in school, and this conflict may inhibit their learning from text. For example, students may believe that, all things being equal, heavier objects fall faster than lighter ones, and ignore instruction that proves they do not (Champagne, Klopfer, & Anderson, 1980). Students may believe that heterosexuals are not at risk for AIDS when they read about taking precautions against AIDS, and therefore ignore the new information they receive through text.

When students' beliefs conflict with the views expressed in a text, the only route to real, lasting change in those beliefs is what social psychologists call the "central" or "systematic" route. Texts *may* be able to promote change through the central or systematic route under certain conditions. For example, if students' beliefs are one-sided or moderate, their beliefs may be changed from reading a text. If the issue is noncontroversial, readers' beliefs may be changed. If the text is clear and comprehensible, readers' beliefs may be changed. If the content of the text is not too conceptually difficult, readers' beliefs may be changed. Although each of these conditions may be necessary for belief change, each one alone is not sufficient. It is very clear from the social psychology literature that the central route to belief change requires *deep thinking, critical reflection, and a weighing of the issues.*

Belief change can also come about even though learners do not think carefully and deeply about the issues. For example, an effective communicator, a simple or comprehensible message can affect beliefs. But, belief change that comes about through these peripheral cues, where no deep thinking or processing is required, is temporary, and learners are likely to return to their previously held beliefs.

For text designers and teachers working with textbooks, the question of how to foster central, not peripheral, change is a critical one in developing and using educational texts. Research in social psychology shows that deep thinking or processing of ideas in the text is essential. However, the research also shows that students, readers, and in fact, most individuals do not tend to think deeply and process information critically unless they have a reason to do so.

What can text designers do to promote deep thinking and thus central change? Text revisers have tried many routes to affect learning from text: refutation text (Maria, 1988), inserting seductive details (Garner et al., 1989), and increasing comprehensibility (Beck, McKeown, Sinatra, & Loxterman, 1991; Graves et al., 1988) are a few examples. We examine each in terms of its potential for promoting belief change.

Science educators and reading researchers have attempted to influence learners' intuitive beliefs about scientific concepts through refutation texts (see, for example, Alvermann & Hynd, 1989; Dole et al., 1991; Maria, 1988). The theoretical base for refutation texts comes from the work science educators have done on conceptual change learning (Posner et al., 1982). Researchers have shown that an effective technique for getting students to change their intuitive beliefs about science concepts is to have them become aware of what they believe to be true and then show them that there is a more plausible alternative (Posner et al., 1982).

Refutation texts are ones in which students' intuitive beliefs about specific concepts are stated so that they can become aware of what they already believe. Further, in refutation texts, students' intuitive beliefs are contrasted with scientific beliefs. For example, in Dole and Niederhauser (1989) text was developed that stated, "Some people think that food is used only in people's stomachs, but this is not true. Food is used in every cell of the body" (p. 7).

The idea that food is used only in people's stomachs was culled from pilot data with sixth-grade students and used to make students aware of what they were most likely to think. The text went on to discuss scientific understandings about where and how food is used throughout our bodies. Results from this and other studies with refutation texts (Guzzetti, Synder, Glass, & Gamas, 1993) indicate that refutation texts tend to be effective in changing students' ideas about scientific phenomena. However, research also shows that large numbers of students continue to maintain their intuitive beliefs despite reading even refutation text (Beck & Dole, 1992).

Perhaps refutation texts are effective in causing change because the statement of both the intuitive belief and its refutation forces the reader to *weigh both sides of an issue*—one of the critical components of the central route to belief change. On the other hand, refutation text has serious problems in its implementation in textbooks, and thus its widespread use is discouraged, at least by some (Dole, Niederhauser, & Hayes, 1991).

Research has shown that individuals tend to think deeply about an issue in which they have a stake in the outcome. For example, students who do smoke are likely to be more attentive to a textbook chapter on smoking and health than students who do not smoke. Perhaps this is why research has shown that interest is a significant factor in text comprehension (Wade & Adams, 1990; Wade et al., 1993). Readers are more likely to engage in the *deep thinking* and *critical reflection* necessary for central change when the text is about a topic they find interesting.

To make texts more interesting, text revisers have tried to "spice up" the text with interesting but unimportant information Garner and her colleagues have called "seductive details" (Garner et al., 1989). For example, Wade et al. (1993) included personal, scandalous details about the personal life of Horatio Nelson in a text about his naval career. These interesting, but unimportant, seductive details were remembered by readers; however, the details did not influence readers' learning of important information. There appears to be growing evidence that inserting seductive details in a text does not facilitate learning of important information (Garner et al., 1989; Wade et al., 1993).

Why does such seductive information not affect comprehension positively? Perhaps seductive details are a type of peripheral cue that may produce peripheral or temporary change, but not central change. One might expect seductive details to pull the reader in to read more carefully and critically. Yet, the research does not support this hypothesis (Wade et al., 1993).

Beck et al. (1991) revised social studies text to be more comprehensible by considering the cognitive nature of the reader and the reading process. For example, in making revisions they considered both text factors, such as text coherence, and reader variables, such as background knowledge, to hypothesize possible comprehension breakdowns. They then revised the text to ameliorate the possible difficulties. Their results and those of others who have attempted to increase the comprehensibility of text (Duffy et al., 1989; Graves et al., 1988) show that texts revised to be more coherent do produce greater recall. As noted earlier, a clear and comprehensible message is more likely to produce central change.

Comprehensibility is essential for central change but, clearly, it is not necessarily sufficient. Conceptually difficult material needs compelling, clear, and coherent explanations to foster understanding from text (Sinatra & Dole, 1993). In our examination of high school biology textbook presentations of evolution, we found that the text presentations lacked both textual coherence and explanatory coherence. That is, the presentation lacked causal connections in terms of text structure, and also failed to provide explanations of how change in species occurs according to evolutionary theory. The result is that the texts are difficult to comprehend and do not provide a compelling account of a major scientific theory. In other words, students may find it difficult to believe the information in the text because the explanation provided is so unconvincing.

Text revision techniques have proven to be somewhat effective under certain conditions. Duffy et al. (1989) and others (Britton, van Dusen, Gulgoz, & Glynn, 1989; Beck et al., 1991) have noted, however, that effective text revisions cannot be produced from a proceduralized list of revision algorithms. We certainly agree with this position. As noted, the social psychology literature suggests that what is most important in promoting the central route to belief change is deep, critical thinking. Revisions that attempt to promote such engaged processing are likely to be more effective than those that do not.

Whether a text has been revised or not, the question for learning from text is: What types of instructional strategies promote active engagement with text and thus have the potential for promoting central change? There are instructional strategies that promote deep thinking and processing through active engagement with text. Palinscar and Brown's (1984) reciprocal teaching research showed the effect on comprehension of teaching readers a questioning and predicting strategy. Readers who use the strategy effectively are clearly engaging with the text in a manner that promotes deeper thinking and processing.

Beck, McKeown, and Worthy (1993) have used a "questioning the author" strategy to promote fifth-graders' active engagement with their social studies textbooks. In this strategy, students are told that textbook authors are not perfect, and that if they as readers do not understand, perhaps the authors failed to make their point clear. The students are then encouraged to problem solve the authors' intended meaning. This instructional strategy clearly fosters a deeper processing of the text than students would have undertaken on their own. It may also promote a sense of "ownership" on the part of readers, that is, a sense that they are in control of their own comprehension process. But, perhaps an important element to the strategy's success is that it promotes the type of *deep thinking* and *critical reflection* necessary for central change.

In sum, for central change to occur when reading text, the text needs to be clear and comprehensible and provide a compelling and convincing argument. Further, readers must care about the issue they are reading about, they must have a stake in the outcome, they must think deeply and reflectively, and they must have ownership in the learning process.

CONCLUSION

Cognitive psychology and social psychology conceptualize the constructs of knowledge and beliefs in similar ways. And yet, while cognitive psychology has had considerable impact on how educators think about learning and teaching, social psychology has not.

Some may argue that students do not have many "beliefs" as they go through school, and therefore the social psychology research does not address issues of learning and teaching. Yet, we know from cognitive research dating back at least to Bartlett (1932) that students do not come to school as blank slates. They hold intuitive "knowledge" about their physical world based on their sensory perceptions and experiences, knowledge about social and political issues, knowledge about religion, knowledge about the nature of their own learning, knowledge about the role of the teacher in the classroom, and knowledge about many of the topics they might read about in and out of school.

Further, as social psychologists point out, learners almost always have an *evaluation* of the knowledge they are presented with in that learners will have a certain commitment to the truthfulness of the knowledge. Either they *believe it* in the sense that they accept it as truth, or they do not.

We believe this is one of the most important points to be gained from social psychology, and represents the important difference between knowledge and beliefs. Knowledge is unexamined information; a belief is a commitment to the truthfulness of that knowledge.

Now, what does this difference between knowledge and beliefs mean for educational researchers studying students and how they learn? We think that when educational researchers discuss *knowledge* that students have, they are almost always discussing *beliefs*. After all, students do evaluate what they hear and read about, and they either accept the information or they do not. So, whether we call it knowledge or beliefs does not seem to us to be central to the research agenda.

Whether we call what students already know *knowledge* or *beliefs*, the impact of what they know is clear from both the cognitive and social psychology research. Both show that learners' knowledge or beliefs tend not to change when new data conflict with what is already known. Both show that learners need to process information deeply and think critically about new data for "conceptual change" or "attitude change" to come about (see also Chinn & Brewer, 1993). Both show that such change is difficult, and in many cases, unlikely.

Cognitive psychologists have avoided hot cognition for many years. Yet, social psychologists studying hot cognition have amazingly similar findings to cognitive psychologists studying cold cognition. Thus, we have to wonder whether the time has come for educational researchers working within a cognitive psychology framework to study affect.

We would argue that there are at least two good reasons why the study of beliefs and other affective factors involved in learning ought to become a part of cognitive psychologists' research agenda. First, there is strong evidence from social psychology that, whether we call what individuals know *knowledge* or *beliefs*, the outcomes are the same. Second, we know that educators working with students are enormously concerned about the many affective factors that influence learning. Many students do not want to learn, or are not motivated to spend time thinking carefully and critically about issues they read about or learn about in school. Thus, the careful study of affective factors involved in learning would have a great deal to say to educators. We believe that research on affective factors, and especially on ways to encourage students to actively engage with material, would be welcomed enthusiastically by those who deal with students every day.

REFERENCES

Abelson, R. P. (1986). Beliefs are like possessions. *Journal for the Theory of Social Behavior, 16*, 223-250.

Alvermann, D. E., & Hynd, C. R. (1989). Study strategies for correcting misconceptions in physics: An intervention. In S. McCormick & J. Zutell (Eds.), *Cognitive and social perspectives for literacy research and instruction* (pp. 353-361). Chicago: National Reading Conference.

Anderson, C. W., & Smith, E. L. (1987). Teaching science. In V. Richardson-Koehler (Ed.), *Educator's handbook: A research perspective* (pp. 84-111). New York: Longman.

Anderson, J. R. (1983). *The architecture of cognition*. Cambridge, MA: Harvard University Press.

Anderson, R. C., & Pearson, P. D. (1984). A schema-theoretic view of basic processes in reading comprehension. In P. D. Pearson, (Ed.). *Handbook of Reading Research* (Vol. 1, pp. 255-292). New York: Academic Press.

Anderson, R. C., & Pichert, J. W. (1978). Recall of previously unrecallable information following a shift in perspective. *Journal of Verbal Learning and Verbal Behavior, 17*, 1-12.

Anderson, R. C., Reynolds, R. E., Schallert, D. L., & Goetz, E. T. (1977). Frameworks for comprehending discourse. *American Educational Research Journal, 14*, 367-382.

Bartlett, F. C. (1932). *Remembering*. Cambridge, England: Cambridge University Press.

Beck, I. L., & Dole, J. A. (1992). Reading and thinking with history and science text. In C. Collins & J. N. Mangieri (Eds.), *Building the quality of thinking in and out of our schools in the twenty-first century* (pp. 3-21). Hillsdale, NJ: Lawrence Erlbaum Associates.

Beck, I. L., McKeown, M. G., Sinatra, G. M., & Loxterman, J. A. (1991). Revising social studies text from a text-processing perspective: Evidence of improved comprehensibility. *Reading Research Quarterly, 24*, 251-276.

Beck, I. L., McKeown, M. G., & Worthy, M. J. (1993, April). *Questioning the author: An approach to enhancing students' engagement with text*. Paper presented at the meeting of the American Educational Research Association, Atlanta, GA.

Britton, B. K., van Dusen, L., Gulgoz, S., Glynn, S. M. (1989). Instructional texts rewritten by five experts teams: Revisions and retention improvements. *Journal of Educational Psychology, 81*, 226-239.

Brown, A. L. (1988). Motivation to learn and understand: On taking charge of one's own learning. *Cognition and Instruction, 4*, 311-321.

Chaiken, S. (1987). The heuristic model of persuasion. In M. P. Zanna, J. M. Olson, & C. P. Herman (Eds.), *Social influence: The Ontario Symposium* (Vol. 5, pp. 3-39). Hillsdale, NJ: Lawrence Erlbaum Associates.

Chaiken, S., & Eagly, A. H. (1976). Communication modality as a determinant of message persuasiveness and message comprehensibility. *Journal of Personality and Social Psychology, 34*, 605-614.

Chaiken, S., & Eagly, A. H. (1983). Communication modality as a determinant of persuasion: The role of communicator salience. *Journal of Personality and Social Psychology, 45*, 241-256.

Chaiken, S., Liberman, A., & Eagly, A. H. (1989). Heuristic and systematic processing within and beyond the persuasion context. In J. S. Uleman & J. A. Bargh (Eds.), *Unintended thought* (pp. 212-252). New York: Guilford Press.

Champagne, A., Klopfer, L., & Anderson, J. (1980). Factors influencing learning of classical mechanics. *American Journal of Physics, 48*, 1074-1079.

Chinn, C. A., & Brewer, W. F. (1993). The role of anomalous data in knowledge acquisition: A theoretical framework and implications for science instruction. *Review of Educational Research, 63*, 1-49.

Craik, F. I. M., & Lockhart, R. S. (1972). Levels of processing: A framework for memory research. *Journal of Verbal Learning and Verbal Behavior, 11*, 671-684.

Dole, J. A., & Niederhauser, D. S. (1989, December). *The effects of considerate and refutation text on learning conceptually easy and difficult science topics*. Paper presented at the meeting of the National Reading Conference, Austin, TX.

Dole, J. A., Niederhauser, D. S., & Hayes, M. T. (1991, April). *The role of reading in conceptual change in science*. Paper presented at the meeting of the American Educational Research Association, Chicago.

Dole, J. A., Sinatra, G., & Reynolds, R. (1991, December). *The effects of strong beliefs on text processing and learning: The case of evolution and creationism*. Paper presented at the meeting of the National Reading Conference, Palm Springs, CA.

Duffy, T. M., Higgins, L., Mehlenbacher, B., Cochran, C., Wallace, D., Hill, C., Haugen, D., McCaffrey, M., Burnett, R., Sloane, S., & Smith, S. (1989). Models for the design of instructional text. *Reading Research Quarterly, 24*, 434-457.

Eagly, A. H. (1974). Comprehensibility of persuasive arguments as a determinant of opinion change. *Journal of Personality and Social Psychology, 29*, 758-773.

Eagly, A. H., & Chaiken, S. (1975). An attribution analysis of the effect of communicator characteristics on opinion change: The case of communicator attractiveness. *Journal of Personality and Social Psychology, 32*, 136-144.

Eagly, A. H., & Chaiken, S. (1993). *The psychology of attitudes.* Ft. Worth, TX: Harcourt, Brace, & Jovanovich.

Eagly, A. H., & Himmelfarb, S. (1978). Attitudes and opinions. *Annual Review of Psychology, 29*, 517-554.

Eaton, J. F., Anderson, C. W., & Smith, E. L. (1984). Students' misconceptions interfere with learning: Case studies of fifth grade students. *Elementary School Journal, 64*, 365-379.

Fazio, R. H. (1986). How do attitudes guide behavior? In R. M. Sorrentino & E. T. Higgins (Eds.), *Handbook of motivation and cognition: Foundations of social behavior* (pp. 204-243). New York: Guilford Press.

Fazio, R. H. (1987). Self-perception theory: A current perspective. In M. P. Zanna, J. M. Olson, & C. P. Herman (Eds.), *Social influence: The Ontario Symposium* (pp. 129-149). Hillsdale, NJ: Lawrence Erlbaum Associates.

Fazio, R. H. (1989). On the power and functionality of attitudes: The role of attitude accessibility. In A. R. Pratkanis, S. J. Breckler, & A. G. Greenwald (Eds.), *Attitude structure and function* (pp. 153-179). HIllsdale, NJ: Lawrence Erlbaum Associates.

Fishbein, M., & Ajzen, I. (1975). *Belief, attitude, intention and behavior: An introduction to theory and research.* Reading, MA: Addison-Wesley.

Fiske, S. T., & Taylor, S. E. (1991). *Social cognition.* New York: McGraw Hill.

Garner, R., & Chambliss, M. J. (in press). Do adults change their minds after reading persuasive text? In A. J. Pace (Ed.), *Beyond Prior Knowledge: Issues in text processing and conceptual change.* Norwood, NJ: Ablex.

Garner, R., Gillingham, M.G., & White, J. (1989). Effects of "seductive details" on macroprocessing and microprocessing in adults and children. *Cognition and Instruction, 6*, 41-57.

Graves, M. E., Slater, W. H., Roen, D. D., Redd-Boyd, T., Duin, A. H., Furniss, D. W., & Hazeltine, P. (1988). Some characteristics of memorable expository writing: Effects of revisions by writers with different backgrounds. *Research in the Teaching of English, 22*, 242-265.

Guzzetti, B. J., Synder, T. E., Glass, G. V., & Gamas, W. S. (1993). Promoting conceptual change in science: A comparative meta-analysis of instructional interventions from reading education and science education. *Reading Research Quarterly, 28*, 117-155.

Hidi, S. (1990). Interest and its contribution as a mental resource for learning. *Review of Educational Research, 60*, 549-571.

Hidi, S., & Baird, W. (1986). Interestingness—A neglected variable in discourse processing. *Cognitive Science, 10*, 179-194.

Hovland, C. I., Harvey, O. J., & Sherif, M. (1957). Assimilation and contrast effects in reactions to communication and attitude change. *Journal of Abnormal and Social Psychology, 55*, 244-252.

Hovland, C. I., Janis, I. L., & Kelly, J. J. (1953). *Communication and persuasibility.* New Haven, CT: Yale University Press.

Krosnick, J. A. (1988). Attitude importance and attitude change. *Journal of Experimental Social Psychology, 24*, 240-255.

Lazarus, R. S. (1982). Thoughts on the relations between emotion and cognition. *American Psychologist, 37*, 1019-1024.

Lazarus, R. S. (1984). On the primacy of cognition. *American Psychologist, 39*, 124-129.

Maria, K. (1988, December). *Helping fifth graders learn with science text.* Paper presented at the meeting of the National Reading Conference, Tucson.

McCloskey, M. (1983). Naive theories of motion. In D. Gentner & A. Stevens (Eds.), *Mental models* (pp. 299-324). Hillsdale, NJ: Lawrence Erlbaum Associates.

McGuire, W. J. (1969). The nature of attitudes and attitude change. In G. Lindzey & E. Aronson (Eds.), *Handbook of social psychology* (2nd ed., Vol. 3, pp. 136-314). Reading MA: Addison-Wesley.

McGuire, W. J. (1985). Attitudes and attitude change. In G. Lindzey & E. Aronson (Eds.), *Handbook of social psychology* (3rd ed., Vol. 2, pp. 233-346). Reading MA: Addison-Wesley.

Meyer, B. J. F., & Rice, G. E. (1984). The structure of text. In P. D. Pearson (Ed.), *Handbook of reading research* (pp. 319-351). New York: Longman.

Milburn, M. A. (1991). *Persuasion and politics.* Pacific Grove, CA: Brooks/Cole Publishing.

Otero, J., & Kintsch, W. (1992). Failures to detect contradictions in a text: What readers believe vs. what they read. *Psychological Science, 3,* 229-235.

Palincsar, A. S., & Brown, A. L. (1984). Reciprocal teaching of comprehension-fostering and monitoring activities. *Cognition and Instruction, 1,* 117-175.

Petty, R. E., & Cacioppo, J. T. (1981). *Attitudes and persuasion: Classic and contemporary approaches.* Dubuque, IA: Brown.

Petty, R. E., & Cacioppo, J. T. (1986). *Communication and persuasion: Central and peripheral routes to attitude change.* New York: Springer-Verlag.

Posner, G. J., Strike, K. A., Hewson, P. W., & Gertzog, W. A. (1982). Accommodation of a scientific conceptions: Toward a theory of conceptual change. *Science Education, 66,* 489-508.

Pratkanis, A. R. (1989). The cognitive representation of attitudes. In A. R. Pratkanis, S. J. Breckler, & A. G. Greenwald (Eds.), *Attitude structure and function* (pp. 71-98). Hillsdale, NJ: Lawrence Erlbaum Associates.

Sherif, M., & Hovland, C. I. (1961). *Social Judgment.* New Haven, CT: Yale University Press.

Sinatra, G. M., & Dole, J. A. (1993, April). *Textbook presentations of evolutionary biology: Issues impeding comprehension.* Paper presented at the meeting of the American Education Research Association, Atlanta, GA.

Spiro, R. J. (1980). Constructive processes in prose recall. In R. J. Spiro, B. C. Bruce, & W. F. Brewer (Eds.), *Schooling and the acquisition of knowledge.* Hillsdale, NJ: Lawrence Erlbaum Associates.

Tesser, A. & Shaffer, D. R. (1990). Attitudes and attitude change. *American Review of Psychology, 41,* 479-523.

Wade, S. E., & Adams, B. (1990). Effects of importance and interest on recall of biographical text. *JRB: A Journal of Literacy, 22,* 331-353.

Wade, S. E., Schraw, G., Buxton, W. M., & Hayes, M. T. (1993). Seduction of the strategic reader: Effects of interest on strategy and recall. *Reading Research Quarterly, 28,* 93-114.

West, L. H. T., & Pines, A. L. (1985). *Cognitive structure and conceptual change.* Orlando, FL: Academic Press.

Vosniadu, S., & Brewer, W. F. (1987). Theories of knowledge restructuring in development. *Review of Educational Research, 57,* 51-67.

Zajonc, R. B. (1980). Feeling and thinking: preferences need no inferences. *American Psychologist, 25,* 151-175.

CHAPTER FOURTEEN

The Role of Belief Systems in Authors' and Readers' Constructions of Texts

Suzanne Wade
Audrey Thompson
William Watkins
University of Utah

Until recently, cognitive researchers have tended to view reading and learning from texts in terms of information processing and retrieval: Reading to learn has meant correctly recovering the facts, ideas, and principles set forth in a text. Generally, the texts in question have been experimental texts, specifically designed to set forth facts to be processed. Because such texts appeared to be neutral—if not objective—repositories of meaning, it was assumed that any beliefs readers displayed were their own contributions, unrelated to the text. Unless readers' beliefs took the form of misconceptions that interfered with learning, beliefs were considered a subjective matter and therefore not relevant to comprehension or learning.

As this volume attests, the role of beliefs in comprehension and learning has started to come under careful scrutiny. Beliefs are now recognized as part of the legitimate meaning-making process, in what Bruner (1990) has called a "renewed cognitive revolution." Bruner describes this new focus as offering a more interpretive approach to cognition—one concerned with the construction of meaning rather than with the processing of information. As a result, *mind*—in the sense of "believing, desiring, intending, grasping a meaning" (p. 8)—is becoming a central concept to be researched and understood. In this volume, authors of the various chapters have drawn on different paradigms and definitions in addressing the question, "What is a belief?" Our own approach, for the purposes of the present study, is to look at beliefs in connection with a belief *system*—an ideology.

Therefore, we will be looking at beliefs as part of a system that includes assumptions, knowledge, commitments, attitudes, and feelings—all of which are caught up in an evaluative framework. As Abelson (1979) notes, "a belief system typically has large categories of concepts defined in one way or another as themselves 'good' or 'bad,' or as leading to good or bad" (p. 358). The evaluative dimension of beliefs may be so embedded, however, as to be effectively invisible—the essential components of a belief system are precisely what we take for granted. That is, we assume that our beliefs are simply "common sense" or the natural order of things. They are what we consider normal, relevant, or self-evident. For example, when professional women first began to protest their male colleagues' assumption that the women would make the coffee, the general response was incredulous. From the point of view of the men, making coffee was simply a woman's job, something so obvious and normal that to raise it to the level of an issue was absurd. For the women, however, the point was not the mere fact of making coffee, but the framework that assumed that it *only made sense* for the women to be responsible for anything resembling domestic chores. In protesting coffee-making, women were calling a whole ideology into question.

When common sense judgments conflict, it becomes easier to recognize them *as* referenced to particular belief systems. However, only those assumptions regarding normalcy and appropriateness that are at odds with the assumptions of the dominant groups will be widely identified as *ideological*. Yet, in fact, any group's belief system, regardless of its political currency, may be described as an ideology. An ideology, as Apple (1979) describes it, is "some sort of 'system' of ideas, beliefs, fundamental commitments, or values about social reality" (p. 20). It is a way of organizing meaning, of making sense of social situations through recourse to a comprehensible and (more or less) coherent world view. In Geertz's (1964) phrase, it is a "system of interacting symbols," though this is not to suggest that such systems are *logically* systemic. As historian Barbara Fields (1982) observes, ideologies "consist of contradictory and inconsistent elements" (p. 154). Their viability, she points out, is a function of their adaptability, rather than of any inherent intellectual quality.

While ideology encompasses beliefs that, at face value, we might not consider political, the term refers to a specifically political function. As Apple (1979) notes, ideology "always deals with legitimation, power conflict, and a special style of argument" (p. 21). Specifically, legitimation refers to beliefs that justify and rationalize vested social, political, and economic interests and roles. It follows, then, that "power conflict is always at stake in ideological disputes" (Apple, 1979, p. 21), since ideology is linked to conflicts between people seeking or holding power in any sphere of activity that deals with the allocation of rewards. Ideologies also have a distinctive language and rhetoric that appear to be economically and culturally neutral, but that often "disguise the real values, interests, and social functioning which underpin them" (p. 22). In education, for example, Apple argues that the language, assumptions, and values of ideologies enable people to "employ frameworks which both assist them in organizing their world and enable them to believe they are neutral participants in the neutral instrumentation of schooling . . . while at the same time, these frameworks serve particular economic and ideological interests which are hidden from them" (p. 22).

The purpose of this chapter is to describe how the ideologies of both authors and readers influence what they find interesting, what they pay attention to, what meanings they construct, and what evaluations they make. In many ways, writing and reading are highly similar. Just as texts are considered to be constructions of meaning on the part of the author, reading is generally understood as the active construction of meaning on the part of the reader. Some researchers have even argued that readers "compose" meaning, much as an author does. For example, Petrosky (1982) has argued that "our comprehension of texts, whether they are literary or not, is more an act of composition—for understanding is composing—than of information retrieval" (p. 19). Similarly, Tierney and Pearson (1984) have claimed that readers, like writers, compose meaning: "From a reader's perspective, meaning is created as a reader uses his background of experience together with the author's cues to come to grips both with what the writer is getting him to do or think *and* what the reader decides and creates for himself" (p. 33).

We begin by describing how texts are ideological, focusing in particular on history texts—both academic works and school textbooks. We then present results of a study that describes how viewers responded to the recent PBS documentary film about the Civil War. In this study, we examine the different ways that individuals with varying backgrounds, interests, conceptions of history, and purposes engage with the text—some responding appreciatively and others resistantly, some engrossed in the storytelling and others distanced and critical. In the last section, we discuss some implications of our study for schooling in a democratic society.

THE IDEOLOGIES OF TEXTS

As cultural and political constructions by authors, texts reflect authors' assumptions, beliefs, commitments, attitudes, and values. Nowhere is this more evident than in history texts. Historian Henry Steele Commanger (1966) offers this debunking of the myth of objectivity:

> Let us admit at once that history is neither scientific nor mechanical, that the historian is human, and therefore fallible, and that the ideal history, completely

objective and dispassionate, is an illusion. There is bias in the choice of a subject, bias in the selection of material, bias in organization and presentation, and inevitably bias in interpretation. (p. 53)

The term *bias* might seem to suggest that, conversely, neutrality *is* possible, but in fact the point being made here is that any text *as* a text—as a framework of meaning—inevitably represents particular assumptions, selections, omissions, interpretations, and organizational decisions. Ideology, then, operates at the level of the text as a whole, not only with respect to content but with respect to the structure (whether argument, narrative, or listing of facts). Ideology may also appear in the form of one or more *subtexts* running parallel (or occasionally counter) to the explicit meaning of the text. As Wineburg (1991) defines them, subtexts are underlying messages or points that supplement the overt meaning of the text. In a recent issue of *The Journal of American History* (1992), William Cronon describes the different political subtexts in histories of the long drought that struck the Great Plains during the 1930s. Historians drew radically different conclusions, depending on whether they believed the dust storms of the 1930s represented (a) a natural disaster with a happy ending ("nature made a mess and human beings cleaned it up"), or (b) a human disaster with a tragic ending (people failed to accommodate themselves to nature, resulting in collapse of the ecosystem), or (c) a human disaster with a happy ending, thanks to the New Dealers with their enlightened perspective of scientific management.

Cronon (1992) argues that historical texts are ideological because historians are naturally drawn to storytelling: "We [historians] configure the events of the past into causal sequences—stories—that order and simplify those events to give them new meanings. We do so because narrative is the chief literary form that tries to find meaning in an overwhelmingly crowded and disordered chronological reality" (p. 1349). In constructing a narrative, the historian decides who or what is included and excluded, relevant and irrelevant. History is thus inevitably political. "Whatever its overt purpose, it cannot avoid a covert exercise of power: it inevitably sanctions some voices while silencing others" (p. 1350).

Of course, *any* text is ideological, including those that adopt a "just the facts" format. Texts such as medical reference works, for example, are no more immune to ideological bias than any other text. In ironic recognition of the pervasive bias in one such text, an anonymous index editor for the standard medical text, *Williams Obstetrics,* included the following entry as part of the index for the book: " 'Chauvinism, male, voluminous amounts, pages 1–1102' " (Shorter, 1992, p. 3). In contrast to "just the facts" texts, though, history texts are not only about "what happened" but about "what history tells us about ourselves." In consequence, they undergo frequent rewritings to accommodate ideological shifts—and thus are more readily identifiable *as* ideological. Every political regime acknowledges the importance of history and history texts in creating support for its partisan agenda (Watkins, 1986). History textbooks for elementary and secondary schools are frequently rewritten and carefully monitored by various political groups. In *America Revised* (1979), Frances FitzGerald has documented how U. S. history textbooks have changed during the course of the 20th century to reflect the prevailing ideology: "Consensus documents, they are themselves a part of history in that they reflect the concerns, the conventional wisdom, and even the fad of the age that produced them" (p. 20). As FitzGerald (1979) points out, the purpose of history textbooks is not to examine but to instruct—"to tell children what their elders want them to know about their country. This information is not necessarily what anyone considers the truth of things. Like time capsules, the texts contain the truths selected for posterity" (p. 47). Similarly, de Castell (1991) argues that school textbooks have a social function: "to represent to each generation of students a sanctioned version of human knowledge and culture" (p. 78).

Just as the historians' accounts of the dust bowl have changed over time, these truths-to-be-taught have also changed. Consider, for example, how differently Reconstruction was been depicted in the textbooks of the mid-60s compared to those of the early 70s. FitzGerald found that the change was not just a shift in emphasis "but a total inversion: the same material is used, nothing has been added, but the interpretation has altered so that—one might say—what was white is now black and vice versa" (p. 85). The earlier texts viewed Reconstruction as an unmitigated disaster brought about by the Radical Republicans who wanted revenge on the South and a permanent electoral majority in the Congress; Reconstruction governments were depicted as run by corrupt "carpetbaggers" and "scalawags," who pillaged the South; and, the Ku Klux Klan was portrayed as an organization of respectable White Southerners—at least initially—joining together for purposes of self-defense against bands of Negroes roaming the countryside. However, when the Klan became lawless, solid citizens of the South forced it to disband—suggesting, it would seem, that the Klan no longer existed. In contrast, textbooks of the 70s viewed Reconstruction in a more positive light: The Radical Republicans were right to want to prevent the reestablishment of slavery by means of the Black Codes and to give Blacks the vote; many of those whom Southerners called carpetbaggers and scalawags were sincere reformers; yes, corruption may have been a problem, but it had always existed in the South; and the Ku Klux Klan waged a campaign of terror to prevent freedmen from voting. Even later editions of the same book can reflect a radically different ideology than the original. As an example, FitzGerald cites a popular eighth-grade history textbook (Casner & Gabriel, 1931/1935, 1938, 1942/1950/1955), which metamorphosed from offering a liberal internationalist interpretation in the 30s to taking a fierce anti-Communist stance in the 50s.

In some cases, the content itself has changed, especially when we consider what is included and excluded and whose voices are heard and whose are silenced. FitzGerald describes one text (Muzzey, 1950) that, having begun its description of the population of the U. S. by saying, "Leaving aside the Negro and Indian population . . . ," then "proceeded to do just that. The Blacks were never treated as a group at all; they were quite literally invisible" (FitzGerald, p. 84). Only in the 1960s did African Americans, Native Americans, and other minority groups suddenly appear in textbooks—usually on sections on the civil-rights movement—and then as if they had no history. Also excluded has been any mention of class conflict, considered by every textbook writer to be un-American (FitzGerald, p. 155). By avoiding mention of conflicts of interest, textbooks promote the perception of an underlying unity such that what appear to be social "problems" can be resolved through the application of more of whatever is said to make America great (for example, more tolerance or, alternatively, more uniformity, depending on the prevailing beliefs).

As Apple (1979) has argued, ideologies have a distinctive language or rhetoric that appears to be neutral but in fact is not. This is certainly true of history textbooks. Textbooks have often used words such as "we," "our," "freedom," and "brave," to encourage readers to identify with the United States. A perusal of titles bears this out: *Our Country's History, The Free and the Brave: The Story of the American People, This is Our Nation*, and *America: Land of Freedom*. And, although at one time school texts were clearly opinioned (FitzGerald, 1979), now the most common rhetorical style is "an objective, unelaborated, straightforward style with an anonymous authoritative 'author' reporting a body of facts in one preposition after another" (Crismore, 1984, p. 279). McKeown, Beck, and Worthy (1993) argue that the neutral "objective" style of textbook prose, which places textbooks above criticism, may cause students to attribute comprehension difficulties to their own perceived inadequacies rather than to problems in the text.

While "fact-stating" textbooks are usually referred to as "expository" texts, Suzanne de Castell (1991, p. 78) argues that they are better described as "documentary" texts, insofar as their primary function is to describe and define reality without recourse to any explicit frameworks of analysis or of argumentation. The analogy de Castell offers is to government documents— in particular, the innumerable forms that define, categorize, and police welfare recipients. But insofar as film documentaries enjoy a reputation for objectivity and for concentration upon "the facts of the case," they too may be said to belong to that documentary tradition.

The recent PBS documentary film series, *The Civil War*, offers a useful case study of the role of ideology in documentary texts—especially as it represents both a "fact-stating" text and a form of popular entertainment meant to appeal to voluntary engagement. Whereas school texts and government literature coerce rather than invite participation, documentary films aimed at a popular audience invite reader responsiveness. *The Civil War*, for example, employs narrative devices to enliven its "facts of the case" structure. One question this approach raises is whether the softening effect of a narrative structure affects viewers' perceptions of the ideological framework that informs the film. In a documentary film of the high quality of *The Civil War*, we certainly expect objective reporting, balanced attention to the facts, and perhaps even the disembodied authority associated with (idealized) textbooks, but of course we also expect to escape many of the secondary qualities of school texts—their tonelessness, for example, and above all their notoriously boring character.

The Civil War more than meets these expectations, if we are to judge by its resounding popular success. In talks and interviews, director Ken Burns has spoken of his concern to produce a fair and even-handed account of the Civil War, and indeed the series enjoyed favorable and prestigious reviews when it was released. It also provided an entertaining and interesting account of the Civil War, evidently prompting renewed and in some cases new interest in U.S. history. It is worth noting that the interest generated by the series was not tied to any apparent controversy. Rather, the film told the story of the Civil War in a way that made mere "raw" facts interesting and relevant.

As our earlier discussion of ideology suggests, this function alone speaks to the film's ideological character: the perception of information as relevant or important depends upon a particular evaluative framework and a specific ordering of assumptions, attitudes, and investments. Interestingly, this documentary appears to link the ideological traditions of two quite separate genres. On the one hand, of course, the film belongs to the "consensus document" genre that FitzGerald identifies with textbooks. On the other hand, it also partakes of the narrative structure of the television minidrama genre. Gerard Jones (1992) offers the following outline of the underlying narrative structure of sitcoms:

> Domestic harmony is threatened when a character develops a desire that runs counter to the group's welfare, or misunderstands a situation because of poor communication, or contacts a disruptive outside element. The voice of the group—usually the voice of the father or equivalent chief executive—tries to restore harmony but fails. The dissenter grabs at an easy, often unilateral solution. The solution fails, and the dissenter must surrender to the group for rescue. . . . The wisdom of the group and its executive is proved. Everyone, including the dissenter, is happier than at the outset. (p. 4)

If we were to deconstruct *The Civil War*, the father figure would be represented by Abraham Lincoln, or, more generally, by the White Northern leaders, who figure as saviors for the sketchily drawn Black figures. The "facts of the case" structure at times simply lends support to the "father knows best" storyline narrative structure, but at times it also runs counter to it. The structure of the text, the various subtexts, and the content of the film, as some of the viewers in our study discuss, all reflect particular ideological assumptions—though no single ideological account of the film is given. Indeed, *The Civil War* might variously be deconstructed from a Southern perspective, an African-American perspective, a Marxist perspective, or a feminist perspective, to name only a few possible frameworks of reference. Yet the presence of a particular ideological framework and content does not mean that the film determines what viewers' responses will be. As becomes apparent in the next section, both appreciative and critical viewers may choose to respond to texts in a variety of ways. Despite the relatively slight attention devoted to Blacks in the documentary, for example, some viewers respond most vitally to the portrayal of Blacks under slavery as that part of the story that they find most inherently dramatic or as that which most moves them. We turn now to describing results of the case study examining viewer responses to *The Civil War.*

A STUDY OF VIEWERS' RESPONSES TO THE *CIVIL WAR*

The purpose of the present study was to examine how an ideological text—specifically, the PBS documentary on the causes of the U. S. Civil War—might be "read" by individuals who vary in background knowledge, experience, interest, and beliefs—in other words, by people with different ideologies. Among other beliefs, such individuals might hold different conceptions of how history should be portrayed; they might construct different interpretations of the meaning of the Civil War in U. S. history (What was it *really* about? Why does understanding it matter?); and they might hold different theories of causality—for example, what caused the Civil War and what happened as a result. And, because the text reflects the filmmaker's own ideology, participants in the study would be expected to be involved in the text differently and to respond to it differently, depending on their purposes for and expectations of viewing and the congruence of their beliefs with those of the filmmaker.

The present study is distinctive in the text research literature because it involved not the reading of a written text but rather the viewing of a video. Specifically, it involved examining the think aloud protocols from six individuals as they viewed the first hour of the Civil War series that was presented on PBS. The topic of the Civil War was chosen because it is considered important in U. S. history and because many people in the United States have some background knowledge of and interest in the topic. In addition, the video was chosen because it represents an attempt to both entertain and educate a wide audience outside of the school context. The video also offers a more public experience than reading, enabling the interviewer to participate in the viewing along with the participant. Finally, the video represents a kind of "alternative text" that may contribute to our understanding of how responses to written text converge and diverge. Whereas a video and a printed text both convey ideas and their relationships through words and images, a video can be considered more controlling, defining, and bottom-up than a printed text, since with the latter readers are better able to control the pace of presentation and to construct their own understandings and mental images based on prior knowledge and experience.

Six individuals, chosen because they had different backgrounds, volunteered to participate in the study. One participant was a historian whose specialty is 19th century African-American political and social history and school curriculum; one was a feminist philosopher with a focus on ethics and pedagogy; one was a homemaker with relatively little background knowledge concerning the Civil War but an interest in biography and autobiography; one was an accountant who is also a history buff with a particular interest in the Civil War; one was a film buff and a doctoral student in music education; and one was a historian whose specialty is educational and welfare policy in the 20th century.[1] Of the group, three were men and three were women; five were White and one was an African American; three were trained as critical theorists and three were not; and four had a great deal of background knowledge and interest related to the Civil War while two did not. All six were Northerners (though from different parts of the country), college-educated, and between the ages of 30 and 45.

Participants met individually with the same researcher in one 2- to 3-hour session. Each was asked the following interview questions at the beginning of the session: Are you interested in the Civil War as a topic? Is this a personal interest (e.g., leisure reading)? Do you consider the Civil War to be important in history? What in particular do you find interesting and important about it? Does the topic relate to your work? If so, how? Participants were then asked to view the video tape of the first hour of the PBS series on the Civil War and encouraged to comment on any aspect of the presentation, content, etc., at any point in the film, rather than at predetermined boundary points (cf. Langer, 1990). Whenever participants wished to verbalize their thoughts, they hit the pause button on the remote control of the VCR. The verbal

---

[1]In the spirit of collaborative research, study participants became involved in the study in various ways after the interviews had been completed. Some chose to read and comment on their individual transcripts, while two became coauthors of this chapter, helping to frame and write the first and last sections and the commentaries. However, as study participants, they did not code the data in the case study itself.

content of the video and the think alouds were tape recorded and transcribed, allowing the researchers to examine where in the video presentation the participant had stopped the film and commented upon it. Following the viewing, participants were asked questions such as the following: What did you find important and interesting in the video? How would you characterize the filmmaker's purpose for creating the video? Do you think the filmmaker achieved that purpose? If so, how? Did you learn anything new from watching this video?

Three qualitative analyses of the data were then conducted. The first analysis involved the previewing interview questions. This information served primarily to develop profiles of the participants in terms of their points of view and their background knowledge of and interest in the Civil War. The second analysis was conducted with the think-aloud data gathered during the viewing. In this analysis, each transcript was read carefully, first separately, then in comparison with the other transcripts in a search for patterns that capture different aspects of the content of the verbal reports. Once categories of responses were identified, the researcher returned to the transcripts to code responses into categories and to select prototypical quotes illustrating each category (Goetz & LeCompte, 1984). The third analysis involved data from the postviewing interview questions. The questions listed above were used as the main categories for organizing the data. Within each category, responses were compared for similarities and differences. In addition, individuals' answers to interview questions were compared to the major points and evaluations they made during the think alouds.

Although there are a number of ways to categorize responses to the film, we focus in this chapter on the kinds of relationships, or *stances*, that might be said to exist between a reader (in this case, a viewer) and a text. A stance can be thought of as the way a reader reads a text—for example, whether appreciatively or resistantly. This is largely affected by the reader's purpose—what the reader wants to get out of the text—and the congruence the reader believes exists between his or her own ideology and goals and the author's. Thus, stances do not represent stable characteristics of readers, nor is one stance necessarily characteristic of a whole reading. Rather, the stance a reader adopts depends on the reading context, the text, and his or her goals at the time.

To characterize reader stances, we have drawn primarily on the work of Rosenblatt (1988) and Vipond and Hunt (1984). Rosenblatt has characterized reading as predominantly *efferent* or *aesthetic*. In efferent reading (after the Latin *efferre*, to carry away), we focus our attention on "the ideas, information, directions, conclusions to be retained, used, or acted on after the reading event" (p. 5). Vipond and Hunt have a similar category called *information-driven* reading. However, they see information-driven reading more as knowledge acquisition that occurs in learning-from-text situations, as in some school learning tasks and laboratory experiments on reading. As they say, "information-driven reading is most likely to occur in contextually isolated situations, when the reader's task is to learn or remember the material and when the text itself is fragmentary or inane" (p. 268).

In contrast, a reader who adopts an aesthetic stance focuses attention on what he or she is experiencing *during* the reading event—"the lived-through experience." Here, the focus is on the sensations, images, feelings, and ideas that are personally relevant. As Rosenblatt describes it, "the aesthetic reader experiences, savors, the qualities of the structured ideas, situations, scenes, personalities, emotion, called forth, participating in the tensions, conflicts, and resolutions as they unfold" (p. 5). One type of aesthetic reading is what Vipond and Hunt (1984) call *story-driven* reading. This is the kind of reading a person would do who is "looking for a 'good read'—interesting, affectively-arousing events" (p. 269). Story-driven reading tends to emphasize plot, characters, and events, rather than the "discourse" in which these narrative elements are presented. As Vipond and Hunt put it, "a person reading in a story-driven way would not find it necessary to construct a model of the author: the story seems to exist, and can be enjoyed, quite independently of any implied author" (p. 269).

What is missing from Rosenblatt's distinction between efferent and aesthetic reading is the analytical, critical approach to a text that some readers may adopt in some reading situations. Readers who have a good deal of topic-related background knowledge, a strong point of view, and/or training in critical theory or critical thinking may search for a text's hidden and latent meanings, or subtexts. As they do so, they question how texts "frame reality and disclose information about their authors' assumptions, world views, and beliefs" (Wineburg, 1991, p. 499). Consistent in some respects with the critical thinking tradition, the emphasis here is on gaining distance from a text, of achieving objective, critical readings. This, of course, assumes that texts have discernible meanings. In attempting to achieve a critical, objective reading of the text, particularly its subtexts, the critical/analytical reader's attention is focused on the structure of a text—its arguments, theoretical underpinnings, and discursive moves. Critical reading is likely to foreground subtexts and structures, and to articulate rhetorical or theoretical frameworks, rather than to accept texts at face value.

Vipond and Hunt refer to what we are calling the critical/analytical approach as *point-driven* reading, which they describe as a search for the author's underlying message and assumptions—not the gist of a text but what the author might be "getting at." This kind of reading is particularly relevant to a study of beliefs because, as Vipond and Hunt note, "a point involves not the exchange of information, but rather the sharing and comparing of values and beliefs. . . . Points aren't 'in' stories, waiting to be identified by perceptive listeners [or readers] but instead are *constructed* by listeners on the basis of various sources of information, only one of which is the text" (pp. 263, 265). Like Wineburg (1991), Vipond and Hunt argue that a comprehender's ability to construct the point of a text is increased when he or she imputes motives to authors—that is, the comprehender assumes that authors *intend* to make points.

As a kind of "lived-through experience," Vipond and Hunt consider point-driven reading to be a form of aesthetic reading, just as story-driven reading is. However, although both story-driven and point-driven readers are likely to be highly, even passionately, engaged during the reading event, we see a distinct difference because of the analytical distancing that is emphasized in critical, analytical, point-driven reading.

Viewers' Responses

From the analysis of the data, two types of stances emerged, which will be referred to as *critical/analytical* and *personal/narrative*. Given our focus on the role of ideology in meaning construction, we first describe the responses of viewers who adopted a critical/analytical stance because they focused so strongly on ideological issues. Then, we describe the responses of viewers who adopted the personal/narrative stance. There was little evidence of information-driven reading in this study, at least as Vipond and Hunt have described it. This may be because participants had at least some background knowledge to begin with and because they viewed it for their own purposes rather than to meet the requirements of an externally imposed task such as a recall test.

Critical/Analytical Responses. Responses of three of the participants (Audrey, whose specialty is feminism and philosophy; Bill, who specializes in African-American history and curriculum; and Harvey, who specializes in 20th-century history) reflect the kind of critical, distanced, point-driven thinking described earlier. Because the understandings and values of the critical/analytical readers often clashed with those of the filmmaker, their reading might also be described as resistant. Most of the critical/analytical responses were evaluative both of the film's content and of the filmmaker's strategies for achieving his purpose. Evaluative responses concerning content were primarily judgments about the film's bias, interpretation of events, and questions of its historical accuracy. For example, Bill noted the discrepancy between the film's and his own interpretation of the meaning of the Civil War: "[The film makers] are framing issues in a certain way. There is a certain political and ideological position. They are talking about the language of freedom and democracy and are not really looking at how the economy and power politics—vested interests—were the underlying factors in the war. . . . I think they are extending some of the misconceptions, giving us a fairy tale view of the Civil War."

Of concern to all the critical/analytical respondents was the film's perpetuation of myths and its tendency to romanticize both the war and its heroes. Audrey saw the film as framing U. S. history as "a story of salvation [of Blacks by Whites] rather than a story of oppression. . . . It is a portrayal of the way that a few brave, strong men were willing to sacrifice their political power or their positions in life for what they saw as right." Harvey provided an example of a particular myth that the film perpetuates: "This myth about Lee is the biggest of them all. There is this myth that Lee was really opposed to slavery and favored the Union until the end. But the history that's been done shows that he wasn't opposed to slavery at all and he wasn't nearly as reluctant an advocate of the South as has been suggested. I think it is sort of this pantheon of American heroes, these American generals and men. It is sort of like they can't accommodate this guy—that he really did believe in slavery and he really did think that the Southern way of life should be preserved. It is part of the process of healing and rewriting history after that period. Many of the issues over which the Civil War was fought, particularly the issue of race and inclusion, were in effect sublimated to what I would argue are Southern interpretations of history."

At the same time, all three believed that the film generally reflected the point of view of the North. As Audrey noted, "Shelby Foote is really the only spokesman for the South who has any credibility. The quotes of Southerners, other than Mary Chestnut, tend to be people who we don't have any sympathy with. So what I'm seeing here is a very Northern bias." Bill also noted that by romanticizing individuals such as Abraham Lincoln, "history is viewed as the result of the whims and acts of great men rather than powerful social and economic forces."

All three respondents also found that the film only touched on important issues such as abolition and slavery, without adequately explaining them. In commenting on such patterns, the respondents attended as much to what was excluded from the film as to what was included. For example, Bill criticized the discussion of slavery as "incomplete." "It doesn't discuss how slavery built up tremendous capital accumulation, the largest accumulation of financial capital in the history of the world, and it catapulted the United States into a whole new economic position, and it made the maintenance and continuation of slavery even more important. So it wasn't just an irrational act or a simple act of cruelty. It was an act of financial investment, and they didn't bring that point forward."

Obvious to all of the respondents was the exclusion of any discussion of race and racism. Harvey, for example, noted that a discussion of racial attitudes is missing in the video: "They talk about slavery . . . but there is very little talk about what White people actually thought about Black people and what they thought about race and the positions of Whites in relation to Blacks." The result, in Bill's view, is that the viewer does not get a "good theoretical and clear understanding of slavery. [Instead, viewers get] a sense of the irrationality of it all . . . and the idea that we have a self-correcting country, that reform is part of the nature of our society, and that we can right all wrongs." All the respondents mentioned in one way or another that the film describes slavery (although inadequately) without discussing racism, which they believe was institutionalized from the very beginnings of the nation and continues in society today. As a consequence, they believe, slavery is presented as an aberration in American society that came to an end with the Civil War. As Bill put it, "It is part of the American folklore that we can make mistakes and that we've had discrimination, we've had slavery, we've had the oppression of women, we've had the denial of people's individual freedoms, but somehow we always get over it. Kind of a fairy tale—we all live happily ever after."

For all three respondents, this was clearly a film about White male heroes. As Audrey noted, the film "ignores anybody else who lived through it. It ignores the slaves, it ignores the women, and suggests that the Civil War was really just about the battles." Concerning the lack of a Black perspective, she went on to say, "Usually the Civil War is talked about in terms of brother fighting brother—in fact, they mention that here—with very little discussion of the fact that Blacks couldn't count on having families at all. . . . There is definitely a choice here that it is going to be framed in terms of the White perspective as to what is a normal way of life." She also found that when Blacks are mentioned, they "are always seen from the White point of view." Bill also criticized the portrayal of the life of the slave as inadequate: Although "you get a sense of the cruelty," the acts of cruelty seem like "isolated kinds of incidents. . . . You didn't get a sense of the destruction of a whole people. You didn't get a sense of the long-term nature. . . . I would have liked them to cultivate some outrage, to really dramatize and underline the indignities." And, Harvey noted that painting the picture of American society as pastoral and harmonious before the war ignores the perspective of the slaves: "If you had been a slave, you wouldn't think that this was a wonderful pastoral, peaceful country."

Audrey and Harvey, in particular, were critical of the film for ignoring the role of women in the war. Audrey, for example, observed, "Now this seems to me a very male-centered treatment of women altogether. Whereas White women, not having the vote, not having a way to make themselves heard politically, threw themselves into oratory and into talking people into taking a stand against slavery." Furthermore, Audrey was aware of the author/filmmaker behind the text as she analyzes how Harriet Tubman is represented in the video: "That seems to me to be a deliberate choice. They had a picture, there are lots of stories about her, and they chose not to talk about her."

The filmmaker's conception of history and how history might be told was also the focus of evaluation. As Bill observed, "Much of the discussion is reduced to personality . . . the Great Man Theory, which separates men from the events that spawned their activities—the context. I think this is a reduction—a kind of trivialization of major events happening in the world." Also from an historian's point of view, Harvey made this comment: "All the stuff that was in there wouldn't really be interesting to an historian. I mean all the kinds of details about the little events in people's lives that may act as a way to involve the person who is watching, but which an historian isn't going to be paying a lot of attention to in terms of thinking about: Why did this happen? What does it represent? What were its outcomes?" From a different point of view, Audrey noted that the way the story was told was "a male way of framing things." Not only do the battles seem to define the Civil War but the war is presented as "an adventure that has a beginning and an end." A more female rendition, she believed, would be more like "an interwoven series of stories where you are seeing what is going on for all the different members of the family at the same time. . . . It leaves things open-ended, showing life as an ongoing set of problems where nothing ever comes to some final resolution." Because of the way the story is framed, Audrey argued, "we don't really have a sense of how people's views changed, how Northern Whites came to see slavery as a problem or as a moral issue. . . . What changed people's minds? If you talk about it just in terms of right or wrong, then those are eternal verities and abstractions that tend to be more in the male framework. The female framework is going to be more a matter of coming to know, coming to understand, coming to decide. Then, you are going to have a historical narrative that has a different shape."

Like the historians in Wineburg's (1991) study, these respondents were highly aware of the filmmaker behind the film, and often commented on his purposes, intentions, and underlying ideology. All agreed that the filmmaker's goal was to appeal to a wide audience. Harvey described the filmmaker as trying to create a personal kind of an involvement with an event over 130 years ago by showing how it affected ordinary people: "It's an attempt to grab people by saying this kind of thing could have happened in your front yard as well." Harvey stated that "it speaks to [the audience] on a level that an analysis of the politics of the war and some grander theoretical scheme wouldn't accomplish." He also surmised that this appeal to a wide audience may be one of the reasons the film romanticizes the war and the individuals who played key roles in it. Unfortunately, according to the critical/analytical respondents, this goal distorts the real meaning of the war. Bill concluded that the filmmaker does not tell the "real story of power and control and the expansion of the Northern corporate economic interests because it is not as endearing as the one about freedom and liberty. It is not as sexy." And Harvey felt that focusing on individuals in history and telling anecdotes "creates a story about the Civil War that is probably involving for people in a way that doesn't really get at what this conflict was really about." Furthermore, Harvey equated the goals of the film with the goals of school history textbooks: "This tendency to mythologize is the same kind of theme that comes through school textbooks. It may not be a conscious attempt [in the film] but there is a sense of building an identity, almost a national identity around these figures and battles—that this is part of who we are as a country." Similarly, Audrey saw the effect of the film's ideology as leaving people with "a sense of how America came out on the right side. We did what was right. We as Whites made the right choice. We made the sacrifices that were necessary. . . . I would think that most Whites watching this would feel self-congratulatory—Whites finally came through for Blacks."

Finally, the critical/analytical viewers were highly aware of the strategies the filmmaker used to achieve his purposes, particularly his presumed desire to engage the audience. These viewers spoke appreciatively of the effective use of the camera as it panned and zoomed over still photographs; of music; poetry; visual imagery; and readings from diaries, letters, speeches, and other documents. But they also noted that the use of music, soft hues, and visual images frequently served to diminish the violence and cruelty portrayed by the content of the photographs or the verbal content that was simultaneously being presented. For example, Harvey found that the soft hues of the photographs that depicted the carnage of the war and the melancholy background music "evoke a kind of sadness about it, but I think maybe it also has the effect of romanticizing it in a way." Harvey described the photos and music themselves as a subtext, sometimes purposely at odds with the subtext of the horror and violence of the war, "creating a nostalgia that almost gets disconnected from the fact that all these people really died in it." He pointed out that many of the original photographs were staged at the time for a political purpose—one couldn't show how horrible and violent the war really was to the people back home. Similarly, Audrey noted that the peaceful image of a sunset over a river counters any mental images of the horrors of slavery that a listener might create as he or she listens to Frederick Douglass's account. Audrey also described some of the pictures of slaves on the plantations as "benign images." Focusing on the brutality of the war more than on the brutality of slavery, she observed, "keeps the focus on Whites."

Commentary. Viewers whose responses demonstrated a critical/analytical orientation adopted a distanced stance—a stance outside of the text—in contrast to viewers who immersed themselves in the film. Distancing allows for specific attention to the ideological framing of the text (though it doesn't guarantee such attention), and in fact these viewers spoke to three levels of ideological decision making on the part of the film's director—those concerning the construction of the text itself, its subtexts, and its content. These viewers also addressed the ways in which the narrative structure was interwoven with factual statements and quotes to either support or undercut particular ideological interpretations.

The text itself was variously identified as ideologically framed in terms of race, class, and/or gender. Thus, for example, both Bill and Harvey pointed out that the construction of the text as a moral narrative about the abolition of slavery ignored the economic conflicts of which slavery was an integral part. In their view, the text is constructed along lines that specifically downplay economic issues. The film is also, in the eyes of all three critical/analytical viewers, a very White text—one that assumes the standpoint of Northern Whites as saviors of the Black slaves. While the story is often sympathetic to Blacks, it more often ignores them or offers an incomplete, simplified, or softened picture of the Black experience. A third textual analysis points to the traditionally male framing of the story in terms of battles, war casualties, laws, policies, and national leadership. Within that framework, the tribulations of people outside the public arena are largely irrelevant—a mere matter of local color. From the perspective of women and children, however—and indeed that of a good number of men—the lived consequences of economic, military, and other policies on the shifting patterns of actual lives *are* the story.

All three viewers also spoke to the interplay between the text and the subtexts which either supported or undercut the dominant message of the film. As Harvey pointed out, for example, the dominant message of triumph over a shameful past is undercut, ironically, by a certain nostalgic appeal. Both Harvey and Audrey also mentioned the ways in which the selection of surprisingly benign images in the film often worked against the overt story of slaughter and oppression. Other images, though, effectively supported the dominant narratives. All three viewers commented on the effect of heavily depicting (or quoting) Northern White male leaders such as Abraham Lincoln—a subtext that served to support various textual themes, including the Great Man Theory, the Civil-War-as-male-narrative theme, and the assumption that the story of the Civil War is a story about Whites.

Finally, each of the viewers also commented on the content of the film in terms of the ideological choices being made—Bill noting the paucity of information or detail about slave life, for example, and Harvey pointing out the film's use of a myth about Lee as if it were fact. Again, the use of imagery was linked to ideology. For example, the choice not to use a picture of or stories about Harriet Tubman, Audrey pointed out, represents a decision not to include Black women in any significant way in the story of "The Civil War."

As we've seen, point-driven viewers were highly critical as they viewed the film. Perhaps as comprehenders search for the underlying point that they believe the author (or filmmaker) is making, they are more likely to distance themselves from the text, to be aware of the author/filmmaker behind the product, and to evaluate the content and the telling of the story (Hunt & Vipond, 1986). In contrast, story-driven readers and viewers—as illustrated in the next section—seem to immerse themselves in the text and to be more interested in plot, characters, and events—elements that create interest and arouse affect.

Personal/Narrative Responses to Text. Most of the responses of the three other participants in the study (John, a Civil War buff; Barbara, who is interested in biography; and Marina, who has a background in music and performance) can be characterized as personal, aesthetic responses that focus on the narrative aspects of the text. (However, Marina also critically analyzed how effectively the filmmaker engaged the viewer emotionally and aesthetically, as we show later). These respondents tended to see the Civil War as a story of events and relationships and evaluated their experience of viewing in terms of personal involvement. Their stance could therefore be described as empathetic in that they wished to immerse themselves in the text and identify with the personalities who were portrayed, rather than assume an analytical distance from the story. For the most part, these viewers' shared conception of history as story-telling—whether about the public events or the private lives of individuals affected by the war—was congruent with the filmmaker's. Partly as a result, perhaps, they tended to respond appreciatively to the film.

These personal, aesthetic, narrative, and empathetic elements are evident in the following comments: As John said, "One of the things that I found so fascinating about the whole war is that there are so many little anecdotes, so many little ironies." He went on to say, "Some people read for escapism—that is why they like fiction. Well, I like nonfiction for the same reasons, because it is escapism. I can think what would it be like if I were there. . . . I would read about [specific incidents] and think, 'Gee, I wonder what I would do in that case.' " Barbara, who focused to a great extent on the social/cultural/psychological aspects of history, stated, "I've always liked the romantic idea that we could go back in time. What was life like back then? What were individual people portrayed in the video like when they were alive?" At another point she said, "history has always interested me because it gives you a measure of a different time in which people had a whole different way of thinking—you can take on a new way of looking and see things from a new perspective." Marina also valued the emotional involvement she experienced while immersed in the film: "When I watch a movie, I forget. I get very much involved in the film. . . . I immerse myself because I love acting, because I love the stage and theater. . . . If the film is good, it brings out something in you emotionally and makes you think about yourself and your relationships with other people and your family and things like that." Like Barbara, Marina wondered, "Wow, what would have happened to me? What would I have been like if I was in America at that time? What would be the things that I would have to deal with? What kinds of decisions would I have to make?"

These viewers also went beyond the text by either elaborating on and embellishing the events and stories presented in it or wishing to know more. Here's an example of what John, the Civil War buff, typically had to say: "I just remember one story that I think he [the filmmaker] may talk about later on, about how they didn't hate each other so much, and in one battle there was trench warfare—I think one of the first times I ever heard about trench warfare—and they got tired of the war, but their commanders were forcing them to shoot at each other. So before they would shoot they would yell at each other to get down. That's just one of the many little interesting stories that made the whole war so fascinating." In contrast, Barbara frequently wished for more details: She'd like to know more about "the way the people thought, the way they dressed, even the food they ate, why they thought the way they thought." Both Marina and Barbara wished that they could have been on the scene to ask questions. For example, after viewing veterans of the Civil War marching in a parade in 1930, Barbara said, "I would have loved to have talked with some of these gentlemen and asked them questions, and also to have been a witness to their reactions to each other—the soldiers from the Confederate side and the soldiers from the Union side. That would have been really intriguing." Similarly, Marina described questions she would have asked some of the historical persons mentioned in the film. For example: "I want to just sit down and talk to this person and say, 'Hey, what did you feel? What were you going through? What happened? What *really* happened? I mean in addition to what did you do? Did you get up in the morning like we do?' " At other times, Marina elaborated on the video by recalling information from other films and referring to information remembered from school history projects.

When these viewers responded to larger issues such as the importance of the Civil War and slavery, they often did so in personal, empathetic terms by both identifying with the people involved and focusing on the personal dimensions of social issues. The following are some of Barbara's reactions to different aspects of slavery that were mentioned in the video: "It makes you wonder what it was that kept them going. What did they consider to be the purpose of their lives?" "I wonder if that child was ever separated from her or his mom. It's sad." "I imagine that is real whipping. I would never, I can't even imagine, you know what I mean, the pain that we endure in our lives—it doesn't seem like it can come anywhere close to that kind of pain." Similarly, Marina commented on "trying to understand how these people felt working those endless 14-hour days by moonlight. That bothers me. I think it should bother all of us—any human being doing those kinds of things to another human being. Because the horrible thing is that it still goes on."

The violence portrayed in the photographs of the war evoked a great deal of emotion in Barbara, who found them effective and necessary. They made her wonder about the kind of rage that would set people against each other and found it "horrifying to see this guy that's dead in the prime of his life. . . . This is real sad, but it's necessary, I think, to personalize it in this way, instead of just hearing the facts. The facts are sometimes cold. They don't speak like this kind of image does about the horrors of war." Thus, unlike the critical/analytical respondents, who saw some of the violence diminished by the music and softening of the photographs, Barbara found violence to be a strong subtext of the film.

Also implicit in some of these respondents' comments are their beliefs about the meaning of the war—particularly the belief that the Civil War marked a turning point in U.S. history, that what had existed before was forever changed. To John, the Civil War meant that the U.S. was no longer a collection of individual states but rather a union in which slavery was eliminated: "The war really shaped America. It decided if we were going to continue as a union and what kind of a role Blacks were going to play in this country. . . . After the Civil War we weren't a collection of states anymore, we were a country, we were America. And, it effectively ended slavery. . . . The whole idea of slavery, it is so different from anything we can conceive of now. How could people really treat other people as slaves?" Barbara had a similar perspective regarding the war's effect on slavery: "It seems so outrageous that Black slavery could even have existed. . . . We think of our government as being based on equality, and certainly we needed to have that war to sort of reestablish that, to sort of look into our souls and see that we were really being hypocritical—holding that to be important to us, but not living that way." Later, she said, "the Civil War was like a cleansing. And, we needed this cleansing."

Like Barbara and Marina, who focus more on the individuals in history rather than on political and economic forces, John talked about what the war might have meant to the average soldier: "For a lot of the people, it was just a sense of adventure. These people didn't know the horrors of war, because war was never as horrible as this. Not many people were killed or even hurt in the Revolutionary War—not like the Civil War. So, it was thought of as kind of romantic. So, as opposed to all these causes and all the issues, a lot of people just went for the adventure—on both sides, I think." This interest in the individual is congruent with the filmmaker's portrayal of history. As John said, "One of the things that make it so interesting about this war, which you get over and over again [in the film], is the really interesting personalities. How many times do they refer to somebody as eccentric? . . . Just by throwing in the little colorful things, it makes it so interesting. I think maybe this is why people enjoyed [the film] so much was that it is a very human interpretation of the whole war." This is not to say that John does not see the cause of the war in terms of political and economic forces. His beliefs about the causes of the war, he acknowledges, are congruent with the filmmaker's: "Well, I was just going to say that part of the whole split was the fact that they just touched on there, that the economies of the North and the South were so different that the political interests were different, and I think this was a big factor also in leading up to the Civil War."

The story-driven orientation does not preclude occasional critical/analytical reading and evaluation. John, for example, wondered if the voice of poor Southern Whites would be heard, and he noticed that "we are not seeing a whole lot of the Southern side of it." And, Barbara is well aware of history as interpretative. In discussing Barbara Field's commentary in the film, Barbara said, "I'm sure that her experience [as an African American] influences her discussion of history. It would be interesting to see how a Black historian, maybe even a Black female historian, would present a history of the Civil War as opposed to a White American."

Of the three respondents, Marina most often was analytical and at times critical. While valuing the aesthetic experience of film, she often stepped out of it to examine the filmmaker's strategies, most of which she appreciated as techniques designed to engage the viewer. However, she was highly critical of the filmmaker's decision to intersperse moving color clips such as scenes of clouds drifting across the moon, preferring instead the original photographs. As she put it, "Color says this is a documentary made in the 1990s—not 'take me back and keep me back there in time.'"

Commentary. While the responses that we have characterized as personal and narrative included occasional critical observations regarding the framing of the text, those critical moments appear to reflect a different set of assumptions and expectations than the critical perspectives found in the critical/analytical approach. Whereas the critical/analytical approach assumes a distanced stance in order to evaluate the text as an ideological construction, the personal/narrative orientation assumes involvement—viewers expect to be caught up in the story. Thus, one form of criticism that these viewers brought up was a dissatisfaction with the story's ability to keep the viewer engaged or to satisfy viewers' expectations that they were hearing the real or the whole story. Marina, for example, criticized the use of color film as jeopardizing the viewer's sense of being suspended in time. John's observation that "we are not seeing a whole lot of the Southern side of it," similarly, may in part reflect an interruption in his appreciative engagement with the film—a sense that the viewer cannot simply yield himself to the story being told as *the* story.

Not all of the critical moments in these viewers' responses represent an interruption of engagement, however. In a few cases, critical observations were used to affirm the text's capacity to engage the viewer, as when Marina noted the successful use of music. In several cases, the viewers also commented on their enjoyment of the experience of immersion, saying for example: "I can think what would it be like if I were there"; "I've always liked the romantic idea that we could go back in time"; and "When I watch a movie, I forget. I get very much involved in the film."

The most striking form of criticism, though, was in these viewers' empathetic response to the horrors of slavery and of war. Unlike the critical/analytical viewers, John, Marina, and Barbara regarded the images of violence and abuse as powerful reminders of the horrors of both war and slavery as institutions. Indeed, they commented specifically on the value of what they experienced as very affecting depictions of the evil of slavery, for example. While two of the viewers saw the Civil War as marking the end of a horrific period in our past, they both still tried to put themselves in the place of people from that time period—John asking, "How could people really treat other people as slaves?" and Barbara acknowledging a "we" relation to the past, noting that "we were really being hypocritical." Their criticism is not only of the institution itself but of humans' willingness to blind themselves to their cruelty. Both Barbara and Marina also tried to imagine themselves into the place of the slaves, wondering "what it was that kept them going" and "how they felt working those endless 14-hour days by moonlight." Such responses have important political implications. As Marina pointed out, slavery is not a thing of the past; the issues are neither dead nor abstract.

In an article entitled "Things So Finely Human: Moral Sensibilities at Risk in Adolescence," Betty Bardige (1988) points out that this kind of empathetic response is commonly discouraged in schools as being insufficiently cognitive. The approved modes of understanding are those which Piaget defined as stages of formal operational thinking, which involves abstract, hypothetico-deductive reasoning (Piaget, 1976/1946) but ignores the emotions (Ginsburg & Opper, 1969, p. 15). Bardige has described two forms of formal operational thinking—"composite picture thinking" and "multiple lens thinking." In composite picture thinking, students look at both sides of the story and "below the surface to understand the thinking and motivations of the people involved" (p. 91). In multiple lens thinking, students consider "situations from several points of view and recognize . . . that what people see is affected not only by where they stand but also by the language and values through which they filter their perceptions" (p. 91). By contrast, students who display empathetic, or "face value thinking," are concerned not to analyze but to respond to what they encounter.

Bardige's study (1988, p. 87), focusing on students in a course called "Facing History and Ourselves: Holocaust and Human Behavior," found that the distanced, analytical style seems to put "moral sensibilities at risk" by allowing, perhaps even encouraging, a "turning away" from the immediacy of pain. Formal cognitive analyses tend to frame social issues in terms of abstractions; the empathetic or face value orientation, by contrast, looks at social issues in terms of lived consequences for actual people—and calls for a personal response. In the student journals that Bardige (1988) examined for her study, students adopting this stance employed language that evinced "empathy, shock, and a call for personal action to stop the violence" (p. 99).

The different cognitive and personal responses were not necessarily mutually exclusive, Bardige found: two might appear in "a single student's journal, sometimes in the same entry" (p. 91). But, with one exception, the "responsive face value language" was found only in the girls' journals, and indeed all but one of the girls used that language at least sometimes (p. 99). Such findings support arguments by Carol Gilligan (1982) and others that mainstream psychology has conceived of cognition too narrowly in defining it in terms of abstract and distanced knowing (a model associated with the public sphere and therefore primarily with men). What both Bardige's study and our own study suggest is that empathetic engagement represents a distinctive kind of "critical" orientation—one that does not take on belief systems as such, but that engages moral beliefs in a vitally responsive way.

Conclusions and Suggestions for Future Research

We began this chapter by arguing that both texts and readers are ideological. Embedded in texts—both those constructed by authors originally and those constructed by readers during the reading process—are beliefs about texts, authors, reading, and the subject matter at hand. In our case study of *The Civil War*, beliefs revolved around issues of objectivity, fairness, completeness, human rights, the interpretation of historical events, causation, the role of individuals in history, and how history should be portrayed, to name but a few. To make their points, authors use strategies that are implicit in the content and structure of the text, or explicit as when a narrator from outside the storyworld offers comments (Hunt & Vipond, 1986). Similarly, comprehenders bring their own attitudes, beliefs, values, and prior knowledge to the texts they transact with. In doing so, they often evaluate the author's evaluations. Examining the responses of people with different points of view and different amounts and kinds of background knowledge and interest in a topic furthers our understanding of individuals' interactions with texts, particularly the evaluative aspects of some stances.

There are a number of limitations to the present study that future research in this area should address. First, only a single text was used; in fact, it is a different medium than is traditionally investigated in text comprehension research. The strategies that filmmakers use to achieve their objectives are in many respects different from those authors have available. For example, the film in this study used music, photographs, and moving clips simultaneously with print, readings from primary source material, and background narration. Thus, studies that compare film and print versions of a variety of texts are needed before we can draw conclusions about individuals' stances toward texts and the kinds of evaluations they tend to make with different types of texts. We also need to expand the scope of the present study by including more individuals in order to verify patterns that seem to be emerging from the data. For example, are there nonacademics, such as community activists and history buffs from different parts of the country, who would adopt a critical/analytical stance toward this particular text? Are there individuals who might adopt a primarily information-driven stance? And, are there gender differences in how individuals might respond to and evaluate the text? We hope that future research along these lines will expand our understanding of text comprehension and ultimately move reading instruction in schools beyond surface-level comprehension and exclusively information-driven reading.

IMPLICATIONS FOR EDUCATION
IN A DEMOCRATIC SOCIETY

Belief systems, we have argued, play a crucial role in the making of textual meaning. On the part of an author, a belief system works to select, organize, and frame materials to form a more or less coherent picture or argument. And of course the publication process also intervenes in—and may largely dictate—the ideological shaping of a text, whether it's a history textbook, a sitcom, a documentary film, or a book review. For readers, belief systems also serve as organizing frameworks—ways to shape attention and expectations, to discern patterns of meaning, and to inform judgments. Here too, the context is part of that ideological shaping. Readers or viewers who approach a text on their own initiative may form different expectations and assumptions than those who are asked or told to read a text; the reading process will also be affected by the social and institutional context (home, street, grade school, high school, research university, police station) and by the purposes and consequences of reading (say, consumer information, entertainment, education, or a tax refund).

The issues addressed in this chapter raise a number of questions for education. For example, what does it mean to read critically? What does it mean to read empathetically? What are the strengths and limitations of each reading style, and can the two approaches coexist without one being subordinated to the other? To what extent does a heightened ideological awareness affect a reader's ability to read appreciatively and empathetically?

Finally, how can we teach reading so that multiple forms of engagement, appreciation, and critical responsiveness become possible?

As the Bardige study indicates, the distanced analytical style may coexist with an empathetic orientation, but it is not clear whether one stance must predominate. Does one serve as a subset of the other? Do they alternate as equally acceptable but nonsimultaneous perspectives, in the manner of Gestalt shift images, as Gilligan (1987) has suggested? Can they work together interactively as mutually informing stances? Or, would each stance have to undergo modifications in order to interweave with the other? As yet, there can be no definitive answers to these questions. Both learning style and epistemology continue to be hotly contested arenas of debate, particularly with respect to issues of race and gender. Some recommendations can be made, though, as to how schools might address ideology as a dimension of reading and of learning.

At the level of the textbooks used in classrooms, it is clear that, by and large, schools have failed to introduce students to ideological complexity. Fiction probably has worked best, thus far, to introduce students to the diversity in ideological frameworks. Schools that have declared themselves antiracist and multicultural, for example, often include a good deal of fiction in order to teach students about perspectives other than their own (cf. Mizzell, Benett, Bowman, & Morin, 1993). In mainstream schools, however, the literary curriculum is likely to be quite heavily censored in favor of traditionalist narratives. In traditional narratives, as Georgia Johnson (1993) notes, "even when a story is set in a 'faraway land' or 'long, long ago' . . . , the experiences of the characters . . . [are] reassuring because the author has presented a world always already known" (p. 22). As a result, students do not enter into perspectives other than their own.

Textbooks are so thoroughly precensored as to render local censorship more or less redundant, though of course by no means unheard of. As discussed earlier in the chapter, ideology pervades school textbooks, but is never brought into the foreground *as* ideology. Race, class, and gender are all commonly subsumed to the dominant ideology, appearing as mere variations on White, middle-class norms. A more defensible ideological stance, both Barbara Fields (1982) and James Anderson (1992) have argued, would put race at the center of history texts. As Fields, who is quoted in the film, wrote in 1982, race developed during the Revolutionary era as an ideological construct to explain and justify slavery:

> Race became the ideological medium through which people posed and apprehended basic questions of power and dominance, sovereignty and citizenship, justice and right. Not only questions involving the status and condition of black people, but also those involving relations between whites who owned slaves and whites who did not were drawn into these frames of

reference, as a ray of light is deflected when it passes through a gravitational field. (p. 162)

She concludes the article with the observation that race *remains* "a predominant ideological medium because the manner of slavery's unraveling had lasting consequences for the relations of whites to other whites, no less than for those of whites to blacks" (pp. 168–169), and she rejects the thesis of slavery as a "tragic flaw" or aberration in American history. Interestingly, Fields is interviewed on-camera in "The Civil War," but the film never takes up her analysis and indeed suggests the opposite: Slavery emerges as the question by which America would define itself, so that, in abolishing slavery, the United States at last lived up to its principles. Most history textbooks assume precisely this perspective.

Like the film, textbooks do acknowledge counterperspectives, yet the subtexts represented by pictures and captions, chapter headings and subheadings, the index, and other extratextual materials often serve to undermine the impact of the apparent counterperspectives. Such patterns are perhaps most apparent in the contrast between the images and the written or voiced narrative of a text. Many textbooks will state a problem ("girls tend to do less well in math and science than do boys"), and then undercut the statement visually (for example, with a picture of a girl performing a science experiment, apparently with perfect competence); similarly, "The Civil War" employs a visual rhetoric at odds with its spoken rhetoric. The modern, colored film footage of rivers and valleys, for instance, suggests a "this land is your land, this land is my land" theme in counterpoint to the overt themes of a nation torn apart. Even when this imagery is literally appropriate to the script (as when a moving picture of a river accompanies Frederick Douglass's observation regarding the "river of blood"), the metaphorical function of the image works to almost opposite effect, as a serene, if mildly melancholy, image of America as Nature.

Such paradoxes and contradictions, ironically, seem to lend credence to the claims of a text to "objectivity." Since "both sides" of a story are shown, the interests of balance appear to be served. Yet, as the critical/analytical viewers' analysis of the film in our study demonstrates, the ideological structure of a text may override its apparent concessions to alternative points of view. In "The Civil War," the fact-stating framework appears to call the heroic narrative into question: Lincoln's original lack of support for the abolitionist cause is noted, for example, as a corrective to the notion that Lincoln was morally flawless. Yet the narrative returns again and again to White leaders in general and to Lincoln in particular as the main characters of the story—those whom the story is really *about*. Indeed, at one point early in the film, when a Black man is quoted as saying that for the slave there was never a dawn, his eloquent characterization of the slave's condition is immediately followed by what the voice-over suggests is a more reliable account—a White man's confirmation that no one would want to be a slave.

Nevertheless, the *appearance* of objectivity often places textbooks above criticism in the eyes of students (Luke, de Castell, & Luke, 1983). Wineburg's (1991) findings support this concern: whereas historians ranked a passage from a textbook as the *least* trustworthy of eight documents (including an excerpt from a fictional work), high school students tended to rate the passage from the textbook as the *most* trustworthy, believing that the textbook contained "straight information" and was "just reporting the facts" (p. 501).

Textbooks themselves, then, need to be rewritten in ways that will more reliably reflect the variety of possible interpretive frameworks to which a text might appeal. The selection of texts for a curriculum also needs to speak to ideological diversity, both in the case of fiction and that of factual materials. At the same time, teachers can address ideology pedagogically, by teaching deconstructive skills (cf. Johnson, 1993) and by attending to students' empathetic responses to reading materials in which social issues are presented in the abstract. Students are not inherently passive readers, though the schools often train them to *become* passive (cf. Anyon, 1981; Davies, 1989). Engaging students as active and vital readers may be the first step towards teaching students to recognize and think about the belief systems through which they learn and make sense of experience.

Current reading programs in schools tend to place students in the position either of identifying with the point of view implicit in a text (a position potentially alienating to many readers) or of resisting the text because they see it as alienating. If reading is to be part of a democratic and pluralistic education, we will need to change the text selection process and may have to reject approaches to reading that are dichotomized as either critical or appreciative (cf. Johnson, 1993). We will also need to reconsider the status of school texts as disembodied, authoritative representations of truth. One possibility is to reconnect reading with writing—that is, with an awareness of the act of constructing meaning—by engaging readers in writing their own texts (cf. Freire, 1970; Rose, 1989).

Rethinking text selection and reading pedagogy is only part of a reconsideration of how we teach thoughtful reading, however. Given the importance of context in reading, we also need to address schooling itself both as an institution and as a physical environment. For example, situations in which readers are directed to work in isolation from one another and in which reading and writing are demarcated as "English" exercises having nothing to do with history or social studies are unlikely to promote communities of readers who can both appreciate and evaluate a variety of texts. Still less, of course, does reading-for-the-test or reading competitively offer an education in reading, though obviously it offers a certain training that pays off in terms of particular socioeconomic values. If "reading" is to be taught as both personal responsiveness and as critical engagement, it will need to be taught across the curriculum as an ongoing project of interpretation, action, and responsibility.

ACKNOWLEDGMENTS

The authors wish to express their appreciation to Stephen Preskill for his assistance.

REFERENCES

Abelson, R. P. (1979). Differences between belief and knowledge systems. *Cognitive Science, 3*, 355-366.

Anderson, J. (1992). *How we learn about race through history.* Keynote Address, University of Utah, Black History Month.

Anyon, J. (1981). Social class and school knowledge. *Curriculum Inquiry, 11*, 3-42.

Apple, M. W. (1979). *Ideology and curriculum.* London: Routledge & Kegan Paul.

Bardige, B. (1988). Things so finely human: Moral sensibilities at risk in adolescence. In C. Gilligan, J. V. Ward, & J. M. Taylor (Eds.), *Mapping the moral domain* (pp. 87-110). Cambridge, MA: Harvard University Press.

Bruner, J. (1990). *Acts of meaning.* Cambridge, MA: Harvard University Press.

Casner, M. B., & Gabriel, R. H. (1931/1935). *Exploring American history.* New York: Harcourt Brace.

Casner, M. B., & Gabriel, R. H. (1938). *The rise of American democracy.* New York: Harcourt Brace.

Casner, M. B., & Gabriel, R. H. (1942/1950/1955). *The story of American democracy.* New York: Harcourt Brace.

Commanger, H. S. (1966). *The nature and study of history.* Columbus, OH: Charles E. Merrill.

Crismore, A. (1984). The rhetoric of textbooks: Metadiscourse. *Journal of Curriculum Studies, 16*, 279-296.

Cronon, W. (1992). A place for stories: Nature, history, and narrative. *The Journal of American History, 78*, 1347-1376.

Davies, B. (1989). *Frogs, snails and feminist tales: Preschool children and gender.* Sydney, Australia: Allen & Unwin.

de Castell, S. (1991). Literacy as disempowerment: The role of documentary texts. In D. P. Ericson (Ed.), *Philosophy of education 1990* (pp. 74-84). Normal, IL: Philosophy of Education Society.

Fields, B. J. (1982). Ideology and race in American history. In J. M. Kousser & J. M. McPherson (Eds.), *Region, race, and reconstruction: Essays in honor of C. Vann Woodward* (pp. 143-77). New York: Oxford University Press.

FitzGerald, F. (1979). *America revised: History schoolbooks in the twentieth century.* New York: Vintage Press.

Freire, P. (1970). *Pedagogy of the oppressed.* Myra Bergman Ramos, Trans. New York: Continuum.

Geertz, C. (1964). Ideology as a cultural system. In D. Aper (Ed.), *Ideology and discontent* (pp. 47-76). New York: Free Press.

Gilligan, C. (1982) *In a different voice: Psychological theory and women's development.* Cambridge, MA: Harvard University Press.

Gilligan, C. (1987) Moral orientation and moral development. In E. F. Kittay & D. T. Meyers (Eds.), *Women and moral theory* (pp. 19-33). Savage, MD: Rowman & Littlefield.

Ginsburg, H., & Opper, S. (1969). *Piaget's theory of intellectual development.* Englewood Cliffs, NJ: Prentice-Hall.

Goetz, J. P., & LeCompte, M. (1984). *Ethnography and qualitative design in educational research.* New York: Academic Press.

Hunt, R. A., & Vipond, D. (1986). Evaluations in literary reading. *Text, 6,* 53-71.

Johnson, G. (1993). *The false promise of pluralism in award-winning children's literature: 1965-1975.* Unpublished doctoral dissertation. University of Utah, Salt Lake City.

Jones, G. (1992). *Honey, I'm home! Sitcoms: Selling the American dream.* New York: St. Martin's Press.

Langer, J. A. (1990). Understanding literature. *Language Arts, 67,* 812-823.

Luke, C., de Castell, S., & Luke, A. (1983). Beyond criticism: The authority of the school text. *Curriculum Inquiry, 13,* 111-127.

McKeown, M. G., Beck, I. L., & Worthy, M. J. (1993). Grappling with text ideas: Questioning the author. *The Reading Teacher, 46,* 560-566.

Mizzell, L., Benett, S., Bowman, B., & Morin, L. (1993). Different ways of seeing: Teaching in an anti-racist school. In T. Perry & J. W. Fraser (Eds.), *Freedom's plow: Teaching in the multicultural classroom* (pp. 27-46). New York: Routledge.

Muzzey, D. S. (1950). *A history of our country: A textbook for high school students.* Boston, MA: Ginn.

Petrosky, A. R. (1982). From story to essay: Reading and writing. *College Composition and Communication, 33,* 19-36.

Piaget, J. (1976/1946). *The psychology of intelligence.* Totowa, NJ: Littlefield, Adams. (First published in 1946. Trans. M. Piercy & D. E. Berlyne).

Rose, M. (1989). *Lives on the boundary: A moving account of the struggles and achievements of America's educational underclass.* New York: Penguin.

Rosenblatt, L. M. (1988). *Writing and reading: The transactional theory* (Technical Report No. 13). Center for the Study of Writing, University of California, Berkeley, and Carnegie Mellon University.

Shorter, E. (1992) Deliverance (Review of *The American Way of Birth,* by Jessica Mitford). *The New York Times Book Review,* 3, 22.

Tierney, R. J., & Pearson. P. D. (1984). Toward a composing model of reading. In J. M. Jensen (Ed.), *Composing and comprehending.* Urbana, IL (ERIC Clearinghouse on Reading and Communication Skills).

Vipond, D., & Hunt, R. A. (1984). Point-driven understanding: Pragmatic and cognitive dimensions of literary reading. *Poetics, 13,* 261-277.

Watkins, W. (1986). *The political sociology of postcolonial social studies curriculum development: The case of Nigeria 1960-1980.* Unpublished doctoral dissertation. University of Illinois at Chicago.

Wineburg, S. S. (1991). On the reading of historical texts: Notes on the breach between school and academy. *American Educational Research Journal, 28,* 495-519.

A Look to the Future:
What We Might Learn
From Research on Beliefs

Claire Ellen Weinstein
University of Texas, Austin

Over the past several decades, I have witnessed many changes in text research—changes that have been mirrored in my own work in the area of learning and study strategies. In many ways, *Beliefs About Text and Instruction With Text* symbolizes the natural progression that has occurred not only in my research but also in the broader research community's understanding of the nature of text and instruction related to effectively interacting with text. When I began studying how people learn and how I could help students and their teachers improve upon the learning process, my focus was on general cognitive strategies (Weinstein, 1978). Such a perspective was commonplace in the literature at that time (cf. O'Neil, 1978). I, like my contemporaries, thought little about students' will to learn or their ability to regulate their own learning, or about their beliefs about text or instruction involving text.

With time, however, it became evident to me and many colleagues that students' success in school could not be explained by cognitive factors alone (McCombs & Manzano, 1990; McKeachie, 1993; Paris, Lipson, & Wixson, 1983; Pintrich & Garcia, 1991; Weinstein, Goetz, & Alexander, 1988; Weinstein & Meyer, 1991; Zimmerman, 1990). Thus, motivation and self-regulation became essential components in my research on learning and study strategies. Reading the chapters in this volume, I have become increasingly aware of the potential role that yet another dimension plays in learning and studying—one's beliefs about text and instruction related to text Like many of the contributors to the volume, I now *believe* that we can no longer ignore the contributions that beliefs make to human development, motivation, learning, and thinking.

The ideas presented in this volume are both important and timely for researchers, educational practitioners, and writers. For instance, several authors have documented that teachers and students hold beliefs that color their perceptions of text, including beliefs about what constitutes text (e.g., Horowitz). Moreover, these beliefs, which are highly resistant to change (e.g., Chambliss), influence the way teachers teach and students learn (e.g., Hutton, Spiesman, & Bott). Further, individuals' beliefs are related to their research orientation (Dole & Sinatra; Wade, Thompson, & Watkins), educational experiences (e.g., Schommer) pedagogical training (e.g., Anders & Evans; Borko, Davinroy, Flory, & Hiebert), and their gender (e.g., Nolen, Johnson-Crowley, & Wineburg).

My task, however, is not to summarize the findings of this ground-breaking volume but to go beyond it by speculating on future research directions. I describe various issues that surfaced for me from my reading of this volume. I have organized these issues on future research into three areas: conceptual issues, methodological issues, and research issues.

CONCEPTUAL ISSUES

Self-Beliefs

As the chapters in this volume demonstrate, a focus on beliefs about text is crucial to deepening our understanding of the interactions among writers of text, readers of text, and those who select texts for educational purposes. However, even with these interactions considered, the picture remains incomplete. Specifically, beliefs about text must be examined within the context of individuals' beliefs about themselves (self-system beliefs), their perceptions of their future possible selves, and their beliefs about the world and how it works. We filter all of our experiences and understandings through many layers. However, it is the beliefs about ourselves that are perhaps the most potent, pervasive, and tacit of our beliefs systems.

The research on self-efficacy beliefs relates in part to this issue of self-knowledge. Yet, the goal of self-efficacy research seems to be to provide one a window to one's self-system beliefs. Self-efficacy, and related research, tends to investigate discrete tasks that are completed in specific times and places. Self-system beliefs affect all that one does and encompass beliefs that are abstracted from a particular time and place.

Although the contributors to this volume have given us glimpses into self-system beliefs, the portrayal remains sketchy at best. Future research will need to take a more extensive and systemic look at self-beliefs and the impact of such beliefs on learning from and instructing with texts.

Interactive Models of Strategic Learning

Despite the many contributions made by the authors in this volume, we are still left with pieces of a very complex puzzle, and with only hints as to what the assembled structure may resemble. This is not to downplay the significant contributions of this volume. Theories and models of the kind that I am advocating are frequently late in developing in a program of research. They sometimes arise after decades of systematic investigation. But, as we look into the future, I would hope for an overarching theory and model of beliefs about text and instruction with text that can encompass the results reported in this book. I would also hope that this model would be interactive and multidimensional. That is, I envision a model that weighs the interplay between, as well as the unique influences of, learners' strategic abilities, desire to learn, and their monitoring and regulation of those processes.

As I stated before, my personal development in the area of learning and study strategies led me to recognize the importance that individuals' self-system beliefs, motivation, affect toward learning, and self-regulation play in learning, along with their general cognitive abilities and skills. These dimensions do not operate in isolation, but interact in critical ways. It is often these interactions, as opposed to any unidimensional effects, that offer some of the greatest insights into the learning process. Now, as we move forward to consider more completely the variable of beliefs in our formulas for learning and instruction, it is essential that beliefs be considered interactively and multidimensionally. Thus, beliefs and their influence on learning and instruction must be embedded in models that stress interactions among skill, will, and self-regulation dimensions.

Learners' Goals

One aspect of beliefs that should be explored in the future relates to learners' personal goals. This includes both short-term and long-term goals and intentions that individuals and groups establish. As Garner and Alexander suggest in their preface, beliefs are dynamic. So are the individuals who hold those beliefs. Goals, in a way, reflect individuals' views of their future selves. Current conceptions of beliefs appear to overlook the particularly powerful impact that these "future selves" have on learning and instruction.

By uncovering goals that people have articulated for themselves, we can place their demonstrated and reported beliefs in a context that extends beyond the immediate. In the chapter on knowing and believing, for example, Alexander and Dochy found that a number of students professed a goal of resisting new information that might conflict with their existing beliefs. The ramifications of such personal intentions can have serious consequences for trying to change students' conceptions. Therefore, I urge researchers to gather data on individuals' goals or intentions, short-term and long-term, and to consider findings on beliefs about text and instruction with text in light of those data.

METHODOLOGICAL ISSUES

Every literature has methodological problems inherent in it, and the emerging literature on beliefs about text is no exception. I was impressed with the creative methodologies applied by the authors of this book to externalize individuals' beliefs. I was also impressed by the placing of those beliefs within meaningful, educational, and sociocultural contexts. Wade et al.'s technique of having adults share their thinking while watching a popular television series on the Civil War, Garner and Hansis's use of street texts, and Gillingham et al.'s triad tasks all represent creative approaches to examining beliefs.

Verbal-Report Data

Still, due to the character of human beliefs (i.e., their idiosyncratic, evasive, and sometimes episodic nature), methodological issues persist and must be directly addressed in future research. For one, because most beliefs research (including the work reported in the current chapters) relies on verbal report data, it remains susceptible to the various problems associated with such introspective data (Ericsson & Simon, 1980; Garner, 1988; White, 1980). Further, language seems particularly inadequate to capture the complex system of beliefs that individuals hold. Filling out the questionnaire for the Alexander and Dochy task, I was reminded of just how difficult it is to talk about beliefs. Although this dependency on verbal reports may never be eliminated as a concern, one step that can be taken to compensate for their potential shortcomings is to seek converging evidence or to triangulate measures (Garner, 1988). The more that alternative data sources can confirm or overlap, the more confidence that researchers and practitioners can have in findings from the beliefs literature.

Social Desirability

One methodological problem that is particularly prevalent in the beliefs literature pertains to the issue of social desirability. When people are asked to discuss or demonstrate their beliefs, there may be a tendency for them to provide responses that would be judged by others as socially acceptable.

Individuals may not even be aware that they are framing their responses in socially desirable ways that may not accurately reflect their true beliefs. Humans, as social psychologists have told us for years, are very adept at fooling themselves, to say nothing of others. Thus, this issue of social desirability is one that is difficult to counter. However, the more that individuals' statements are judged against their actions, and using multiple methods, the more that this influence of social acceptability can be reduced.

Transparency of Items

Related to this issue of social desirability is one that I would label the transparency of items. As one who has long been involved in the construction of scales and measures of learning and strategic behavior, I am well aware of how researchers may contribute to the problem of social desirability by developing items that are rather transparent in their intentions. Like the old vaudeville quip, "Have you stopped beating your wife?", there may be no way for the respondent to frame an answer that is not unduly influenced by the tone and bias embedded in the item itself. Items that may appear to be well constructed can still have a desirable response that is rather evident to a reasonably intelligent, socially attuned individual. I found little evidence of such transparent items in the current collection of research, however, those researching beliefs about text will need to be vigilant in this regard.

Independent Measures of Reality

Finally, whenever we attempt to investigate a phenomenon as elusive as beliefs, we must remember that independent measures of reality do not exist. In an experimental sense, you cannot control or hold constant beliefs, and from the chapters in this book (e.g., Garner & Hansis) it would certainly seem hard to manipulate individuals' beliefs. Thus, while we can theoretically and philosophically separate beliefs from other interrelated constructs, such as knowledge or motivation, it seems virtually impossible to do so, in any true sense, pragmatically or empirically. What we can do, at a minimum, is seek to devise a "clean" system of interrelated tasks that provides us rich glimpses at beliefs with the understanding that purity is an ideal and not an absolute in this research.

RESEARCH ISSUES

Individual Differences

How are beliefs shaped by one's gender, childhood environment, parents' income level, or one's ethnicity? One of the themes that emerged from this volume was the relationship between gender and beliefs (e.g., Alvermann

& Commeyras). In addition, Horowitz's chapter showed the possibilities of research on beliefs with subjects from ethnically diverse backgrounds. I found these lines of inquiry fascinating and would urge future researchers to explore the influences that individual differences have on beliefs about text and instruction with text. I feel that such an exploration will be particularly warranted in the future as we acquire a general framework against which individual differences can be compared. That is, once we have established a base of knowledge about beliefs that we hold to be consistent and reliable (e.g., beliefs are resistant to change), we can begin to venture beyond the global questions about beliefs and explore the less charted territory of individual differences. Adding such variables into the equation of beliefs will, of course, complicate the picture further. Therefore, it is important to introduce such variables in some manner that will permit us to discern the patterns that emerge. Should we move too quickly to explore variations, in other words, we could risk losing the "big picture," into which the individual manifestations of beliefs about text fit.

Social Context

More and more researchers in learning and instruction are coming to realize how much social factors impact human thoughts and actions, including beliefs. As Dole and Sinatra point out, some fields of research (e.g., social psychology) came to this realization long before those of us in cognitive or experimental psychology. It is evident, however, that social context has a major role to play in the development of one's beliefs, and the more that we can understand the nature of that role, the more that the work on beliefs can inform educational practice. My own interest in improving schooling makes me especially interested in knowledge about how the beliefs of role models or others in power relations with students (e.g., teachers, parents, peers) shape or alter learners' beliefs. Since all of learning is situated, it is essential that future research on beliefs consider the impact of contextual norms on the individual's system of beliefs. I can recognize in my own system of beliefs, for example, the impact that my parents, my faith, and my mentors have had on me. How does my own experience compare to those of others? Is there a way to assess the influence of these social contextual factors on the individual's belief system?

Generic Beliefs Versus Situational Specificity

There has been a period in the study of learning and study strategies when researchers wrestled with the issue of general vs. domain-specific strategies (Alexander & Judy, 1988). Today, there is a general perception that both types of strategies have crucial roles to play in the learning process, and, in fact, may be different points of a continuum that measures the domain of applicability of a strategy. I expect, however, that a similar kind of debate will be waged in the area of beliefs about text and instruction with text. When researchers begin to refine the questions they ask about beliefs, I anticipate that some will posit questions about the interaction between epistemic and episodic beliefs; that is, how do more generic beliefs that people hold affect situational beliefs and vice versa.

It is likely that one's epistemic beliefs such as those discussed by Schommer (this volume) take on certain characteristics when they are manifest in differing situations. For example, a physicist may epistemically believe in a "theory of everything" (e.g., Grand Unification Theory) having faith that the universe can be accounted for mathematically. Yet, given governmental budget cuts for research associated with particle physics, this scientist may believe that such a theory may not receive empirical support for many years to come. It might also be that beliefs are not as situationally dependent as certain theories of learning and instruction seem to suggest (e.g., Greeno, 1991). Or, maybe situations are so contextually rich, so dynamic, and so complex that their power to impact epistemic beliefs is dissipated. The interplay between generic and situationally specific beliefs will need to come under greater scrutiny, however, if the foregoing questions are to be addressed.

SUMMARY

It is an enviable position to have the final word in an edited volume such as this one that not only offers new insights into beliefs about text and instruction with text, but which also promises to pave the way for future programs of research on beliefs. While the exploration of beliefs has been an integral part of human inquiry for centuries, the promise of this work is that it brings the study of beliefs more centrally into the work on learning and instruction. Certainly, if we are to continue to grow and develop in our understanding of human learning, then we must embrace the role that beliefs about text and instruction with text plays interactively and multidimensionally in that process.

REFERENCES

Alexander, P. A., & Judy, J. E. (1988). The interaction of domain-specific and strategic knowledge in academic performance. *Review of Educational Research, 58,* 375-404.

Ericsson, K. A., & Simon, H. A. (1980). Verbal reports as data. *Psychological Review, 87,* 215-251.

Garner, R. (1988). Verbal-report data on cognitive and metacognitive strategies. In C. E. Weinstein, E. T. Goetz, & P. A. Alexander (Eds.), *Learning and study strategies: Issues in assessment, instruction, and evaluation* (pp. 63-76). San Diego: Academic Press.

Greeno, J. G. (1991). Number sense as situated knowing in a conceptual domain. *Journal for Research in Mathematics Education, 22,* 170-218.

McCombs, B. L., & Marzano, R. J. (1990). Putting the self in self-regulated learning: The self as agent in integrating will and skill. *Educational Psychologist, 25,* 51-69.

McKeachie, W. J. (1993). *Teaching tips: A guidebook for the beginning college teacher* (9th Ed.). Lexington, MA: D. C. Heath.

O'Neil, H. F., Jr. (1978). *Learning strategies.* New York: Academic Press.

Paris, S. G., Lipson, M. Y., & Wixson, K. K. (1983). Becoming a strategic reader. *Contemporary Educational Psychology, 8,* 293-316.

Pintrich, P. R., & Garcia, T. (1991). Student goal orientation and self-regulation in the college classroom. In M. Maehr & P. R. Pintrich (Eds.), *Advances in motivation and achievement: Goals and self-regulatory processes* (Vol. 7, pp. 371-402). Greenwich, CT: JAI Press.

Weinstein, C. E. (1978). Elaboration skills as learning strategy. In H. F. O'Neil, Jr. (Ed.), *Learning strategies* (pp. 31-55). New York: Academic Press.

Weinstein, C. E., Goetz, E. T., & Alexander, P. A. (1988). *Learning and study strategies: Issues in assessment, instruction, and evaluation.* Academic Press.

Weinstein, C. E., & Meyer, D. K. (1991). Implications of cognitive psychology for testing: Contributions from work in learning strategies. In M. C. Wittrock & E. L. Baker (Eds.), *Testing and cognition* (pp. 40-61). Englewood Cliffs, NJ: Prentice Hall.

White, P. (1980). Limitations of verbal reports on internal events: A refutation of Nisbett and Wilson and of Bem. *Psychological Review, 87,* 105-112.

Zimmerman, B. J. (1990). Self-regulated learning and academic achievement: An overview. *Educational Psychologist, 25,* 3-17.

Author Index

Subject Index